MW01200689

# Great Lakes Creoles

A case study of one of America's many multi-ethnic border communities, *Great Lakes Creoles* builds upon recent research on gender, race, ethnicity, and politics as it examines the ways that the old fur-trade families experienced and responded to the colonialism of United States expansion. Lucy Eldersveld Murphy examines Indian history with attention to the pluralistic nature of American communities and the ways that power, gender, race, and ethnicity were contested and negotiated in them. She explores the role of women as mediators shaping key social, economic, and political systems, as well as the creation of civil political institutions and the ways that men of many backgrounds participated in and influenced them. Ultimately, *Great Lakes Creoles* takes a careful look at Native people and their complex families as active members of an American community in the Great Lakes region.

Lucy Eldersveld Murphy is Associate Professor of History at the Ohio State University, Newark.

# Studies in North American Indian History

*Editors*

Frederick Hoxie, *University of Illinois, Urbana-Champaign*
Neal Salisbury, *Smith College*
Tiya Miles, *University of Michigan*
Ned Blackhawk, *Yale University*

This series is designed to exemplify new approaches to the Native American past. In recent years scholars have begun to appreciate the extent to which Indians, whose cultural roots extended back for thousands of years, shaped the North American landscape as encountered by successive waves of immigrants. In addition, because Native Americans continually adapted their cultural traditions to the realities of the Euro-American presence, their history adds a thread of non-Western experience to the tapestry of American culture. Cambridge Studies in North American Indian History brings outstanding examples of this new scholarship to a broad audience. Books in the series link Native Americans to broad themes in American history and place the Indian experience in the context of social and economic change over time.

### Also in the Series

# Great Lakes Creoles

*A French-Indian Community on the Northern Borderlands, Prairie du Chien, 1750–1860*

## LUCY ELDERSVELD MURPHY

*The Ohio State University, Newark*

# CAMBRIDGE
## UNIVERSITY PRESS

32 Avenue of the Americas, New York, NY 10013-2473, USA

Cambridge University Press is part of the University of Cambridge.

It furthers the University's mission by disseminating knowledge in the pursuit of education, learning, and research at the highest international levels of excellence.

www.cambridge.org
Information on this title: www.cambridge.org/9781107674745

First published 2014

Printed in the United States of America

*A catalog record for this publication is available from the British Library.*

*Library of Congress Cataloging in Publication data*
Murphy, Lucy Eldersveld, 1953–
Great Lakes Creoles : a French-Indian community on the northern borderlands, Prairie du Chien, 1750–1860 / by Lucy Eldersveld Murphy, Associate Professor of History, Ohio State University, Newark.
pages   cm. – (Studies in North American Indian history)
Includes bibliographical references and index.
ISBN 978-1-107-05286-4 (hardback) –
ISBN 978-1-107-67474-5 (pbk.)
1. Creoles – Wisconsin – Prairie du Chien – History.   2. Prairie du Chien (Wis.) – History.   3. Prairie du Chien (Wis.) – Race relations – History.   I. Title.
F589.P8M87   2014
305.8009775'74–dc23        2014002459

ISBN 978-1-107-05286-4 Hardback
ISBN 978-1-107-67474-5 Paperback

*For my family, past, present, and future.*

# Contents

# Tables

# Figures

# Acknowledgments

This project has taken over a dozen years, even though I have had an amazing amount of help from all kinds of people. The administration at Ohio State University, Newark, where I work, has given generous support in the form of travel and research funds and leaves of absence. Two fellowships at the Newberry Library in Chicago in 1998–9 and 2006–7 provided wonderful opportunities to find sources, reflect on the project, and engage with other scholars in a nurturing environment. I am grateful to the National Endowment for the Humanities, the Lloyd Lewis Fellowship, and the Committee on Institutional Cooperation American Indian Studies Consortium for funding them, and to the entire Newberry family for creating and sustaining such an awesome site of learning. The Newberry's librarians were extremely helpful, particularly John Aubrey, whose expertise in this area is legendary. Since the mid-nineteenth century, the Wisconsin Historical Society has saved and shared an amazing assortment of the Midwestern past. There, Genealogy Reference Librarian James L. Hansen has been an extraordinary resource, given his great knowledge of the old fur-trade families and his generous willingness to share what he knows.

Numerous friends and colleagues have read drafts of my chapters and conference papers and given their advice and suggestions. They include Rebecca Kugel, Richard Shiels, Allan Kulikoff, Wendy Hamand Venet, Joan Jensen, Frederick Hoxie, Daniel Usner, John Brooke, Randy Roth, Michael Les Benedict, Rowena McClinton, Jennifer Brown, Lisbeth Haas, and one anonymous reviewer. I have done my best to revise according to their good advice but am sure I have fallen short in some respects; I truly appreciate their wise assistance. I am also grateful for many conversations about fur-trade families, colonization, race and ethnicity, and other related topics with OSU colleagues and friends Katherine Borland, Alcira Dueñas, Judy Wu, Lilia Fernandez, Marti Chaatsmith, Christine Ballengee Morris, Margaret Newell, Chad Allen, Peter Hennen, and Kathryn Magee Labelle. Many other friends, fellow conference participants, and Newberry Fellows shared ideas and suggestions, including Theda Perdue, R. David Edmunds, Neal Salisbury, Susan Sleeper-Smith, Heather Devine, Anne Hyde, Jacqueline Peterson, Carolyn Podruchny, Sherry Ferrell Recette, Pierre Lebeau, Denys Delage, Laurier Turgeon, Diana Robin, Kathleen Conzen, Jameson Sweet, Clara Sue Kidwell, Theresa M. Schenck, and Leslie Choquete. Furthermore, Linda Waggoner, Tanis Thorne, Nicole St-Onge, Dennis Au, and Carl Ekberg gave helpful guidance and even shared research materials. James McClurken kindly trained me in land research methods. And it was my privilege to have had many long conversations about this project with the late Helen Tanner, who knew *everything* about Great Lakes ethnohistory.

In Prairie du Chien, Michael Douglass, former director of the Villa Louis Historic Site, gave me encouragement, allowed access to the site's archives, drove me around to historic places, and helped me to connect with local people who could assist me with my research. Susan Caya-Slusser, the present director, was one of them, as were president of the Prairie du Chien Historical Society Mary Antoine, Josh Wachuta, Myra and Chuck Lang, Marcella Cornford, and Dean Cornford. Sandy Halverson at St. Gabriel's Church was also very helpful.

The Barrette family – Phil and Doris Barrette, Geri Curley, and Rosemary Stephens – greeted me at my first meeting with them by giving me a copy of a photograph of Euphrosine Antaya Powers, whose importance I had yet to understand. They and their relative Virginia Barrette Powell were extremely generous in sharing family documents and pictures over the years. Similarly, the late Mary Valley and her daughter Bette Valley Beneker befriended me and helped me to understand the values, history, and culture of the people of the Fourth Ward. Mike Valley and Lori Valley Frisbee were also very kind in chatting with me about the history of their family and community.

Dale Klemme and Cheryl Mader live in the old home of Euphrosine Antaya and Strange Powers. They kindly invited me over to see the historic "French" log construction of the dwelling, to marvel at the many artifacts Dale has found under the house, and to sup with them. Dale also chatted with me at length about the Fourth Ward removal project of the mid-twentieth century.

The efforts of my talented, smart, and wonderfully organized student assistants contributed significantly to this project. Dr. Cecily Barker McDaniel crunched and organized the census data when she was a graduate student at Ohio State. Undergraduate student assistants Christa Hupp, Trisha Bradley, Alicia Barringer, Danielle Nelson, Lori Carter-Devereaux, and Megan Cromwell assisted in numerous ways.

Earlier versions of parts of Chapters 4 and 6 found their way into two articles, "Public Mothers: Native American and Métis Women as Creole Mediators in the Nineteenth-Century Midwest" (*Journal of Women's History,* special issue titled "Revising the Experiences of Colonized Women," 14, no. 4 [Winter 2003]: 142–166) and "Women, Networks, and Colonization in Nineteenth-Century Wisconsin" (in *Contours of a People: Metis Family, Mobility, and History,* edited by Nicole St-Onge, Carolyn Podruchny, and Brenda MacDougall [Norman: University of Oklahoma Press, 2012]). I am grateful for the constructive feedback I received on them from Claire Robertson, Carolyn Podruchny, Nicole St-Onge, and Brenda MacDougall.

I am blessed to be working with editor Debbie Gershenowitz of Cambridge University Press whose wise enthusiasm is just what I needed to bring this project to completion. Working with Debbie and her able assistant Dana Bricken has been a real joy.

My wonderful family members have pitched in many times over the years: my children Bethany and Colin and my daughter-in-law Dannielle all spent time with me in archives, as did our dear friend Kate Stevenson. My mother Molly Wilson Magee joined me on some of my earliest trips to Prairie du Chien and Platteville, assisting me in visiting key sites and sifting through old court records. My father Samuel J. Eldersveld cheered me all along the way, always happy to discuss my research, especially when it touched on politics. My brother Sam encouraged (no doubt with some apprehensions) my efforts to quantify political data; Els Niewenhuijsen expressed enthusiasm for the project, and my aunt Wilma Phillips was always rooting for me. Cousins Mary and Dave Vanderhart sheltered me with much interest when I conducted research in and near our nation's capital and politely refrained from expressing their wonder that this project was taking so darn long. Our newest family members, son-in-law Guillermo Gomez and grandchildren Finnegan, Alice, and Kellan, provided additional love and distractions – the perspective we all truly need.

My terrific husband Tom has abided this amazingly drawn-out project with humor, affection, support, patience, and ideas, reading multiple drafts and helping to clarify my prose and data. He has been my strongest cheerleader, central to all I do.

I share credit for whatever virtues this project may have with these amazing relatives, friends, and scholars while reserving to myself blame for its shortcomings. I thank them all from the bottom of my heart.

# Introduction

## "Indian Extraction"

On the occasion of his ninety-fifth birthday, Louis Barrette (Figure I.1) gave an interview to a reporter from the Crawford County, Wisconsin, *Press,* laying out his personal and family history, and that of his community. It was 1919, and the unnamed reporter was impressed with the old man's longevity and spunk, commenting, "Louis Barrette is a wonderfully preserved old gentleman and although he is about to begin his 96th year of life he is quite spry; has fairly good sight and a good appetite; he delights to help about with the chores on his son's farm"[1] Barrette was forthright about his origins, explaining that he "was born in what is now the city of Prairie du Chien," in 1824. He added, "His mother before him was born here, too, as was also his grandmother, the latter of Indian extraction, and he and his children, grand-children and great-grand-children are proud of it."[2]

---

[1] "Lewis Barrette to Celebrate His 95th Birthday," Crawford County [WI] *Press*, Prairie du Chien, February 26, 1919, Wisconsin Historical Society Library, F 902/3BA, 44.

[2] "Lewis Barrette to Celebrate." During the period of our study, people in the Great Lakes region and elsewhere used the terms "Canada" and "Canadian" in sometimes vague ways to refer to the lands and peoples of northern sections of French North America, and later of that same region after it came under the government of Great Britain. Governmental administrative units changed during the eighteenth and nineteenth centuries before the creation of the Dominion of Canada in 1867. During the nineteenth century, the British Province of Quebec became Upper Canada (a region north of Lake Erie and Lake Ontario) and Lower Canada (a region along the St. Lawrence River). In the Wisconsin region, the word Canadian referred to people from those areas, or even the Red River region northwest of Prairie du Chien. D.G.G. Kerry, *Historical Atlas of Canada*, 3rd rev. ed. (Don Mills, Ontario: Thomas Nelson, 1975); William G. Dean et al., eds., *Concise Historical*

1

FIGURE I.1. Louis Barrette, age ninety-five, 1919. Courtesy of Phil Barrette.

Barrette was born into one of the town's many fur trade families. "There were very few whites in 'Prairie des Chens' [*sic*] in those earlier days," he explained, "but there were Indians a plenty from the various tribes of the northwest who came here to barter with the tradesmen." Louis's wife, Caroline Powers (Figure I.2), was also a local woman, the daughter and granddaughter of Meskwaki women and Canadian fur trade workers. Louis and Caroline had lived through an era of amazing transitions in this pivotal village. From an eighteenth-century Native marketplace and French Canadian trade center, the community had gone through intense political, economic, and demographic changes to become

*Atlas of Canada* (Toronto: University of Toronto Press, 1998); Helen Hornbeck Tanner, ed., *The Settling of North America: The Atlas of the Great Migrations into North America from the Ice Age to the Present* (New York: Macmillan, 1995), 59; J. M. Bumsted, *A History of the Canadian Peoples*, 4th ed. (Don Mills, Ontario: Oxford University Press, 2011), 107.

FIGURE I.2. Caroline Powers Barrette and children. Courtesy of Mary Barrette.

a bigger, busier, and more diversified "American" commercial center and farm town.

There were other fur trade communities undergoing these transitions, towns such as Green Bay, Detroit, St. Louis, Vincennes, and Sault Ste. Marie. Over fifty centers around the Great Lakes region had been created during the late eighteenth and early nineteenth centuries when market towns were established by European and Euro-American (and a few African American) fur traders, most of them French speakers. They married local Native women, raising families of mixed-ancestry children and developing a multi-ethnic Creole culture.[3] A very conservative estimate

[3] Jacqueline Peterson, "The People in Between: Indian-White Marriage and the Genesis of a Métis Society and Culture in the Great Lakes Region, 1680–1830" (Ph.D. diss., University of Illinois at Chicago Circle, 1981); Jacqueline Peterson, "Many Roads to Red River: Métis Genesis in the Great Lakes Region, 1680–1815," in *The New Peoples: Being and Becoming Métis in North America*, edited by Peterson and Jennifer S. H. Brown (Winnipeg: University of Manitoba Press, 1985; rept., St. Paul: Minnesota Historical

puts their population at 15,000. Prairie du Chien was just one of these peltry centers.

Diverse communities and multi-ethnic families were common in many parts of North America during the eighteenth and nineteenth centuries, according to the scholarship of the past three decades. In numerous studies, we have come to see that American towns and crossroads and kinship networks were much more complex in their gender and ethnic relations than we once realized.[4]

---

Society Press, 2001). Population data are on p. 63. On Métis and fur-trade families and communities, see also Jennifer S. H. Brown and Theresa Schenck, "Métis, Mestizo, and Mixed-Blood," in *A Companion to American Indian History*, edited by Philip J. Deloria and Neal Salisbury (Malden, MA: Blackwell, 2002), 321–338; Sylvia Van Kirk, *"Many Tender Ties": Women in Fur-Trade Society* (Winnipeg, MB: Watson and Dwyer, and Norman: University of Oklahoma Press, 1980); Jennifer S. H. Brown, *Strangers in Blood: Fur Trade Company Families in Indian Country* (Vancouver: University of British Columbia Press, 1980); Rebecca Kugel, "Reworking Ethnicity," in *Enduring Nations: Native Americans in the Midwest*, edited by R. David Edmunds (Urbana: University of Illinois Press, 2008), 161–181; Tanis Chapman Thorne, *The Many Hands of My Relations: French and Indians on the Lower Missouri* (Columbia: University of Missouri Press, 1996); Susan Sleeper-Smith, *Native Women and French Men: Rethinking Cultural Encounter in the Western Great Lakes* (Amherst: University of Massachusetts Press, 2001); Carl J. Ekberg, *French Roots in the Illinois Country: The Mississippi Frontier in Colonial Times* (Urbana: University of Illinois Press, 1998); Catherine J. Denial, *Making Marriage: Husbands, Wives and the American State in Dakota and Ojibwe Country* (St. Paul: Minnesota Historical Society Press, 2013); and Lucy Eldersveld Murphy, *A Gathering of Rivers: Indians, Métis, and Mining in the Western Great Lakes, 1737–1832* (Lincoln: University of Nebraska Press, 2000).

[4] Anne F. Hyde, *Empires, Nations and Families: A History of the North American West, 1800–1860* (Lincoln: University of Nebraska Press, 2011); Fredrika J. Teute and Andrew R. L. Cayton, eds., *Contact Points: North American Frontiers, 1750–1830* (Chapel Hill: University of North Carolina Press, 1998); Juliana Barr, *Peace Came in the Form of a Woman: Indians and Spaniards in the Texas Borderlands* (Chapel Hill: University of North Carolina Press, 2007); James F. Brooks, *Captives and Cousins: Slavery, Kinship, and Community in the Southwest Borderlands* (Chapel Hill: University of North Carolina Press, 2002); Tiya Miles, *Ties that Bind: The Story of an Afro-Cherokee Family in Slavery and Freedom* (Berkeley: University of California Press, 2005); Tiya Miles, *The House on Diamond Hill: A Cherokee Plantation Story* (Chapel Hill: University of North Carolina Press, 2010); Jean M. O'Brien, *Dispossession by Degrees: Indian Land and Identity in Natick, Massachusetts, 1650–1790* (New York: Cambridge University Press, 1997; rept., Lincoln: University of Nebraska Press, 2003); O'Brien, *Firsting and Lasting: Writing Indians Out of Existence in New England* (Minneapolis: University of Minnesota Press, 2010); Daniel H. Usner Jr., *Indians, Settlers, and Slaves in a Frontier Exchange Economy: The Lower Mississippi Valley before 1783* (Chapel Hill: University of North Carolina Press, 1992); Jay Gitlin, *The Bourgeois Frontier: French Towns, French Traders and American Expansion* (New Haven, CT: Yale University Press, 2010); Antonia Castañeda, "Presidarias y pobladoras: Spanish-Mexican Women in Frontier Monterey, Alta California, 1770–1821" (Ph.D. diss., Stanford University, 1990); Albert Camarillo, *Chicanos in a Changing Society: From Mexican Pueblos to American Barrios in Santa*

Today, more than three million Americans who are not tribal members descend from Native American ancestors, according to the U.S. Census Bureau.[5] The actual number is probably much higher. Many of them descend from these Great Lakes Creole communities of the nineteenth century. While we know a great deal about the tribal histories of the nineteenth century, and while scholars are beginning to identify and describe the forgotten, diverse families and communities of that era, there has not been much in the way of a systematic look at how these multi-ethnic people fared after Anglo-American settlers became the majority and their institutions gained control.[6] This project aims to address that lack.

Historically, most colonization has consisted of projects designed to enrich a parent country by exploiting the resources of another region, including the labor of its people. In addition, many of these projects sought to cultivate the indigenous people as a market for consumer products, religion, and other cultural change, while preventing other nations from gaining a foothold in the region. The French and British colonial

*Barbara and Southern California, 1848–1930* (Cambridge, MA: Harvard University Press, 1979, 1996); Douglas Monroy, *Thrown among Strangers: The Making of Mexican Culture in Frontier California* (Berkeley: University of California Press, 1990); Peterson, "Many Roads to Red River: Métis Genesis in the Great Lakes Region, 1680–1815"; Deena J. González, *Refusing the Favor: The Spanish-Mexican Women of Santa Fe, 1820–1880* (New York: Oxford University Press, 1999); Anna-Lisa Cox, *A Stronger Kinship: One Town's Extraordinary Story of Hope and Faith* (Lincoln: University of Nebraska Press, 2006); Albert L. Hurtado, *Intimate Frontiers: Sex, Gender, and Culture in Old California* (Albuquerque: University of New Mexico Press, 1999); Gary Nash, "The Hidden History of Mestizo America," *Journal of American History* 82, no. 3 (Dec. 1995): 941–964.

[5] The 2010 Census counted 2.9 million people who identified as American Indian or Alaska Native, and 2.3 million others who gave that as their race in combination with one or more additional races. The Bureau of Indian Affairs states that it serves 1.9 million American Indians and Alaska Natives who are members of federally recognized tribes. Thus, there are at minimum 1 million Native people who have been detribalized or whose tribes are not recognized by the federal government, and at least 2.3 million others whose mixed-ness challenges demographers and historians trying to fathom the complex patterns of their lives and relations. This does not begin to count the many other Americans with Native and other ancestors who today identify as white, African American, Hispanic, or Asian American. U.S. Census Bureau, "Overview of Race and Hispanic Origin: 2010," March 2011, http://www.census.gov/prod/cen2010/briefs/c2010br-02.pdf, consulted Nov. 16, 2012; U.S. Department of the Interior, Indian Affairs, "Who We Are," http://www.bia.gov/WhoWeAre/index.htm, consulted Nov. 16, 2012.

[6] Among the few are Sleeper-Smith, *Native Women and French Men*; Bruce M. White, "The Power of Whiteness, or the Life and Times of Joseph Rolette, Jr.," *Minnesota History* 56, no. 4 (Winter 1998–99): 179–197; Thorne, *The Many Hands of My Relations*; Gitlin, *The Bourgeois Frontier*; Martha Harroun Foster, *We Know Who We Are: Métis Identity in a Montana Community* (Norman: University of Oklahoma Press, 2006); Jean O'Brien, *Dispossession by Degrees*, and Linda Waggoner, *The Civilized Band: The Minnesota Ho-Chunk Who Became Naturalized Citizens in 1870* (forthcoming).

projects in the Great Lakes area had been related to the fur trade and had focused on exploiting as natural resources the pelts of mammals in a system that recruited indigenous people to gather the furs and to process them in a preliminary way before they were shipped to Europe. Native hunters, trappers, and hide-processors were needed to make the system work. But a new phase of exploitation, settler colonialism, was introduced when the regime changed. Settler colonialism specifically targets the land and seeks to remove the indigenous people so that colonizers can move onto that land to create permanent societies.

Enormous change came to the old fur trade communities of the Midwest, as the War of 1812 clamped U.S. sovereignty onto the border regions of Wisconsin and Michigan, which had been considered part of New France until 1763, and then the British Province of Quebec until the American Revolution. Within a generation, settler colonialism brought a rush of land-hungry migrants as the opening of the Erie Canal and termination of the Black Hawk War prompted thousands of English-speaking Yankees (that is, New Englanders and New Yorkers) and western Europeans to swarm into the region.

But people were already here: thousands of American Indians lived in their own communities, while in the old fur-trade towns thousands more fur-trade families were composed of Native wives, Euro-American husbands, and children of mixed ancestry.

While previous colonization had brought small numbers of men intent on buying and exporting animal peltry without displacing Indian people, now migrants sought to force the tribes to the margins and plant themselves on Native ground. Government, economy, gender, and social relations – all were overturned or shaken. As the United States took control of the Great Lakes area in the early nineteenth century, territorial officials established its government in the old francophone fur-trade communities.

What this meant for the residents was that they eventually became minorities in their own communities. The "Americans" brought a new government and court system, English as the court language, Protestant churches, and different forms of business and other economic practices. They also backed this up with the presence of the army and pressed thousands of the Creoles' Indian relatives to give up their lands and move away. The fur trade went into decline.

I became interested in this history while working on a previous book about the Wisconsin and Illinois frontier during the century before the Black Hawk War of 1832. Inspired by new research into the fur trade and its communities and families, I began to wonder what happened to them during the changes of the mid-nineteenth century. Were their experiences similar to those of the Anglo-American and western European "pioneers"? Intrigued by apparent similarities between this midwestern borderland and the American Southwest after the Mexican-American War, I wondered, what was it like to become a minority in your own hometown? Did the new government feel like a protective cloak or a restrictive leash? Was it hard to keep the land? How did the old fur-trade families respond when the commerce in peltry shifted to the northwest and declined? How did the new régime affect gender roles and women's status? Then, as I read more about similar families north of the Canadian border in the mid- to late nineteenth century, about the Riel conflicts of 1869–70 and 1885, I wondered why the mixed ancestry peoples *south* of the Canadian border did not develop an identity as *Métis*, like their northern cousins. In western Canada, some people of Indian and European ancestry who had been brought together by the fur trade became a separate group with a clear indigenous ancestry, and they are recognized today as aboriginal by the government and society. In the United States, however, this was not the case, although some of the descendants of Canadian Métis refugees became part of the Turtle Mountain Band of Chippewa Indians of North Dakota or migrated to Montana.[7]

Prairie du Chien, it turns out, provides a fine opportunity for a case study. Considered the second oldest non-Native town in Wisconsin, it is well documented in numerous archives. Local and state historians and archivists preserved many of the town's records in the Wisconsin Historical Society's several libraries and in local repositories during both the nineteenth and twentieth centuries. The old courthouse and register of deeds office, both located in Prairie du Chien itself, still hold myriad useful documents. More information is scattered in courthouses and libraries around the Midwest, while descendants of some families have collected and saved family treasures and traced their private histories with the help of talented genealogy librarians and researchers, and have kindly shared them.[8]

## Community Study

Community studies like this one can show how regional, national, and international forces, events, and institutions (colonization, the War of

---

[7] Foster, *We Know Who We Are: Métis Identity in a Montana*.
[8] The Barrette and Valley families have been especially generous.

1812, democratic territorial governments, for example) played out at the ground level. They offer opportunities for scholars to explore the impacts of larger trends on the lives of individuals, families, and local groups. In some ways, this book follows paths blazed by a range of earlier scholars, people who have written about new communities at different locations and in different time periods in American history.[9] Like them, I have narrated key events in Prairie du Chien's transitions, such as the establishment of local government, participation in territorial politics, and the creation of the court system, and have examined occupational and farming developments. I have retold the most interesting and significant stories I have found, but also described and analyzed the salient economic, social, and demographic trends, using quantitative as well as qualitative sources. To tie these themes together, I focus on a few important and representative kinship groups: the Rolette-Dousmans, the Brisboises, and the Antaya-Powers families, but of course their many neighbors play significant roles in this study as well.

As a community study, this project provides new insight into a number of arenas. First, while it examines the introduction of American-style democracy and the implementation of governmental forms emerging from the Revolution as well as related social and economic adaptations, it complicates these topics by introducing variables of race, ethnicity, and culture in unusual ways. Second, gender dynamics are central to this analysis, consistently impacted by issues of indigeneity. Third, this community's history has the added significance of experiencing multiple waves of conquest, colonization, and settlement. Rather than starting from "scratch" like other settlements created by Anglo-Americans, the Yankees who arrived with and after the War of 1812 grafted their society and institutions onto an established community that was already integrated into an international economy. And during the course of the nineteenth century, massive demographic changes took place, including federal government policies to remove the American Indians living

---

[9] For example, Kenneth A. Lockridge, *A New England Town: The First Hundred Years* (New York: Norton, 1970); Merle Curti, *The Making of an American Community: A Case Study of Democracy in a Frontier County* (Stanford, CA: Stanford University Press, 1959); Don Harrison Doyle, *The Social Order of a Frontier Community: Jacksonville, Illinois, 1825–70* (Urbana: University of Illinois Press, 1978); John Mack Faragher, *Sugar Creek: Life on the Illinois Prairie* (New Haven, CT: Yale University Press, 1986); John L. Brooke, *Columbia Rising: Civil Life on the Upper Hudson from the Revolution to the Age of Jackson* (Chapel Hill: University of North Carolina Press, 2010); Albert Camarillo, *Chicanos in a Changing Society*.

nearby, the very people whose economic activity had sustained Prairie du Chien for a century. Thus, this study of Prairie du Chien's old fur-trade families provides both a standard community study and additional layers of complexity.[10]

## Borderlands

The old Midwestern fur-trade towns had much in common with other communities across North America, whose founding pre-dated American settlement, places such as colonial Santa Fe, New Mexico; Santa Barbara, California; St. Augustine, Florida; and New Orleans, Louisiana, where people of many cultures came into contact and contests of social, economic, and political control were played out. A few decades later, after the Mexican-American War, Texas, California, Arizona, and New Mexico would experience some of the same conflicts and challenges faced by Creoles in the north. Like these other borderlands, the Great Lakes region experienced multiple waves of colonization and immigration, having been part, first, of New France, then of British North America before the United States took control in the late eighteenth and early nineteenth centuries.

It is also helpful to consider this topic in the context of the major demographic transitions taking place in the Americas. After thousands of years as the western hemisphere's only peoples, Native Americans' absolute and proportionate population decreased after the arrival of Europeans and Africans, due both to imported diseases and to the violence of conquest and colonization. In the late eighteenth century, Native people became a minority of the overall population of the Americas.[11] These demographic changes, of course, were played out with many variations at the local and regional levels, based on local and regional events.

---

[10] Historian John Mack Faragher has argued that projects of this sort are valuable for facilitating the comparison of various frontiers, in part because of their scale. In a 1992 essay, he pointed out, "A community approach also has the advantage of focusing on groups that encompass within their manageably small spheres a critical mass of interrelating social and cultural parts that reflect their larger societies." He went on to compare in a preliminary way American open country farm settlements such as Sugar Creek, Illinois, with Mexican villages and métis communities. The present study should contribute to this larger comparative project. John Mack Faragher, "Americans, Mexicans, Métis: A Community Approach to the Comparative Study of North American Frontiers," in *Under an Open Sky: Rethinking America's Western Past*, edited by William Cronon, George Miles, and Jay Gitlin (New York: Norton, 1992), 92.

[11] Colin McEvedy and Richard Jones, *Atlas of World Population History* (New York: Facts on File, 1978), 280.

Where there were multiple waves of colonization, intermarriage, and several immigrant groups, the dynamics of population changes became complex and created conflicts over the control of resources and politics.

The mixed-ancestry peoples of two different regions invite comparison with the experiences of the fur-trade families in the Great Lakes and northern Mississippi River area. They are first, the Métis of what became the Canadian West and, second, the Californios, Hispanos, and Spanish-Mexican residents of the U.S./Mexican border region. In New Spain, the Great Lakes Region, and the areas north and west of the Great Lakes, people had experienced the multiple "cycles of conquest" (referenced in the title to Edward Spicer's classic study of Indian-white relations in the Southwest from 1533 to 1960).[12] In all three geographic areas, Europeans had created colonial societies among indigenous people and had developed mixed cultures. Later, all three regions were re-colonized by Anglo-American or Anglo-Canadian settlers bringing the domination of different nations and raising questions about the future roles of border residents in the new régimes.

But although Great Lakes Creoles experienced settler colonialism in some of the same ways, there were key differences, which led to alternate outcomes for them in terms of identity, rights, and assimilation. Northwest of the Great Lakes, many fur-trade families of mixed ancestry identified themselves as Métis, rose up against the Canadian government, and became racialized as non-white aboriginal peoples – a very different situation from the experiences of the Creoles in the American Great Lakes region.[13] In the American Southwest after the Mexican-American War, Spanish-Mexican and mestizo peoples became stigmatized as non-white and/or non–Anglo-Saxon, and suffered racist discrimination. Both the Métis and the Hispanics would be chronically impoverished through the

---

[12] Edward H. Spicer, *Cycles of Conquest: The Impact of Spain, Mexico, and the United States on the Indians of the Southwest, 1533–1960* (Tucson: University of Arizona Press, 1962).

[13] Harriet Gorham, "Families of Mixed Descent in the Western Great Lakes Region," in *Native People, Native Lands*, edited by Bruce Alden Cox (Ottawa, Canada: Carleton University Press, 1988), 37–55; Jennifer S. H. Brown, "The Métis: Genesis and Rebirth," in *Native People, Native Lands*, edited by Bruce Alden Cox (Ottawa, Canada: Carleton University Press, 1988), 136–147; Jennifer Brown and Theresa Schenck, "Métis, Mestizo, and Mixed-Blood," in *A Companion to American Indian History*, edited by Philip J. Deloria and Neal Salisbury (Malden, MA: Blackwell, 2002), 321–338; Chris Andersen, "*Moya 'Tipimsook* ('The People Who Aren't Their Own Bosses'): Racialization and the Misrecognition of 'Métis' in Upper Great Lakes Ethnohistory," *Ethnohistory* 58, no.1 (Winter 2011): 37–63.

middle of the twentieth century.[14] The Creoles of the Great Lakes region would face conquest, prejudice, ethnic marginalization, and economic challenges, and they would become minorities in their own communities, but they would not become a racialized outgroup. An extended comparison between the Creoles and these two other groups will be found in the conclusion to this book.

## Government

In Michigan Territory, which included what is now Wisconsin from 1818 to 1836, the American government needed allies, so it defined the electorate in an inclusive way in order to achieve the critical mass of participants required to legitimize its rule. Unlike so many American places, here men with some non-European ancestry were encouraged to participate in politics.[15] But the Creole residents of Prairie du Chien during the period of this study went from being in the majority in their towns to ethnic minorities due to massive in-migration of English-speaking "Americans" and Europeans. During this same period, officials of Michigan Territory introduced new forms of government that were based upon *democracy* in electoral politics – with its concept of majority rule – and upon a court system with a need for *consensus* on the part of juries. Creole men sometimes seized opportunities for political participation to assert their own concepts of justice and governance, concepts that reflected their experiences with indigenous as well as French Canadian political cultures.

## Families and Land

In coping with the challenges of the nineteenth-century transitions, two of the most important resources people had were land and family. Families are a central focus of this study, and it is based in part on a significant amount of genealogical reconstruction in order to understand

---

[14] Albert Camarillo, *Chicanos in a Changing Society;* Mario Barrera, *Race and Class in the Southwest: A Theory of Racial Inequality* (Notre Dame, IN: University of Notre Dame Press, 1979); Miroslava Chavez-Garcia, *Negotiating Conquest: Gender and Power in California, 1770s to 1880s* (Tucson: University of Arizona Press, 2004), 143–150; Reginald Horsman, *Race and Manifest Destiny: The Origins of American Racial Anglo-Saxonism* (Cambridge, MA: Harvard University Press, 1981), 279; Jerome R. Adams, *Greasers and Gringos: The Historical Roots of Anglo-Hispanic Prejudice* (Jefferson, NC: McFarland, 2006), chapters 19–24.

[15] See, for example, Brooke, *Columbia Rising: Civil Life on the Upper Hudson from the Revolution to the Age of Jackson.*

both kinship networks and the cultural influences people brought to this community. This type of research allows for a more gendered approach to a community study as care has been taken to follow the relationships and experiences not only of men but also of women whose names often changed at marriage; this allows for women to be included in nominal linkage analyses, a research method where names are checked in several census documents and their data compared. Furthermore, this helps to reveal the indigeneity of so many family members.

That indigeneity continued to matter to Creole people even as they became a minority in their town. When Louis Barrette stressed to his interviewer that his mother and grandmother had been born in Prairie du Chien and that he had Indian ancestry, he was making a proud statement about his indigenous roots and articulating his sense of belonging rightfully to this place. This indigeneity provided a connection to the land, a connection that is vital to understanding the transitions taking place at Prairie du Chien during the nineteenth century.

After the War of 1812, when the United States moved to solidify its control over this region, the government individualized the common lands and began to evict the Native peoples. To the extent that many intermarried Native women and their families were able to gain title to parcels of these Native homelands, they gained both political legitimacy and an important economic resource that could help them to weather the enormous demographic, economic, and political changes that would take place during the century. Tribal members would be dispossessed and removed to make way for Euro-American and European settlers, but by virtue of their marriages to "white" men, these women and their kin would be permitted to stay, although in a changing society. Those with access to land would have a much better chance of persisting in this place than those without it, because the land would provide homes, resources, and alternatives to occupations in the peltry business. Little wonder that Louis Barrette proudly pointed out to his interviewer that his father was "a landed man." Louis's parents, in fact, created one of the most successful farms in the community. Some Creoles gained land titles and used the land in a variety of new ways as they adapted to change. Their efforts are explored in this study.

Land also provided political legitimacy. As historian Lauren Basson has pointed out in a recent study of the legal status of mixed-ancestry individuals in the nineteenth-century United States, European American colonial settler states focused on dividing and privatizing land as part of the evolution of capitalism and linked citizenship to individual property ownership. She argues that national ideals "worked together to produce a system that destroyed indigenous relationships to the land and replaced them with policies and practices that divided the land, dissolved tribal affiliations, and strengthened the definition of a racially exclusive European American public whose good the land would serve."[16] Thus, real estate ownership was a key factor for marginal people because political philosophy and legal prescriptions linked the elective franchise and civil rights – for men – to individual landholding.[17] Because voters (always male) were defined first as land owners and later as men who paid taxes on property, owning land qualified men to participate. Under American law, when women married, they lost the ability to control their land and other property, a legal situation that was complicated for Native women. At the same time that legal concepts regarding democracy were evolving, American society was developing the policies and practices that would seize Native people's land and keep these groups as outsiders in the body politic. For these reasons, land plays a significant role in this study.

## Gender

In some ways, women and men experienced the new order similarly, but there were significant differences as well. Opportunities for political participation were opened to many Creole men who had not been politically active before. In fact, when it came to the courts, they might be compelled to participate. (They could be subpoenaed to serve on a jury, for instance.) On the other hand, women's opportunities to participate in politics were restricted. Furthermore their property rights were eroded.

In the early decades of the nineteenth century, virtually all the women at Prairie du Chien were Native-descended, and for many women, their ancestors linked them to this very landscape. Unlike the immigrants, they found that the *border* crossed *them* (rather than vice versa), but the shifting border brought a new government causing significant reductions in women's rights. Yankee migrants also introduced restrictive idealized gender roles, which new laws supported, so Prairie du Chien's women developed other ways of influencing, mediating, and serving their communities. As women became officially subordinated to men in new ways,

---

[16] Lauren L. Basson, *White Enough to Be American? Race Mixing, Indigenous People, and the Boundaries of State and Nation* (Chapel Hill: University of North Carolina Press, 2008), 15–21; quote is on p. 19.

[17] Basson, *White Enough to Be American?*, pp. 15–21.

Prairie du Chien's men found that democratic political practices increased
the authority of men who had been accustomed to deferring to elites,
blurring the old hierarchies.

## Identity and Identification

What terms should we use when referring to these old fur-trade families, whose ethnic and cultural background was so mixed? The interview with Louis Barrette makes clear that there was no set vocabulary to
refer to people like him. The author called Louis "a real pioneer," mentioned that his "father was one of the first white settlers," stated that his
grandmother was "of Indian extraction," and referred to Louis as one of
"the French teamsters." Regarding his wife Caroline Powers Barrette, the
reporter explained that her grandfather "was one of the three first white
settlers here" and added that "the present generation of the Barrettes
have French, English and Indian lineage."[18] "Pioneer," "settler," "white,"
"Indian," "French," "English," "lineage," "extraction" – all of these terms
were used to discuss this family.

But the absence of a set of widely accepted terms is part of the point –
these people resisted being pigeonholed; they avoided being racialized.
They never referred to themselves as Métis, unlike some of the mixed people of the Canadian West who developed a sense of "peoplehood," during
the nineteenth century and twice rose in resistance against the Canadian
government. Sociologist Chris Andersen cautions scholars against using
the term Métis for groups of people who did not identify themselves in
this way.[19] In some respects, the people of Prairie du Chien adopted the
thinking of their Native relatives and assigned identities based upon kinship, lifestyle, and culture, not race.[20]

In the nineteenth century, *outsiders* used many different terms to
describe these individuals and their families, including half-breed, French,
Canadian, *habitant*, or Creole. Except for the first, these terms included

---

[18] "Lewis Barrette to Celebrate." The reporter even spelled his given name two different
ways: Lewis and Louis!

[19] Chris Andersen, "*Moya 'Tipimsook.*"

[20] Rebecca Kugel, "Leadership within the Women's Community: Susie Bonga Wright of
the Leech Lake Ojibwe," in *Midwestern Women: Work, Community, and Leadership
at the Crossroads*, edited by Lucy Eldersveld Murphy and Wendy Hamand Venet
(Bloomington: University of Indiana Press, 1997), 17–37; Theresa Schenck, "Border
Identities: Métis, Halfbreed, and Mixed-Blood," in *Gathering Places: Aboriginal and Fur
Trade Histories*, edited by Carolyn Podruchny and Laura Peers (Vancouver: University of
British Columbia Press, 2010), 233–248.

people of both mixed and unmixed ancestry. For example, an 1840 news-paper article about Prairie du Chien stated that "the population consisted almost exclusively of Canadians of French descent, and half-breed Indians" and also referred to residents as "the old French settlers."[21] "The Americans generally consider the Canadians as ignorant," remarked an Italian traveling in the region in 1828. "Whether this be true, I know not; but I do know that I invariably found them very polite and obliging, even among the lower classes."[22] Yankee politician James Duane Doty used the term "old Inhabitants" in reference to Green Bay residents, probably as an Anglicization of the French word *habitants*.[23] Treaties provide examples of the term "half-breed" in use: one typical instance was an 1830 document in which the "Sioux" provided land to "the half breeds of their Nation."[24] For the most part, the word "half-breed" was not inclusive enough to cover all the people of these old fur-trade communities and was only used to refer to those with mixed ancestry; it carried a pejorative meaning. Ultimately, for Anglo-Americans, the essential point was that the old residents of Prairie du Chien were not exactly Indian, but were culturally different from the Anglos and *were already there* when the United States took over.

Creole society was extremely complex. A typical fur-trade family might include a French Canadian husband (who might or might not have had some intermarried Native ancestors), a wife of mixed Sauk and Meskwaki or Ho-Chunk ancestry, with kin, servants, and/or other employees who might have Pawnee, Dakota, Menominee, Odawa, Scottish, or even African ethnic heritages. Their neighbors might represent yet other ethnicities. This variety bothered some bigoted Anglo-Americans: Caleb Atwater, for example, an agent sent as part of an 1827 treaty delegation, described the people of Prairie du Chien in this way: "They are a mixed breed, and probably more mixed than any other human beings in the world; each one consisting of Negro, Indian, French, English, American,

---

[21] "Prairie du Chien," *Wisconsin Enquirer*, Madison, Feb. 26, 1840, 2: 14, p. 1, reprinted from the Galena, Illinois, *Gazette and Advertiser*.

[22] Giacomo Constantino Beltrami, *A Pilgrimage in Europe and America* (London: Hunt & Clarke, 1828), 2: 174.

[23] James Duane Doty, Green Bay, to Joseph Brisbois, Prairie du Chien, May 3, 1831, Letterbook, pp. 148–149, Doty Papers, Bentley Library, microfilm.

[24] Treaty with the Sauk and Foxes, etc., July 15, 1830, 7 Stat. 328./ Proclamation, 24 Feb. 1831, Charles J. Kappler, ed., *Indian Affairs: Laws and Treaties*. Vol. 2, Treaties, p. 307. Originally GPO: 1904, now available at http://digital.library.okstate.edu/kappler/consulted Oct. 29, 2010. The word choice was clearly made by the interpreters and officials.

Scotch, Irish, and Spanish blood! And I should rather suspect some of them, to be a little touched with the Prairie wolf. They may fairly claim the vices and faults of each, and all the above named nations and animals, without even one redeeming virtue."[25] In a way, the Creoles of the nineteenth century were analogous to the category of "Hispanic" today: people of many "races" from a variety of national backgrounds who generally speak a colonial language (for Hispanics, Spanish; for Creoles, French) and who tend to be Roman Catholic. While the people of Prairie du Chien did not all share identical ancestry, during the period of this study, they did share some common experiences.

## Racialization

Racialization is the process of creating categories of human beings based on perceived differences in skin color, other physical characteristics, and/or ancestry, a process that often results in social and legal inequality for those not perceived to be "white."[26] Even though many people such as Louis and Caroline Powers Barrette had some Native ancestry, they and Prairie du Chien's other Creoles were generally able to avoid being racialized as "non-white."

As social definitions in the United States were being increasingly racialized during the nineteenth century, mixed communities like these did not fit into the neat categories that people in the eastern states were developing. The U.S. federal census forms in the mid-nineteenth century, for example, were not designed to record the complex families and ancestries of these people. There was a column in which census takers were supposed to record a person's "color," but the only options were "White, black, or mulatto," so in the Great Lakes region, they generally left the column blank unless someone was "black or mulatto," making others "White" by default.[27]

Decades earlier, the Anglo-American John W. Johnson had given up and used his imagination, writing in a letter from Prairie du Chien,

---

[25] Caleb Atwater, *Remarks Made on a Tour to Prairie du Chien in 1829* (Columbus, OH: Isaac Whiting, 1831), 180.

[26] Yehudi O. Webster, *The Racialization of America* (New York: St. Martin's Press, 1992); Robert Miles and Stephen Small, "Racism and Ethnicity," in *Sociology Issues and Debates*, edited by Steve Taylor (New York: Palgrave, 2000), 141–143.

[27] For example, Population Schedules of the Eighth Census, 1860 manuscript, Crawford County, WI, microfilm M653, Reel 1402; U.S. Census Office, *Population of the United States in 1860* (Washington, DC: Government Printing Office, 1864), 534.

"I have spent a winter of more pleasure than one could calculate on from the society around me, *we* (I use this word meaning the americans here) had to immagin them to be a white people, their manners were very much in favor under this impression."[28]

As we shall see, political realities were behind the ability of the old fur-trade families to avoid being racialized, even though they would be marginalized and sometimes ostracized in Prairie du Chien. Johnson was a minor government official who was part of an effort to secure the allegiance of the local tribes to the United States, an effort that badly needed the support and assistance of the Creoles. A Missouri slaveholder with a Sauk-Meskwaki wife and several mixed children, Johnson was clearly ambivalent about the concept of race and recognized the need for pragmatic flexibility in its application, a flexibility that would ultimately benefit the Creoles.

As they became legally "white," many Creoles maintained a sense of themselves as people somewhat different from the incoming Anglo-Americans and Europeans. And sometimes people like Louis Barrette would make a point about their mixed European and Native ancestry, even boldly stating that they were proud of it, repudiating the racism of others. But whiteness carried benefits and prerogatives that people like Barrette would not reject.

### Creoles and Creolization

Anglo-Americans might not have been able to racialize the residents of the fur-trade towns, but they did sense that they were very different culturally. One of the terms the Anglos used was "Creole." In the most neutral sense, this term was one that had come to convey the idea that the people and their culture were *already in place* before the arrival of the Yankees. Anglos and others used the word in the same way that vacationers today might speak of "the locals" when away from home – to refer to residents who had arrived beforehand and established a society of their own.

Folklorist Nicholas R. Spitzer traces the word *creole* to the Portuguese crioulo ("native to a region") and finds, "It is especially significant for folklorists (given our penchant for expressive culture) that the root verb in Latin, crear, means 'to create.' Indeed creole peoples are often the makers of memorable and significant new cultural expression." He points

---

[28] John W. Johnson to George C. Sibley, April 28, 1817, Prairie du Chien, Sibley Papers, Missouri Historical Society collections, St. Louis.

out that although "European control of the word creole initially defined 'native to a region' as a white person of European descent born and raised in a tropical colony ... this meaning shifted in practice to include people of non-European origin, and especially those perceived as having multiracial, 'mixed' ancestry."[29]

Because Native people and fur-trade families thought of themselves and each other more often in reference to culture than color, this is appropriate. The word Creole best reflects the idea that people of many backgrounds created a culture with roots in several cultures, but also with elements original to itself, and that this culture was in place before the United States took control of the region. I use the word *métis* (with a lower case m), only when I seek to describe someone's ancestry as part Native, for these people never used the term themselves.

Strictly speaking, French dictionaries defined Creoles as people of pure European ancestry born in colonies, but actual usage changed over time and varied from place to place and user to user. A study of Mississippi Valley French during the eighteenth and early-nineteenth centuries found that the noun *Créole* was formally defined as "a white person born in America of European ancestry," but was sometimes applied to American-born blacks. Furthermore, when not capitalized and used as an adjective, *créole* meant "anything produced by Creoles, anything native to the land of the Creoles."[30]

However in communities in which many people were of mixed ancestry but where cultural elements such as French language and Christianity were prevalent and unifying characteristics, the term Creole became both more inclusive as to ancestry while also retaining the sense that the people had been born *in the region*. In the upper Mississippi Valley the word Creole was used infrequently, but inclusively. In Illinois, a 1797 census divided the adult males into four categories: "*français, creole, canadien, américain.*" Historian Carl Ekberg found that some people of mixed ancestry were certainly included in the category of *creole*.[31] Anglos were also using the term *Creole* to describe the residents of the fur-trade

---

[29] Nicholas R. Spitzer, "Monde Créole: The Cultural World of French Louisiana Creoles and the Creolization of World Cultures," *Journal of American Folklore* 116, no. 459 (Winter, 2003): 59. See also Gitlin, *Bourgeois Frontier*, 191, n 2.

[30] John Francis McDermott, *A Glossary of Mississippi Valley French, 1673–1850* (St. Louis: Washington University Studies, 1941), 60–62.

[31] "Etat et dénombrement de la population du Poste de la Nouvelle Bourbon des Illinois," compiled by Pierre-Charles de Lassus de Luzières in 1797 and located in the Archivo General de Indies in Seville, legajo 2365; Carl Ekberg, personal correspondence with Lucy Murphy, October 27, 2006. Thanks to Carl Ekberg for sharing this source.

communities as early as the late eighteenth century. For example, the English commandant at Mackinac, Arent Schuyler DePeyster wrote in a report to the governor of Canada, General Frederick Haldimand, in 1780 about the dangers of Sioux attacks upon the "Habitations of the Creoles."[32]

This usage continued and increased in the nineteenth century. To illustrate, in 1819 the Detroit *Gazette* printed a description of Edward Tanner's travels through Wisconsin and mentioned the residents of Prairie du Chien: "In the settlement are about fifteen hundred inhabitants ... who are principally Creoles."[33] In the preface to their 1987 book, *The Wisconsin Creoles*, genealogists Les and Jeanne Rioux Rentmeester documented nineteen examples of the use during the eighteenth, nineteenth, and early twentieth centuries of the word *Creole* to refer to the francophone, often mixed ancestry, peoples of Wisconsin. For them, "The first 200 years of Wisconsin's recorded history ... is dominated by French-Creoles, a mixture of French newcomers with the Indian natives."[34] The *Iowa Patriot* newspaper in 1839 reprinted a short article, previously published in the New Orleans *Picayune*, defining the word: "A Creole is but a native of the state or country where he or she may have been born."[35] In other words, the term had come to refer to the people *who had been living in the region* and had established communities and cultures well before the high tide of Anglophone in-migration began in the early to mid-nineteenth century.

When casting about for a respectful label that will allow us to describe the experiences of the old fur-trade families, one searches for a term they used for themselves. What should we call people like Louis and Caroline Powers Barrette? They did not call themselves or each other Métis. It is hard to find more than a few sources in which the residents of the fur-trade communities of the Midwest used terms to refer to themselves as a group distinct from others. An 1887 interview with septuagenarian Andrew J. Vieau, a former fur trader and son of the founder of

---

[32] Arent Schuyler DePeyster to General Frederick Haldimand, June 8, 1780, Historical Society of Wisconsin [WHC] (1892), 12:50.

[33] The article was apparently extracted from the report of a committee that interviewed Tanner about his travels. The committee is given as "Messrs. Woodward, Rowland, and Shattuck." "Wisconsin in 1818 by Edward Tanner," originally published in the Detroit *Gazette*, January 8 and 15, 1819, rept. Historical Society of Wisconsin (Madison: David Atwood, State Printer, 1879), 8: 289.

[34] Les and Jeanne Rentmeester, *The Wisconsin Creoles* (Melbourne, FL: Privately published, 1987), v–iii. Quote is from p. v.

[35] The Iowa *Patriot*, June 6, 1839.

Milwaukee, referred to the "French Creoles" of Green Bay.[36] It is unclear whether the francophone Vieau or the Anglo interviewer chose this word. Joseph Brisbois, a Prairie du Chien justice of the peace and francophone member of an old fur-trade family, used the word "Inhabitants," which may be an Anglicization of the French word *habitants*.[37] Jeanne Rioux Rentmeester, herself a descendant of mixed ancestry, promoted the use of the word Creole. This book will use the word *Creole* (and sometimes *habitant*) when referring to these very complex old fur-trade family members, including people of mixed as well as unmixed Native, European, and occasionally African ancestry. Thus, it might include people of purely European, Native, or African ancestry, or any mixture of these, based upon culture and community membership.

## Creolization

The concept of creolization is helpful for understanding the syncretic culture, values, and behaviors of the old fur-trade families of this study. Historian David Buisseret emphasized the definition of "creole" as "something that is born or developed in the New World," and explained that creolization "describes that 'syncretic expression' in which new cultural forms came to life in the New World." Native people as well as those of European and African ancestry sometimes participated in this process, he argued, as did even "later, resident Creoles." And the process of creolization was ongoing, varied, and might be faster or slower, depending on certain variables.[38] This is an apt characterization of some of Prairie du Chien's agricultural, political, and judicial practices, and women's activities in social and medical mediation.

Although most often used when examining language, literature, and performance arts, the concept of creolization can be used to illuminate mixed, evolving cultural forms with political agendas. As a response to colonization, the term sometimes describes "the emergence of cultural phenomena borne out of the necessity to rise above dominance through

---

[36] Reuben Gold Thwaites, "Narrative of Andrew J. Vieau, Sr.," *Collections of the State Historical Society of Wisconsin* (Madison: Democrat Printing, State Printers, 1888), 11: 234.

[37] Joseph Brisbois, Prairie du Chien, to Morgan L. Martin, Member of the Legislative Council, Detroit, December 10, 1832, Green Bay and Prairie du Chien Papers, Wisconsin Historical Society, micro. page 144 (frame 340).

[38] David Buisseret, Daniel H. Usner Jr., Mary L. Galvin, Richard Cullen Rath, and J. L. Dillard, *Creolization in the Americas* (College Station: Texas A&M University Press, 2000), 6–7.

asserting the local voice," according to scholars Robert Baron and Ana C. Cara. People of different backgrounds have used this process to create challenges to colonial elites and their institutions, Baron and Cara argue, including "maneuvers, tactics and schemes designed to steal power away from 'top-down' monolithic impositions."[39]

Prairie du Chien's old fur-trade families did draw upon multiple cultural traditions in their responses to the political – as well as social and economic – changes of the nineteenth century. Their participation in local government and their actions in the courts reflected indigenous as well as Euro-American values and often expressed resistance to federal and territorial political power, demonstrating their own form of creolization.

This book is organized both thematically and chronologically. Power can be used as an overarching organizational tool, since we can differentiate between authority – that is, the power over others – and autonomy, the power over oneself. The first four chapters of this work explore the contests for authority between Creoles and Anglo-Americans while the last two examine the ways that Creoles sought social and economic autonomy. Chapter 1 provides background on the community, narrates the conquest of Prairie du Chien and creation of the United States Army fort there, and discusses the ways that many of the old families were able to gain legal title to land. Next, Chapter 2 examines the initiation of democratic electoral politics, local participatory government, and the ways that territorial administration affected Prairie du Chien's Creoles. The establishment of the courts system is the topic of Chapter 3, where we see the ways that Creole officials, litigants, jurors, and others both resisted and adapted to the new forms. Chapter 4 turns the lens toward women, those who were newly and formally excluded from the new democratic forms.

The final two chapters are concerned with Creoles' efforts to sustain themselves as their community weathered enormous political, economic, and social changes. Chapter 5 focuses on the effects of Indian removal, the decline of the fur trade, and the challenges of the in-migration of non-Creoles into Prairie du Chien. It also examines the shifts in occupational patterns, concluding with a look at the many Creoles who made their living at mid-century in farming. Chapter 6 returns to the issues of land loss and retention and adds an examination of the ways that Creoles

---

[39] Robert Baron and Ana C. Cara, "Introduction: Creolization and Folklore – Cultural Creativity in Process," *Journal of American Folklore* 116, no. 459 (Winter, 2003): 4–5.

organized their homes on the land, creating ethnic neighborhoods. It continues with a discussion of Creole persistence and migration patterns; a separate conclusion takes a comparative look at Great Lakes Creoles, Canadian Métis, and Hispanics of the Southwest.

This book asks a series of questions. What happened to people like Louis and Caroline Powers Barrette, their families, and their many neighbors from the old fur-trade community? Thousands of people like them lived in the Midwest when the United States colonized the region, beginning with the Revolutionary War. But we still do not know very much about how families like the Barrettes weathered the changes of the nineteenth century. Few scholars have studied the ways that these families responded to the challenges of changing politics, economies, and social patterns. We also know very little about the process of assimilation of Native people into mainstream society. Furthermore, although scholars have studied Indian land loss through treaties, allotment, and termination, the process by which individual Native-descended families lost, acquired, or saved land has not received much scholarly treatment.

This project is formed around three basic themes: community, government, and economy. Along the way, it also touches on gender, race, and ethnicity. It is a community study, a case study that also examines the implementation of American democratic forms of government and social relations in a region with different political and judicial traditions. In addition, it follows the economic transitions of an important commercial center in an emerging agricultural region situated on America's most important river.

My main points are these: First, many Native-descended people and other Creoles maintained ties to the land, although it was individualized. Besides providing linkages to the indigenous past, land also provided sustenance, and for the men, political legitimacy. Although economic and demographic shifts were stressful, many Creoles stayed and adapted, especially those with access to real estate. In addition, land ownership protected many Creoles from *economic* subservience, helping them to avoid being classed as a racialized out-group.

Second, Creole men participated in *politics*, adapting institutions to their own notions of justice, often to the consternation of Anglo political elites. The Creoles avoided being racialized because of democratic political realities, because during the demographic transition, the Anglos needed them to be on their side of the emerging color line, opposite Indians. Disgruntled Anglo officials, however, used *ethnic* discrimination to diminish the participation of many Creoles in the consensus-driven institution of courts. Still, they retained essential political rights and insider status that would eventually permit their assimilation.

Third, Creole men and women experienced settler colonialism in different ways. While men gained opportunities for civic engagement, women experienced a decline in property rights and loss of an approved political voice. New governmental institutions rigidly restricted women's participation and opportunities for formal authority, and changes in marriage practices reduced some opportunities for women to serve their communities in familial roles. Traditionally, intermarriage had served to acculturate and assimilate newcomers into Native (and then fur-trade) communities as wives became interpreters and intermediaries, but when intermarriage declined, Creole women developed patterns of outreach and mediation across cultural lines at the juncture of ideals of womanhood. They found ways to gain approval and to smooth relationships with hospitality, charity, healing, and midwifery. In so doing, they minimized the divisions between Creoles and the newcomers, reducing the likelihood that Creoles would become *socially* isolated enough to be excluded from the ascendant "American" society.

Finally, although most Creoles were geographically marginalized into ethnic "French" neighborhoods, they differed from other multicultural mixed-ancestry groups in nineteenth-century North American history such as the Métis of Canada and the Mexican Americans of the Southwest by being more fully incorporated into the settler society that the Anglo-Americans created. Economic, social, and political developments contributed to Creoles' ability to situate themselves as insiders who would remain and eventually assimilate after the fur trade was gone and the Indians removed. Men and women both contributed to this outcome. In some ways they continued old cultural patterns, and in others they reacted, adapted to, and shaped the new political, social, and economic realities. The following chapters explore their experiences.

# 1

## "The Rightful Owners of the Soil"

### Colonization and Land

In 1781 Michel Brisbois watched a colorful ceremony take place at Mackinac Island situated between the upper and lower Michigan peninsulas. The twenty-two-year-old fur-trade clerk from Maska near Montreal looked on as British Governor Patrick Sinclair presided over a council in which Meskwaki leaders formally approved the multi-ethnic commercial center 500 miles away at Prairie du Chien and confirmed the community's right to occupy nine square miles of ground located just north of the junction of the Wisconsin and Mississippi rivers. Representing the Prairie's Creole residents, three French Canadian fur traders thanked the Meskwakis and gave them numerous trade goods in payment.[1]

Brisbois was surely paying close attention and understood the layered realities evident as the council proceeded. This ceremony affirmed (as Prairie du Chien residents would later explain) that the Meskwakis were the "rightful owners of the soil," but also recognized that they had been

---

[1] Lyman C. Draper, ed., "Traditions and Recollections of Prairie du Chien. Related by Hon. B. W. Brisbois," *Wisconsin Historical Collections* (hereafter, *WHC*), Vol. 9 (1882), 282–302; see 282–283. (*The Wisconsin Historical Collections* are sometimes known as *Collections of the State Historical Society of Wisconsin*) Peter Lawrence Scanlan, *Prairie du Chien: French, British, American* (Menasha, WI: Collegiate Press, 1937), 70; Pierre Lapointe deposition, Oct. 23, 1820, William Woodbridge Papers, Burton Historical Collection, Detroit Public Library. The payment may actually have come from the British government through the generosity of Governor Sinclair, which sometimes got him into trouble. David A. Armour, "Sinclair, Patrick," *Dictionary of Canadian Biography Online*, http://www.biographi.ca/009004-119.01-e.php?&id_nbr=2660, accessed December 3, 2012. Two decades later, this approbation was reaffirmed when, according to trader Michel Brisbois, a Meskwaki leader named Nanbouis "ratified at Cahuhoukey [Cahokia] ... an ancient sail [*sic*] of said Prairie to the French." Michel Brisbois deposition, Oct. 21, 1820, William Woodbridge Papers, Burton Historical Collection, Detroit Public Library.

24

colonized by the French, who in turn had lost a war with the British. Thus the three French Canadian representatives tacitly acknowledged the hegemony of the British while gaining the public permission of the Meskwakis, preferring the British over the United States as the Revolutionary War inflamed the tense Ohio country to the east. And Sinclair's participation meant that the British government had no objection to the existence of this Creole fur-trade town. However, the British control over the upper Mississippi Valley was weak at best. The ceremony took place at Mackinac Island rather than at Prairie du Chien because British officials generally avoided the region west of Green Bay due to Native hostility.

Most of those present would also have realized that kinship networks made this multi-ethnic community possible, relationships created during the previous quarter century when Native women had married the fur traders. Of the three men representing Prairie du Chien's Creoles, two had become kin by marrying into the Meskwaki band. The third had a Dakota wife from a nearby village, as did the interpreter.[2] These wives and their children represented a continuing Native presence on the land even as Prairie du Chien was being colonized. A half century later, political necessity would compel the new American nation to confirm real estate titles to the Creole fur-trade families whose Native women linked them to the soil. These deeds would prove to be crucial in sustaining them and maintaining them on their ancestral land.

Not long after the ceremony, Brisbois stepped into a canoe and commenced the long journey from Mackinac Island to Prairie du Chien, where he planned to add his labors to the commercial efforts there. Brisbois was only one of thousands of men who left their homes along the St. Lawrence River during the eighteenth and nineteenth centuries and traveled widely around the Great Lakes region selling kettles, beads, guns, cloth, and many other items to Native peoples in exchange for furs and other items of Native production. Most would return to their homes after a term of service, but some, like Brisbois, would remain permanently in the Great Lakes region, marry and settle down to raise families.[3]

---

[2] Thomas Forsyth, "A List of the Sac and Fox half breeds who claim land according to the Treaty made at Washington City with the Chiefs Sac and Fox Tribes on 4th August 1824," Thomas Forsyth Papers, Lyman Draper Manuscripts, microfilm, State Historical Society of Wisconsin, Madison, 2T:20, 22; M. E. Fraser, "Early Families of Prairie du Chien," [1919] Wisconsin Historical Society, Madison, SC 2743, pp. 21, 32; Scanlan, *Prairie du Chien,* 70.

[3] Carolyn Podruchny, *Making the Voyageur World: Travelers and Traders in the North American Fur Trade* (Lincoln: University of Nebraska Press, 2006).

The fur trade was an extractive form of colonialism, one that exploited both the natural resources of the land – its beavers, otters, muskrats, and other mammals – and the labor of the Native people who collected and processed the pelts. The Europeans involved certainly participated in order to enrich themselves and their masters, and they were backed up by the coercive authority of military and diplomatic personnel. Unlike many other colonial extractive endeavors around the world such as mining and plantation agriculture, however, the peltry business required cooperation between free peoples. Initially, traders visited Native communities to make their sales, but eventually they established commercial posts on Native ground. These hamlets would not require much land, would not require the removal of the Indians, and in fact would perish if the tribes moved away. Land, thus, was not a key resource to be exploited in this form of colonialism.

No doubt Brisbois's companions Pierre Antaya, Basil Giard, Augustin Ange, and the others explained the region's customs and history to the young man during their journey to Prairie du Chien. Survivors of a conflict with the French that had raged for a quarter of a century, Meskwaki Indians had built a village where the Wisconsin River runs into the Mississippi in 1737 after the Fox Wars (1712–37).[4] So many had died and been captured – some of them sold into slavery, others scattered as refugees far and wide – that there had been in that year fewer than 200 Meskwakis left in this area.[5] Weary of war, the people agreed to trade with their old enemies, the French, in order to achieve the peace they longed for. By the 1750s the Meskwakis were actively involved in the fur business at the behest of Frenchmen such as Joseph Marin, who was both a leading fur trader in the region and a politico-military appointee in charge of La Baye (later known as Green Bay, Wisconsin) and the upper Mississippi Valley. His soldiers built a fort near the Meskwaki village in the mid-1750s; French Canadian fur traders set up shop and traded here but also sent salesmen to tribal villages and campsites to exchange European products for furs and other Native goods. [6]

[4] Helen Hornbeck Tanner, ed., *Atlas of Great Lakes Indian History* (Norman: University of Oklahoma Press, 1986), 42.

[5] R. David Edmunds and Joseph L. Peyser, *The Fox Wars: The Mesquakie Challenge to New France* (Norman: University of Oklahoma Press, 1993), 221; Brett Rushforth, "Slavery, the Fox Wars, and the Limits of Alliance," *William and Mary Quarterly*, 3rd Series, 63, no. 1 (January 2006): 53–80.

[6] Louise Phelps Kellogg, *The French Regime in Wisconsin and the Northwest* (1925; reprint, New York: Cooper Square, 1968), 379–380; Kenneth P. Bailey, ed. and trans., *Journal of Joseph Marin, French Colonial Explorer and Military Commander in the Wisconsin*

The French lost control of most of their North American possessions to the British in the Seven Years War, also known as the French and Indian War (1754–1763), but the British Army abandoned the Wisconsin region after Indian attacks on Michilimackinac and threats against Green Bay in 1763.[7] Not surprisingly, French traders who resented British rule were attracted to the region by the power vacuum. Before the late eighteenth century, most fur-trade couples resided at least part of the year in Indian villages, but after the Seven Years War more and more mixed couples and their children moved to newly established villages where they created a culturally syncretic society and economy based on the fur trade. Between 1763 and 1830, there were at least fifty-three fur-trade settlements in the western Great Lakes region, according to a study by historian Jacqueline Peterson.[8] These communities included Detroit, Mackinac Island, Vincennes, St. Louis, Green Bay, and Prairie du Chien.

These commercial centers served a diverse indigenous population that included not only Meskwakis, Sauks, and Ho-Chunks, but also Dakotas, Menominees, Potawatomis, Ojibwes, Kickapoos, Illini, and Iowas (see map, Figure 1.1). Prairie du Chien's closest neighbors included as of 1768 about 1,500 Meskwakis (a remarkable resurgence made possible by intermarriage, a healthy birth rate, and the return of refugees), 2,000 Sauks, and 1,500 Ho-Chunks.[9]

Native lifeways were based on an economic system that optimized the use of the land's abundant natural resources by seasonal migrations. The Sauk leader Black Hawk explained the traditional rhythms of the region's many Native peoples in his autobiography. In the spring, he said, people returned to their planting villages and the women would "open the [caches], and take out corn and other provisions, which had been put up in the fall," and then women prepared their fields and planted corn, beans, squash, melons, and other crops, tending them until they had a good start. Festivals celebrated the season, and people who had

---

*Country, Aug. 7, 1753–June 30, 1754* (n.p.: Published by the editor, 1975), 106–161. This history is explored in more detail in Lucy Eldersveld Murphy, *A Gathering of Rivers: Indians, Métis, and Mining in the Western Great Lakes, 1737–1832* (Lincoln: University of Nebraska Press, 2000), ch. 1.

[7] Louise Phelps Kellogg, *The British Regime in Wisconsin and the Northwest* (Madison: State Historical Society of Wisconsin, 1935), 22.

[8] Jacqueline Peterson, "The People in Between: Indian-White Marriage and the Genesis of a Métis Society and Culture in the Great Lakes Region, 1680–1830" (Ph.D. diss., University of Illinois at Chicago Circle, 1981).

[9] Tanner, *Atlas of Great Lakes*, 66; Edmunds and Peyser, *The Fox Wars: The Mesquakie Challenge to New France*, 220–221.

FIGURE 1.1. Western Great Lakes fur-trade territory. Detail of an illustration from "Trade Territory of St. Louis in the Late XVIII Century," 1939, in James B. Musick, *St. Louis as a Fortified Town* (St. Louis, MO: Press of R. F. Miller, 1941).

not seen each other for many months "recount[ed] to each other what took place during the winter."[10] During the summer, the young men went west to hunt deer and buffalo; other men, women, and children set off in small groups to fish and gather wild rushes for mats, herbs, roots, bark, and wild foods, while some women went to the lead mines near the Mississippi to dig for ore. In early August, people reconvened in their villages, exchanged the products they had collected, cheered and wagered on sports such as lacrosse games and horse racing, and then harvested their crops. Festivals celebrated the earth's bounty. In the fall, traders sold the people guns, ammunition, kettles, blankets, clothing, and other products on credit. When the weather cooled, Indians dispersed in small bands to their winter hunting camps until March, when they moved to their maple sugar camps for a month of sap boiling before it was time to return to their villages and begin again.[11]

Furs were only one of many products Native people developed for subsistence and commercial purposes. In the region around Prairie du Chien, Native peoples diversified their economies in the late eighteenth and early nineteenth centuries as more non-Native people came into the region to trade or settle. In the late eighteenth century some of the Sauks, Meskwakis, and Ho-Chunks had developed lucrative lead mining concerns to the south of Prairie du Chien, enterprises which a few traders would facilitate as brokers of the smelted lead. By the early nineteenth century, Native women had increasingly commercialized the production of maize, maple sugar, feathers, and moccasins, and Native men became increasingly involved in providing services to Europeans and Euro-Americans.[12]

## "The Great Mart"

When Michel Brisbois arrived in Prairie du Chien in 1781, he found it situated on a beautiful floodplain stretching a third of a mile from the water's edges east to high steep hills, where one could gaze westward across calm inlets to tree-covered islands or between them to the wide swift river and farther shores, or watch for travelers approaching on the waters from three directions. Flotillas of canoes often appeared out of the

[10] Donald Jackson, ed., *Black Hawk, An Autobiography* (1833; reprint, Urbana: University of Illinois Press, 1990), 90.
[11] Jackson, *Black Hawk*, 89–95.
[12] Murphy, *A Gathering of Rivers*, ch. 5.

north, south, or east bringing visitors or kinfolk with news, commerce, and entertainment. The French called the town by the name of its leader, a man they knew as *Chien*, the Dog.[13]

We can get a sense of what Prairie du Chien was like when Michel Brisbois arrived on the scene thanks to the explorer Jonathan Carver who visited Prairie du Chien in 1766 and recorded his impressions. "This town is the great mart where all the adjacent tribes, and even those who inhabit the most remote branches of the Mississippi, annually assemble about the latter end of May, bringing with them their furs to dispose of to the traders," he wrote.[14] Impressed by the beauty of the landscape, he commented, "this is one of the most delightsom[e] settlements I saw during my travels." Carver was told that the community had been led, until his recent death, by a chief who had many wives and dozens of children, a man who had been a peacemaker and a promoter of "trade and commerce among the whole nation."[15] Here, on the outskirts of a Meskwaki village built where the Wisconsin River runs into the Mississippi, families carried on the brisk business of exchanging European-made kettles, blankets, traps, guns, hoes, and beads for Native products such as beaver and raccoon pelts, maple sugar, maize, moccasins, and venison. This town developed as a market center for Native customers and as a depot for traders going west of the Mississippi.

During the 1760s it was the location of huge annual trade fairs – exciting festivals where hundreds of Native people from many tribes camped, feasted, danced, and competed in lacrosse matches, horse races, and games of chance.[16] Indian bands worked jointly to maximize profits by creating a consortium. Carver explained, "It is not always that they conclude their sale here; this is determined by a general council of the chiefs who consult whether it would be more conducive to their interest to sell their goods at this place, or carry them on to Louisiana, or Michilimackinac. According to the decision of this council they either proceed further, or return to their different homes."[17]

During the 1770s Prairie du Chien became a place where rendezvous took place at least twice a year: in the fall when Indians stopped to get

---

[13] Lyman C. Draper, ed., "Traditions and Recollections of ... B. W. Brisbois," 283.

[14] Norman Gelb, ed., *Jonathan Carver's Travels through America, 1766–1768* [1788] (New York: John Wiley, 1993), 76.

[15] John Parker, ed., *The Journals of Jonathan Carver and Related Documents, 1766–1770* (St. Paul: Minnesota Historical Society Press, 1976), 88.

[16] Gelb, *Jonathan Carver's Travels*, 76.

[17] Gelb, *Jonathan Carver's Travels*, 76.

ammunition and other goods on credit as they began their travels to the winter hunting grounds, and then again in the spring when they arrived to pay their debts with furs and other products, and shopped for bargains with their extra pelts.[18]

In some ways Prairie du Chien was uniquely positioned to become an attractive home for enterprising families. Its location at the confluence of the Wisconsin and Mississippi rivers meant that it was situated along a waterway that connected the Great Lakes (and hence the St. Lawrence and the Atlantic) to the Mississippi, the continent's central artery, from which one could access the upper reaches of the Midwest, the Illinois country, the Missouri River, and of course, the central South to the Gulf of Mexico. The region was rich in resources of the rivers, lakes, forests, prairies, and lead mines and was within trading distance of mineral resources such as Lake Superior's copper, and Minnesota's catlinite, many prime hunting areas, and farming villages such as Saukenuk (present day Rock Island).

Furthermore, since the 1760s Prairie du Chien had been a place of peace, a safe haven reserved for the purposes of trade. "Whatever Indians happen to meet at La Prairie le Chien," Carver noted, "though the nations to which they belong are at war with each other, yet they are obliged to restrain their enmity, and forbear all hostile acts during their stay there. This regulation has been long established among them for their mutual convenience, as without it no trade could be carried on."[19] Thus, it was a good place for traders like Michel Brisbois to settle with their Native wives, children, and other kinfolk and employees, people who assisted in providing food, clothing, other provisions, and labor in the business of the fur trade.

Another stimulus to the growth of Prairie du Chien as a Creole town was the rise of St. Louis, 400 miles south on the Mississippi River. During the last two decades of the eighteenth century, that community developed as a financial and trade center importing products from both the upper Missouri River region and the lower Mississippi Valley, including New Orleans. Before this, traders had relied solely on receiving goods from Mackinac and Montreal, making Prairie du Chien's remoteness a hindrance to the trade. But after St. Louis became a depot, it provided an alternate market for furs and a source of goods, so that Prairie du

---

[18] Peter Pond, "Journal," *WHC* 18 (1908), 44.
[19] Gelb, *Jonathan Carver's Travels*, 95.

Chien's merchants could import and export from both St. Louis and Mackinac. [20]

Although Prairie du Chien had seemed to be a single Native community in the 1760s, by the time Brisbois arrived in 1781, the "great mart" at the northern outskirts of the Meskwaki town was evolving into a distinct fur-trade village, as Euro-American and métis traders established stores and homes there. Brisbois soon met the local residents, including a large Meskwaki family of Des Chiens at the Prairie, descended from the chief of that name.[21]

Pokoussee was probably among their daughters and she would play a central role in maintaining a Meskwaki presence on the land. She had recently married Pierre Peltier *dit* Antaya, one of the three negotiators Brisbois had met at Mackinac Island. (Many families in the Great Lakes area had alternate surnames, and the word *dit* was sometimes used to note the alternative name or alias used by a person or family.) Pokoussee and Pierre began to raise a family eventually consisting of twelve children.[22] Pierre had followed in his father's footsteps in entering the trade by 1762, and by 1779 – before moving to Prairie du Chien – had been a trader for one of Mackinac's general store companies. This branch of the Peltier family had used the alias "Antaya" for several generations in Quebec before Pierre arrived in Prairie du Chien, but this name probably recommended him to the Meskwaki community because of its similarity to the Meskwaki word, "netaya," which means "my pet, dog, or horse." Or perhaps there was already a long-term connection between this Canadian family whose name suggests dogs, and the Dog Prairie.[23]

Together with other bicultural, biracial families, Pokoussee and Pierre made their community an important fur-trade center, with strong links to Meskwaki, Sauk, Dakota, Ho-Chunk, and other Midwestern tribes. Marriages like Pokoussee and Pierre Antaya's were a way to create

---

[20] Tanis Chapman Thorne, *The Many Hands of My Relations; French and Indians on the Lower Missouri* (Columbia: University of Missouri Press, 1996), ch. 2.

[21] Michel Brisbois deposition, Woodbridge Papers.

[22] Thomas Forsyth, "A List of the Sac and Fox half breeds," 1824, 2T, 22; Forsyth, "List of Sac and Fox half-breeds who claim Lands … ," 1830 Kansas State Historical Society, Records of the Superintendent of Indian Affairs, St. Louis, Vol. 32, 10–15; James L. Hansen, "The Pelletier dit Antaya Families of Prairie du Chien" (forthcoming).

[23] Scanlan, *Prairie du Chien*, 71. Ives Goddard, ed., *Leonard Bloomfield's Fox Lexicon*, Critical Edition (Winnipeg: Algonquian and Iroquoian Linguistics, 1994), 230. Antaya may have had a similar meaning in another Algonquian dialect, as well.

ties between people of different cultural traditions. Unlike many ethnic groups, Indian peoples in the Midwest had approved of – and even encouraged – intermarriage. During the fur-trade era, traders learned that their Native customers expected them to marry local daughters, creating bonds of obligation to their in-laws and their communities. Native wives became interpreters who learned and taught both their own Native families and their husbands about each other's expectations and cultures. Their bicultural children grew up to continue the patterns of mediation. The intermarriages and resulting kinship connected the Native people and the traders; these relationships were the bases of the Indians' willingness to allow Prairie du Chien and other Creole towns to take root in their backyards.

Although most of the male residents had French or French Canadian roots, Prairie du Chien's population was quite multi-ethnic. A visitor noted, "Indians are numerous … the French I believ[e] have most of them Indian wives."[24] The town's diversity is evident in the records of an 1817 visit by the Reverend Joseph Marie Dunand. The priest stayed for a month, performing 135 baptisms and fourteen marriages, recording the names and other information regarding children and parents who participated in the ceremonies, including tribal affiliations, in many cases. These together with land claims and other records allow us to reconstruct a partial census of the community, of slightly less than half the population, which was estimated at about 600 (see Table 1.1).

Here was an extremely mixed community of people bringing diverse experiences, languages, religious views, and cultural practices to their involvement in an international business and its related activities. (The category "mixed" here masks the diverse specific backgrounds of many residents as well.) The Native women and their children maintained connections to their tribal communities (with the likely exception of the Pawnee, who like the Mandan man was or had been a slave), keeping open lines of communication between their hometowns and the cosmopolitan Prairie du Chien. In a way, these women were delegates in a regional United Nations, playing important social, economic, and political roles. While as many as half of the men may have been exclusively European in their ancestry, only a handful at most of the women would have been considered "white" by those who thought about this racial concept.

---

[24] Willard Keyes, "A Journal of Life in Wisconsin One Hundred Years Ago kept by Willard Keyes of Newfane, Vermont," *Wisconsin Magazine of History* 3, no. 3 (March 1920): 353.

TABLE 1.1. *Prairie du Chien Ethnicity, 1817*

**Wives and mothers**

11 Dakota
5 Meskwaki
2 Ojibwe
1 Pawnee
1 Sauk
1 Menominee
1 Ho-Chunk (Winnebago)
17 Mixed
2 Afro-French
3 French
3 Not Ascertained

**Daughters**

57 Mixed
7 Afro-French
6 French
1 Not Ascertained
**118 Total females**

**Men**

5 French
54 Mixed
3 Afro-French
6 Anglo-American (including 1 Jew)
1 Mandan Indian
65 Not Ascertained
**133 Total males**

*Sources:* Hansen, "Prairie du Chien's Earliest Church Records, 1817," *Minnesota Genealogical Journal* 4 (1985): 329–342; James H. Lockwood, "Early Times and Events in Wisconsin," *WHC* 2 (1856): 125–126; M. M. Hoffmann, *Antique Dubuque, 1673–1833* (Dubuque, IA, 1930), 51–59; and U.S. Congress, American State Papers: Documents, Legislative and Executive, of the Congress of the United States ..., 38 vols., Class VIII, Public Lands, 8 vols., ed. Walter Lowrie et al., (Washington, DC, 1832–1861) (hereafter cited as *ASPPL*, 5: 47–98, 270–272, 283–328. Thanks to James L. Hansen for help gathering information about these people.

    While the Antaya family represents a Meskwaki-French union dating to about 1780, an even more ethnically complex kin group can be seen in the Brisbois family. By 1790, Michel Brisbois had married "*á la façon du pays*" – according to the custom of the country without a license or priest – Chambreywinkau, a beautiful Ho-Chunk woman who was the sister of one of the principal chiefs of the tribe,

Merchistay.[25] By marrying into this elite Native family situated nearby, Michel increased his prestige among his customers, his network of kin connections and allies, and his chances of being respected by fellow traders. And he gained the partnership of a woman who had been raised to assume a role of authority and mediation in her world. She would be able to teach him about her people and her culture, and to serve as a go-between in diplomacy, hostess in the social and political realm, and fellow in the commercial business of exchanging European products – cloth, kettles, guns, traps, beads, and so forth – for furs, maple sugar, and game. They had three children, but, as sometimes happened, after about five years, Chambreywinkau and Michel dissolved their marriage; eventually she returned to live with her Ho-Chunk kin.[26] In Native communities here, divorce was an option for incompatible spouses, and sometimes fur-trade couples did separate.[27] Years later, their daughter Angelique Brisbois took after her parents as both a trader and mediator.[28] Their son Michel Jr. married Pokoussee and Pierre Antaya's daughter Catherine and was also an intermediary. He worked for the British Indian service, and then after the War of 1812 as an interpreter for the Americans under William Clark.[29]

Domitille Gauthier was fifteen years old when she became Michel Brisbois's second wife in 1796.[30] She was a member of a well-connected Mackinac Island family that had been trading in the Great Lakes region for at least four generations. Her mother Marie Madeleine Chevalier was the great-granddaughter of an Illini woman who had begun the family tradition of marrying French Canadian men, and her father's Odawa grandmother Domitille (also known as La Blanche) had been the

---

[25] Draper, ed., Brisbois, "Traditions," 283; Les and Jeanne Rentmeester, *The Wisconsin Creoles* (Melbourne, FL: Privately published, 1987), 207–208; Linda M. Waggoner, ed., *"Neither White Men nor Indians:" Affidavits from the Winnebago Mixed-Blood Claim Commissions, Prairie du Chien, Wisconsin, 1838–1839* (Roseville, MN: Park Genealogical Books, 2002), 35, 82.

[26] Draper, ed., Brisbois, "Traditions," 283.

[27] Jackson, *Black Hawk*, 91; Perrot, "Manners, Customs, and Religion," Vol. I, 64; Marston, "Memoirs Relating to the Sauk and Foxes," Vol. II, 167. Black Hawk commented in his autobiography, "If we were to live together and disagree, we should be as foolish as the whites. No indiscretion can banish a woman from her parental lodge – no difference how many children she may bring home, she is always welcome – the kettle is over the fire to feed them," 91.

[28] Waggoner, *"Neither White Men,"* 82.

[29] Hansen, "The Pelletier dit Antaya Families of Prairie du Chien"; Draper, ed., Brisbois, "Traditions," 284; he was shot by an unknown assailant while hunting about 1820.

[30] Peterson, "The People in Between," 161.

daughter of a chiefly family. That the teenage bride was named after her elite Odawa great-grandmother certainly escaped no one.[31] Domitille and Michel would have eight children, and the younger generation, like their parents, would be prominent in Prairie du Chien.[32]

Domitille's father, former British Indian agent (Claude) Charles Gauthier de Verville (1738–1803) was connected to an extraordinarily diverse assortment of people.[33] He had cousins and children among the Menominees, Odawas, Dakotas, and Ho-Chunks, and perhaps even the Meskwakis or Sauks.[34]

Domitille's sister Madeleine would marry Henry Monroe Fisher and move to Prairie du Chien around 1800.[35] Henry had been born in upstate New York shortly before the American Revolution broke out, but he made his way west and became an appointee at Prairie du Chien under the British regime. He served as a Justice of the Peace and a Captain of Militia in the British Indian Department. Henry and Madeleine had four children before their marriage ended in either divorce or her death. Henry's second wife was Marianne La Sallière, a distant cousin of his first wife; their daughter Elizabeth Thérèse was born in 1810 and would in the 1880s write memoirs providing vivid descriptions of life in the old fur-trade towns of the Midwest.[36] Thus, the Brisbois family network linked members to most of the tribes in the Great Lakes region and to Anglophones as well as Francophones. Networks like these were the foundation of social, political, and commercial life in the region.

## Creole Culture

Like Green Bay, St. Louis, Detroit, and Michilimackinac, and dozens of other towns that grew out of the fur-trade era in New France, Prairie du

---

[31] "The Mackinac Register," Marriages, *WHC*, Vol. 18, 499, 490, 492; Peterson, "The People in Between," 161; Susan Sleeper-Smith, "Women, Kin, and Catholicism: New Perspectives on the Fur Trade," *Ethnohistory* 47, no. 2 (Spring 2000): 432–438.

[32] Rentmeesters, *Wisconsin Creoles*, 207–208; Fraser, "Early Families of Prairie du Chien," 11.

[33] Edmunds and Peyser, *The Fox Wars*, 202 (on Gauthier as a British Indian agent); Peterson, "The People in Between," 161; Rentmeesters, *Wisconsin Creoles*, 252–253.

[34] Peterson, "The People in Between," 161; Mary Ellen Kelly, descendant, correspondence with the author, February 27, 2008; Rentmeesters, *Wisconsin Creoles*, 253.

[35] Peterson, "The People in Between," 161. Elizabeth Baird, "Memoranda," Henry S. Baird Papers, Wisconsin Historical Society, Madison, Box 4, Folder 1, no date.

[36] Elizabeth Baird, "Memoranda"; Rentmeesters, *Wisconsin Creoles*, 246; Virginia Dousman Bigelow Papers, Villa Louis, Wisconsin Historical Society, Prairie du Chien; Elizabeth T. Baird, "O-De-Jit-Wa-Win-Wing; Comptes du Temps Passe," Henry S. Baird Collection, State Historical Society of Wisconsin, Madison, Box 4, Folder 9, ch. 15.

Chien developed a culture that combined elements of both Native and European traditions, demonstrating the creative and syncretic aspect of creolization. There one might hear French spoken, but also Meskwaki, Dakota, Ho-Chunk, Ojibwe, and a number of other languages. Native-descended wives and mothers continued Native maple-sugar making, often taking their chickens (a European introduction) with them to the sugar camps. Catholic Easter celebrations included French crêpes with maple syrup and Easter eggs. Although some husbands plowed fields with their oxen or horses and planted European crops, many wives prepared Native-style gardens and grew the "three sisters" – corn, beans, and squash – as their Native mothers and grandmothers had taught them without the need for plows or livestock to pull them. They negotiated culture at the family level as well as community wide. This type of "middle ground" was based on personal, social, and economic relationships rather than the political and diplomatic associations examined by historian Richard White.[37]

At least thirty-nine Creole households were established before 1800, land claims testimony would later suggest.[38] "The houses are well built after the Indian manner, and pleasantly situated on a very rich soil from which they raise every necessary of life in great abundance" Carver noted. "I saw here many horses of a good size and shape."[39] The *habitants* built homes near the Mississippi River; common fields were an important aspect of the settlement.

The fur-trade families initially adopted modified indigenous dwelling styles. Carver described them as "built of hewn plank neatly joined, and covered with bark so compactly as to keep out the most penetrating rains," with overhanging roofs in front that formed a sort of inset porch.[40]

[37] Some works on this topic include Peterson, "The People in Between"; Clara Sue Kidwell, "Indian Women as Cultural Mediators," *Ethnohistory* 39 (1992): 97–107; Sylvia Van Kirk, *Many Tender Ties: Women in Fur-Trade Society* (Norman: University of Oklahoma Press, 1980); Jennifer S. H. Brown, *Strangers in Blood: Fur Trade Company Families in Indian Country* (Vancouver: University of British Columbia Press, 1980); Tanis Chapman Thorne, *The Many Hands of My Relations; French and Indians on the Lower Missouri* (Columbia: University of Missouri Press, 1996); Susan Sleeper-Smith, *Native Women and French Men: Rethinking Cultural Encounter in the Western Great Lakes* (Amherst: University of Massachusetts Press, 2001); Carl J. Ekberg, *French Roots in the Illinois Country: The Mississippi Frontier in Colonial Times* (Urbana: University of Illinois Press, 1998); Murphy, *A Gathering of Rivers*. The reference is to Richard White, *The Middle Ground: Indians, Empires, and Republics in the Great Lakes Region, 1650–1815* (New York: Cambridge University Press, 1991).

[38] *ASPPL*, Vol. 5, 47–98, 270–272, 283–328.

[39] Gelb, *Jonathan Carver's Travels*, 76.

[40] Gelb, *Jonathan Carver's Travels*, 74.

This type of housing could be built without the need for Euro-American carpenters or nearby sawmills. By the early nineteenth century, some of the elites had houses of squared log construction, a distinctive French Canadian style. When Zebulon Pike visited in 1805 and 1806, he noted that "part of the houses are framed, and in place of weather-boarding there are small logs let into mortises made in the uprights, joined close, daubed on the outside with clay, and handsomely whitewashed within."[41] He added, "The inside furniture of their houses is decent and, indeed, in those of the most wealthy displays a degree of elegance and taste."[42]

Creoles were known for being both charming and fun-loving. Pike commented that "they possess the spirit of generosity and hospitality in an eminent degree."[43] Particularly during the long winters when time could hang heavy, they filled up their lives with sleigh rides, dancing to local fiddlers, horse racing, drinking, and card parties. Those with larger homes more often hosted and might clear the furniture out of one room to create a dance floor, and set up a babysitting area in another.[44] A comment about a party at Green Bay could have been written for Prairie du Chien: "Nothing could exceed the mirth and hilarity of the company. No restraint, but of good manners – no excess of conventionalities – genuine, hearty good-humor and enjoyment ... with just enough of the French element to add zest."[45]

Weather permitting, sports were popular. Willard Keyes, a Vermont-born man who arrived at Prairie du Chien in 1817, noted that the residents enjoyed several types of recreation: "the people are galloping about on French Ponys[,] playing at ball, billiards [etc.]" but disapproved because "the Sabbath appears to be a day of recreation and amusement among them."[46] When Pike first arrived at the Prairie, his men were soon challenged to entertain the locals by proving their athletic talents, and he proudly reported that his men "beat all the Villagers jumping and hopping."[47] Native athletes sometimes held lacrosse games at the Prairie.

---

[41] Elliott Coues, ed., *The Expeditions of Zebulon Montgomery Pike* (New York: Francis P. Harper, 1895), 303–304.

[42] Coues, *Expeditions of Pike*, 303–304.

[43] Coues, *Expeditions of Pike*, 304–305.

[44] James H. Lockwood, "Early Times and Events in Wisconsin," *WHC*, Vol. 2 (1856), 120; Elizabeth T. Baird, "O-De-Jit-Wa-Win-Wing."

[45] Juliette Kinzie, *Wau-Bun; The "Early Day" in the North-West* [1856] (Urbana: University of Illinois Press, 1992), 19.

[46] Keyes, "A Journal of Life in Wisconsin," 353.

[47] Donald Jackson, ed., *The Journals of Zebulon Montgomery Pike* (Norman: University of Oklahoma Press, 1966), 23.

Pike observed one such match in 1806 in which one team consisted of Dakotas and the other of Ho-Chunks and Meskwakis, and he reported, "It is an interesting sight to see two or three hundred naked Savages contending on a plain who shall bear the palm of victory; as he who drives the ball round the Goal, is much shouted by his companions." Notwithstanding Pike's use of the pejorative term "Savages," he found the game very entertaining, and opined that the Dakotas won more "from their superior skill in throwing the Ball, than superiority of foot," since he thought the Ho-Chunks and Meskwakis were "the swiftest Runners."[48] Native women also sometimes played lacrosse in Prairie du Chien and around the region.[49]

### Strange Powers, Voyageur and Baker

In January of 1806, a young man with the wonderful name of Strange Powers went to Montreal and signed on to become a *voyageur* and to travel for the next two years to Michilimackinac and *"Dependances du Sud,"* the southern dependencies.[50] Thousands of Canadians entered the fur trade in this way in the eighteenth and nineteenth centuries, paddling the canoes and providing the physical labor supporting the elite peltry merchants.[51]

Strange's father John Powers from New England had taken the Loyalist side when the Revolutionary War broke out, enlisting in Boston in 1775 in the 84th Regiment of Foot (Royal Highland Emigrants) and went to Canada by early September of that year. John was discharged from the regiment in June of 1784, and lived in Sorel (also known as Fort William Henry), where in 1786 little Strange was born and baptized in Christ's Church Anglican. John and Magdalene Powers seem to have given their son a name that had been in the family: another Strange Powers (perhaps a grandfather), a mariner and also a Loyalist, had died

---

[48] Jackson, *Journals of Pike*, 125–126. Quote is from 126.

[49] Thomas Vennum Jr., *American Indian Lacrosse, Little Brother of War* (Washington: Smithsonian Institution Press, 1994), 184–185; George Catlin, *Catlin's Letters and Notes on the North American Indians [1841]* (North Dighton, MA: JG Press, 1995), Vol. 2, 164–166.

[50] Voyageur Contracts Database, Centre du Patrimoine, Société Historique de Saint-Boniface, Saint-Boniface, Manitoba, Banq, Greffes de notaries, Microfilm number M620/1535 02497, http://shsb.mb.ca/en/Voyageurs_database, accessed July 8, 2011. His name was mis-transcribed as Strange Rose.

[51] Podruchny, *Making the Voyageur World*.

in Rhode Island in 1777.[52] As a voyageur, Strange Powers the younger (who was sometimes known as Strange Pose or Poze) became acquainted with the western Great Lakes region, and eventually went to work for Michel Brisbois at Prairie du Chien in the business of making bread and hardtack biscuits to provision travelers, as Brisbois began to diversify his commercial efforts.[53]

Everyone loved bread.[54] For Euro-Americans, the leavened loaves were an essential but gendered part of life, something their mothers had created, but Prairie du Chien was a village of brown women whose Native mothers had made unleavened corn bread instead. They didn't know how to work with yeast. Some of the residents grew a little wheat, so about 1809 Henry Fisher set up a horse mill to grind it, and people imported barrels of flour as well.[55]

These elements combined to inspire Michel Brisbois to supplement his extensive trading business by opening a bakery and hiring Strange Powers to work there. Not only did they sell the bread, but they traded bread tickets worth fifty loaves for each 100 pounds of flour, and the tickets became a kind of local money. An early resident recalled that they "made a convenient change to buy trifles of the Indians with." He added, "None of the inhabitants pretended to make their own bread, but depended entirely upon the bake-house."[56] Powers later explained that the bakery was worth "between three & four dollars per day" in profits to Brisbois.[57] Having found a niche for himself, Strange Powers would marry into the Antaya family.

[52] British Military C Series, RG 8, I, Vol. 505, 127–128, National Archives of Canada Microfilm C-3043, Microfilm C-2861; and Vol. 506, 93, Microfilm C-3043; Anglican Church register for William Henry, Quebec National Archives microfilm 128.41, cited in Alison Hare, "John Powers of Sorel," 2001, private collection of Virginia Barrette Powell. Regarding earlier Strange Powers, personal correspondence, Virginia Powell to the author, January 24, 2011. Thanks to her for sharing this information.

[53] For example, see Isaac Lee map, "Plan of the Settlement at Prairie du Chien," 1820, Wisconsin Historical Society WHi-79654 (this map was first published in *ASPPL* facing 5, 270); Hansen, James L. "The Pelletier dit Antaya Families of Prairie du Chien." Strange was unable to write his own name, Strange Powers Deposition, Feb. 29, 1832, Burton Historical Collection, William Woodbridge Papers, Detroit Public Library; on biscuits, Mary Elise Antoine personal correspondence with the author, July 26, 2012.

[54] Kinzie, *Wau-Bun* [1992], 92.

[55] Lockwood, "Early Times," 125; William Arundell, "Indian History," [written 1809] *Galena (IL) Miners' Journal*, October 30, 1830, State Historical Society of Wisconsin, Madison, File 1809 (typescript); Lyman C. Draper, transcriber and ed., John Shaw, "Shaw's Narrative," *WHC*, Vol. 2 (1856), 227.

[56] Lockwood, "Early Times," *WHC*, Vol. 2, 125.

[57] Strange Powers Deposition, Woodbridge Papers.

## A Conquered People

The American conquest of Prairie du Chien did not really take place until the War of 1812. Even though Prairie du Chien became nominally part of the new United States at the end of the Revolutionary War under the Treaty of Paris (which was ratified in 1784), most residents continued to feel loyalty to British Canada. British officials did not vacate their posts around the western Great Lakes region until after Jay's treaty was signed in 1795. As historian Alice E. Smith explained, "it was soon apparent that the British would interpret loosely the treaty promise to evacuate the posts 'with all convenient speed.'"[58] When the Wisconsin region fell within Indiana Territory in 1800, Governor William Henry Harrison sent commissions to Prairie du Chien for five local men to be sworn in as justices of the peace and officers of the militia, but these appointees may not have exercised a great deal of authority. According to Prairie du Chien's local historian Peter Scanlan, "probably these appointments remained only paper appointments, with law and order in the hands of the traders much as before."[59] Zebulon Pike paid a few visits to Prairie du Chien in 1805 and 1806 as he was checking out the new territories and making himself generally obnoxious to Indian and *habitant* alike but did not leave in place any military unit.[60]

Not until the War of 1812 did the United States try to assert real control over the Prairie. On June 2, 1814, General William Clark led a squad of men up the Mississippi from St. Louis and they began to build Fort Shelby at Prairie du Chien. Once its construction was well under way, Clark left the soldiers under the command of Lieutenant Joseph Perkins and went back downriver. Two and a half weeks later, Perkins raised the American flag over the new fort. Two small cannons armed the structure, while a gunboat moored nearby kept watch, carrying two cannons, several howitzers, and most of the ammunition and other provisions sent to sustain the garrison.

But then a British force of 530 Indian warriors and 120 Creole and Anglo fur-trade workers under trader William McKay attacked on July 17. Among their number were Michel Brisbois Jr. (Chambreywinkau's

---

[58] Alice E. Smith, *The History of Wisconsin*, Vol. I (Madison: State Historical Society of Wisconsin, 1973), 73; Carl J. Ekberg, *French Roots in the Illinois Country: The Mississippi Frontier in Colonial Times* (Urbana: University of Illinois Press, 1998), 103.
[59] Scanlan, *Prairie du Chien*, 166–167. Quote is on 167.
[60] Scanlan, *Prairie du Chien*, 113–116.

son) and a trader named Joseph Rolette; the attack damaged the gunboat so that its captain to save it cut the cable and retreated downstream.[61]

Little Bernard Brisbois, eight years old, watched from a distance as his brother and the other men prepared to shell the American vessel, and he would later remember that the Americans had fired on him. He had climbed a fence near the family home, he recalled, "to get as good a view as he could" of the gunboat. "Those on the boat noticing his too inquisitive observations, fired a rifle shot at him, the ball passing between his legs, and lodging in his father's house," he told an interviewer.[62] Whether the soldiers actually took aim at the little boy or he was simply caught in the crossfire, the impression of American aggression stayed with him.

The British force laid siege to the fort for three days and exchanged sporadic small arms fire, forcing its surrender on July 19, 1814. The battle of Prairie du Chien had been noisy but there were no deaths and only eight minor injuries. The British renamed the fort McKay, and a garrison composed of volunteers under the leadership of Captain Andrew Bulger suffered through the fall and winter with inadequate supplies and low morale.[63]

The war caused hardships for Prairie du Chien's residents, due in large part to an interruption in trade, which meant not only that the peltry business suffered but also that it became more difficult to import some of their food. While the townspeople's sympathies were generally with the British, they were ill-equipped to help support the garrison. In a letter from Prairie du Chien, trader Duncan Graham, a captain in the British Indian Department, wrote, "Let a person turn his head what way he will, he can find nothing but misery, famine and distress in all their various shapes, staring him in the face.... By a proclamation issued some time ago, all the inhabitants of this place are requested to deliver one fourth part of all the wheat in their possession into the king's store. This appears to be a hard task for these poor, distressed people."[64] Many *habitants*, no doubt, had mixed feelings when news came that the war was over and the Treaty of Ghent (concluded on Christmas eve of 1814) ratified the hegemony of the United States over Prairie du Chien.

Some certainly gave sighs of relief when the demanding British evacuated after burning the fort, but there was wonder as they looked up

---

[61] Smith, *The History of Wisconsin*, Vol. I, 87–88.

[62] Draper, ed., Brisbois, "Traditions," 295.

[63] Smith, *The History of Wisconsin*, Vol. I, 88–90.

[64] Duncan Graham to John Lawe, March 14, 1815, *WHC*, Vol. 10, 127–132, quoted in Smith, *The History of Wisconsin*, Vol. I, 90–91.

into the night sky to see the stars falling as a meteor shower provided a cosmic comment on the change of régimes. What did it portend?[65] Most of Prairie du Chien's British traders left for northern trading posts, while the French Creoles generally decided to stay and weather the political changes.[66]

The war disrupted many families because of their political loyalties, among them the Brisbois and Fishers. Henry Fisher's wife Marianne LaSallière and baby daughter Elizabeth had taken refuge with her family at Mackinac Island, which was in the United States. Their marriage did not survive this separation. Siding with the British, Henry Fisher took his sons Henry and Alexander and nephew Michel Brisbois Jr. and went north of the border to Red River to work for the Hudson's Bay Company, not to return for many years.[67] He left his daughter Jane and son George to be raised by Michel and Domitille Brisbois.[68]

## Consequences of Conquest

The United States' conquest would have enormous consequences for the *habitants* and the tribes. In some ways, the transfer of power to the Americans signified the same types of changes that had taken place when the British took over from the French. There would be new government officials and policies, expectations for military assistance, and efforts to gain the allegiance of the tribes and the Creoles. Eventually, however, it became clear that the War of 1812 had ushered in the era of settler colonialism and that land would be a central issue.

The government wanted to pacify the Indians and secure the support and loyalty of the Creoles. Taking the advice of Governor Lewis Cass, policymakers decided to focus on trying to win the allegiance of the region's Indians using three tactical institutions: military posts at key locations, Indian agencies, and government-owned trading posts to be called "factories" staffed by men known as "factors."[69] Prairie du Chien's location at the end of the Fox-Wisconsin riverway that connected the

---

[65] Draper, Brisbois, "Traditions," 297; Smith, *The History of Wisconsin,* Vol. I, 90.

[66] Smith, *The History of Wisconsin,* Vol. I, 91. Some had to leave because they had sworn oaths of allegiance to the United States as appointees and feared being charged with treason for having supported Britain in the war.

[67] Rentmeesters, *Wisconsin Creoles,* 246; Scanlan, *Prairie du Chien,* 116. Michel Brisbois Jr. was actually the nephew of Fisher's first wife.

[68] Rentmeesters, *Wisconsin Creoles,* 246.

[69] Bruce E. Mahan, *Old Fort Crawford and the Frontier* [1926] (reprint, Prairie du Chien: Howe Printing, 2000), 67–68.

Great Lakes to the Mississippi was considered to be a top strategic priority, so it would be the site of all three: a new fort, an Indian agent, and a "factory." Even before the army, the first agent of the American government to arrive in May of 1816 was the factor John W. Johnson, the American husband of the Sauk and Meskwaki woman Tapassia, whom he had espoused while working at Fort Madison in Iowa. Without local Native in-laws, it is doubtful that Johnson would have been accepted here. He was soon competing for Native customers with the established traders, not always successfully.[70]

The "factories" that the U.S. policymakers had created to win Indian customers away from the British did not always prosper, mainly because the goods they sold were of inferior quality. One of the American-born traders, James Lockwood, explained that Congress's "humane purpose of preventing the British traders from extortions on the Indians, and of counteracting British influence over them" was not effective, "and through the bad management of the traders, the Government of the United States was made to appear contemptible in the eyes of the Indians." While the U.S. factors were peddling "sleazy and cheap" merchandise, British goods were much superior.[71]

More striking changes came with the army of occupation in the following month. "The officers of the army treated the inhabitants as a conquered people, and the commandants assumed all the authority of governors of a conquered country," an early resident later recalled.[72] The Great Lakes region **was** a conquered country, and like other subjugated and colonized regions throughout history, it was about to experience profound political, economic, social, and demographic change.

The presence of the army was the most immediate fact demonstrating that the United States was now going to dominate Prairie du Chien and its neighboring provinces. Until the War of 1812, colonial powers had been mostly far away and had asserted control imperfectly. The French fort built in 1753 had been staffed for only a short time; the British had appointed a few local men to civil roles, but they had exercised great autonomy and the British authorities had not interfered with the town's main activities of trade and subsistence agriculture. After the American Revolution, other men received civilian commissions and Zebulon Pike stopped by for two days, but generally speaking, life had not been much

---

[70] Mahan, *Old Fort Crawford*, 70; Forsyth, "A List of the Sac and Fox half breeds," 1824.

[71] Lockwood, "Early Times," 130; Kellogg, *British Regime*, 261–264; George Hunt, "A Personal Narrative," *Michigan Pioneer and Historical Collections* 8 (1885): 663.

[72] Lockwood, "Early Times," 128–129.

affected. There had not even been any Christian missionizing, and those who wanted the services of a priest had traveled to St. Louis or Mackinac. Most local disputes had been mediated by local elites, although a few had been taken to far away venues.

As Wisconsin historian Alice E. Smith argued, "During the three decades of changing territorial status [from the Revolution through the War of 1812], the United States had exercised a minimum of control over the region between Lake Michigan and the Mississippi.... The central government of the United States, occupied with such weighty matters as internal organization, bringing the Ohio Valley Indian tribes to terms, and maintaining survival during the reverberations of the Napoleonic conflict, could give no serious attention to the upper Mississippi fur-trade frontier."[73] But now the new United States was flexing its muscles and by building Fort Crawford signaled that it was going to impose its institutions, laws, leadership, and culture on the region. Other forts were established up and down the Mississippi and around the Great Lakes as well.[74]

Brevet Brigadier General Thomas A. Smith of the United States Army aimed to assert American control in no uncertain terms over this region which had been contested ground between the United States and Great Britain for more than two generations. He arrived at Prairie du Chien on June 20, 1816, to build the new fort and assert American sovereignty over the land.[75]

When he arrived to stake American claims to the region and the real estate, Smith was surprised to find Prairie du Chien inhabited by about 600 people.[76] He viewed the towns' residents as "intruders," as squatters who had "in violation of the laws taken possession of public lands," and he reported to his superiors:

I would have destroyed the settlement, and delivered the male part of the inhabitants to the civil authority to be prosecuted for the intrusion, but for the impression that they could be made useful in provisioning a post so remote. The officer left in command was authorized to carry this view of the subject into effect whenever he should deem it expedient.[77]

---

[73] Smith, *The History of Wisconsin,* Vol. I, 203.
[74] Tanner, *Atlas,* 106–107.
[75] Mahan, *Old Fort Crawford,* 70.
[76] Population figures based on Coues, *Expeditions of Pike,* 304; Daniel S. Durrie, "Annals of Prairie du Chien," *Early Out-Posts of Wisconsin* (Madison: State Historical Society of Wisconsin, 1873), 5.
[77] Thomas A. Smith to John Calhoun, September 2, 1819, extract, *ASPPL,* Vol. 5, 320.

But the residents of Prairie du Chien were not squatters. Smith clearly did not care that they lived in a town with a history dating back to the mid-eighteenth century, and that the Creoles had collectively gained not only the permission of the Meskwakis but also the recognition of the British colonial government for their presence on the land. Smith also did not understand the roles of women in this community: he assumed that only the male inhabitants could be useful, completely missing Prairie du Chien women's centrality in society and economy, including agricultural production.

Although Jay's Treaty of 1794 had stipulated that all residents of the region were to have U.S. citizenship unless they chose otherwise and would have the right to trade, the officers at Prairie du Chien did not honor many of these rights. Smith and Indian Agent Major Richard Graham challenged the resident traders to show licenses and confiscated the goods of all whose documents were not in order. They commandeered several houses for the use of the army; factor John W. Johnson was ordered not to pay rent for the trading house he had leased.[78] At the location selected for the new Fort Crawford, the commanding officer ordered the resident families to take down their houses and rebuild them on the outskirts of town.[79]

Smith decided to make an example of Michel Brisbois Sr. and charged him with having supported Britain during the war; Strange Powers was also detained and the two were confined and sent under guard to St. Louis to face trial.[80] Domitille and the children and other members of the household were turned out of their house, which was seized by the commanding officer along with the bakery and winters' supply of cordwood. Later, Michel was acquitted, having been defended by Thomas Hart Benton, and he returned with Strange Powers to try to restore order to his household and business.[81]

Colonel Talbot Chambers, who arrived in the spring of 1817 as commanding officer, was particularly harsh. Prairie Du Chien's historian Peter Scanlan aptly commented that Chambers "showed himself very arbitrary and treated many of the Canadian-French as traitors."[82] He arrested the American Fur Company's clerks and sent them to St. Louis for trial and

---

[78] Mahan, *Old Fort Crawford*, 70–71.
[79] Mahan, *Old Fort Crawford*, 71–73; *ASPPL*, Vol. 5, 63–64; 91–92, 321.
[80] Brisbois, "Traditions and Recollections"; Strange Powers deposition, Woodbridge Papers.
[81] Mahan, *Old Fort Crawford*, 71; *ASPPL*, Vol. 5, 63–64; 91–92, 321.
[82] Mahan, *Old Fort Crawford*, 72–73; Scanlan, *Prairie du Chien*, 124.

banished trader Joseph Rolette to an island in the Mississippi for the winter of 1816–17.[83] Chambers sometimes drank to excess, and one day in 1817 while intoxicated, he "chased a young female into the house of Jacque Menard, with no good motive for doing so," according to a witness. Menard intervened, so Chambers ordered his men to bind, strip, and whip him.[84] "Instances of high handed oppression and injustice were … frequently committed by some military martinet, upon the persons, liberty or property of those whom they were sent to protect," summarized Henry Baird, a lawyer who spent some time in Prairie du Chien serving the circuit court.[85]

In the meantime, Native people continued to come to Prairie du Chien to exchange furs and other items for manufactured goods, and the traders who could manage to get licenses continued to supply them, while also sending their traveling assistants, clerks, and *voyageurs* abroad to do business with their Native clientele.

## Land Claims

Native people would look back on the American takeover as the moment when their land became vulnerable. In 1829 at a Prairie du Chien treaty council, the Ho-Chunk orator, Huwanikga, the Little Elk, gave a speech recounting the history of all three phases of colonization of the region. He spoke fondly of the French who had married into Native communities and adopted aspects of their culture and who "wanted to buy no land of us!" He had kind words for the English who came to trade and to recruit Native men for military projects, "but never asked us to sell our country." But he spoke bitterly of the American land hunger. Finally, he explained, "came the 'Blue coat,' and no sooner had he seen a small portion of our country, than he wished to see a map of THE WHOLE of it; and, having seen it, he wished us to sell it ALL to him."[86]

Recognizing the vulnerability of their land tenure, the Creoles petitioned the government, asking Congress to confirm their land titles. In 1816, they told their history in a document that acknowledged both

---

[83] Scanlan, *Prairie du Chien*, 125; Lockwood, "Early Times," 129.

[84] Scanlan, *Prairie du Chien*, 125; Shaw, "Shaw's Narrative," 229–230. Eventually Chambers was dishonorably discharged from the army for cruelly punishing his men, then went to Mexico and joined the army there. "Shaw's Narrative," 230.

[85] Henry Baird, "Early History and Conditions of Wisconsin," *WHC*, Vol. 2 (1856), 84.

[86] Caleb Atwater, *Remarks Made on a Tour to Prairie du Chien in 1829* (Columbus, OH: Isaac Whiting, 1831), 121–122.

French colonialism and the sovereignty of the local tribes and dated the establishment of the Creole town from the construction of Marin's fort. "The government of France, then master of all the country upon the Mississippi, established a military post near the mouth of the Ouisconsin, of which Mons. De Marin was the commandant, and ... many families settled themselves in the vicinity of the post with the assent of that officer, and [with] the approbation of the neighbouring Indians, the rightful owners of the soil, formed there the village of Prairie Du Chien," they wrote.[87] Creoles in other fur-trade communities around the Great Lakes had similar concerns. There was a very real danger that the residents of Prairie du Chien would be evicted or would become landless, marginal people under the new regime, as American officials were intent on pushing Native people aside, individualizing real estate holdings, and providing land for westward-moving settlers. And married women were especially at risk because the American legal system of *coverture* turned their property over to their husbands.

This was a key moment in the determination of land rights. Settler colonialism is a form of imperialism where a shift from extractive economic processes carried out with the participation of indigenous people gives way to a system in which Native people are forced off the land to make way for settlers wanting exclusive use of the soil.[88] In similar contexts a few decades later, similar peoples of mixed cultures and ancestries leftover from previous waves of colonization would fare poorly and lose their lands to new Anglo-American and Anglo-Canadian regimes. To the north, in Red River, Manitoba, and Saskatchewan, the Métis rose in resistance when it became clear that the Canadian government had no intention of recognizing their rights to the ribbon lots they had established over the years. After much suffering, the Métis would emerge mostly landless and consistently poor from struggles against the tide of

---

[87] "The Petition of the Inhabitants of Prairie du Chien," 1816, Wisconsin Historical Society Library, http://content.wisconsinhistory.org/u?/tp,72459, accessed 7 May 2012. The petition gave 1755 as the construction date of the fort, although they may have been alluding to a fort Marin had built south of Prairie du Chien during autumn 1753; another fort was built at Prairie du Chien sometime after that. Bailey, *Journal of Joseph Marin*, 62, 67, 92.

[88] Patrick Wolfe, "Settler Colonialism and the Elimination of the Native," *Journal of Genocide Research* 8, no. 4 (December 2006): 387–409; James Belich, *Replenishing the Earth: The Settler Revolution and the Rise of the Anglo-World, 1783–1939* (Oxford, UK: Oxford University Press, 2009), 23; Margaret D. Jacobs, *White Mother to a Dark Race: Settler Colonialism, Maternalism, and the Removal of Indigenous Children in the American West and Australia, 1880–1940* (Lincoln: University of Nebraska Press, 2009).

new settlement. To the southwest in California, New Mexico, Texas, and Arizona, most of the Hispanic landowners would find themselves forced off the real estate coveted by newcomers, generally Anglophone American settlers. For these Hispanic people, the loss of land would mean persistent poverty and for many, a dependent economic status and permanent role as unskilled wage workers. For Métis and Hispanic border peoples, the experience of being dispossessed helped to solidify a collective self-consciousness as outsiders, an identity that Anglophone settlers would emphasize and use to support discrimination. These outsider identities would be racialized as non-white. [89]

But many Creoles in the region around the Great Lakes and the upper Mississippi Valley, *were* able to gain title to the land in fur-trade towns. This was because some Creole families adapted their ideas about land and found ways to maximize their eventual holdings, and consequently their ability to retain Native ground. But this was also because the government needed Creole support for the new regime and used land rights as one incentive to persuade the *habitants* to tolerate and even to participate in the American colonization of the region and the tribes. Policymakers at both the national and the territorial level realized that in order to govern and control the thousands of Indians living in the region, and in order to introduce and successfully establish the new organs of government, they would need the Creoles as allies and participants. They were willing to pay for allegiance with a few real estate deeds.

In 1820, Michigan Territory's officials decided it was time to figure out who owned what land, so that the rest of it could be surveyed and sold to

---

[89] J. M. Bumsted, *A History of the Canadian Peoples*, 4th ed. (Don Mills, Ontario: Oxford University Press, 2011), 212; Alexander Begg, *The Creation of Manitoba* (Toronto: A. H. Hovey, 1871), 110–111, 255–256, reproduced in Victoria Community Network, http://victoria.tc.ca/history/etext/metis-bill-of-rights.html accessed Nov. 20, 2012, and Canada History, http://www.canadahistory.com/sections/documents/thewest/metisbill-rights.htm, accessed Nov. 20, 2012; Maggie Siggins, *Riel: A Life of Revolution* (Toronto: HarperCollins, 1994), 95–97; Brown, "The Métis: Genesis and Rebirth"; Jennifer Brown and Theresa Schenck, "Métis, Mestizo, and Mixed-Blood"; Rupert's Land Act, 1868, William F. Maton, The Solon Law Archive, http://www.solon.org/Constitutions/Canada/English/rpl_1868.html, accessed Nov. 5, 2012; Albert Camarillo, *Chicanos in a Changing Society*; Mario Barrera, *Race and Class in the Southwest: A Theory of Racial Inequality* (Notre Dame, IN: University of Notre Dame Press, 1979); Miroslava Chavez-Garcia, *Negotiating Conquest: Gender and Power in California, 1770s to 1880s* (Tucson: University of Arizona Press, 2004), 143–150; Reginald Horsman, *Race and Manifest Destiny: The Origins of American Racial Anglo-Saxonism* (Cambridge, MA: Harvard University Press, 1981), 279; Jerome R. Adams, *Greasers and Gringos: The Historical Roots of Anglo-Hispanic Prejudice* (Jefferson, NC: McFarland, 2006), chs. 19–24.

new "settlers."[90] No doubt the officials had been influenced by the efforts of French elites from Louisiana and St. Louis who, according to historian Jay Gitlin, had been petitioning, writing letters, and meeting with U.S. officials to secure their property rights for two decades.[91] Colonel Isaac Lee of Detroit accepted the assignment to visit the old fur-trade communities at Green Bay and Prairie du Chien to interview the residents and draw lines on a map indicating whose land was where.[92] He was chosen because he could speak both French and English, because he was well connected, and because he didn't have anything else pressing that he needed to do for the next year or so.[93]

Off he went in the summer of 1820, traveling by canoe from Detroit around the Great Lakes to Green Bay, and down the Fox and Wisconsin rivers, arriving in Prairie du Chien in October, a time of year when the town was surrounded by the breathtaking beauty of autumn's colors: leaves glowing with warmth on sunny crisp days, and the *habitants* finishing their harvest, counting their trade receipts, or helping Native customers equip themselves for their winter hunting seasons.[94] When Lee arrived, he went house-to-house, introducing himself and explaining his assignment and the process he would use to determine who would receive land titles.[95] He would collect testimony from the residents, record it, translate it if necessary, and submit it to commissioners at Detroit. They would make recommendations to the federal government.

As early as 1709, French-American communities had been conceptualized and drawn by mapmakers as including "long lots," or "ribbon lots," parcels of narrow land holdings fronting on a river (or sometimes a road) and extending back a long ways. This form of landholding afforded residents access to the transportation networks and proximity to their neighbors, but gave sufficient land to permit some farming and cutting of wild hay for livestock. This land pattern probably originated in eastern Europe and moved west; it is still seen in parts of Normandy, according to David

---

[90] Scanlan, *Prairie du Chien*, 184–189.

[91] Jay Gitlin, *The Bourgeois Frontier: French Towns, French Traders and American Expansion* (New Haven, CT: Yale University Press, 2010), 57–64.

[92] Smith, *The History of Wisconsin*, Vol. I, 65–66.

[93] William Woodbridge, Peter Audrain, and Jonathan Kearsley to Isaac Lee, Instructions. Detroit, August 8, 1820, Woodbridge Papers, Burton Historical Collection, Detroit Public Library.

[94] He interviewed the local residents who had been there for many years to be sure the Indian title had been extinguished.

[95] Isaac Lee, "to the commissioners of the land District of Detroit" [April 1822], Woodbridge Papers, Burton Historical Collection, Detroit Public Library.

Buisseret, a scholar of the cartography of French America.[96] Historian Carl Ekberg, who has written at length of this land system, pointed out that it was used "everywhere in North America where there was the least bit of French influence," along the St. Lawrence River, around the Great Lakes, in the Red River of the north, through the Illinois Country including St. Louis, and in Louisiana.[97]

When Isaac Lee got to Prairie du Chien and began talking to people, he expected to find privately held land, in long lots. People who had lived along the St. Lawrence River or in the Illinois country were used to the long lots, but many residents had their own conceptions of appropriate land tenure. Instead, their settlement pattern seems to have been both communal and Native.

The Prairie du Chien parcels that would become known as "farm lots" were generally not places where people lived. The town contained four clusters of dwellings: a "Main Village" on the island with about three dozen claimants, an "Upper Village" north of the island along the river where seven families lived, and two clusters of homes along the slough that separated the island from the mainland when the river was high (see map, Figure 1.2).

More problematic still was the fact that residents seemed to possess a sense of collective ownership of much of the prairie, in line with Native concepts of community proprietorship of a village or region. The town had long been viewed this way both by Europeans and by Creoles. A traveler had commented forty years earlier that Prairie du Chien was "a town of considerable note, built after the Indian manner."[98] Echoing this, Denis Courtois (who had lived there since 1791) told Lee in 1820, "the Prairie des Chien has formerly been occupied something like an Indian Village ... that the whole of Prairie des Chien has been occupied by little improvements and as a common since his arrival in this Country."[99] In her memoir, Theresa LaPointe Barrette recalled that her parents married at Prairie du Chien in 1803, and that "in those days, when they wanted land, all they had to do was take possession of it."[100] Native communities,

[96] David Buisseret, *Mapping the French Empire in North America* (Chicago: Newberry Library, 1991), 29.

[97] Ekberg, *French Roots*, chs. 1–2. Quote is on 9.

[98] John Long, *Voyages and Travels in the Years 1768–1788* (Chicago: R. R. Donnelly, 1922), 185, quoted in Ekberg, *French Roots in the Illinois Country*, 103

[99] Denis Courtois, deposition Oct. 21, 1820, Woodbridge Papers, Detroit Public Library, Burton Historical Collection.

[100] "Reminiscence of Theresa Barrette," in Consul Willshire Butterfield, *History of Crawford and Richland Counties* (Springfield, IL: Union, 1884), 564–565.

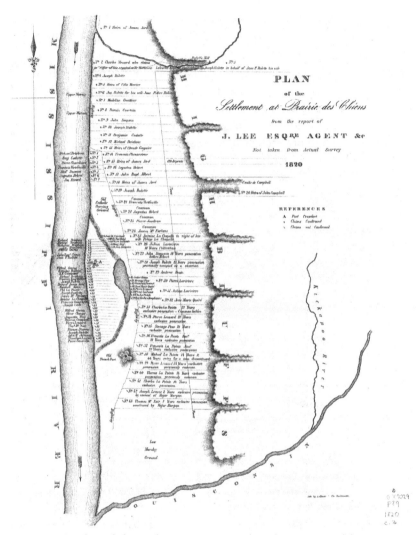

FIGURE 1.2. Plan of the settlement at Prairie des Chiens. Created by Isaac Lee, 1820. Wisconsin Historical Society WHi-79654. This map was originally published facing 5: 270 in U.S. Congress, *American State Papers: Documents, Legislative and Executive, of the Congress of the United States ...*, 38 vols., Class VIII, Public Lands, 8 vols., ed. Walter Lowrie et al. (Washington, DC, 1832–1861).

of course, had communal land bases, in which families had the right to use certain areas for specific purposes such as farming, fishing, sugar making, or other activities, and common areas available to all.[101]

---

[101] William Cronon, *Changes in the Land: Indians, Colonists, and the Ecology of New England* (New York: Hill and Wang, 1983), 59–70; Cronon, *Nature's Metropolis: Chicago*

Lee himself reported at length on communal village landholding patterns. He wrote, "the whole extent of the prairie on which is situated the village of Prairie des Chiens, excepting so much of it as is fenced and in the exclusive possession of individuals, is claimed by the villagers and inhabitants of that settlement as a common appurtenant to the village, and that many objections were urged against some of the claims preferred, lest they should ultimately be found to encroach upon that common." He wondered if he should trust these witnesses, since they "felt equal interest in establishing the claim," so he made a special effort to press key male informants on this issue: "I made diligent inquiry ... especially among the oldest and most intelligent of the inhabitants," he explained, and had become convinced that "from the earliest periods in the history of this settlement, all that part of the said prairie not enclosed ... was ... and is used as a common ... in which all the inhabitants are acknowledged to have an equal interest."[102] Lee might have been familiar with the concept of commons which had been practiced both in colonial New England and New France but which had pretty much faded in those areas by this time, according to historian Allan Greer.[103] Prairie du Chien's open-field farming used together with closely spaced houses located elsewhere was characteristic of francophone settlements only in the Illinois County and Prairie du Chien and was not practiced in this combination elsewhere, according to Ekberg.[104]

The areas in Prairie du Chien that were *not* considered to be part of the common were fairly small, perhaps even less than half the land, before Lee forced the issue. Lee's map shows a single fence running north and south along the length of the prairie, enclosing perhaps one quarter of the land between the bluffs and the river. Another map, done by survey in 1828, shows a similar long fence, plus fences enclosing a field, another around a house (and perhaps a garden), and two other relatively small areas. They seem to have been designed to enclose areas where crops were planted, and to keep animals out. Lee's map also indicates at least four areas that had been commons at one time.[105]

*and the Great West* (New York: W.W. Norton, 1991), 27, 394, n. 11; Allan Greer, "Commons and Enclosure in the Colonization of North America," *American Historical Review* 117, no. 2 (April 2012): 365–386.

[102] *ASPPL*, Vol. 5, 308.

[103] Greer, "Commons and Enclosure," 374–375.

[104] Ekberg, *French Roots*, 28–30.

[105] Isaac Lee map, "Plan of the Settlement at Prairie du Chien," 1820; Lucius Lyon, Prairie du Chien map, 1828, Villa Louis Historic Site library, Prairie du Chien.

Clearly, individually owned private property was not the universal norm in Prairie du Chien. As a multi-ethnic Creole French-Indian town, it incorporated some elements of both Native and Euroamerican practices, cultural traditions, and expectations. The idea of commons seems to have been accepted by residents of both backgrounds. Prairie du Chien's blended families included people from both heritages, and its settlement patterns reflected practices familiar to Indians and francophones alike. Individual land rights in the American cultural and legal frameworks would have been a new concept for many of them. This put them particularly at risk for losing land rights.

The residents may have had some difficulty both understanding the requirements of the new land ownership system and planning how to maximize their land retention, given Lee's (and their own) preconceived notions about land ownership. They requested that a common be maintained in the central part of the community, but this request was not honored.[106]

As Isaac Lee went from house to house, he explained his mission and the rules governing who could claim what and how they had to justify their claims. The rules stated that claimants had to prove that they had possessed the land before 1796 (the year Jay's Treaty was finalized), or obtained parcels of land legally from someone who did.[107] So neighbors seem to have conferred and negotiated privately about the allotment of the land. Claimants had to ask their friends and employees to testify on their behalf. Certainly many were coached by the most authoritative or knowledgeable among them, about what they had to say: that so-and-so had been there since 1795 or had inherited or bought the land from a certain person who had been there since then. For example, for the parcel designated as Farm lot No. 1,

Dennis Courtois, ... being duly sworn, deposeth and saith that the above-described tract of land was occupied in [1791] by Joseph Creely, who sold to Jean Marie Cardinal, who sold to Stephen Hempstead, who sold to Joseph Rolette, who sold to James Aird, deceased; that the above-described tract of land, called the Grand farm, has been continually occupied by the aforesaid persons from [1791] to the present time.[108]

Later on because of some problems regarding the 1796 requirement, at Lee's request, Congress passed a law in 1823 permitting titles to be issued

---

[106] *ASPPL*, Vol. 5, 97.
[107] Frederick N. Trowbridge, "Confirming Land Titles in Early Wisconsin," *Wisconsin Magazine of History* 26, no. 3 (March 1943): 314–322, see especially p. 316.
[108] *ASPPL*, Vol. 5, 308–309.

to people who possessed the land as of 1812, as long as they had not been disloyal to the United States.[109]

Further complicating the landholding picture was the fact that some Native- descended women claimed lots. Native wives like Pokoussee came from communities in which mature women had a substantial amount of autonomy in their personal lives and economic activity, both because they controlled key resources and forms of production and because the norms of Midwestern Native societies emphasized both communalism and individual autonomy for women and men.[110] Native women managed their production of foods such as corn, beans, squash, and maple sugar, and they were considered to own the usufruct rights to the fields and sugar groves in which they worked.[111] And wives *as mothers* owned the family's property. A knowledgeable Indian agent reported that, "It is a maxim among the Indians that every thing belong[s] to the woman or women except the Indian [man]'s hunting and war implements, even the game, the Indians bring home on his back."[112]

Native wives did much of the farming in the early years. In fur-trade towns, residence was seasonal for *voyageurs,* but their female family members often stayed behind when the men were gone for extended periods to trade. An observer could have been describing Prairie du Chien

---

[109] Trowbridge, "Confirming Land Titles," 321; Isaac Lee "To the Commissioners of the land District of Detroit," April 1822, Woodbridge Papers, Burton Historical Collection, Detroit Public Library.

[110] Tanis C, Thorne, "For the Good of Her People: Continuity and Change for Native Women of the Midwest, 1650–1850," in *Midwestern Women: Work, Community and Leadership at the Crossroads,* edited by Lucy E. Murphy and Wendy Hamand Venet (Bloomington: Indiana University Press, 1998), 95–120; Rebecca Kugel, "Leadership within the Women's Community: Susie Bonga Wright of the Leech Lake Ojibwe," in *Midwestern Women,* 17–37. Political traditions acknowledged Native women's right to have a voice in community decision making, and some tribes included women's, as well as men's, formal political organizations and roles.

[111] Nancy Oestreich Lurie, "Indian Women: A Legacy of Freedom," in *Look to the Mountain Top,* edited by Charles Jones (San Jose, CA: Gousha, 1972), 29–36; "Journal of Peter Pond," in *WHC,* Vol. 18 (1908), 335; Thomas Forsyth, "An Account of the Manners and Customs of the Sauk and Fox Nations of Indian Tradition," in *The Indian Tribes of the Upper Mississippi Valley and Region of the Great Lakes,* edited by Emma Helen Blair (Cleveland: Arthur H. Clark, 1911), 2, 218; Greer, "Commons and Enclosure," 370. For an extended discussion of Native women's status, see Lucy Eldersveld Murphy, "Autonomy and the Economic Roles of Indian Women of the Fox-Wisconsin Region, 1763–1832," in *Negotiators of Change: Historical Perspectives on Native American Women,* edited by Nancy Shoemaker (New York: Routledge Press, 1994).

[112] Forsyth, "An Account of the Manners and Customs," 2, 218.

when he commented about Green Bay that "All these enclosures of men more or less employed as laborers by the traders were cultivated by their women, whom they called *wives*, but really Indian women with whom they lived after the Indian custom."[113] By the time Lee arrived, some farmers had moved up from the Illinois country and many husbands were also involved in various aspects of growing crops and animal husbandry, but the traditions of Native women's leadership and proprietary rights would certainly have persisted, at least for some families.[114]

But Lee's project challenged these norms and seems to have inspired creative adaptation on the part of many residents. They learned that under the U.S. laws, wives' land would be recorded as belonging to their husbands. Because wives could not independently own property, claims for land belonging to wives had to be entered by their husbands.[115] The claims map labeled each lot by its claimant, such as "Charles Menard who claims in right of his reputed wife Marianne Labuche Menard," and "Joseph Rolette for his wife Jane Fisher Rolette." Another is marked "Antoine LaChapelle in right of his wife Pelige La Chapelle." Fifteen-year-old Theresa La Pointe, unmarried, also put in a claim; the widow Madeleine Gauthier filed a claim as well.[116] Some husbands didn't mention their wives' names. Through their dealings with Lee, families and kin groups came to understand that the new legal system expected the land to be individualized and that Lee expected it to be expressed in long lots privately held by males – or by single women. So families devised ways to slice up their lands to official satisfaction, most to be listed under the names of the family's men.

Many of the claimants were men with Native wives and other kin, genealogical research shows. For example, Basil Giard had been one of the three men sent as representatives to the 1781 meeting that secured formal approval for the community at Prairie du Chien to be situated on Native land. His wife was Macoutchequoi, a Meskwaki woman, and they had two daughters, Louise (also known as Lisette) born in 1788 and Mary, born in 1794.[117] Lisette's husband François Chenevert claimed Farm Lot 14, stating he had received it from Giard, but probably

---

[113] "Lawe and Grignon Papers, 1794–1821," *WHC*, Vol. 10 (1888), 140.

[114] Mary Elise Antoine, *Prairie du Chien* (Charleston, SC: Arcadia, 2011).

[115] Nancy F. Cott, *Public Vows: A History of Marriage and the Nation* (Cambridge, MA: Harvard, 2000), 11–12.

[116] Isaac Lee map, "Plan of the Settlement at Prairie des Chiens."

[117] Forsyth, "A List of the Sac and Fox half breeds," 1824, 2T: 22; Scanlan, *Prairie du Chien*, 70.

Macoutchequoi had a hand in this land transfer to her daughter and son-in-law.[118] Cheenawpaukie was another Meskwaki woman living in Prairie du Chien in the early 1820s; her husband Augustin Hebert claimed a village lot, Farm Lot 16, and part of the old common, Farm Lot 22. Similarly, just south of Hebert's third claim was land patented to Pierre Jeandron, husband of Kaywiscoquai, who was also Meskwaki.[119] Pierre Courville, who had a child with a woman who was half Meskwaki, also claimed a lot in the village.[120]

The most interesting cases of creative efforts to maintain control of land come from the Antaya family. As we have seen, Pokoussee, a Meskwaki, had married Pierre Antaya, but he had died in 1816. Like Basil Giard, Pierre had been one of the three men to whom the Meskwakis gave permission for a trade town to be established, and no doubt his marriage to Pokoussee was an important part of the agreement. Pierre and Pokoussee had a large number of children, mostly daughters. On the southern end of the prairie, on or near where the Meskwaki village had been, their sons-in-law and other relatives sat down with Isaac Lee and claimed lot after contiguous lot, thirteen in all, or *30 percent* of the Prairie du Chien farm lots, plus seven smaller homesteads.

The family's nucleus was in the cluster of dwellings known as the Village of St. Friole, which grew up on the slough along the western section of some of these farm lots. Here were the houses of three of Pokoussee and Pierre's daughters, of the widower of a fourth, a granddaughter, two Antaya cousins, and another man whose relationship to the clan is unclear. They were Catherine Antaya and her husband Andre Basin, Euphrosine Antaya and her husband Strange Powers, Theotiste Antaya and her husband François Provost, Jean Marie Queré (whose mother may have been an Antaya), Pokoussee and Pierre Antaya's granddaughter Julie Crelis and her husband Pierre Lessard, Marie Antaya (Pierre's niece) and

---

[118] *ASPPL,* 308–312. The American State Papers transcript of the testimony states that Chenevert claimed he got the land from Jean Baptiste Giard, but there seems not to have been a person by that name. Wisconsin Historical Society genealogist James L. Hansen suggests that the transcriber made a mistake. James L. Hansen, personal correspondence with the author, July 13, 2011. It is also possible that Basil was sometimes called Jean Baptiste. Eventually the Giards moved across the river to Iowa. Scanlan, *Prairie du Chien,* 71.

[119] Isaac Lee map, "Plan of the Settlement at Prairie du Chien," 1820, Forsyth, "A List of the Sac and Fox half breeds," 1824, 2T: 22.

[120] Isaac Lee map, "Plan of the Settlement at Prairie du Chien," 1820; Forsyth, "A List of the Sac and Fox half breeds," 1824, 2T: 22. Her name is not given. Their child was Antoine, born in 1805. His claim may not have been confirmed.

her husband François LaPointe, Charles LaPointe (widower of Josette Antaya), and Jacques Bartholome *dit* Monplaisier (whose connection to the family, if any, is unclear).[121]

Like the house lots mentioned earlier, most of the farm lots on the southern part of Prairie du Chien were claimed by – and patented to – men whose wives were Pokoussee and Pierre Antaya's daughters. Their neighbors were other relatives[122] (see Figure 1.3).

We may imagine an Antaya family meeting at which the kinfolk had discussed the situation and decided on a strategy that allocated certain parcels to certain family members, and then instructed the husbands and cousins to step forward at Isaac Lee's hearings and make their claims. It is possible that Pokoussee had even presided.[123] At least some of these people, it seems, considered this Pokoussee's land to be handed down to her many descendents.

Although the community had recognized both common areas and some individualized parcels, only the latter were confirmed. Responding to Lee's recommendations, Congress approved most of the claims and confirmed the concept of long lots for Prairie du Chien by 1828, although it did not recognize the concept of commons.[124] Isaac Lee's map with its distinctive long lots continued to influence land conceptualizations and land ownership in Prairie du Chien. Today, Prairie du Chien's plat maps still use these long lots as part of the town's legal layout.[125] Congressional refusal to approve a continuation of the commons at Prairie du Chien is consistent with the government's project of dispossessing the Indians. As Greer points out, "where land was cleared and bounded for settler use, natives were generally excluded."[126] And so the Native ground-turned-Creole business center was divided and registered in the names of Native women's husbands.

---

[121] James L. Hansen, "Prairie du Chien's Earliest Church Records, 1817," *Minnesota Genealogical Journal* 4 (1985): 329–342, 340, 332; Hansen, "The Pelletier dit Antaya Families," *ASPPL*, 323–328. On Queré, Rentmeesters, *Wisconsin Creoles*, 324.

[122] Strange Powers, Michael Brisbois Jr., Andre Basin, Pierre La Riviere, and Charles La Pointe claimed and received title to the lots. Their wives were Pokoussee and Pierre Antaya's daughters Euphrosine, Catherine (who married Brisbois first, then Basin), Marguerite, and Josette Antaya, respectively. Hansen, "The Pelletier dit Antaya Families."

[123] Hansen, "The Pelletier dit Antaya Families." Pierre Antaya had died a few years before Lee's first visit to Prairie du Chien and Pokoussee had married Etienne Precour in 1817 or before. Precour did not claim a lot, however.

[124] Lee, "Plan of the Settlement"; *ASPPL*, Vol. 5, 308.

[125] Crawford County Wisconsin Land Atlas/Plat Book, (St. Cloud, MN: Cloud Cartographics, 2001).

[126] Greer, "Commons and Enclosure," 375.

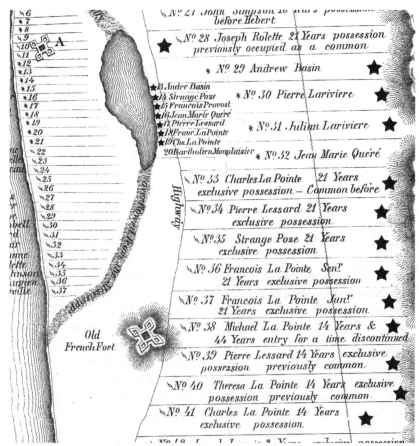

FIGURE 1.3. Antaya Kin Map. The lots marked with a star were claimed by sons-in-law and other relatives of Pokoussee and Pierre Antaya. Queré was probably another relative. Euphrosine Antaya actually claimed and received title to Farm Lot 28 near the top of the map, incorrectly indicated on this map as going to Joseph Rolette. The Antaya family cluster of village lots would be called St. Friole. The Antaya farm lots were at or near the old Mesquaki village site. [Detail from "Plan of the Settlement at Prairie des Chiens."]

Thus, the government individualized the land and then confirmed the Creoles in their right to the village and farm lots on the Prairie du Chien. *Eighty-six percent* of the village lots and *81 percent* of the farm lots went to French Creoles, and most of the rest went to Anglophone fur traders who had Creole families.[127] Their ability to avoid dispossession would

[127] Lucius Lyon, "Private Claims at Prairie du Chien," map, 1828, U.S. Dept. of the Interior, Bureau of Land Management archives, Springfield, Virginia.

provide a buffer against the economic and political changes to come. The many who could retain the land would be able to avoid becoming part of an underclass.

In other Creole towns around the Great Lakes and upper Mississippi Valley region, similar processes concluded with fur-trade families gaining and maintaining legal title to ribbon lots under the American regime. For example, the government confirmed many Creoles' real estate holdings in Detroit, Green Bay, St. Louis, Vincennes, and Kaskaskia.[128]

## Earthworks

Surveyors would soon be tramping through the fields and groves marking the boundaries of the newly defined lots with piles of stones and notches in trees. In the land records and deed books, Native people's continuing presence in this Creole community would be obscured by the names of European-descended men. But the land itself bore witness to a long Native presence, a continual reminder that this was Native land, and that Indian people had lived here for thousands of years.

A few years after Isaac Lee drafted his sketch of land claims at Prairie du Chien, Lucius Lyon was appointed to survey the lots more carefully and accurately. Interestingly, Lyon added details on Indian earthworks in the area, recognizing in at least a small way that centuries before he and Isaac Lee had divided Prairie du Chien into long lots, Native peoples in the Midwest had marked the land with earthworks in a wide range of styles. Other maps also record the presence of mounds that persisted into the nineteenth century, even if they do not persist to the present day.[129]

Native people in the area had reverence for the earthworks and may have tried to protect them.[130] Many of those mounds were on land claimed by Antaya husbands and kin Pierre Lessard, Francois LaPointe

---

[128] Buisseret, *Mapping the French Empire* 53, 71; Buley, *The Old Northwest* I, 121; Ekberg, *French Roots*, 67, 85, 99; Gitlin, *Bourgeois Frontier*, 58–64.

[129] Lucius Lyon, Prairie du Chien map, 1828, Villa Louis Historic Site library, Prairie du Chien; Albert Coryer map, Villa Louis Historic Site library, Prairie du Chien; James Duane Doty Papers, WIS Mss DD, Box 2, Folder 1, Wisconsin Historical Society Library, Madison. Many mounds can still be seen across the Mississippi River at Pike's Peak State Park and Effigy Mounds National Monument in Iowa.

[130] Some Ho-Chunks, for example, considered themselves the descendants of mound-builders. Albert Yellow Thunder, "Winnebago Chief Writes of Tribal History, Culture," *Wisconsin Rapids Daily Tribune*, Jan. 8, 1927, p. 8. Thanks to Patricia Mason for bringing this article to my attention.

Jr., and Michel and Theresa LaPointe.[131] Judge James Duane Doty (more about him later) recognized the significance of Native earthworks, if not so benignly as Lyon. In 1824, Doty bought land from Antaya husbands Strange Powers and Pierre Lessard, on which three large earthworks were located, and drew a map of it. Perhaps he was tired of holding court in the local taverns and barns; certainly he hoped to make money in real estate. So he gave some of the land to the county government urging that a courthouse be built *on top of* these mounds, which would have increased the value of his landholdings nearby while sending a symbolic message about the dominance of the new regime over the lives and heritage of the old *habitants* and their Native kin. The local community never liked the idea and never got around to building a courthouse there – perhaps there was a sense that the mounds were sacred and therefore were an inappropriate place for a courthouse – so the federal government bought it for a new military fort built between 1829 and 1834, thus making an even stronger statement about U.S. domination.[132]

## Using the Land's Resources

In spite of the conquest and colonization of Prairie du Chien, those who were able to gain individual ownership of the land found that they had resources that could not only sustain them with food but also help them to weather life's storms and achieve some of their personal goals. In the years after official deeds were issued, early records reveal Creoles using the land in a variety of ways. It was divided and handed down to the younger generation, used to secure support for sick, elderly and mentally incompetent relatives, loaned to a friend, sold to fund a marital separation, posted as security, and used for speculation. For example, in 1826, Augustin Hebert filed papers saying that François Vertefeuille could build a barn and stable on his farm lot, giving him permission to stay there until his children "shall be of age in consideration of [his] friendship." Vertefeuille had a small lot nearby, where his home was located.[133] In 1832 when Joseph Rolette was suing Charles Menard and several other men for a large debt, Menard and his wife Marianne Labuche Menard, afraid of losing their farm, took out a mortgage from Hercules Dousman

---

[131] Lyons, Prairie du Chien map.

[132] James Duane Doty Papers, WIS Mss DD, Box 2, Folder 1, Wisconsin Historical Society Library, Madison; Scanlan, *Prairie du Chien*, 137; Mahan, *Old Fort Crawford*, 126–139.

[133] Deed Book A, Crawford County Register of Deeds, 147–148.

on Farm Lot #2, on which their home was located; Dousman presumably covered their obligation. They paid him back with one dollar and two pairs of oxen, two cows, four heifers, three horses, and one colt.[134] In this way they avoided losing their land to Rolette, for whom Dousman worked. The Menards were able to keep the land in the family at least until 1869.[135] Dousman also profited: with loans and transactions like these, he increased his local political and economic power.

Creoles used land transfers to help care for family members. For example, Denis Courtois was feeling his sixty-six years in 1834 and was worrying about his son Charles, who was mentally ill. So he made a bargain with his son-in-law, Jean Baptiste Pion (husband of Theotiste Courtois). Denis gave half of Farm Lot 8 to Pion in exchange for a promise to take care of the old man and his son and to give them $10 per year.[136] To further illustrate, when Jane Fisher Rolette separated from Joseph Rolette, he deeded six lots to her cousin and guardian Bernard W. Brisbois for her use and posted a "penal bond of $30,000."[137] In another case, Charles LaPointe Sr. in 1829 gave one of his farm lots to his granddaughter Verronica Ranger, stating that since she was young, he would "give full power and authority to Louise Deschampt," Veronica's mother.[138] He gave another parcel of land to his son Charles Jr. not long afterward.[139] In 1840, François Chenevert and his wife Louise Giard "in consideration of the natural love and affection which they ... have and beareth unto" their four sons, divided up Farm lot 11, giving each a quarter.[140]

## Conclusion

During the second half of the eighteenth century, what had once been a thriving Meskwaki village and rendezvous ground became the fur-trade

---

[134] Deed Book A, Crawford County Register of Deeds, 435–441.

[135] Mortgage Book F, Crawford County Register of Deeds, 155.

[136] Eventually, another Courtois daughter and her husband Oliver Cherrier got the land. Deed Book B, Crawford County Register of Deeds, 50–52; James L. Hansen, ed., "Prairie du Chien and Galena Records, 1827–29," *Minnesota Genealogical Journal* 5 (May 1986): 18; Albert E. Coryer, Interview, broadcast, and anecdotes, Wisconsin Historical Society Library, Madison.

[137] Deed D, Crawford County Register of Deeds, 292–294.

[138] Deed Book A, Crawford County Register of Deeds, 231.

[139] Deed Book A, Crawford County Register of Deeds, 232; Hansen, "The Pelletier dit Antaya Families."

[140] Deed Book A, 364; Rentmeesters, *Wisconsin Creoles*, 223. Louise was a daughter of Basil Giard and Macoutchequoi. Forsyth, "A List of the Sac and Fox half breeds," 1824. They had purchased the lot from Joseph Rolette and Jane Fisher Rolette in 1832.

town of Prairie du Chien. By the 1750s, traders and their families had settled near the French fort there at the Meskwaki town, and Indians had in
1781 granted formal permission for European-descended men and their
families to establish their own settlement. By 1810, there was no longer
a distinctive Meskwaki village there: these Native people had instead
located their towns just to the south along the Mississippi.[141]

But there were still Native people living on the Prairie, the wives and
children of traders who, as representatives of the community, sought and
received the blessings of "the rightful owners of the soil." These women
and children would continue their connections to their tribes and would
also continue as co-owners in fact of this land, even when their husbands
and fathers would be the official, nominal titleholders. Thus the settlement at Prairie du Chien was both a Native place and a site of colonization; a foothold for the conquerors and but also a reserve for Native
descendants.

After the conquest, the United States intended to give individual land
titles to Euro-Americans and they did. Uncomfortable with communally
owned land, Congress dismissed requests to continue the practice of commons but granted titles to individual parcels for people who seemed part
of the non-Native cultures, who could help to support the new government. Newly and uncertainly dominant, the young United States needed
these Creoles, people on the margins between Indian and white worlds,
to help them achieve the critical mass of population that would allow
them to dominate and control the other peoples of the Midwest.

The Creoles could have been racialized as non-white. Some officials
such as Caleb Atwater had noticed that the people of Prairie du Chien
had intermarried extensively and were "a mixed breed," a situation that
irritated him.[142] But these very mixed people were needed as allies of
the United States, a need that triumphed at least temporarily over the
emerging and evolving racialization of American society. When John
W. Johnson wrote that the "Americans" had to imagine the Creoles as
"a white people," he was clearly thinking about the fluid boundaries of
racial definitions and was ambivalent about them.[143] And policymakers
at the territorial and national level were willing to go along with him.
This tendency to "imagine" the Creoles to be "a white people" was only

---

[141] Tanner, *Atlas of Great Lakes Indian History,* 98.
[142] Atwater, *Remarks Made on a Tour to Prairie du Chien,* 180.
[143] John W. Johnson to George C. Sibley, April 28, 1817, Prairie du Chien, Sibley Papers,
Missouri Historical Society Collections, St. Louis.

one part of a complex and shifting set of ideas, relationships, and identities that would be shaped by politics, economics, love, and kinship for the next four decades. For their part, the Creoles would counter many of the Anglo-American institutions, values, and practices with their own, and they would adapt to others, just as they adapted to Isaac Lee. In the meantime, the land was carved up and left in the hands of men with European names. Behind the scenes were their neighbors, wives, and partners, the children and grandchildren of the "rightful owners of the soil."

# 2

## "To Intermeddle in Political Affairs"

### New Institutions, Elections, and Lawmaking

In 1822, the newly created Borough Council of Prairie du Chien passed a law against "white persons ... skulking or sneaking about after 10 oclock at night."[1] This remarkable ordinance, passed by the leaders of the Creole fur-trade community, is the most unique but not the only expression of resistance to a new political order imposed by the United States on a region that had both a strong Native American presence and a long allegiance to the French and British Canadian provinces. It marked the first phase of a series of Creole political adaptations that allowed them to express local values, thwart racialization, and express consensus before factionalism and demographic change altered their options within the democratic system.

The new régime brought major changes in government to Prairie du Chien at the local, territorial, and national level, changes that would affect the *habitants* personally, economically, and politically. It would alter their social relationships, shift local power dynamics, challenge their worldviews, and provide avenues for expression in unexpected ways. During the 1820s and '30s, the ethnically and racially mixed residents of this old fur-trade town experimented with Yankee-style democracy and courts, mixed them with American Indian political practices and fur-trade traditions, and came up with surprising results. In some ways, we may see their actions as critiques of colonization and assertions of alternative concepts of governance; and in others, we can observe the

---

[1] "By-Laws enacted and passed by the Warden and Burgesses for the Borough of Prairie des Chiens," March 20, 1822, Register of Deeds Office, Crawford County Courthouse, Book: Deeds B (in the back, upside down), Section 15.

processes of assimilation and acculturation. In addition, their participation in the political and judicial system may help to explain why they did not develop an identity as indigenous Métis people like their Canadian cousins. But it is a complex story.

As previously mentioned, the United States nominally gained hegemony at the end of the American Revolution but ruled only loosely until after the War of 1812, when the young nation asserted its intentions to dominate the region.[2] The project of imposing control was a delicate one for U.S. officials: many of the Creoles had supported the British in the War of 1812 and resented Yankee intrusion and settlement. People like Michel and Domitille Brisbois, Pokoussee, and Pierre Antaya could influence both Native and Creole views and relationships with officials. The United States had to find ways to create the mechanisms of government that would control the old residents, protect the "rights" of U.S. citizens to "settle" the region, and "develop" the region's resources. Especially during the early years when the Yankees were a small minority of the population, their success depended upon the cooperation of the Creoles. In order to recruit the loyalty of the Creoles and to avoid provoking overt resistance, it was necessary to allow them to participate in the process, but only enough that they would not be able to thwart the colonizers' goals.

During the first phase of U.S. occupation, the army had built forts in the western Great Lakes region and maintained garrisons in the old fur-trade communities, ruling as conquerors. But during a second phase, officials established civil, democratic institutions and initially sought to include longtime French Creole residents as voters, jurors, and local officials. (Prairie du Chien was part of the Northwest Territory when it was created in 1787, then joined Indiana Territory in 1800, Illinois Territory in 1809, and Michigan Territory in 1818.[3] See map, Figure 2.1.) About 1820, word had come to the Prairie that the Yankees had organized Michigan Territory and would expect the francophone Creoles to participate in representative government and to obey territorial laws made in far-away Detroit. During the early 1820s, a few Anglo settlers and an itinerant judge named James Duane Doty (see Figure 2.2) arrived in

---

[2] Alice E. Smith, *The History of Wisconsin* (Madison: State Historical Society of Wisconsin, 1985), Vol. I, 36–94, 203.

[3] Smith, *The History of Wisconsin*, Vol. I, 200–201; Clever Bald, *Michigan in Four Centuries* (New York: Harper & Brothers, 1954) 105; R. Carlyle Buley, *The Old Northwest*, 2 vols. (Indianapolis: Indiana Historical Society, 1950), Vol. I, 62–63. Kugel "Reworking Ethnicity: Gender, Work Roles, and Contending Redefinitions of the Great Lakes Métis, 1820–42," (pp. 160–181).

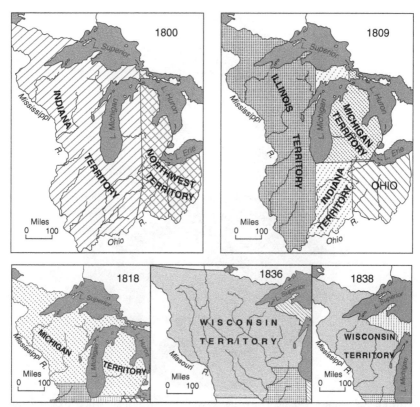

FIGURE 2.1. Territorial changes, 1800–1838. Based upon Alice E. Smith, *The History of Wisconsin* (Madison: State Historical Society of Wisconsin, 1985), I: 201.

Prairie du Chien with a list of new laws and tried to tutor the Creoles in justice and democracy, often with a patronizing and condescending attitude that must have been maddening.[4] Doty, an ambitious and arrogant young circuit court judge who had been raised in New York before seeking his fortune in Detroit, spent the winter of 1823–24 at Prairie du Chien.[5]

We may imagine how it seemed to the residents of old Great Lakes communities such as Green Bay, Mackinac, River Raisin, and Prairie du Chien. The army had conquered them and, in James Lockwood's

[4] Alice Elizabeth Smith, *James Duane Doty: Frontier Promoter* (Madison: State Historical Society of Wisconsin, 1954), chs. 4–5.

[5] Smith, *James Duane Doty, Frontier Promoter,* 30, 35.

FIGURE 2.2. James Duane Doty. Doty was an older man when this portrait was taken, but he was only twenty-four years old when he arrived in Prairie du Chien as a judge of the Additional Court. Wisconsin Historical Society, Image ID 11337.

words, "treated the inhabitants as a conquered people." [6] The new Anglo-American judge and lawyers came into town and established a court and political system different from the one they had been accustomed to, and began imposing laws and procedures created in Detroit or Washington, DC. Even though some of the Creoles were invited, and even summoned, to participate in the process, the meddling and imposition of the new régime grated. Running for a territorial office in Detroit, John R. Williams (whose mother Marie Cecilia Campau was Creole) expressed this resentment in his appeal for the votes of the heavily "French" River Raisin/

[6] James H. Lockwood, "Early Times and Events in Wisconsin," *Wisconsin Historical Collections* (hereafter *WHC*), Vol. 2 (Madison: Wisconsin Historical Society,[1856]; reprint, 1903), 128.

Monroe region. He wrote, "Be assured that the contest is really among us all, natives of the country, and the foreigners who are striving already insolently to despoil us of our rights and natural privileges."[7]

In the beginning, new governmental forms and processes were not at all clear, because Prairie du Chien's residents were extraordinarily remote from the seats of territorial government. It took more than two years for copies of Michigan Territory's laws to reach Prairie du Chien after the town became part of it. During the 1820s, it sometimes took six or seven months for the news of new statutes passed in Detroit to reach Green Bay and Prairie du Chien.[8] But in the years after 1818, laws made in those remote locations would increasingly affect the *habitants* as Michigan Territory's officials asserted control, creating local offices and courts.

Both outsiders and local men started the gears of new civil institutions. Newcomers such as Judge Doty, "factor" John W. Johnson, and Indian agent Nicolas Boilvin represented the territorial and federal governments, and (their superiors assumed) knew how things were supposed to work. But territorial governors also sent commissions to prominent local men to serve as justices of the peace, captains of the militia, and officials in other capacities. In this way, Creoles could be recruited into supporting the new regime.[9] By the mid-1820s, many appointees to local positions around the territory included men of both purely European and mixed ancestry.[10]

In the first phase of American territorial government, rule was by appointed – not elected – officials who could adopt only laws that had already been adopted by established states. A governor and ruling council passed laws and served as justices. This was a familiar pattern to the Creoles who were conversant with the British Canadian political system that had maintained for them the nondemocratic French governance. Before the establishment of U.S. control over the region, the French Canadian version

[7] John R. Williams to François Navarre, August 31, 1819 (Navarre Papers, Burton Historical Collection), cited in Russell E. Bidlack, *The Yankee Meets the Frenchman, River Raisin 1817–1830* (Ann Arbor: Historical Society of Michigan, 1965), 17; thanks to Dennis Au for Williams's mother's name.

[8] James Duane Doty to James Clark, March 16, 1830, James Duane Doty Papers, letter-book, 49–51, microcopy, Bentley Historical Library, Ann Arbor, Michigan.

[9] James L. Hansen, "Crawford County Public Office Appointments," unpublished paper, in possession of James Hansen; Peter Lawrence Scanlan, *Prairie du Chien: French, British, American* (Menasha, WI: Collegiate Press, 1937), 166–172. On other parts of the territory: "Executive Records," *Michigan Pioneer Collections*, Vol. 36 (1908), 121–131.

[10] Affidavit of Thomas Sheldon; Oct. 31, 1825, *Territorial Papers of the United States* (hereafter, *TPUS*), Vol. 11, 774.

of the *Coutume de Paris* had been the law of the land, and the elite traders had served as ad hoc officials and magistrates. There had been no elections; instead there had been a hierarchy of power at the top of which was the fur-trade elite, reflecting employer-employee relations.[11]

The *habitants*, however, through their trade-related travels and experiences in Native communities were also familiar with Native political systems of the region. Indian communities made decisions in village meetings where men and women could voice their opinions, and leaders sought consensus on important issues. Consensus was both a philosophy of community decision making and a goal to be reached in village meetings.[12] A former Indian agent knowledgeable about the Sauk and Meskwaki Indians, for example, wrote "All questions relating to the nations are settled in council by the Chiefs.... In all Indian councils ... the whole number of chiefs present must be of the same opinion otherwise nothing is done."[13] Native leadership was based upon the respect of the community for leaders' experience, talent, and kinship connections. Women as well as men might have significant political influence, but usually male leaders were the ones to interface with outsiders. Charles Eastman, a Dakota Indian physician and ethnographer, wrote that "a woman who had attained to ripeness of years and wisdom, or who had displayed notable courage in some emergency, was sometimes invited to a seat in the council."[14] Native leaders, however, did not have coercive authority: they had influence. Ideally, important decisions were made in council by consensus of the entire community, including women.[15]

---

[11] *History of Crawford and Richland Counties*, 359–364; Smith, *The History of Wisconsin*, Vol. 1, 203–207. In her study of fur-trade workers and their employers, historian Carolyn Podruchny explains that "masters and servants accepted their positions as rulers and ruled," and that they shared "a deeply held belief in the legitimacy of paternalism." Carolyn Podruchny, *Making the Voyageur World: Travelers and Traders in the North American Fur Trade* (Lincoln: University of Nebraska Press, 2006), 136.

[12] Thomas Forsyth, "An Account of the Manners and Customs of the Sauk and Fox Nations of Indians Tradition," in *The Indian Tribes of the Upper Mississippi Valley and Region of the Great Lakes*, edited by Emma Helen Blair (Cleveland: Arthur H. Clark, 1911) Vol. II, 187; Charles A. Eastman, *The Soul of the Indian, An Interpretation* (1911; reprint, Lincoln: University of Nebraska Press, 1980) 42; examples may be found in Ellen M. Whitney, comp. and ed., *The Black Hawk War, 1831–1832*, 2 vols. (Springfield: Illinois State Historical Library, 1973); and Kenneth P. Bailey, ed. and trans., *Journal of Joseph Marin, French Colonial Explorer and Military Commander in the Wisconsin Country, Aug. 7, 1753–June 30, 1754* (n.p.: Published by the editor, 1975).

[13] Forsyth, "Account of the Manners," Vol. II, 187.

[14] Eastman, *The Soul of the Indian*, 42.

[15] Anthony F. C. Wallace, "Prelude to Disaster: The Course of Indian-White Relations Which Led to the Black Hawk War of 1832," in *The Black Hawk War, 1831–1832*,

Native communities had hierarchies of status and influence rather than coercive power, at the top of which were men and women notable for their age, wisdom, family, skill, and achievements. However, there was also a sense of equality, as a longtime resident of the region commented in the eighteenth century: "The chiefs who are most influential and well-to-do are on an equal footing with the poorest, and even with the boys – with whom they converse as they do with persons of discretion."[16] Another observer commented that "this feeling is general among all the savages, each man is master of his own actions, no one daring to contradict him."[17] Tribal town meetings with broad-based community input and ideologies recognizing some types of equality had parallels in the Yankee political system.

Thus, the *habitants* had experience with two quite opposite forms of governance. They were used to authoritarian and hierarchical systems like the one implemented by the commandants of Fort Crawford, but they were also familiar with Native political systems similar to new American forms of government: the town meeting and the jury.

## Self-Government

When self-government first came to Prairie du Chien at the local level with the creation of the borough council, it was new, but had a certain familiarity. Prairie du Chien's borough charter in 1821 was adapted from models in Massachusetts and Ohio, adopting New England–style town meetings. It established a governing board consisting of a warden and two burgesses, a clerk, a treasurer, and a marshal, elected by freeholders.[18] The earliest elected borough council members were three fur traders. This format introduced the novelty of self-government and elections, but the town meetings shared some aspects of Indian village councils.[19]

edited by Ellen Whitney (Springfield: Illinois State Historical Library, 1978), Vol. I, 4–7; Nicolas Perrot, "Memoir on the Manners, Customs, and Religion of the Savages of North America," in *The Indian Tribes of the Upper Mississippi Valley and Region of the Great Lakes* [1911–1912], edited by Emma Helen Blair (Lincoln: University of Nebraska Press, 1996), Vol. I, 136, 145; Claude Charles Le Roy, Bacqueville de La Potherie, "History of the Savage Peoples Who Are Allies of New France," in Blair, *Indian Tribes*, Vol. I, 303.

16  Perrot, "Manners, Customs, and Religion," Vol. I, 136.
17  Potherie, "History of the Savage Peoples," Vol. I, 303.
18  "By-Laws enacted and passed by the … Borough of Prairie des Chiens … [1821]"; Scanlan, *Prairie du Chien*, 190–191.
19  Michael Zuckerman, *Peaceable Kingdoms: New England Towns in the Eighteenth Century* (New York: Alfred A. Knopf, 1970).

It is clear from its earliest records that residents provided vigorous feedback to the borough council, apparently in open meetings. Some of the earliest laws modeled on New England ordinances focused on safety and good order. They included speed limits and parking regulations for horses, and rules about regular cleaning of chimneys – these laws seem to have been accepted by the *habitants*. For example, an ordinance stated "that no person shall be permitted to ride or drive his horse, mare, or gelding through the streets of this village; faster than a common traveling gait under the penalty of a fine of one dollar."[20] Another mandated that "all persons being concerned in a common field with a neighbor or neighbors" had to keep their fences in good condition.[21] Another measure specified that Indians should not camp in a certain neighborhood (apparently near the fort).[22]

The borough council repealed six unpopular ordinances within months of their passage in 1822, suggesting that local residents were willing to challenge their new council when it did not express the community's will. Compensation for the town clerk was reduced, and a boat tax and flour regulation and inspection ordinances were repealed at the second and third town meetings, suggesting community outrage at the new measures.[23] A law against haystacks standing south of Fort Crawford was repealed at the next town meeting in 1823 as well.[24] The haystack ordinance might have been intended to reduce the likelihood of fire threatening the fort, but the *habitants* seem to have been unwilling to tolerate the inconvenience and were not particularly interested in protecting the fort anyway.

Among the first laws passed in 1822 was the ordinance stipulating that "all white persons seen skulking or sneaking about after 10 oclock at night within the enclosing of any lot in this village without the permission of the owner ... shall pay a fine" of from two to five dollars.[25]

---

[20] "By-Laws enacted and passed by the ... Borough of Prairie des Chiens ... 20th day of March 1822." Sect. 7.

[21] "By-Laws, enacted and passed by the ... Borough of Prairie des Chiens," December 7, 1822.

[22] "By-Laws, enacted and passed by the ... Borough of Prairie des Chiens," March 20, 1822.

[23] "By-Laws enacted and passed by the ... Borough of Prairie des Chiens," March 20, 1822, May 6, 1822, and December 7, 1822. Ordinances repealed were Numbers 10, 11, 12, 13, 14, and part of 19.

[24] "By-Laws enacted and passed by the ... Borough of Prairie des Chiens," December 7, 1822 and October 23, 1823.

[25] "By-Laws enacted and passed by the ... Borough of Prairie des Chiens," March 20, 1822, Section 15.

What was this ordinance all about? It reflects the concerns of the town's brown wives, daughters, and sons, and resentment against the army; and together with other laws and court cases of that time, provides an interesting expression of community values that drew heavily from tribal political philosophies. It also reveals a conflict between local and territorial laws, and demonstrates a local definition of "whiteness" at odds with that of American territorial and congressional lawmakers.

The "white persons skulking" law was adopted in a community with many tensions. When it was passed, residents still resented the presence of the U.S. Army at Fort Crawford because officers and enlisted men treated the Creoles harshly, abusing them, both while soldiers were acting in an official capacity and while off duty.[26] One resident later remembered that the army commandants imposed martial law on this conquered territory, "arraigning and trying the citizens by courts-martial, and sentencing them to ignominious punishments."[27] For example, Charles Menard had been charged with peddling alcohol to soldiers; he was "tried by court-martial, whipped, and with a bottle hung to his neck, marched through the streets, with music playing the *Rogue's March* after him." Throughout, Menard maintained his innocence.[28] Another Menard, as discussed in the previous chapter, had been whipped for defending a girl from sexual assault by the commanding officer. So the Creoles found ways to use the new government to express their sense of justice and to protect their community.

Many of the Creoles came from intermarried fur-trade families; most of the men had Native or métis wives. All would have been aware that Native communities expected women to express their political views, whether in their families or in political meetings. Some Anglos thought the Native women in the Great Lakes region were notably – perhaps excessively – assertive, and their husbands remarkably patient with their assertiveness. Longtime Indian agent Thomas Forsyth, for example, was amazed that Indian men could "listen to a woman scold all day" without becoming aggravated.[29]

---

[26] Scanlan, *Prairie du Chien*, 123. *TPUS*, Vol. 10, 803–804; Michigan Territory "Records," Vol. 1, 61; Smith, *The History of Wisconsin*, Vol. I, 201.

[27] Lockwood, "Early Times," 128–129.

[28] Lockwood, "Early Times," 129; Willard Keyes, "A Journal of Life in Wisconsin One Hundred Years Ago," *Wisconsin Magazine of History* 3, no. 3 (March 1920): 339–363, and 3, no. 4 (June 1920). Keyes recorded on December 5, 1817, "A French Citizen confined and punished at the fort for selling whiskey to hirelings and soldiers contrary to orders." Keyes, "A Journal of Life in Wisconsin," 356.

[29] Thomas Forsyth, "Account of the Manners," Vol. II, 215. He added, "They will scold their husbands for getting drunk or parting with a favorite horse or wasting any property

The "white persons skulking law" was probably enacted in response to the concerns of brown wives, mothers, and daughters complaining about men who intimidated or threatened them. The threat of sexual assault was very real. After all, even the army's commanding officer had chased a local female. It is likely that Prairie du Chien's women had voiced their concerns about "whites" to their husbands, sons, and brothers and to the members of the borough council. Maybe the women came to the town meeting, or perhaps they lobbied the burgesses behind the scenes and sent their men to speak up. For these women, it must have been unnerving to sense that "white" men were lurking in the darkness outside their homes. (Ironically, this inverts the pioneer trope of Indians skulking around frontier cabins, threatening white wives and children. Keyes, for example, complained of "the tawny Savage of the wilderness, sculking [*sic*] in the thicket," causing "terror" to "those unacquainted with their manners.")[30] It is interesting, too, that this law expresses the concept of "whites" as dangerous "others."

But the threat of a fine did not seem sufficient to deter white skulkers. So, the following year in 1823, "An Act to establish a Patrol" was passed. This act made clear that it was soldiers from the local Fort Crawford who were skulking around disturbing the peace, particularly when intoxicated. The ordinance empowered the Warden (chairman of the borough council) to organize local men into nightly patrols when necessary. It also mandated that "whenever the cry of 'soldiers,' is made or any public disturbance is heard in the night times within said Borough, the Warden or either of the Burgesses shall have power to call upon any or all of the inhabitants of said Borough to assist in resisting, seizing and quelling those who may have caused such disturbances." In these and other ordinances, this community codified color and culture into their laws in ways that suggested that Indians were less dangerous than "white persons" (especially soldiers). These soldiers were no doubt the "white persons" the council worried about, men who were not only outsiders but also part of the conquering army.[31] Furthermore, other laws and court cases reveal deep divisions between Creoles and Yankees in legal philosophy, while demonstrating Creole willingness to use the borough council to protest and control the behaviors of soldiers and army officers.

---

to purchase spirituous liquor, will scold their children for wasting or destroying any property," 218.

[30] Keyes, "A Journal of Life in Wisconsin," 353.

[31] "By-Laws enacted and passed by the ... Borough of Prairie des Chiens," 1823.

Which brings us to drinking, where legal philosophies and efforts to control soldiers' behavior converged. Prairie du Chien's residents, visitors, and soldiers from Fort Crawford frequently spent their Sundays and holidays drinking and with activities such as ball playing (probably lacrosse), billiards, horse racing, boxing, and gambling. Both Euro-American and Native dancing were common in town, some of it accompanied by strong drink.[32] Willard Keyes, a Vermont man who lived there from 1817 to 1819, commented disapprovingly about local activities on the Sabbath, "it is the custom with many here to spend this day in riot and drunkenness."[33] Apparently the soldiers imbibed more excessively than the Creoles: New Yorker John Shaw, who spent some time in Prairie du Chien about 1816, commented, "The traders were polite and kind, and their hospitality was both general and generous; and while they drank freely, it was regarded as disgraceful to get drunk."[34] Many of the soldiers, however, in spite of the territorial laws, regularly drank to excess.[35] Lieutenant Colonel Willoughby Morgan, commander of Fort Crawford, wrote in 1824, "the Soldiers find Such facilities for obtaining Spiritous liquors that they become dissipated and at times quite unmanageable."[36] A few years later, future president of the United States Zachary Taylor, then commander of Fort Crawford, complained that "every other house at least is a whiskey shop, owing to which circumstance & the drunken materials the rank, & file of our army are now composed of ... I had more trouble ... with soldiers than I ever before experienced."[37] Between 1790 and 1840, American alcohol consumption reached unprecedented levels, and soldiers were among the heaviest of drinkers, according to a study by historian W. J. Rorabaugh. Beginning in 1810 in the Northeast and slowly gathering steam, however, an organized Temperance movement led by evangelical Protestant Christians would influence many people's attitudes and behaviors, causing both conflicts and a dramatic decrease in consumption by mid-century. These drinking-related issues in the early

---

[32] Keyes, "A Journal of Life in Wisconsin," 353, 354, 358, 443, 444, 445, 452, 453.

[33] Keyes, "A Journal of Life in Wisconsin," 354.

[34] John Shaw, "Shaw's Narrative," *WHC*, Vol. 2, 226.

[35] Bruce E. Mahan, *Old Fort Crawford and the Frontier* (Iowa City: State Historical Society of Iowa, 1926), 262–263; Henry Baird, "Early History and Condition of Wisconsin," *WHC*, Vol. 2 (1856), 89–90.

[36] Willoughby Morgan to Brigadier General Jessup, April 12, 1824, Record Group 92, Records of the Office of the Quartermaster General. Consolidated Correspondence File. 1794–1915, Box 430, Entry 225, NM-81, National Archives, Washington, DC.

[37] Zachary Taylor to Major General T. S. Jessup, December 15, 1829, Zachary Taylor Papers, Founders Library, Northern Illinois University (microfilm, series 2, reel 1, p. 2).

1820s in Prairie du Chien thus took place during the early years of a heated national controversy.[38]

Creoles and Yankees had two *different, opposing* approaches to controlling the consumption of alcoholic beverages to prevent revelry from becoming riot. The local community targeted *drunks* rather than *vendors* for control. Some of the tipplers who frequented Prairie du Chien were Native. Prairie du Chien's first alcohol-related ordinance stipulated that that "any Indian intoxicated in the streets making a noise and disturbing the peace shall subject himself to imprisonment and there remain until he gets sober."[39] The wording of this ordinance made the incarceration seem voluntary, imposed no fines, and avoided any language of coercion.

This law corresponds to Native views of drinking and to the practices of Great Lakes fur traders, according to historian Peter Mancall. Traders often used liquor as an enticement to trade, and Indians were generally willing to forgive people who misbehaved while drunk. When drinkers became violent, Mancall wrote, "communities accepted the idea that liquor was responsible for their actions; it made no sense to punish the person who committed the crime when the true offender was alcohol."[40]

While *Indians* were to be jailed until they sobered up (and, by implication, released in the morning), the 1823 ordinance aimed at *soldiers* empowered patrols composed of male residents to detain intoxicated and suspicious persons overnight until officials could bring the offenders before a magistrate "to be disposed of according to law."[41] (Many of the magistrates were Creole.) These regulations were much more coercive and punitive than the law regarding intoxicated Indians, suggesting that the local community felt drunken soldiers and other "white persons" were more dangerous than tipsy Indians.

But laws were also made by the territorial council, which reflected Yankee rather than Creole views. If Prairie du Chien's Creoles believed the laws should focus on controlling antisocial drinkers, Yankees like Judge Doty and the territorial lawmakers viewed drinking *establishments* as wicked. Doty told grand jurors in 1824 that "Taverns are for

---

[38] W. J. Rorabaugh, *The Alcoholic Republic: An American Tradition* (New York: Oxford University Press, 1979), 5–8, 144, 248, ch. 7.

[39] "By-Laws enacted and passed by the Warden and Burgesses," 1822, Section 26.

[40] Peter C. Mancall, "Men, Women, and Alcohol in Indian Villages in the Great Lakes Region in the Early Republic," *Journal of the Early Republic* 15 (Fall 1995): 425–448, quote on 432; Peter C. Mancall, *Deadly Medicine: Indians and Alcohol in Early America* (Ithaca: Cornell University Press, 1995), 79–82. Quote on 80.

[41] "By-Laws enacted and passed by the ... Borough of Prairie des Chiens," November 20, 1823.

the convenience of travelers, and under proper regulations can never be sunk into grog-shops; and if any one should assume this latter character, it becomes a crying evil, and demands your immediate interference." Moreover, he described grog-shops and "irregular taverns" as "those places of resort for the idle and intemperate, and haunts of dissipation and almost every species of crime."[42]

Additional territorial laws followed suit. Rather than targeting drunks, an 1816 territorial law prohibited sales of alcoholic beverages to minors, apprentices, soldiers, militiamen while in service, and to Indians. An 1819 act required vendors of individual drinks to be licensed.[43]

By targeting taverns, these laws threatened local institutions facilitating social and even political activities. Taverns in the Old Northwest were community centers, where neighbors socialized, travelers found bed and board, religious services and courts were convened, people danced, joked, brawled, and of course, drank.[44] Harry Ellsworth Cole's study of early Wisconsin taverns described the "picturesque scenes" at these businesses in Prairie du Chien and Green Bay: "Costumes of the people ranged from army uniforms worn by soldiers and Parisian gowns of certain ladies of fortune, to buckskin garments and moccasins of [I]ndians.... This variety and contrast in raiment produced a kaleidoscope of color, cut, and texture."[45] One of Prairie du Chien's inns was run by James Reed, whose stepson Antoine Grignon later recalled, "Around the fireplace in his tavern was often gathered an interesting throng of hunters, trappers, traders and Indians, and the usual town loafers. Many strange tales of frontier life and backwoods lore were told."[46]

---

[42] *U.S. v. J. Barrell*, May 1824, Michigan [Territory] Circuit Court (Iowa County) Criminal Case files, 1824–36, Wisconsin Historical Society Library, Platteville, Iowa Series 20, folder 4; Elizabeth Gaspar Brown, ed., "Judge James Doty's Notes of Trials and Opinions: 1823–1832," *American Journal of Legal History* 9, no. 1 (January 1965): 33.

[43] *Laws of the Territory of Michigan, 1871*, Vol. I, 201, 407. Another law passed in 1821 reiterated the ban on selling liquor to Indians, but also stipulated that anyone who did so had to give back to the Indian whatever had been given in exchange. *Laws of the Territory of Michigan, 1871*, Vol. I, 923. Eventually, the Borough Council did pass an ordinance requiring people to have licenses to sell whiskey in quantities less than three gallons. This took place after Doty moved to the Prairie and his influence is likely. "By-Laws enacted and passed by the ... Borough of Prairie des Chiens," December 4, 1823.

[44] Harry Ellsworth Cole, *Stagecoach and Tavern Tales of the Old Northwest* (Cleveland: Arthur H. Clark, 1930), 17, 237–298. A more recent study by Elliott West made similar conclusions about the far west: *The Saloon on the Rocky Mountain Mining Frontier* (Lincoln: University of Nebraska Press, 1979).

[45] Cole, *Stagecoach and Tavern Tales*, 181.

[46] Eben Pierce, "Indians Knew Reed as a Fearless Man," *Galesville Republican*, July 15, 1915.

Taken together, the actions of the borough council tell us several things about the residents: they had grievances against the army of occupation; they had views about drinking that were more like those of the Indians than the Yankees; and they used the language of racialization, but not in the same ways as most Anglos because their perspectives on race were different. Reading between the lines of local laws, we can discern the protests of female residents, who identified lurking predators as "white persons" and outsiders in contrast to less threatening "Indians," who were familiar and often kin.

Familiarity with Native political formats such as consensus-based village councils probably helped the Creole population to adapt the New England town meeting format to meet their needs. Prairie du Chien's *habitants* used the borough council to express resentment against and fear of the army garrison occupying their village and to organize patrols. Speedy repeal of unpopular ordinances makes clear that residents spoke their minds when given a chance to influence the town governance. Like Native village councils, the town meeting forum offered opportunities for vigorous feedback and debate, and for the creation of consensus. It also formalized conventions regulating the common field. And the contrast between local and territorial laws about drinking provides an example of the very different ways that people of differing cultures addressed social problems and methods of social control. The tensions evident here would be played out in the courts, the topic of a later chapter.

Prairie du Chien's borough council was a men's council not unlike many one could find in Indian communities around the Midwest. Here the village's most respected men presided, but everyone could attend, listen to deliberations, give their opinions, and influence the decision-making process. It was a forum where community values and concerns could be expressed, and we see them in the measures that were passed.

### "In a Suffering Condition": The Glass Family

Another men's council was created to govern the county of Crawford, an enormous region encompassing roughly the western half of what is now the state of Wisconsin. Prairie du Chien's elite served on the Crawford County Commission – three at a time. In 1824, residents tried to use this institution to ameliorate the tribulations of the needy.[47] The Glass family

---

[47] *Laws of the Territory of Michigan* (Lansing: W. S. George, 1871 and 1874), Vol. I, 661; Vol. II, 279.

crisis provides a glimpse into the ways that the new laws both created problems and – with the new organs of government – provided a menu of options to solve them.

Joseph Glass, when our story opens in January of 1824, was in jail awaiting trial for selling liquor by small measure without a license. He had been caught in the snare of a law made in faraway Detroit seeking to control alcohol vendors, a law at odds with the local philosophy about how best to control antisocial intoxication. Unable to afford the bail, Joseph was stuck, biding his time in custody until the court would meet six months hence. He couldn't work, so his wife Eve and three children were "in a suffering condition."[48] Although the Glass family was neither Creole nor Indian, it appears that their Creole neighbors came to their aid.

It would not seem that Joseph and Eve Glass would have aroused the sympathies of the *habitants*. He had served in the army for five years, apparently as a private, having finished his time in September of 1823 a few months before he was arrested for the crime of unlicensed liquor sales. They were outsiders: Eve Rager had married Joseph in Ohio in 1810, and there did not seem to be any kin connections between them and the fur-trade community.[49] They were, in other words, lately part of the conquering army, and Joseph was seemingly one of those "white persons" that the *habitants* were so concerned about. In fact, if Joseph did indeed sell liquor to some of the "white persons" from the fort, they might well have troubled the Creoles with their skulking. However, the Glass family caught the attention of their neighbors and elicited pity.

Working behind the scenes to help the hungry family was Madame Marie Chalifoux Vertefeuille, who was Menominee and French.[50] She had asked Indian agent Nicolas Boilvin to help them out, but although he gave them some food, they were so needy that something else would have to be done. So, prompted by Madame Vertefeuille, Boilvin contacted

---

[48] Doty, Notes on Trials and Decisions (January 12, 1824), Mss. DD Box 3, typescript 22. Genealogy Buff.com, "Miscellaneous Pickaway County, Ohio, Marriages," accessed 8–25–09; correspondence from James L. Hansen, Wisconsin Historical Society, 3–16–2007.

[49] "Register of Enlistments in the U.S. Army," Genealogy Buff.com, "Miscellaneous Pickaway County, Ohio, Marriages," accessed Aug. 25, 2009; correspondence from James L. Hansen, Wisconsin Historical Society, accessed March 16, 2007.

[50] Les and Jeanne Rentmeester, *The Wisconsin Creoles* (Melbourne, FL: Privately published, 1987), 221.

the Crawford County Commission, the new governing body set up by Michigan Territory, whose duties included taking care of the poor.[51]

Nicolas Boilvin was a French Canadian who had first arrived in the Midwest in 1774 as a teenager, allied himself with the United States at an opportune moment, and by 1808 was a U.S. government-appointed Indian agent living at Prairie du Chien, where the next year he added to his roles that of justice of the peace. He had extensive knowledge of tribal cultures in the region, and his first wife, Wizak Kega, had been Ho-Chunk.[52] Boilvin as an official thus tried to get the gears of government – this new men's council – to move as a means of resolving the Glass family's crisis.

The commissioners called a special meeting because the family "was supported by private charity and other improper resources."[53] Commissioners Joseph Rolette and James Lockwood constituted a quorum in the absence of the third commissioner. Boilvin explained to them, "Mrs. Glass sent Mrs. Vertefeuille to ask me for a little provisions for her Children .... I told Bourgignon to give them some provisions when she sent for them and since that time I see the children almost every morning go to the Kitchen for something."[54] Colonel Willoughby Morgan of Fort Crawford testified that several officers had come to him, having said there was a rumor "that Mrs. Glass was in a suffering condition, for Wood and perhaps for Provisions," and requested permission to provide her with both at their own expense. Morgan agreed and offered to make a donation as well.[55] No doubt the military officers were particularly sympathetic since Joseph Glass had been a soldier. But the Glass family's problems exceeded the ability of charitable individuals to help out.

Boilvin asked the commissioners to allocate some funds to help them. Instead, the panel took a look at the territorial laws explaining the commission's duties and decided to take the Glass children away from their parents and indenture them to others until they would attain adulthood. Indentures were arranged for the children: John Glass to Colonel Willoughby Morgan, Jane Glass to Judge Doty, and Harriet Glass to a

---

[51] Wisconsin Territorial Papers, County Series, Crawford County, Proceedings of the County Board of Supervisors, Nov. 29, 1821–Nov. 19, 1850 (Madison: Wisconsin Historical Records Survey, 1942) (hereafter, CC Supervisors), 5–6; *Laws of the Territory of Michigan* Vol. I, 531–532.

[52] Peter L. Scanlan, "Nicolas Boilvin, Indian Agent," *Wisconsin Magazine of History* 27, no. 2 (December 1943): 145–169.

[53] CC Supervisors, 5.

[54] CC Supervisors, 6.

[55] CC Supervisors, 5.

Creole fur trader.[56] This was a severe mandate and it was certainly *not* what Madame Vertefeuille and Monsieur Boilvin intended.

The Glass family fortunes continued to plummet: three days later Governor Lewis Cass's brother attacked the still-imprisoned Joseph Glass and tried to kill him. According to court records, Captain Charles L. Cass aimed a loaded pistol at Joseph's chest; when it apparently misfired, Cass beat him.[57] Relations between the U.S. Army and the local citizens had been extremely tense for eight years, and this was just another example of the army's extensive abuse of civilians (even though Glass was himself a former soldier).

We may imagine the community uproar that ensued. Instead of helping to feed the Glass family, the commissioners were taking away their children and giving one of them to the obnoxious Yankee judge, Doty, and another to an officer of the hated conquering army. On top of that, the governor's own brother had attacked the children's father!

Behind the scenes, people were negotiating. Someone tried to use Judge Doty's court to block the transfer of the Glass children with an injunction, but Doty refused to interfere.[58] Doty affirmed the right of the commissioners to remove the children, who were "under age and very young," from their mother, who was not only poor, but whose "general reputation [was] that of an immoral woman." Doty added the opinion that even if money had not been an issue, the parents' morals could be grounds for removing the children. Doty wrote:

It may well be doubted whether parents, whatever may be their wealth or degree in life, who notoriously train their children up to vice and immorality, conducting before them in an indecent and shameless manner, and who are in the daily violation of the most positive rules of morality, as well as the laws provided by the Legislature of the Country, are entitled, by any law, to the possession of their children.... [I]n the *morals* of an individual, the *society* has certainly a deep interest.[59]

[56] CC Supervisors, 6; *Laws of the Territory of Michigan*, 1871, Vol. 1, 531–532, for the law permitting the commissioners to take this action. The man to whom Harriet Glass was indentured was probably Pierre LaRiviere.

[57] *United States v. Charles L. Cass*, Indictment for an assault with intent to murder upon Joseph Glass, May 11, 1824, Wisconsin Historical Society, Crawford County Circuit Court records, Iowa Series 20, Folder 17.

[58] Doty Papers. James Duane Doty Trials and Decisions. Wisconsin Historical Society Library, Mss. DD. Box 3, Circuit Court of the U.S., pp. 22–26, January 12, 1824. Because the records are fragmentary, it's unclear whether it was Brisbois, Vertefeuille, or someone else seeking an injunction to keep the children with their mother.

[59] Doty Papers, James Duane Doty Trials and Decisions, Mss. DD Box 3, Circuit Court of the U.S., Wisconsin Historical Society Library, Madison, typescript, 22–24.

The community, however, seems to have disagreed strongly with Doty.

Even if the court couldn't be used to help the Glass family, another solution was forthcoming. Within three weeks, the county commissioners had a change of heart and called another emergency meeting. This time, the third commissioner, Creole Denis Courtois, was able to attend and may have exerted an influence. Public pressure and backstage negotiations had convinced the commissioners to reverse the order taking the children from their mother. The attack on Joseph Glass by the governor's brother had probably added to public opinion that injustice had been done to his family and may have influenced the commissioners further.

So the commissioners voted to cancel the order to bind out the Glass children, after fur trader Michel Brisbois signed a security bond promising that "Joseph Glass and Eve his wife shall well and sufficiently provide for themselves and children" and "that said Children would not become chargeable to the County."[60] The commissioners decided to release Joseph Glass on bail pending his trial, no doubt with the expectation that as a free man he could support his family so they wouldn't need charity. When at his trial he was later convicted of the liquor license violation and reimprisoned because he couldn't pay the $50 fine, the county commissioners settled for $25 and set him free.[61] What was the point of keeping a man in jail if it meant that his family would suffer enough to cause a community crisis? It seems that the county commissioners (two thirds of whom were Creole) had discovered that they had the power to mitigate not only their own rulings but also the rulings of the courts.

The misfortune that had stalked the Glass family had been created by the new institutions and processes of the American state. The territorial legislature's mandate requiring the licensing of liquor sales created a catch-22 that jailed a man too poor to pay his bail. This prevented him from earning either the bail money or a living for his family. The territorial law providing for indentures of poor children exacerbated the crisis. But a group of Creoles rallied to their defense – Vertefeuille, Boilvin, Brisbois, and probably Courtois and Rolette – adapting the new Yankee institutions to untangle their crisis.

Prairie du Chien's *habitants* were experimenting with the new institutions in this situation, trying out the county commission and the courts,

[60] Wisconsin Historical Society Library: Crawford Series 4 Crawford County Clerk, Board Papers 1817–1848 Box 1 Folder 1; CC Supervisors, 7.
[61] CC Supervisors, 8.

and testing the utility and flexibility of territorial laws. Here we see a crisis being mediated by a Native-descended woman, Marie Vertefeuille, and an elite Creole, Indian Agent Nicolas Boilvin, who sought the assistance of the new county government to help a family whose father ran afoul of representatives of *other* U.S. institutions: the army and the courts. Yet when the county commission's decision did not resolve the situation in a satisfactory way, someone stepped forward to renegotiate. When Judge Doty wouldn't help out, Brisbois guaranteed that the children would not go hungry if their parents were allowed to keep them. And though the court convicted the unlucky Joseph Glass in June, the commissioners asserted their right to show mercy, deviated from the exact letter of the law, and moderated the court's penalty. Vertefeuille was playing a traditional Native and Creole women's role as mediator. Boilvin interceded with a local men's council (the county commissioners) to seek a solution to a community problem. When the new institutions exacerbated rather than solved the Glass family's problems, Creole community members creatively negotiated behind the scenes to negate the institutional decisions and find a compromise. In a sense, they were creolizing those institutions.

If this incident is any indication, the Creoles were adapting well, experimenting with ways to achieve their goals – peace, justice, and local autonomy – in the context of new political realities. These events demonstrate the persistence of Native and Creole values in the old fur-trade community at Prairie du Chien, of ideals such as compassion for the poor, female mediation, elite patronage, and an unwillingness to surrender complete control to outsiders such as the Yankees Cass and Doty. It also demonstrates that ethnic categories were fluid enough that Creoles could sympathize with and help the Glasses, even though the Glasses were not Creole.

### "Without Even One Redeeming Virtue": Prejudices

Many of the newcomers who made their homes in Prairie du Chien were unprepared to accept the Creoles on equal terms. Ideas about whiteness differed in Prairie du Chien – where so many of the residents had Native kin and ancestors – from concepts held by Anglos coming in from the east. Outsiders brought biases against people based upon color, religion, and ethnicity. There were, of course, many Indian haters among the newcomers. Willard Keyes, for example, wrote about "the Tawny Savage" remarking that "their mode of living and eating is disgusting to those

who have any sence [*sic*] of decency or cleanliness."[62] Others disliked
Creoles in particular.[63] One point of criticism was intellectual attainment.
"The Americans generally consider the Canadians as ignorant," remarked
an Italian traveling in the region in 1828. "Whether this be true, I know
not; but I do know that I invariably found them very polite and obliging, even among the lower classes."[64] In the East, the evolving norms
regarding race and social status relegated people who were not "white"
to the bottom levels of the hierarchy. As a result, Anglos who arrived in
Creole communities sometimes were surprised by what seemed to them a
disjunction of color and status, race and class. James L. Lockwood later
remembered his amazement at finding Indian wives and biracial children
among the elites of the community. He wrote:

to see gentlemen selecting wives of the nut-brown natives, and raising children of
mixed blood, the traders and clerks living in as much luxury as the resources of
the country would admit, and the *engagees* or boatmen living upon soup made of
hulled corn with barely tallow enough to season it ... all this to an American was
a novel mode of living.[65]

Another newcomer in 1836 wrote a flippant letter to a friend that Prairie
du Chien's elite fur traders were "as fat, ragged and black as their great-
grandfathers were. (if they ever had any)."[66]

Thus, many newcomers responded to the Creole communities with an
awareness that people who seemed to be "nut-brown" or "black" were
among those who married "gentlemen." In addition, some expressed a
special distaste for people of mixed background.[67] As we have seen, Caleb
Atwater, an agent sent as part of an 1827 treaty delegation, complained
that the people of Prairie du Chien were excessively intermarried, writing

[62] Keyes, "A Journal of Life in Wisconsin," 353.
[63] R. David Edmunds, "'Unacquainted with the laws of the civilized world': American attitudes toward the métis communities in the Old Northwest," in *The New Peoples: Being
and Becoming Metis in North America*, edited by Jacqueline Peterson and Jennifer S. H.
Brown (1985; reprint, St. Paul: University of Minnesota Press, 2001) 185–193.
[64] Giacomo Constantino Beltrami, *A Pilgrimage in Europe and America* (London: Hunt &
Clarke, 1828), Vol. 2, 174.
[65] Lockwood, "Early Times," 110.
[66] J. H. LaMotte to William Beaumont, September 2, 1836, Beaumont Papers, Missouri
Historical Society.
[67] R. David Edmunds, "Unacquainted with the laws of the civilized world," 185–193;
Thomas N. Ingersoll, *To Intermix with Our White Brothers: Indian Mixed Bloods in the
United States from Earliest Times to the Indian Removals* (Albuquerque: University of
New Mexico Press, 2005), 79–81.

that they were "without even one redeeming virtue."[68] Ethnic and cultural differences continued to inspire bigotry in those who wrote for the Prairie du Chien newspaper at mid-century. An article in the *Crawford County Courier* in 1853, for example, referred to the Creoles as "this class of persons – perfectly destitute of ambition or worthy pride," and exulted that energetic Yankees were moving in, so that "where sloth, stupor and vice once ruled, now sturdy farmers, and busy mechanics are instilling a new life."[69] Issues of inclusion emerged in political as well as social situations.

## "The Great North American Family": Voting and Whiteness

Creoles of mixed ancestry narrowly avoided being racialized in 1825 during a heated territorial election controversy, the results of which allowed Creoles to remain insiders to the body politic. Yankee prejudices about Indians and Creoles influenced discourse about the composition of the body politic. While Prairie du Chien's residents were thinking about "white persons" and "Indians" and writing ordinances that affected them differently and while Anglo-American settlers were moving in with their own prejudices, differing concepts of ethnicity and race intruded into legislation and practice at the territorial level. We must shift our gaze eastward momentarily to focus on the evolution of legislation about voters.

Voting laws in the early nineteenth century presented an evolving set of ideas about race, ethnicity, and class on the part of lawmakers at the federal and territorial level. Majority rule, of course, presented the dilemma: a majority of whom? It behooved those Anglo-American elites promoting the political development of the region to be very inclusive. The Northwest Ordinance provided for the territory to progress through three stages to eventual statehood, based upon the numbers of "inhabitants" counted there – 5,000 persons in a county could elect delegates to a territorial legislature; 60,000 in the territory could progress to statehood.[70] They needed Creoles to swell their ranks, to speed these population-based processes toward statehood, and to help them implement the government.

---

[68] Caleb Atwater, *Remarks Made on a Tour to Prairie du Chien in 1829* (Columbus, OH: Isaac Whiting, 1831), 180.

[69] "Local Business," *Crawford County Courier*, Prairie du Chien, May 17, 1853, p. 2.

[70] The Northwest Ordinance, section 9 and article 5, full text online at http://www.ourdocuments.gov/doc.php?doc=8&page=transcript, accessed August 12, 2011.

When created in 1796, the legal code of the Northwest Territory had been less concerned with *race* than with status, gender, and property, stipulating that voters should be "free male inhabitants" who owned at least fifty acres of land and were either citizens or resident for at least two years.[71] (The governor and other officials should own more land: 1,000 or 500 acres, respectively.)[72] The term "free" presumably excluded slaves as well as indentured servants. By 1818, after Ohio, Indiana, and Illinois became states, Michigan Territory took up the remainder of the Old Northwest, including present-day Michigan, Wisconsin, and part of Minnesota.[73] Without reference to race or color, then, the laws had permitted men who had not been purely European in ancestry to vote.

It was then that Congress introduced race into the voting laws by allowing the territory to elect a nonvoting delegate to Congress, permitting "every free white male citizen of said territory" over the age of twenty-one to vote if he had paid a county or territorial tax and lived there for one year.[74] Land-owning requirements were dropped but because taxes were levied on land or other property, this requirement disenfranchised the poor and dependent. And of course, it continued to prevent women from voting.

Ethnicity would also complicate political issues. In the southern and eastern parts of Michigan Territory, voting for congressional delegates seemed to reveal ethnic fault lines, especially in the mid-1820s. Based upon strong French-Canadian support in Monroe County (south of the Detroit area), William Woodbridge was elected as congressional delegate in 1819, and, as author Russell E. Bidlack has argued, "for a number of years thereafter, Michigan politicians recognized that to win the French vote in Monroe County was often to win the election."[75]

---

[71] *Laws of the Territory of the United States North-west of the Ohio* (Cincinnati: W. Maxwell, 1796), vi–vii.

[72] *Laws of the Territory of the United States North-west of the Ohio*, iv – v.

[73] Bald, *Michigan in Three Centuries*, 105; Buley, *The Old Northwest*, Vol. I, 62–63. Between 1809 and 1818, Illinois Territory included what is now Wisconsin.

[74] "An Act authorizing the election of a Delegate from the Michigan territory to the Congress of the United States," *Laws of the Territory of Michigan, condensed, arranged, and passed by the Fifth Legislative Council. Together with the Declaration of Independence; the Constitution of the United States; the Ordinance of 1787; and the acts of Congress, relative to said territory.* (Detroit: S. M'Knight, 1833), 35–36. In 1823 Congress amended the law to specify that people must be citizens of the United States to vote in all elections in Michigan Territory, clearing up the question of whether a person could be a citizen of the Territory without being a citizen of the United States. *Laws of the Territory of Michigan ... ,* 36. TPUS, Vol. 11, 719.

[75] Bidlack, *The Yankee Meets the Frenchman*, 18. The first delegate to Congress, Woodbridge, who was also secretary of the territory, resigned in response to criticism of his dual roles,

In 1823, the Reverend Gabriel Richard, French pastor of Ste. Anne's Catholic Church of Detroit, was elected to the congressional delegate seat based upon strong Creole support in Detroit's Wayne and River Raisin's Monroe counties, horrifying Yankees who had strong prejudices against both French Creoles and Roman Catholics. Comments by a few Protestants and Catholics about Richard's lack of political experience, antiquated unfashionable attire, and difficulty with the English language suggest that the priest did not create in Washington the type of impression that some territorial residents wished the rest of the nation to have of those who lived in Michigan territory. Implied was the anti-Catholic and anti-French prejudice simmering behind their remarks.[76]

So the campaign for territorial representative in 1825 between Richard, Austin Wing, and former Green Bay Indian Agent John Biddle was especially contentious. When preliminary returns seemed to show that Biddle had won by a small margin, Wing challenged the election results, arguing that many people had been permitted to vote at Sault Ste. Marie (an old fur-trade town in the Upper Peninsula) who were not eligible, including recently discharged soldiers, noncitizens, nonresidents, those who had not paid taxes (or who had paid them with work on the roads instead of cash), and those who were not "white."[77]

The most interesting challenge was based on the charge that "half-breeds" had been permitted to vote at the Sault in violation of the stipulation that voters should be "white." Canvassers William Woodbridge and Robert Abbott, the secretary and treasurer, respectively, of Michigan Territory, assumed the task of determining the final vote tally while the governor was on an extended tour of the territory and thus unavailable (and also conveniently able to avoid the controversy).

Men of mixed ancestry had been involved in politics from the beginning of U.S. hegemony in the old Northwest Territory, and in the year 1825, this did not change. In the middle of a contested election, however, voters of mixed ancestry were in danger of being disqualified on

---

and Solomon Sibley replaced him. When in 1822 some citizens again tried to effect a transition to the second phase of territorial status by way of a petition, others organized a meeting to oppose this shift, arguing that government by a governor and judges was adequate and there was no need for a territorial legislature. Buley, *The Old Northwest*, Vol. II, 33–34. In 1823, Congress provided that Michigan Territory would be ruled by a governor and an assembly to consist of eight men selected by the president from eighteen nominated by voters.

[76] Frank B. Woodford and Albert Hyma, *Gabriel Richard, Frontier Ambassador* (Detroit: Wayne State University Press, 1958), 119, 127.

[77] *TPUS*, Vol. 11, 730.

"racial" grounds. A six-year resident of Michigan Territory affirmed, the "population of mixed blood ... have never been denied the right of white men; that he has repeatedly known persons of this description to vote, to set as Jurors, and that they have also held, and do now hold, county offices – viz, Justices of Peace, Coroner &c."[78] In spite of this long-standing inclusive practice, Wing's followers brought twelve depositions to the attention of the canvassers to prove that (in the words of one deponent) "halfbreeds, or Indians of the half blood," had been permitted to vote.[79] Another man said two election inspectors told him that "twenty Indians of the half breed, whose mothers were squaws, were permitted by the inspectors to vote."[80] Some deponents also mentioned that the voters in question had Native wives, which presumably made them more "Indian" than "white." Thus, they considered the men in question in the *context of their families*, implying that the women in voters' lives affected their appropriateness to assume the franchise, proposing a link between personal intimacies, racial status, and voting rights. By this logic, men who married "out" risked losing their membership in the dominant group. This flew in the face of the previously inclusive government practices.

A vigorous discussion among supporters of different candidates, deponents, and politicians ensued in testimony and affidavits concerning the question of whether people of mixed ancestry should be allowed to vote. Some of Wing's supporters characterized "half-breeds" as members of "wandering" Indian families, living in "camps," and following lifeways unlike those of "whites," doing work outside the wage or market economy, thus defining race according to kin ties and specific elements of culture: dwellings and occupations.[81] For example, one man generalized about "half breeds" that "they do not cultivate the soil, nor are engaged in mechanical or other occupations peculiar to the whites – but in general procure their subsistence by hunting and fishing."[82]

---

[78] Affidavit of Thomas C. Sheldon, Oct. 31, 1825, *TPUS*, Vol. 11, 774.

[79] *TPUS*, Vol. 11, 774, 779–780, 774, 738.

[80] *TPUS*, Vol. 11, 739. Rayna Green, "The Pocahontas Perplex: The Image of Indian Women in American Culture," *Massachusetts Review* 16 (Autumn 1975): 698–714; David D. Smits, "The 'Squaw Drudge': A Prime Index of Savagism," *Ethnohistory* 29, no. 4 (Autumn, 1982): 281–306.

[81] These depictions, of course, overlook the extent to which many Euro-Americans still followed patterns of subsistence to a very great extent, and the difficulty of farming in the cool climate.

[82] *TPUS*, Vol. 11, 742, 748.

But some Biddle supporters argued that the "half breeds" were *not* as Wing's followers had characterized them. These deponents argued that the mixed voters *"live in houses, cultivate the earth, and labor by the day or month,* and pay their taxes when called upon, as other citizens of the United States do." They added that those of mixed ancestry "supply wood, hay, and other articles for this market." Others testified that the "half breeds (so called,)" "dress[ed] like white men," spoke French or English, practiced the Roman Catholic religion, and that "debts are collected by law of them." [83]

The two canvassers both believed that all voters should have at least some European ancestry. They agreed that Sault Ste. Marie voter Peter Pond, who "is generally understood [to be] a mixture of Negro and Indian blood," should not have voted.[84] They stated that Congress clearly intended "free, white, male citizens" to include "those only who may derive their descent from European ancestors." They added,

It is evident to us, that it was as foreign from the intention of the general government to admit Indians to the privilege of voting, as to extend that franchise to the descendants of African parents: both are excluded, for neither of them form component parts of the great North American family.[85]

They rejected the argument that the exclusion should apply only to Negroes because of the heritage of slavery, recognizing that Indians had also been enslaved. They then acknowledged the political sovereignty of Indian tribes, noting "they have to some purposes an independent political existence.... [T]hey constitute every year parties to new treaties with this nation." [86] They added, "It is puerile to suppose that Congress could have intended to confer upon a Wyandot or Chippewa Indian a right to vote at our elections, or in any wise to intermeddle with our political affairs."

On the other hand, the two canvassers disagreed with each other about the suitability of "half breeds" to vote. Reasoning that "white citizen" meant persons whose ancestors were European, "one member of this board is of opinion that *no one,* having any Indian blood in his veins, can be entitled to vote.... Education does not alter the cast, nor any mixture of blood constitute of a part Indian, a 'free, white citizen,'" he believed.[87]

[83] *TPUS,* Vol. 11, 748.
[84] *TPUS,* Vol. 11, 743.
[85] *TPUS,* Vol. 11, 730.
[86] *TPUS,* Vol. 11, 730–731.
[87] *TPUS,* Vol. 11, 731.

The other member of the board, however, was persuaded that a man of mixed Native and European ancestry should be allowed to vote, if he was

born and educated in a condition of estrangement from all nations and tribes of Indians, by education, social habits and associations in strict connexion with the communities composed of the descendants of European ancestry, if he were not party, as of Indian descent, to any treaty, nor in any wise recognized as a constituent member of the tribe, and, especially, if the father were of European descent, and legally intermarried with the Indian mother.[88]

In addition to arguing for identity based upon community membership and culture, he appealed to the logic of patriarchy, elaborating upon this by rejecting the application to people of Indian and European ancestry the doctrine of *partus sequitur ventrem,* which was used to ensure that children inherited their slave mothers' unfree status. If the parents were legally married, "the child should follow the condition of the father."[89] This controversy thus reveals the new government's intrusive interest in people's intimate lives.[90]

In the end, the deciding factor for the two 1825 canvassers was the issue of whether Sault Ste. Marie voters had paid a tax, rejecting the suggestion that road work could be considered a form of tax payment, and cited records that showed only five of those who voted had paid a territorial tax, and only nine had paid a county tax, including one "half-breed Indian." They therefore rejected fifty-two votes (49 for Biddle and 3 for Wing), accepting only nine of the Sault Ste. Marie votes, giving those nine to John Biddle. Tellingly, among those nine men whose votes were accepted was one "half-breed Indian."[91]

The officials thus stopped short of excluding Native-descended Creoles from voting, using the class-related issue of tax paying to sidestep the issue of "whiteness." Wing's supporters were happy because the result favored their candidate. But men like Woodbridge and Biddle knew that Creole voters, including those of mixed ancestry, could be persuaded to vote for Anglo candidates like them, so it should not surprise us that a back door was left open into "white" status, to be kept ajar for future

---

[88] *TPUS*, Vol. 11, 731.
[89] *TPUS*, Vol. 11, 731.
[90] Ann Laura Stoler, "Tense and Tender Ties: The Politics of Comparison in North American History and (Post) Colonial Studies," *Journal of American History* 88, no. 3 (December 2001): 829–865.
[91] *TPUS*, Vol. 11, 724–725.

political needs. And soon after, laws were added to allow men who paid their taxes with road work to vote in the future.[92]

Congress ruled in February of 1826 in response to this controversy that men of mixed Native and European ancestry should be permitted to vote, if they were "civilized," and not tribal members. "If, by his manner of living and place of abode, [a man] was assimilated to, and associated with, the great body of the civilized community; had never belonged to any tribe of Indians, as a member of their community; and being possessed of the other necessary qualifications, no good reason is perceived against such a person being considered as a qualified elector."[93] Thus "whiteness" depended on lifestyle, community membership, and detribalization. This was an important decision for the Great Lakes Creoles, central to their ability to avoid being racialized as a non-white outgroup like the Canadian Métis or the Hispanics of the Southwest later in the century.[94]

The result was the election of Austin E. Wing as a delegate to Congress. Congress tinkered with the results a bit, but accepted Wing, who served there from 1825 to 1829, and then as a Representative from Monroe from 1831 to 1833. Biddle served from 1829 to 1831.[95]

At the local level, judges of election had a great deal of discretion about who could vote. No one complained to the canvassers in 1825 about the Prairie du Chien electorate, but several of the men who voted there were part Native. One, for example, was Simon Barth, the son of an Ojibwe mother.[96] Other men such as Michel and Joseph Brisbois and George Fisher had Native ancestry several generations back.[97] And men with African ancestry were also sometimes accepted by local judges of

---

[92] "An Act to provide for the election of a Delegate in the Congress of the United States," 1[1827], *Laws of the Territory of Michigan,* Vol. II, 564.

[93] U.S. House of Representatives, 19th Congress, 1st Session. [Rep. No. 69.] "Michigan Election," February 13, 1826. Online Databases, Ohio State University Library, "Serial Set," 7.

[94] For a different interpretation of this controversy, see Michael Witgen, *An Infinity of Nations: How the Native New World Shaped Early North America* (Philadelphia: University of Pennsylvania Press, 2012), 364–366.

[95] Biographical Directory of the United States Congress, for Wing, http://bioguide.congress. gov/scripts/biodisplay.pl?index=W000631; for Biddle, http://bioguide.congress.gov/ scripts/biodisplay.pl?index=B000441, accessed Nov. 22, 2006.

[96] *TPUS,* Vol. 11, 898; James L. Hansen, "Prairie du Chien's Earliest Church Records, 1817," *Minnesota Genealogical Journal* 4 (November 1985): 7.

[97] Jacqueline Peterson, "The People in Between: Indian-White Marriage and the Genesis of a Métis Society and Culture in the Great Lakes Region, 1680–1830" (Ph.D. diss., University of Illinois at Chicago Circle, 1981), p. 161.

election: voters Claude Gagnier and François Duchoquette were both Afro-French, these half-brothers being the sons of Marianne Labuche, an important midwife and healer of French African heritage.[98] Many, if not most, of the Prairie du Chien voters had wives who were Native or mixed, including Hyacinthe St. Cyr, whose wife was Keenokou of the Ho-Chunk nation; Pierre Charlefou, whose wife Lizette was Dakota; and François Chenevert, whose wife, Louise Giard, was half Meskwaki.[99] Wing's supporters probably did not complain about Prairie du Chien because it was too far west to be well-enough known or accessible to the men pressing the challenge. Furthermore, they could get the votes they needed by a challenge in only the northern community.

But the lawmakers did not exclude Native-descended Creole men from voting for practical reasons. Men of mixed ancestry had indeed been included in the eastern part of the territory as officials and jurors and even as voters for half a dozen years or more. To disenfranchise them would have alienated a group that the Anglos needed as allies to rule the territory and control the Indians. Additionally, for the *habitants*, ethnic categories and loyalties had not hardened: Creole voters outside southeastern Michigan had not voted strictly along religious or national lines: most had supported either Biddle or Wing over Reverend Richard. Thus, those building political coalitions had reason to assume that they might include métis men among their allies. And soon enough, the Creoles would become a small enough minority that they would be unable to influence the outcome of territorial elections even if they voted as a bloc.

### "The Independence of Self-Government": Elections, Voters, and Consensus

In Prairie du Chien during the 1820s and '30s residents continued to familiarize themselves with the new structures of government, evolving slowly away from French Canadian authoritarianism but retaining patterns of political consensus until elites' conflicts shifted political dynamics.

One novel practice, individualized balloting, was introduced for some men. The town meeting format of the borough council began the first

---

[98] Correspondence of James L. Hansen, Wisconsin Historical Library, Nov. 28, 2006; Lockwood, "Early Times," 125–126.

[99] Hansen, "Prairie du Chien's Earliest Church Records," 4, 9; Linda M. Waggoner, ed., *"Neither White Men nor Indians:" Affidavits from the Winnebago Mixed-Blood Claim Commissions, Prairie du Chien, Wisconsin, 1838–1839* (Roseville, MN: Park Genealogical Books, 2002), 39; Forsyth "A List of the Sac and Fox half breeds."

year, 1821, with appointed officials and open meetings characterized by vigorous discussion, but soon the "Freemen of said Borough" by written ballots selected their officers.[100] This anticipated congressional approval, designed, in part, to encourage the political acculturation of the Territory's Creoles. In 1824, the Legislative Council of Michigan Territory successfully urged Congress to allow *local* officials to be elected, arguing that the population "of French descent," who were "not yet fully conversant with the nature of our institutions," would as local voters learn "to appreciate their value."[101] The 1819 voter definition – free white male, over twenty-one, paid a tax, one-year residence – was extended to all elections in the territory.[102] By December of 1822 Prairie du Chien had elected its officers: three prominent fur traders. They were Joseph Rolette as Warden, Michel Brisbois as 1st burgess, and James H. Lockwood as 2nd burgess.[103]

The ideas of representative government and majority rule did take some getting used to. Creoles seemed, to some outsiders, to vote too frequently according to the advice of their patrons. James Lockwood, an ambitious young man from New York state, a protégée of James Duane Doty, later recalled that the Creoles did not seem to adopt Yankee concepts of the franchise. He wrote:

Of all the foreigners that came to this country, the Canadians of French extraction seemed to have the least idea of the privileges of American citizenship. It appeared almost impossible to instil [*sic*] into their minds anything of the independence of self-government.... They do not consider it a privilege to vote for the officers who are to govern them; and consider it only desirable to use the elective franchise in order to gratify some friend who has asked them to vote for himself or his candidate; and when so requested, they are too polite to refuse, unless a previous promise had been made to some other.[104]

And the Creoles often did vote in unison, or nearly so. Yet, as historian Jeremy Mumford has pointed out, even if they voted as a bloc, this was neither irrational nor pointless, and many other ethnic groups shared similar voting patterns.[105] Indeed, bloc voting would seem to be in the spirit of consensus decision making so valued by Native communities.

---

[100] "An Act to Incorporate the Borough of Prairie du Chien," 1821.

[101] Memorial of the Legislative Council [of Michigan Territory] to Congress, August 5, 1824, *TPUS*, Vol. 11, 604–605.

[102] *Laws of the Territory of Michigan* (Detroit: Sheldon & Reed, 1820), 15.

[103] "By-Laws enacted and passed by the … Borough of Prairie des Chiens," December 7, 1822.

[104] Lockwood, "Early Times," 141.

[105] Jeremy Mumford, "Metis and the Vote in 19th-Century America," *Journal of the West* 39, no. 3 (Summer 2000): 41.

Voters practiced consensus politics at the local level. The Township of St. Anthony was created in 1828 to replace the Borough of Prairie du Chien, and like the borough format, it provided opportunities for local men to elect some of their representatives in town meetings. At the first meeting on April 7, by "viva voce" vote, they unanimously elected three "supervisors" (apparently the name for council members), three assessors, a clerk, a tax collector, two overseers of the poor, three commissioners of highways, three constables, two fence viewers, a pound master, and an overseer of the road. Some men held more than one role; for example, Joseph Brisbois was both an assessor and clerk; Pierre Lariviere was an assessor and an overseer of the poor, and Strange Powers was both Pound Master and Overseer of Roads. (It is unclear how many voted.)[106]

The consensus evident in the unanimous election of these officials was also reflected in the communal measures passed at this meeting. Voters uniformly agreed that "all horses, mares, geldings, all horned cattle and all other domestic animals shall be free commoners." Although Congress had not approved the residents' request for communally owned sections of the village, many Prairie du Chien farmers shared fences. In a town with common fields (which might be individually owned but were contiguous and fenced around the whole), it was important to keep free-roaming livestock out of the arable fields, so the residents unanimously ordained that "all fences that are in common shall be put in good order by the 25th of April."[107]

Beginning in 1829, paper ballots were cast in the town meetings and votes for local officers tended to show consensus. For example, that year Rolette, his brother-in-law Jean Brunet, and Indian Agent Joseph Street were all unanimously elected as supervisors; all the other officers were elected either unanimously or very nearly so.[108] But by 1830, turnout for the town meetings could be low – why? Was it because of the typical near-unanimity, or was the apparent consensus the result of some voters using their absences to avoid emerging political rifts?

---

[106] "Election Record of the Territory," [1823–37].

[107] "By-Laws, enacted and passed by the ... Borough of Prairie des Chiens," December 7, 1822.

[108] "Election Record of the Territory," [1823–37]; 20 voters elected the supervisors; three men were unanimously elected as assessors; Joseph Brisbois received 20 votes for clerk, two others received 20 votes for constable; two men received 18 votes for commissioner of highways, and so forth. Only Daniel Curtis had little support: he received only 2 votes for tax collector.

Soon after local government was established, voters also began participating in territorial elections and they did seem to vote together most of the time. Voters may have been swayed more by personal relationships than issues, as Lockwood suggested, and we get a fleeting glimpse of women and family networks behind the scenes.[109] For example, in 1829, Green Bay resident Henry Baird received thirty-nine votes for one of two seats on the territorial legislative council (his part-Odawa wife was the half-sister of Jane Fisher Rolette), and Robert Irwin Jr. (whose aunt was part Menominee, like Marie Vertefeuille) got thirty-seven votes for a different legislative seat, while two other candidates polled four and two votes, respectively.[110]

Biddle, Wing, and Richard ran against each other several times for the position of delegate to Congress, but they seldom split the electorate. In 1823, for example, John Biddle got eighty-two out of eighty-three Prairie du Chien votes for delegate to Congress.[111] (That year, 82 men voted for other offices, and all voted the same.)[112] (See Table 2.1). In 1825, Wing made a slightly better showing, but still polled only nineteen out of seventy-six votes, the rest going to Biddle. Thereafter, support vacillated between Biddle and Wing, perhaps reflecting changes in the political clout of their local promoters, Rolette and Lockwood, respectively. Notably, there was little support for Father Richard, the French Catholic priest, among the largely Catholic Prairie du Chien voters, demonstrating that religion and ethnicity were not the sole factors swaying voter decision making. But these territorial elections, like the local contests,

---

[109] This was the case in Sault Ste. Marie. James L. Schoolcraft wrote to Henry R. Schoolcraft from Sault Ste. Marie on May 15, 1835, complaining of the recent election. "Our election can only be considered as a strife between the friends of the opposing Candidates; it was not Conducted by a *political principle*." TPUS, Vol. 12, 920–921.

[110] Crawford County Clerk Board Papers, 1817–1848, Series 4, Box 1, Folder 1, Wisconsin Historical Society Library; Elizabeth Baird, "Memoranda," Henry S. Baird Papers, Wisconsin Historical Society, Madison, Box 4, Folder 1, no date; Rentmeesters, *Wisconsin Creoles*, 274.

[111] Some support for Biddle may have been based upon kinship, too. Biddle was the cousin of Edward Biddle of Mackinac, whose Odawa wife Agathe Bailly had relatives at Prairie du Chien. Keith R. Widder, *Battle for the Soul: Metis Children Encounter Evangelical Protestants at Mackinaw Mission, 1823–1837* (East Lansing: Michigan State University Press, 1999), 51, 54; Donald Chaput, "Bailly, Joseph," *Dictionary of Canadian Biography Online* (University of Toronto/Université Laval, 2000), Vol. VI; Elizabeth T. Baird, "Reminiscences of Early Days on Mackinac Island," *Wisconsin Historical Collections*, Vol. 14 (1898), 43; "1821: Wisconsin Traders' Letters," *Wisconsin Historical Collections* Vol. 20 (1911), 197, n. 55; James L. Hansen correspondence, July 14, 2009.

[112] "Election Record of the Territory," [1823–37], Fort Crawford Museum Archives, Prairie du Chien. [#1998–006.024].

TABLE 2.1. *Territorial Elections at Prairie du Chien*

| Year | Mo. | Number of Voters | Biddle | Wing | Richard | Lyon |
|------|-----|------------------|--------|------|---------|------|
| 1823 | September | 83 | 82 | 1 | 0 | |
| 1825 | April | 76 | 57 | 19 | 0 | |
| 1825 | June | 73 | | | | |
| 1827 | May | 13* | 0 | 13 | | |
| 1829 | July | 42 | 38 | 3 | 1 | |
| 1831 | July | 36 | 0 | 36 | | |
| 1833 | July | 72 | | 69 | | 3 |

* The 1827 returns may be incomplete.

Note: The 1825 election was not for representative to Congress but is included to show voter turnout.

Sources: "Election Record of the Territory" [1823–37], Fort Crawford Museum Archives, Prairie du Chien [#1998–006.024]; Crawford County Clerk Board Papers, 1817–1848, Series 4, Box 1, Folder 1, Wisconsin Historical Society Library.

expressed consensus among those who cast ballots in Prairie du Chien. In this way, the *habitants* mirrored the ideal decision making of Native communities.

### "Fully Conversant with the Nature of our Institutions": Voter Turnout

When consensus broke down, some Creoles withdrew from politics. Enthusiasm for electoral democracy had been strong in the early years but soon dropped, probably due – at least in part – to the personal dangers of patronage politics. Voter turnout at Prairie du Chien was good during the three elections that took place in 1823 and 1825, when eighty-three, seventy-six, and seventy-three men cast their ballots, but after that it declined, probably affected by animosities among elites. During the mid- to late 1820s, political and personal rivalries created conflicts at the local level in Prairie du Chien, tensions that might explain some of the decline in voting. Joseph Rolette (Figure 2.3) was at the center of three feuds that would affect Prairie du Chien's politics.

Joseph Rolette had been born in Quebec in 1781 and arrived in Prairie du Chien in 1804 as a fur trader, an occupation he continued until his death in 1842.[113] Most of the time, Rolette had a charming, friendly

---

[113] Martinus J. Dyrud, "King Rolette, Astor Fur Trader on the Upper Mississippi," unpublished manuscript, Villa Louis archives; Scanlan, *Prairie du Chien*, 85. His given name was actually Jean Joseph Rolette III. Dyrud, "King Rolette," 2.

JOSEPH ROLETTE

FIGURE 2.3. Joseph Rolette. Courtesy Villa Louis Historic Site, Prairie du Chien.

personality; he was intelligent, witty, and hospitable. He was also well connected: his first wife, Margaret Dubois, was part Dakota; his second wife, Jane Fisher (Figure 2.4) was the niece of Domitille Brisbois. This short, handsome, and successful businessman was also extremely ambitious and had a strong temper – if crossed, he could be petty and vindictive. For a long time, he was one of the most important men in Prairie du Chien and aspired to lead it from the very front.[114]

In his memoir, Lockwood admitted that he and Rolette were rivals, "opposing candidates for the rank and consideration of the first man of our little village," and they each asked voters to support their favorite candidates.[115] At one election (probably 1825), Lockwood recalled,

[114] Dyrud, "King Rolette," 2; Lockwood, "Early Times," 173–174; James L. Hansen, "The Rolette Family of Prairie du Chien," unpublished genealogy, courtesy of the author.
[115] Lockwood, "Early Times," 175.

FIGURE 2.4. Jane Fisher Rolette Dousman. Wisconsin Historical Society Image ID 2622, Courtesy Villa Louis Historic Site, Prairie du Chien.

a farmer "by the name of Barrette, whose vote had been solicited both by Mr. Rolette and myself ... being engaged in getting in his spring crop of grain, and thinking if he went to the election he would offend one or the other of us ... concluded it would be wisest to remain at home, and work on his farm."[116] In the spirit of the Creole culture's emphasis on avoiding conflict, Barrette thus declined to vote at all. But, Lockwood claimed, Rolette was angry enough with Barrette that he tried to punish him by bringing a complaint in court, alleging that Barrette's stud horse had been running wild in violation of local ordinances. A local jury acquitted Barrette.[117] Yet the incident reveals the dangers of voting – or

---

[116] Lockwood, "Early Times," 142. Indeed, Pierre Barette did not vote for the Legislative Council in 1825, although he had voted in the territorial election of 1823. *TPUS*, Vol. 11, 918;
[117] Lockwood, "Early Times," 143–144.

not voting – in a deferential society, where elites might retaliate against voters. Barrette's neighbors on the jury refused to punish him, but the vengeance of Rolette is instructive. The Lockwood-Rolette rivalry may have soured some voters on the electoral process and kept them from the polls.

About the same time, Rolette found himself in the middle of a feud with the Brisbois family, a conflict that would further challenge local political consensus. Rolette had married Domitille Brisbois's niece Jane Fisher in 1818, but sometime during the next dozen years, their marriage fell apart. In 1834 Jane and Joseph separated, with her cousin Bernard W. Brisbois taking the role of her trustee.[118] The Brisbois-Rolette discord was probably based both on the marital strife and other factors.

Rolette had already picked a fight with Bernard's brother Joseph Brisbois. Outraged that Rolette had accused him of malfeasance as county clerk, Joseph wrote in 1832 to a friend, "I am not surprise[d;] since four year he try to find some charge, so that he may have a man under his controle, to do what he please with him &c as he was custome to do with the clerk previous to my entering in those Office, but I will much surprise if there any charge against me, … all the Inhabitants of this County will support me if it was necessary to be recommended."[119] Brisbois, who was also a justice of the peace and register of probate, continued as county clerk in spite of Rolette's challenge, probably because he did have the broad community support he claimed.[120]

These conflicts of Rolette's were of a piece with a rift between Rolette and another important man. James Lockwood's mentor was Judge James Duane Doty, who had developed a strong animosity toward Rolette and actively sought to hurt him politically. Because of a power struggle with Rolette during the winter and spring of 1823–24, Doty had moved his family from Prairie du Chien to Green Bay, although he continued to preside at the circuit court in Prairie du Chien during its yearly session.[121]

---

[118] Martin Dyrud, "King Rolette," unpublished manuscript, Villa Louis archive, Prairie du Chien, timeline 1834, 1836 [no page numbers].

[119] Joseph Brisbois, Prairie du Chien, to Morgan L. Martin, Member of the Legislative Council, Detroit, December 10, 1832, Green Bay and Prairie du Chien Papers, Wisconsin Historical Society Library, micro. p. 144 (frame 340).

[120] Hansen, "Crawford County Public Office Appointments."

[121] Albert G. Ellis, "Life and Public Services of J. D. Doty," WHC, Vol. 5 (1868), 372.

Doty needed Creoles to support his political goals as did so many other Anglo politicians. Seven years later in 1831, Doty was helping to organize an anti-Rolette political party at Green Bay and trying to recruit the Brisbois family in order to expand the party to Prairie du Chien. He explained to Joseph Brisbois in an 1831 letter, "The people of this county [Brown] have determined ... to free themselves from the shackles of him & his intriguers. A party has been organized, under the title of 'the friends of the country,' at the head of which are the old Inhabitants of this county. John Lawe, Judge Porlier, and every member of the Grignon family are in its front rank." Doty added, "It is hoped that the County of Crawford will abandon the evil of its ways and step forward in support of our ticket. Depend upon it[:] you can never destroy the baneful influence of the little nabob unless you do so."[122] Doty used the term "old Inhabitants," as an Anglicization of the French *habitants*, using ethnicity for political appeal. The Lawes, Porliers, and Grignons were longtime Creole fur traders; Doty's reference to them in this letter to the Creole Brisbois was an effort to demonstrate Creole support for his side. And Doty's efforts paid off: in 1833 when Doty – now a Green Bay resident – ran for a seat on the territorial legislative council, all seventy-two of the Prairie du Chien voters cast their ballots for him. In the next year's township elections, Rolette was elected pound master (the man in charge of stray animals), a truly ignoble post for a man who had until 1831 been one of the township's supervisors and had held top leadership positions in most areas of local and county government during the 1820s.[123] Prairie du Chien's Creole voters had supported Rolette during times of patronage politics and community consensus, but conflicts eroded his base.

Democracy empowered non-elite *habitant* men who had used the franchise enthusiastically to support the hierarchy's status quo for the first few years. But when new Anglo elites emerged and when feuds created political discord, voters were turned off, particularly at the local level. As the Rolette-Brisbois rift threatened to split the vote, and the Rolette-Lockwood/Doty rivalry made some of Prairie du Chien's men anxious to

---

[122] James Duane Doty, Green Bay, to Joseph Brisbois, Prairie du Chien, May 3, 1831, Letterbook, 148–149, Doty Papers, Bentley Library, microfilm. It is interesting that one of the men in opposition to this party and supporting Rolette, according to Doty in this letter, was Henry Baird, whose wife Elizabeth was related to Rolette's wife Jane on their father's side.

[123] "Election Record of the Territory" [1823–37], Fort Crawford Museum Archives, Prairie du Chien [#1998–006.024].

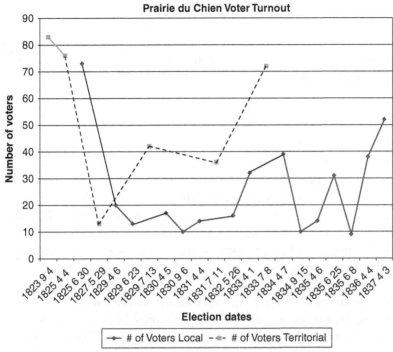

FIGURE 2.5. Prairie du Chien voter turnout, 1823–1837. From "Election Record of the Territory" [1823–37], Fort Crawford Museum Archives, Prairie du Chien [#1998–006.024]; Crawford County Clerk Board Papers, 1817–1848, Series 4, Box 1, Folder 1, Wisconsin Historical Society Library.

avoid insulting any of the elites, voter turnout dwindled, at least until the tax controversy of 1835 (see Figure 2.5 on Voter Turnout).[124]

## The Poor Tax Controversy

Voter consensus broke down in 1835. On Saturday, June 6 of that year, a town meeting had as its primary goal the election of a Register of Deeds. Only nine men appeared, and after the election, these nine took up the issue of funding for the community's paupers.

When sick, elderly, and mentally incompetent people had no one to look after them, territorial law provided that local officials place them with residents who were given money to help cover the cost of their care.

---

[124] Fort Crawford Archives, "Election Record of the Territory" [1823–37].

In 1834, Justice of the Peace Hercules Dousman ruled that Catherine Pelotte "was entitled to relief as a pauper in the consequence of her being an idiot and having no estate upon which she can subsist," so he named Bernard Brisbois as her guardian and ordered the local government to pay him four dollars per month for her upkeep.[125]

The money had to come from the public coffers, which were not well enough endowed. So someone proposed a new revenue measure, and all nine of the men present at the 1835 township meeting voted to establish "a poll tax of one dollar on each free male inhabitant of the age of twenty one years or upwards for the year 1835 for the use and maintenance of the poor." (Notably, one did not have to be "white" to pay a tax but did have to be male.) Bernard Brisbois, Amable Grignon, and Pierre Lachapelle joined five non-Creoles (and one whose name is illegible) in passing this tax. Probably, this was the first revenue measure to be instituted that was neither a property tax nor a fee for services such as registering legal documents.

Once the word got out about the tax, there was evidently a community uproar because another town meeting was called three weeks later on June 28. This time, there was a much stronger turnout: thirty-one men came to vote, and twenty-two of them voted against the tax, at least fourteen of them Creole. We may imagine the vigorous debate that must have taken place on this issue – some of it in French, some in English. Town Clerk Thomas Posey recorded that "It is therefore ordered a majority of the electors concurring that the order or rule adopted … levying a poll tax of one dollar … be and the same is hereby recinded." [*sic*][126]

At this point, some of the voters seem to have left the meeting because when a second measure proposed a tax of 37 1/2 cents per adult male "for the use and maintenance of the poor of said township," only sixteen voters remained to vote and all approved the measure.

Why was this measure so controversial? Was it the tax itself, the idea of using public funds to care for the poor, or resentment directed against Catherine Pelotte or Bernard Brisbois? More likely the vote reflected resistance to the institutionalization of a function – charity – that had heretofore been handled informally within the community with significant female participation (a topic to be considered in a later chapter). The

---

[125] "Register of Paupers Admitted to relief by the Director of the poor for the Township of St. Anthony and County of Crawford," Fort Crawford Archives.

[126] "Election Record of the Territory" [1823–37]. This is the only one of the election records reporting how specific men voted on any issue or candidate.

Glass family fiasco of the previous decade had taught Prairie du Chien residents to be wary of government direction of charity. It is unclear, though, whether the poor tax issue reflected an element of ethnic or partisan tension. Although the township officers presiding in 1835 when the tax was first passed were all Anglos and included James Lockwood, Creoles did not bloc vote the issue: *habitant* voters could be found on both sides.

But there were demographic changes afoot that were evidently affecting the balance of power in Prairie du Chien, and the 1835 controversy may have been a wake-up call for the *habitants*. Perhaps they had learned the downside of apathy. In 1836, when they remembered how the previous year's low turnout had adversely affected them, the number of men who appeared to vote for local officials increased to thirty-eight. (This was the year that the Creoles became a minority in Prairie du Chien.) Out of those thirty-eight voters, only fifteen had French surnames. We don't know who ran for office or how the voters aligned themselves, but the results of the election meant that the town board of supervisors was again composed of three Anglos (Thomas P. Street, James H. Lockwood, and Samuel Gilbert). Joseph Brisbois, however, was elected town clerk again. Lesser roles were mixed but tended to relegate the *habitants* to the bottom: George Fisher and Toussaint Dubeau were constables, Julien Lariviere the pound master, and the fence viewers were Jean Brunet, Francois Chenevert, and Strange Powers. Dousman and Lockwood were highway commissioners.[127]

So the next year, in 1837, twenty-six men with French names were among the fifty-two who showed up to vote at the town meeting to elect township and county officers. This time Bernard Brisbois and Hercules Dousman were elected as two of the three supervisors, and Joseph Brisbois was both township clerk and county treasurer.[128]

Creole political power would soon take a nosedive. The system of majority rule meant that demographic change could wreak havoc in the balance of power. Migration into western Wisconsin had been increasing ever since the end of the War of 1812. After the Black Hawk War of 1832 and subsequent removal of the Sauks and Meskwakis, more and more "settlers" came into the region to take the Indian lands, most of them from the eastern United States, but some were from northern and

[127] "Election Record of the Territory" [1823–37]. In 1837, the town meeting reduced the poor tax to 12 1/2 cents per adult male.
[128] "Election Record of the Territory" [1823–37].

TABLE 2.2. *Prairie du Chien Creole Proportion of the Population*

|  | French Surname |
|---|---|
| 1817: Men identified by name in sources: n = 60/72 | 83.3% |
| 1820: Household heads, U.S. Census: n = 39/53 | 73.6% |
| 1830: Household heads, U.S. Census: n = 45/62 | 72.6% |
| 1836: Household heads, Wisc. Census, County n = 79/157 | 50.3% |
| 1840: Household heads, U.S. Census, County n = 63/187 | 33.7% |
| 1850: All residents (Creoles*) n = 425/1406 | 30.2% |
| 1860: All residents (Creoles*) n = 380/2,398 | 15.8% |

* "Creoles" includes residents with French surnames who were born in Wisconsin, Michigan, Minnesota, Missouri, Illinois, or Canada before 1820, their children, and/or those who were known from genealogical and treaty records to be members of fur-trade families. Data for the years before 1850 were for those with French surnames. All residents appeared in the records without ethnic or racial designations or as "white."

*Sources*: James L. Hansen, "Prairie du Chien's Earliest Church Records, 1817," *Minnesota Genealogical Journal* 4 (1985): 329–342; James H. Lockwood, "Early Times and Events in Wisconsin," *State Historical Society of Wisconsin* 2 (1856): 125–126; Hoffmann, *Antique Dubuque*, 51–59; Lowrie et al., ed., *Public Lands*, 5: 47–98, 270–272, 283–328; Donna Valley Russell, ed., *Michigan Censuses 1710–1830* (Detroit: Detroit Society for Genealogical Research, 1982), 146–147; Elizabeth Taft Harlan, Minnie Dubbs Millbrook, and Elizabeth Case Erwin, trans. and eds., *1830 Federal Census: Territory of Michigan* (Detroit: Detroit Society for Genealogical Research, 1961); [C.W. Butterfield,] *History of Crawford and Richland Counties, Wisconsin* (Springfield, IL: Union Publishing Company, 1884), I, 294–295; Population Schedules of the Seventh Census, 1850, manuscript, Crawford County, WI, microfilm M432, Reel 995; Population Schedules of the Eighth Census, 1860 manuscript, Crawford County, WI, microfilm M653, Reel 1402; U.S. Census Office, *Population of the United States in 1860* (Washington, DC: Government Printing Office, 1864), 534.

western Europe as well. By 1850, 80 percent of Wisconsin's population had been born outside the state, and about one third of all were foreign born. The largest numbers of outsiders hailed from New York, Ohio, Vermont, Pennsylvania, Massachusetts, and Maine. Very few came from the southern states.[129] In the mid-1830s, Creoles became a minority in their hometown (see Table 2.2).

By the end of 1836, the year Wisconsin became a territory separate from Michigan, Prairie du Chien was no longer predominantly Creole. The political implications of becoming a minority would be enormous and are clearly reflected in the decline of Creole officeholders. In 1825, six out of eleven men having official roles were Creole according to the records of the Crawford County Commissioners.[130] Ten years later, four

[129] Smith, *The History of Wisconsin*, Vol. I, 467–468.
[130] CC Supervisors, 20–26.

out of six men mentioned in the county minutes were Creole, some in more than one office; and eleven out of twenty township officials were Creole.[131] However, by 1845, Anglo immigration had led to the political marginalization of the old fur-trade families: among sixty-two men mentioned in the commissioners' records as having official roles in government, there were only seven Creoles.[132] Thus, Creole political authority dwindled as more and more settlers made Prairie du Chien and the surrounding area their home.[133] The Creoles retained their voting rights and their designation as "white," but their political influence was impaired. With very few exceptions, Anglophone settler men would henceforth make the bulk of local laws and policies.

## Conclusion

In the Northwest Territory and its subsequent governmental permutations, U.S. officials incorporated the old fur-trade families' men into the body politic because they needed their participation to legitimize the government and, practically speaking, to operate the government. They also needed Creoles' loyalty as long as Native Americans were a large presence in the territory.

Given the population of the region – a large number of Indians, a smaller but significant number of Creoles, and a tiny population from the original thirteen United States – the "Americans" needed the support and participation of the Creoles to make the system work and to dominate the Indians, so Creole men were urged to vote and serve on juries. Although Congress and the territorial governments were codifying restrictions based upon evolving concepts of race, and laws increasingly excluded from political rights those who were not "white, Creole men survived a challenge to their racial status and were permitted – even required – to participate in government as officials, voters, and jurors. Many Creoles were métis; even more had Native or métis wives, yet they could vote and serve as jurors and officials if by any stretch of imagination they qualified as freeholders or taxpayers or citizens.

---

[131] CC Supervisors, 76–81; "Election Record of the Territory" [1834].

[132] CC Supervisors, 167–218.

[133] Ronald Formisano noted a similar decline in Creole voters and elected city council members in southeastern Michigan during the 1830s through 1850s. He also noted cultural conflicts between Creoles and Yankees that affected local politics. *The Birth of Mass Political Parties: Michigan, 1827–1861* (Princeton, NJ: Princeton University Press, 1971), 171–179.

Because the new institutions required their participation in order to function, Creoles exerted some agency in these roles. They were sometimes able to protect neighbors from skulkers or against aspects of the new institutions that seemed harsh or unjust, such as the binding out of poor children or the incarceration of men unable to post bail for unlicensed tavern keeping. They could express communal agricultural practices and force the reconsideration of unpopular laws. Drawing on experience with Native political and judicial practices, the Creoles used the new forms of governance to critique colonization, assert their choices about local laws, and express their own sense of justice.

The new legal and political system imposed an Anglo-Yankee social and political hierarchy on the Native people and Creoles. This political colonization of the region redefined and formalized many relationships among men by way of official roles. Some of the leadership and mediation activities that men and women had previously performed (often informally) were taken over by the territorial, county, and local administrations. Since these roles were legally restricted to men, they became more gendered. Where *elite* men and women had previously exerted authority, the new roles of voter and juror extended formal influence to some non-elite men, shifting the basis of authority from elite status (derived from prestige, kin connections, age, accomplishments, and economic authority) to maleness and "white"-ness, in addition to citizenship. Yet, some Creole men and women still mediated and negotiated outside of the official channels.

But Creoles found ways to use forms such as the borough and town councils and county commission to express their own concerns and to address local issues in ways that reflected their own culture and experiences. Some of the new political processes had a familiar ring. As fur-trade workers and kin to Native people, Creoles had experienced not only the nondemocratic political system of francophone Canada, but also consensus-based Native political systems.

Where Creole men initially participated with some enthusiasm in the electoral process, they expressed consensus in their decision making during the early years. The dangers of deferential politics soon depressed participation, however. Once Rolette's feuds heated things up, voter turnout began to decline. The Poor Tax controversy of 1835 fractured the remaining consensus while reversing voter apathy. Yet by the mid-1830s the in-migration of Yankee settlers and western Europeans increased to the point that Creole voters became a minority, reducing Creole political power. Throughout, the Creoles experimented with the new systems of governance and then adapted to them, in a process of institutional assimilation.

To the north, in the British colonies that would coalesce into the nation of Canada by 1869, Métis identity developed in part because of concerns over land titles and autocratic governmental policies. Scholars point to the resistance led by Louis Riel as expressions of Métis frustration with government policies that these people had no part in creating, frustrations that brought the Métis together and gave them a shared sense of "peoplehood" (to use sociologist Chris Andersen's term). Creoles in Manitoba and Saskatchewan would come to think of themselves – and others would come to think of them – as an indigenous solidarity group.[134]

For the Creoles of Prairie du Chien, the issue of "whiteness" arose in the local and territorial politics of the early 1820s. The "white persons skulking" law revealed Creole ambivalence about this racial category and an initial tendency to view "white persons" as dangerous and violent outsiders. Yet Creole men were swept into this category by the needs of the colonizing government, and many gained title to community lands. They might be disparaged and demographically overwhelmed by hordes of Yankee settlers, losing much of their political clout to sheer numbers. Technically, though, they were still insiders.

---

[134] Jennifer S. H. Brown, "The Métis: Genesis and Rebirth," in *Native People, Native Lands*, edited by Bruce Alden Cox (Ottawa, Canada: Carleton University Press, 1988), 136–147; Jennifer Brown and Theresa Schenck, "Métis, Mestizo, and Mixed-Blood," in *A Companion to American Indian History*, edited by Philip J. Deloria and Neal Salisbury (Malden, MA: Blackwell, 2002), 321–338; Chris Andersen, *"Moya 'Tipimsook* ('The People Who Aren't Their Own Bosses'): Racialization and the Misrecognition of 'Métis' in Upper Great Lakes Ethnohistory," *Ethnohistory* 58, no. 1 (Winter 2011): 37–63; J. M. Bumsted, *A History of the Canadian Peoples*, 4th ed. (Don Mills, Ontario: Oxford University Press, 2011), 212; Alexander Begg, *The Creation of Manitoba* (Toronto: A. H. Hovey, 1871), 110–111, 255–256, reproduced in Victoria Community Network, http://victoria.tc.ca/history/etext/metis-bill-of-rights.html, accessed Nov. 20, 2012, and Canada History, http://www.canadahistory.com/sections/documents/thewest/metisbillrights.htm, accessed Nov. 20, 2012; Maggie Siggins, *Riel: A Life of Revolution* (Toronto: HarperCollins, 1994), 95–97.

# 3

## "Damned Yankee Court and Jury"

### More New Institutions, Keeping Order and Peace

On May 11, 1824, a grand jury in Prairie du Chien indicted Governor Lewis Cass's brother for assault. Captain Charles L. Cass of the Fifth Regiment, U.S. Infantry, stationed at Fort Crawford had apparently attacked Joseph Glass, who was in jail at the time.[1] The Glass family, of course, had been the objects of community assistance (mentioned in the previous chapter) after the father's incarceration had caused them economic distress and officials had threatened to take the children from their mother. Public pressure had caused the county commission to find a way for Glass to get out of jail and the children to stay with their parents.

The mercy shown to Joseph Glass was one method of resolving the whole affair, but there was also the second issue, the matter of the beating he had received from Charles Cass on January 12. So Prairie du Chien community members used another new institution, the grand jury, to address the violent behavior of Captain Cass. As they had with the new electoral system, the *habitants* found ways to make the unfamiliar court system both familiar and useful. They could have let the matter go out of deference to the governor. After all, Charles Cass wasn't in Prairie du Chien anymore by the time the grand jury met. Five months after the attack when the circuit court finally convened, he seems to have left town

---

[1] *U.S. v. Charles L. Cass*, May 11, 1824, Wisconsin Historical Society Library (hereafter WHSL), Madison, 20, Folder 17. On Charles L. Cass as Lewis Cass's brother, Willard Carl Klunder, *Lewis Cass and the Politics of Moderation* (Kent, OH: Kent State University Press, 1996), 48, n. 55 (p. 326). James Duane Doty, "Notes on Trials and Decisions," Wisconsin Historical Society Library (hereafter WHSL), Madison, WI, Mss DD, Box 3, typescript, 22.

after resigning from the army.[2] But the predominantly Creole grand jury was not going to let the matter go: they were still angry.[3]

The court system with its reliance on juries was brand new in Prairie du Chien in 1824. In May of that year the grand jury of Judge James Duane Doty's court was under the leadership of foreman Alexis Bailly, a twenty-six-year-old fur trader of Odawa, Scottish, and French ancestry. Under Bailly's leadership, the grand jury indicted Captain Cass.[4] The indictment stated that Cass "did make an assault with intent to murder upon Joseph Glass in the peace of God and our ... Territory ... with a certain pistol ... terrified and affrighted the said Joseph Glass ... willfully and of malice aforethought to kill and murder." Cass's gun had misfired, so then he beat Glass. According to the indictment, Cass's actions were "contrary to the statute of this Territory and against the peace and dignity of the United States and of this Territory."[5]

This was a strong public statement of protest against not only Captain Charles Cass but also both the army and the governor. It demonstrated, on the part of local residents, a savvy appropriation of the jury form and the formulaic language of the court to issue a public rebuke. It also expressed a blatant lack of deference to Governor Cass and to the army.

[2] Charles Lee Cass resigned on May 1, 1824. Francis B. Heitman, *Historical Register and Dictionary of the United States Army* (Washington, DC: Government Printing Office, 1903), Vol. I, 289.

[3] Juries "comprised nearly the entire adult male population" of Prairie du Chien, according to former judge Ira Brunson. Ira B. Brunson, "Judicial History of Prairie du Chien, Wis., 1823–1841," manuscript, Wisconsin Historical Society Library, Madison.

[4] *U.S. v. Charles L. Cass*, May 11?, 1824, Michigan. Circuit Court. (Iowa County) Criminal Case Files, 1824–36, Wisconsin Historical Society Archives, Platteville, Iowa Series 20, Folder 17; Doty, Notes on Trials and Decisions, Mss. DD Box 3, typescript, 22. The indictment states that Cass was "late of Prairie du Chien," suggesting that he no longer lived there; Donald Chaput, "Bailly, Joseph," *Dictionary of Canadian Biography Online* (University of Toronto/Université Laval, 2000), Vol. VI, accessed July 14, 2009; Elizabeth T. Baird, "Reminiscences of Early Days on Mackinac Island," *Wisconsin Historical Collections* 14 (1898), 43; "1821: Wisconsin Traders' Letters," *Wisconsin Historical Collections* 20 (1911), 197, n. 55; James L. Hansen, correspondence with author, July 14, 2009. In some ways, Bailly was a typical Prairie du Chien Creole, ethnically mixed at least three ways: his mother was Bead Way Way, also known as Angelique McGulpin, the half-Ottawa daughter of a Scottish fur trader, and his father Joseph was a French Canadian, also in the fur trade. Alexis Bailly had joined the trade as a clerk to Joseph Rolette in 1821. His family was spread across Michigan from Michilimackinac to St. Joseph and into northern Indiana; he himself would soon marry into the Dakota-French Faribault family, and later move to Minnesota, serving in the Territorial Legislature there during the 1860s. Donald Chaput, "Bailly, Joseph"; "1821: Wisconsin Traders' Letters," *Wisconsin Historical Collections* (hereafter *WHC*), Vol. 20 (1911), 197, n. 55.

[5] *U.S. v. Charles L. Cass*, May 11?, 1824. The incident occurred on January 12.

Events like the indictment of Cass that took place in Prairie du Chien's courts reveal the contests and mechanisms of the process of colonization and the imposition of control by the United States and the Territory of Michigan over the *habitants*. After the Revolution but before the War of 1812, the Creoles had been quite autonomous. Although a few men had been given commissions as justices of the peace, government had been fairly casual and ad hoc. Most residents had maintained allegiance to British Canada. The previous chapter examined the evolving legislative side of the new government at Prairie du Chien; this chapter looks at the court system to examine the ways that agents of the new régime sought to establish mechanisms for control as they attempted to force the *habitants* to obey laws and participate in processes created elsewhere. It also discusses how *habitants* took some of the power back, "asserting the local voice" (to use Baron and Cara's phrase) in their own form of creolization, challenging the colonizers.

The case *U.S. v. Cass* took place at Prairie du Chien during the first session of the Additional Circuit Court of Michigan Territory for Crawford County. Idealistic officials of the new government, including Judge Doty, tutored the *habitants* in the workings of the new judicial system. Doty assured jurors and others attending court that *this* institution was not only just but also an improvement over the previous régimes: "The criminal jurisprudence of this country ... is ... a more perfect system than older governments ... can boast."[6] But in many parts of the territory, Creoles blasted the new system. In a memoir, Ebenezer Childs remembered the first jury trial at Green Bay. He himself was the plaintiff in a suit against "a Frenchman." Childs recalled of the Creole defendant, "He and his friends were outrageous in their denunciations of the d – d Yankee court and jury."[7]

The jurors were at the nexus of a paradox: the American conquest and colonization of the region was coercive by its very nature, but at the same time, it brought two new institutions that invited – and occasionally required – the participation of the Creoles. One was the unfamiliar institution of the ballot, with its concept of majority rule; the other was a court system that incorporated the locally novel process – trial by jury – based upon the concept of *consensus*, which was very familiar to the *habitants*.

---

[6] Elizabeth Gaspar Brown, ed., "Judge James Doty's Notes of Trials and Opinions: 1823–1832," *American Journal of Legal History* 9, no. 1 (January 1965): 31.

[7] Ebenezer Childs, "Recollections," *WHC*, Vol. 4, 166.

Like many other cases in the early United States court system in this region, the case of *U.S. v. Cass* was a contest of power between the new régime and the local community. The contest was made more complex because the new system permitted – sometimes even insisted on – participation by the colonized people in the process of administering the colonizers' institutions of government. This also allowed, paradoxically, for the *habitants* to express their own ideas about justice and mediation.

Under the new court system, Creole officials and jurors actively sought to find fair and equitable solutions to community problems, as they and their neighbors were adjusting to the new political reality of domination by the United States over their community and economy. Their ideas of what was fair and equitable differed on occasion from the norms of Anglo-American officials. Sometimes Creole actions can be seen as rebukes to the new régime or as resistance to the processes of colonization or prescribed adjudication. However, their independence and cultural differences eventually led officials to manipulate the system in order to marginalize the Creoles and so solidify their own control. By examining this history in the context of demographic change, we may understand the shift from an inclusive system to one that no longer needed the participation of most Creoles to maintain legitimacy and control.

## Systems of Justice

Before the United States took over, several systems of justice had operated in the Midwest. Native tribes in the Great Lakes region had chiefs, councils of chiefs or elders, and family, clan, and band leaders who worked to solve community conflicts.[8] Individually or in council, chiefs and elders worked with people in conflict to find solutions or compromises acceptable to all that would reduce tensions, provide some restitution to injured parties, and promote community harmony. According to legal

---

[8] Charles A. Eastman, *The Soul of the Indian: An Interpretation* [1911] (Lincoln: University of Nebraska Press, 1980), 108–110; Paul Radin, *The Winnebago Tribe* [1923], (Lincoln: University of Nebraska Press, 1990), 161; Nicholas Perrot, "Memoir on the Manners, Customs, and Religion of the Savages of North America," in *The Indian Tribes of the Upper Mississippi Valley and Region of the Great Lakes* [1911–1912], edited by Emma Helen Blair (Lincoln: University of Nebraska Press, 1996), Vol. I, 141; Thomas Forsyth, "Account of the Manners and Customs of the Sauk and Fox Nations of Indians Tradition," in *The Indian Tribes of the Upper Mississippi Valley and Region of the Great Lakes* [1911–1912], edited by Emma Helen Blair (Lincoln: University of Nebraska Press, 1996), Vol. II, 186–187; Vine Deloria Jr. and Clifford M. Lytle, *American Indians, American Justice* (Austin: University of Texas Press, 1983), 85.

scholar Sydney L. Harring, Native American law historically addressed the "immediate need ... to resolve the legal problem so that the community could move forward – together."[9] As such it was a restorative justice system.

Legal philosophies in these communities differed from those of Europeans and Euro-Americans, as legal scholars Vine Deloria Jr. and Clifford Lytle pointed out. "The primary goal was simply to mediate the case to everyone's satisfaction. It was not to ascertain guilt and then bestow punishment upon the offender," they argued.[10] "Under the traditional tribal system of justice," Deloria and Lytle explained, "the ultimate decision was seldom made by a judge. Rather, the job of the mediator or reconciling chief was to create an atmosphere for participant decision-making."[11] Since community ideals emphasized an individual's membership in and responsibility to his or her family, clan, village, and tribe, misconduct was not to be dealt with individually but by the communities involved.[12] Consensus was a basic philosophy of community decision making and a goal often reached in village meetings in which women as well as men participated.[13]

French legal culture was decidedly different. Under the autocratic French system (which was continued under the British), the *Coutume de Paris* (formally known as the Customary Civil Laws of the Paris *Prévôté* and Viscounty) was the official legal code.[14] According to historian Peter M. Moogk, the French legal code as adopted in New France was based on the idea that basic universal principles of behavior ought to apply without exception. In this system, judges "identified the general principle

[9] Sidney L. Harring, "Indian Law, Sovereignty, and State Law: Native People and the Law," in *A Companion to American Indian History*, edited by Philip J. Deloria and Neal Salisbury (Malden, MA: Blackwell, 2002), 445.

[10] Deloria and Lytle, *American Indians, American Justice*, 111.

[11] Deloria and Lytle, *American Indians, American Justice*, 112.

[12] Eastman, *The Soul of the Indian*, 94; Rudy Al James, "Traditional Native Justice: Restoration and Balance, not 'Punishment,'" in *Unlearning the Language of Conquest: Scholars Expose Anti-Indianism in America*, edited by Wahinke Topa (Austin: University of Texas Press, 2006), 113.

[13] Forsyth, "Account of the Manners," Vol. II, 187; Eastman, *The Soul of the Indian*, 42; examples may be found in Ellen M. Whitney, comp. and ed., *The Black Hawk War, 1831–1832*, 2 vols. (Springfield: Illinois State Historical Library, 1973); and Kenneth P. Bailey, ed. and trans., *Journal of Joseph Marin, French Colonial Explorer and Military Commander in the Wisconsin Country, Aug. 7, 1753–June 30, 1754* (n.p.: Published by the editor, 1975).

[14] Peter N. Moogk, *La Nouvelle France: The Making of French Canada – A Cultural History* (East Lansing: Michigan State University Press, 2000), 62; Allan Greer, *The People of New France*, 118.

pertinent to the case and then applied it." This legal system was also in contrast to English Common Law with its emphasis on legal precedents and current practice.[15] Trials did not involve any type of jury in decision making.

Theoretically guided by the *Coutume* during the French régime, military commandants adjudicated conflicts at Green Bay's fort in an autocratic manner, according to historian Louise Phelps Kellogg, but these officers seldom visited Prairie du Chien. Absent such military personnel and under the British régime, the elite fur traders passed judgment and settled disputes. Kellogg argued that "a kind of traders' code developed, unwritten but powerful, according to which life in the Indian country was regulated and misdeeds punished. As far as it had any legal foundation this code was based upon the sacredness of contract, and rested upon the engagement bonds made by the *voyageurs* when entering the employ of the *bourgeois* or of one of the great companies."[16] The *Coutume*'s emphases on general principles rather than precedents or the details of statutes guided official and unofficial magistrates. In disputes between Indians and traders, elites from both communities typically negotiated resolutions. In the Creole towns, however, elite traders and other leaders sometimes handed down decisions autocratically to the lesser *habitants*.

Before 1824, then, fur traders such as those on the *Cass* jury had experienced French and British Canadian colonial judicial systems and had also witnessed Native legal practices during their visits to Indian villages; many had also learned Indian and Creole legal philosophies from their kin. Thus, they were familiar both with council or elder mediation and with autocratic justice handed down by elites based upon contract or ideal principles.

The court systems under the *United States* formalized the roles of mediation and coercion in different ways. They evolved as the region in question went from being under the jurisdiction of the Northwest Territory (1787), to Indiana Territory (1800), Illinois Territory (1809), the Territory of Michigan (1818), the Territory of Wisconsin (1836), and finally Wisconsin statehood (1848).[17] Early territorial laws were measures

---

[15] Moogk, *La Nouvelle France*, 64–65.

[16] Louise Phelps Kellogg, *The French Régime in Wisconsin and the Northwest* (New York: Cooper Square, 1968), 398–399; Carolyn Podruchny, *Making the Voyageur World: Travelers and Traders in the North American Fur Trade* (Lincoln: University of Nebraska Press, 2006), 136.

[17] Alice E. Smith, *The History of Wisconsin* (Madison: State Historical Society of Wisconsin, 1985), Vol. I, 683.

that had been adopted in any of the original states; Michigan Territory formally repudiated the *Coutume de Paris* in 1810.[18]

The new system also introduced a hierarchy of courts. The appointed justices of the peace and their courts were at the lowest or most "inferior" level. These men, many of whom were Creole, seem to have continued the French legal tradition of focusing on basic principles rather than the details of statutes.[19] In these ways, familiar legal practices continued.

County courts – the next level up from the justice's court – were led by judges who were "learned" but not lawyers. They met once or twice a year to try more serious crimes, and heard appeals from the justices' courts.[20] At the top of the territorial judicial hierarchy were the circuit courts (an arm of the territorial Supreme Court), the judge arriving once or twice each year, accompanied by some circuit-riding lawyers. The circuit courts heard appeals from lower courts, had concurrent jurisdiction with county courts, and tried capital cases and civil cases worth over $1,000 in penalties.[21] James Duane Doty was the first to serve as a circuit judge in what is now Wisconsin; his court serving Michigan Territory's Crawford, Brown, and Michilimackinac counties was referred to as the additional court.

A key difference between the new legal system and the old French Canadian tradition was the addition of juries. The right to trial by jury was – and is – guaranteed by the U.S. Constitution, and American policy-makers meant to extend its blessings to the territories. For the American colonizers, recruiting the colonized as jurors could be an important way to lure the Creoles into the new body politic. In this system, the concept of a jury of one's peers could seem to give the community input into the imposition of the new regime, even though few Creoles were able to participate in writing the new territorial legal codes.

In the Supreme, circuit, and county courts, juries were regularly impaneled, and in the inferior courts of the justices of the peace,

---

[18] *Laws of the Territory of Michigan, condensed, arranged, and passed by the Fifth Legislative Council. Together with the Declaration of Independence; the Constitution of the United States; the Ordinance of 1787; and the acts of Congress, relative to said territory* (Detroit: S. M'Knight, 1833), 563.

[19] Henry Baird, "Recollections," *Wisconsin Historical Collections*, Vol. 4, 209; *History of Crawford and Richland Counties, Wisconsin* (Springfield, IL: Union Publishers, 1884), Vol. I, 364.

[20] Before 1827, in some circumstances it required two county court judges to try a case. *Laws of the Territory of Michigan*, Vol. 1 (1871), 184, 716; Vol 2 (1874), 624; *History of Crawford and Richland Counties*, Vol. I, 365.

[21] Ira Brunson, "Judicial History," Vol. 1, 10; Henry Baird, "Recollections," *WHC*, Vol. 4, 209.

defendants could request a jury. Grand juries were gathered once or twice each year at the county level to make decisions about indictments, and petit juries heard the cases. Jurors would have to leave their work and homes to attend court, although they would be paid, typically a dollar or two for their service. Jurors were required to be qualified to vote, which meant that they were male citizens, taxpayers, at least twenty-one years old, and of European or mixed Native and European ancestry.[22]

For Creoles, the juries must have resembled Indian village councils, in which pressing issues were discussed for as long as was needed to reach consensus. In their work as traders, *voyageurs*, and occasionally officials, these men had much experience visiting, observing, and participating in Native village life. Most were intermarried into one or more Native communities; many were the sons and grandsons of tribal members, and they knew the ways that wise leaders could work together with community members in council and behind-the-scenes negotiations to solve important problems without resorting to coercion. In Native political practice, if one person refused to go along with an important decision, mediation continued until a solution to the problem was reached. Similarly, petit juries required consensus. There was a key difference in the consensus objectives of the two systems: while Native communities used consensus to make political decisions or solve conflicts, the U.S. system expected juries to come to consensus about the *facts* of a case and then apply the law as instructed by the judge.[23] However, Creole juries often tended more to the former than to the latter.

---

[22] An 1820 law stated that all jurors must be qualified to vote for the delegate to Congress, reiterated in the 1827 and 1833 laws. In 1821, the grand jurors were required to be freeholders, a measure not reiterated in later jury laws. The 1827 statute expected jurors to be "judicious persons" and allowed them to be challenged by either party for not having a "competent knowledge" of the English language, another measure not reiterated in the law of the following year. The 1833 law expected jurors to be "of good character" and raised the age qualification from 21 to 25 years. *Laws of the Territory of Michigan*, Vol. 1 (1871), 490–493, 789–790; Vol. 2 (1874), 467; Vol. 3, 1242. Each year beginning in 1827, the Crawford County Board of Supervisors (also known as commissioners) drew up lists of jury members from names provided by the tax assessors, selecting the men who would be required to serve during the county court sessions. Wisconsin Territorial Papers, County Series, Crawford County, "Proceedings of the County Board of Supervisors, Nov. 29, 1821–November 19, 1850" (Madison, WI: Wisconsin Historical Records Survey, 1941), hereafter "CC Supervisors." County commissioners/supervisors were elected, beginning in 1825 (although they had been appointed before that time). *Laws of the Territory of Michigan*, Vol. 2 (1874), 279; Vol. 1 (1871), 661.

[23] Thanks to Michael Les Benedict for pointing out this difference.

## Imposing Control

In 1823, Judge James Duane Doty came into the Creole communities of Michilimackinac, Green Bay, and Prairie du Chien as judge of this additional circuit court to implement the "American" court system.[24] Ambitious, energetic, and anxious to get every detail right while (he hoped) teaching the *habitants* to obey and appreciate the "American" system of justice, the young man from northwestern New York by way of Detroit was in many ways a typical instrument of colonization. Arrogant, dedicated to the institution, and apparently unaware of Native and Creole traditions of negotiation and mediation, Doty arrived to set up his court as the supreme authority, trying the most important cases and superseding the decisions of the lower courts and their judges. Although local magistrates and other elites had adjudicated disputes in the region for a long time before the War of 1812, Doty felt his mission was to bring justice to the wilderness.[25]

Not surprisingly, Doty's attitudes and actions and his court itself were obnoxious to many of the old residents in his new jurisdictions. In an 1856 speech, lawyer Henry Baird recalled that although the inauguration of Doty's additional circuit court established the "civil code and civil authority" (in Baird's view protecting the liberties and property of citizens), many of the Creoles resented the change. He said, "this innovation on the primitive rights of the old settlers, was viewed by them with great jealousy. They looked upon it as a ... serious infringement on their long established customs; and they heartily wished the court, and ... the lawyers too, anywhere but amongst themselves."[26]

Thus, there would be several sources of conflict. Creoles resented Doty's ability to overrule local county court judges and justices of the peace. Doty's elite judicial position ranked him above men who were older than he was and often more familiar with the community. In a culture that valued and respected elders, Doty's youth – he was twenty-four years old when appointed to this position in 1823 – must have added to the tension of colonization. This young man lectured to, overruled, and punished his elders – in blatant contradiction to both Creole and

[24] Alice Elizabeth Smith, *James Duane Doty, Frontier Promoter* (Madison: State Historical Society of Wisconsin, 1954), 30, 35.

[25] Albert G. Ellis, "Life and Public Services of J. D. Doty," *WHC*, Vol. 5 (1868), 372.

[26] Henry Baird, "Early History and Condition of Wisconsin," *WHC*, Vol. 2 (1856), 90–91; Ellis, "Life and Public Services of J. D. Doty," also discussed the animosity between Doty and "the leading Indian traders," in Prairie du Chien, 372.

Native social and political patterns, in which leaders gained their authority from years of generosity, networking, problem solving, mediation, wise advice to others, and economic or military prowess. Kin ties had also been required for local prominence. Doty had demonstrated none of these attributes before assuming such a high position in these communities. To make matters worse, not only was his wife Sarah Collins Doty an outsider from New York rather than a local daughter, but she was a snob, refusing to socialize with the other residents after moving to Prairie du Chien in the fall of 1823.[27] The behavior she modeled was completely opposite to that expected of Native and Creole wives of men with political clout. Elite women in communities such as Prairie du Chien ideally served as intermediaries, connecting people of different families, tribes, and cultural backgrounds with charity, hospitality, leadership, and assistance with conflict resolution, a topic to be addressed in a later chapter.[28]

Doty's inflexible interpretations of the statutes, forcing obedience to the régime, only exacerbated problems with the Creoles. In many cases, Doty argued that local and county institutions had not done their work in the exact ways mandated by the territorial legislators and the governor. Never mind that local judges were hampered by the fact that printed copies of the laws often did not arrive in Wisconsin until long after they had been passed, and some of them were changed often, making it all the more difficult for inexperienced jurists and other officials to avoid having their decisions negated by Doty on technicalities. And, as Henry Baird conceded, many of the territorial laws of that time "were crude and ill-devised."[29]

Although Doty's inflexibility must have seemed, to the Creoles, contrary to common sense and reason, his objectives went beyond finding just solutions to community conflicts: he was also implementing the new government's institutions and forcing the local people's acquiescence to the authority of the territory and the United States.

---

[27] Smith, *James Duane Doty, Frontier Promoter*, 39, 53.

[28] For further discussion of women's ideal roles, see Lucy Eldersveld Murphy, "Public Mothers: Native American and Métis Women as Creole Mediators in the Nineteenth-Century Midwest," *Journal of Women's History*, special issue on "Revising the Experiences of Colonized Women," 14, no. 4 (Winter 2003): 142–166; Eastman, *Soul of the Indian*, 41, 42, 102.

[29] Henry Baird, "Early History," 95. During the early territorial period, the legislative council could only adopt laws already adopted in other states. Smith, *History of Wisconsin*, Vol. I, 207.

Cultural differences and racism probably added to the tension. As Doty lectured them in the courtroom, Creoles heard official attitudes about Native people, including their friends and kinfolk. For example, he addressed a grand jury in Green Bay on June 15, 1830, with regard to the rights of Indians under the law. Although Doty supported both the legal doctrine of sovereignty for tribes (he believed Indians should adjudicate Indians' crimes committed in their own country based on their own traditions of justice), and their right to bring suits in court, his message was nevertheless mixed.[30] He stated that Native tribes' rights to their lands "have never been 'secured' or 'granted' to them by any Treaty with the United States" (an inverted logic from a Native point of view).[31] If anyone had trouble following Doty's rambling legal arguments, it would be hard to miss his statement that "the Indian who is barely human" must be in a state of "dependence and pupilage" with "the whites."[32] For those with Native mothers, wives, grandparents, and other family members, such a statement must have rankled. In addition, his vigorous prosecution of men who were married according to the "custom of the country," was extremely troubling.

One way Doty asserted the domination of the new government over the lives of the *habitants* was through his campaign to enforce the new laws about sex and marriage. As he inaugurated the Additional Circuit Court of Michigan Territory at Prairie du Chien and Green Bay, Doty instructed the grand juries to indict thirty-one men for fornication, including many of the Creole elites, because their marriages had been contracted according to the "custom of the country" without formal licenses or contracts, often according to Native norms.[33] These indictments contained strong language, alleging, in a typical example, that "Augustin Asselin ... of Lewd, Lascivious, depraved and abandoned mind and disposition, and wholly lost to all sense of decency, morality and religion ... with a woman

---

[30] Doty, "Notes on Trials and Decisions," WHSL, typescript, 121–127; Patrick J. Jung, in "Judge James Duane Doty and Wisconsin's First Court: The Additional Court of Michigan Territory, 1823–1836," *Wisconsin Magazine of History* (Winter 2002–2003): 32–41, argues that Doty's "views concerning Indian societies were particularly progressive for his day," 35.

[31] Doty, "Notes on Trials and Decisions," WHCL, typescript, 122.

[32] Doty, "Notes on Trials and Decisions," WHCL, typescript, 123.

[33] Jung, "Judge James Duane Doty," 31; Jacqueline Peterson, "The People In Between: Indian-White Marriage and the Genesis of a Métis Society and Culture in the Great Lakes Region, 1680–1830" (Ph.D. diss., University of Illinois at Chicago Circle, 1981), counted thirty-six at Green Bay, 1; see also Bethel Saler, "Negotiating the Treaty Polity: Gender, Race, and the Transformation of Wisconsin from Indian Country into an American State, 1776–1854" (Ph.D. diss., University of Wisconsin, 1999), 259.

by name the *little Pine alias La grosse Boulanger* of Lewd and dissolute habits, ... did comit whoredom and Fornication ... and dreadfull filthy and Lewd offences."[34] This harsh language was used against local couples, many of whom had been together for years and were the parents of children.

Such indictments, besides asserting the right of the new government to dictate the terms of their intimate relationships and challenging the very bases of their families insulted Creole mothers and fathers, and attributed "evil" and immoral motives to them. Such language may have been derived from court practices of the northeastern states, but it harked back to earlier times. By the 1820s, those states' courts seldom prosecuted fornication, and the New York Supreme Court had issued a ruling legalizing common law marriage, a decision that was widely accepted.[35]

Thus, the new additional court was not simply extending into the Wisconsin region of Michigan territory the legal practices of eastern states, but asserting the new régime's control and at the same time making a complex statement about Creole couples and intermarriage. Not only did these indictments allow men like Doty to express emerging Victorian morality about marriage and sexuality, but they had more serious implications for Native women and their property. Within a few days, most of the couples indicted for fornication did marry as the statute prescribed. Fornication indictments, by forcing marriage according to the laws of the territory, ultimately made Native and métis women subject to the laws of the United States, forced *coverture* on them, and gave their property to Euro-American and métis men. It also gave the colonizers authority over their children.[36]

Ironically, Doty eventually lost his job over the issue of marriage. Among the many people Doty had antagonized were numerous military officers, whose power over civilians Doty sought to minimize. One of them was Colonel David Twiggs (who himself had a child by an "illegal" relationship with Julia Grignon, of Ho-Chunk and French heritage).

---

[34] *United States v. Augustin Asselin*, Indictment for fornication, May 9, 1825, Iowa Series 20, WHSL, Platteville.

[35] William E. Nelson, *Americanization of the Common Law: The Impact of Legal Change on Massachusetts Society, 1760–1830* (Cambridge, MA: Harvard University Press, 1975), 110; Kermit L. Hall, *The Magic Mirror: Law in American History* (New York: Oxford University Press, 1989), 154. The case was *Fenton v. Reed*, 1809.

[36] Lucy Eldersveld Murphy, "Women, Networks, and Colonization in Nineteenth-Century Wisconsin," in *Contours of a People: Metis Family, Mobility, and History*, edited by Nicole St-Onge, Carolyn Podruchny, and Brenda Macdougall (Norman: University of Oklahoma Press, 2012).

Twiggs wrote to President Andrew Jackson in 1831 after the death of Rachel Jackson, saying that he had heard Judge Doty make disparaging remarks about Mrs. Jackson's character. The president, of course, was still bitter over the public scandal that had erupted over the question of whether he and his wife had been legally married, feeling that the viciousness of the controversy had hastened her death. Doty was soon removed from office and David Irvin of Virginia appointed in his stead.[37]

Whatever satisfaction Doty's removal may have brought, American courts still enforced the laws of the new régime. For Creoles, the meaning of the new judicial system emerged as judges instructed jurors and others attending court about the new laws and suggested the wording of indictments that the judges often instigated. Indictments were ways to impose the rule of the new government on the local people, including Creole elites as well as the common *habitants*. Even if the accused were not convicted, the written accusations and summonses to appear asserted the regime's power to legislate, evaluate, and punish, and they were methods and goals at variance with community preferences for mediating disputes. Indictments for selling liquor mandated submission to government licensing; suits for debt ensured that the government could regulate property and obligation. Fornication and adultery charges asserted the new territorial government's right to regulate people's intimate relations while humiliating Creoles who followed Native domestic patterns. Court-ordered marriages brought Native women within the control of U.S. and territorial laws. But in order for the system to function, it required the cooperation of the local people as grand jurors to indict and as petit juries to convict.

## Creoles in Court

By including their men in the judicial system from the beginning, government officials sought the cooperation of many Creoles. Some elite men were appointed to positions as justices of the peace and county court judges during the early years. (Generally speaking, however, men whose mothers were wholly Native seemed to have less-powerful roles than

[37] Smith, *James Duane Doty*, 93–95; "A Famous French-Winnebago Resident," typescript, Henry S. Baird Papers, Box 4, Folder 4, Wisconsin Historical Society (no date; author was probably Henry or Elizabeth Baird). Doty later served in Congress and as governor of Wisconsin Territory and then Utah Territory. Smith, *James Duane Doty*; "James Duane Doty," Topics in Wisconsin History, Wisconsin Historical Society, http://www.wisconsinhistory.org/topics/doty/, accessed August 24, 2011.

those who were second- or third-generation métis or wholly European in ancestry.) Between 1818 and 1836, out of twelve justices of the peace who served in Prairie du Chien, five were Creole. Out of eight county court judges appointed during that time, five were Creole.[38] Throughout the territory, men of mixed ancestry were active in a wide range of political roles. For example, Joseph Brisbois (whose mother, Domitille, had been of French, Odawa, and Illini descent) served as justice of the peace and clerk of the Crawford County court and as a representative in the Wisconsin Legislative Assembly in 1839–40. He was also appointed to serve as an associate justice of the county court for at least one year in the mid-1830s.[39]

If the justices of the peace and judges of the county courts included some elite Creole men drawn from their own communities, the lawyers were outsiders, virtually all Anglos.[40] Wholly *Native* men and women appeared in courtrooms as defendants and witnesses, but never as jurors, lawyers, or judges. Similarly, all women could be defendants, witnesses, and plaintiffs, but otherwise they were kept on the margins of the proceedings.

Creole men, whether mixed in their ancestry or not, made up the vast majority of Prairie du Chien's jurors in the early years, from 1823 to about

---

[38] James L. Hansen, comp., "Crawford County Public Office Appointments," extracted from Clarence E. Carter, ed., *Territorial Papers of the United States*, 28 vols. (Washington, DC: U.S. Government Printing Office, 1934–68) (hereafter *TPUS*),Vols. 10–12, and Michigan Territory, "Records of Acts and Proceedings of the Executive Department," Library of Congress, "Early State Records," [microfilm], unpublished. Before the War of 1812, when Prairie du Chien was in St. Clair County, Indiana Territory, Governor William Henry Harrison had appointed justices of the peace who were in the trade and married to Native or mixed-ancestry women, but were Anglos. William Wesley Woollen et al., ed., "Executive Journal of Indiana Territory, 1800–1816," *Indiana Historical Society Publications* 3, no. 3 [Indianapolis] (1900): 110–112, 122. Thanks to Jim Hansen for sharing this information.

[39] "The Mackinac Register," *WHC*, Vol. 18, 490, 492; B. W. Brisbois, "Traditions and Recollections of Prairie du Chien," *WHC*, Vol. 9 (1882), 282–316; Peterson, "The People in Between," 161; Susan Sleeper-Smith, "Women, Kin, and Catholicism," in *Native Women's History in Eastern North American before 1900: A Guide to Research and Writing*, edited by Rebecca Kugel and Lucy Eldersveld Murphy (Lincoln: University of Nebraska Press, 2007), 234–255. *History of Crawford and Richland Counties*, Vol. I, 355; Hansen, comp., "Crawford County Public Office Appointments."

[40] Brunson, "Judicial History," 6,7,11,12. The exception was Theophilus LaChappelle, who was Dakota and French, a lawyer who during the 1840s represented Crawford County in the Wisconsin Territory Legislative Council, then became insane, murdered a man, and was institutionalized for the rest of his life. Brunson, "Judicial History;" *History of Crawford and Richland Counties*, 356; Elizabeth Baird, "Reminiscences of Life in Territorial Wisconsin," *WHC*, Vol. 15 (1900), 255.

TABLE 3.1. *Petit Jurors, Prairie du Chien, 1823–1833, Percent Creole*

| Year | Number | Percent |
|------|--------|---------|
| 1823 | 9/12   | 75.0%   |
| 1826 | 28/36  | 77.8%   |
| 1831 | 8/12   | 66.7%   |
| 1832 | 13/22  | 59.0%   |
| 1833 | 11/12  | 91.7%   |

*Source*: 1823 and 1826 data from Ira B. Brunson, "Judicial History"; 1831 and 1833 data from Crawford County Court Records, sample cases; 1832 data are from Crawford County Courthouse, "Book A, 1830–32," 2 cases.

1836. During the 1820s, juries in county court cases ranged from 75 percent to almost 94 percent Creole, according to jury lists recorded by former county court justice Ira Brunson.[41] In the early 1830s, between 59 percent and 91 percent of petit jurors were Creole, according to a sample of cases recorded in the Crawford County Courthouse.[42] (See Table 3.1.)

Ultimately, the *habitants* were not as easy to control as Cass, Doty, and other officials had hoped; trials often raised complex issues and revealed complicated dynamics of personal and institutional power.

### "Contrary to Law and Evidence": John Barrell and James Reed

Sitting in a makeshift courtroom in Prairie du Chien on a spring day in 1824, Judge James Duane Doty was disgusted as foreman John Kinzie read the verdict of the predominantly Creole jury in the case of the *U.S. v. Barrell*. These were fur traders and *voyageurs*, most of them men who had lived here through the last years of the British régime and the conquest of the Great Lakes region by the United States. Most of them had supported the British in the War of 1812.[43]

---

[41] Brunson, "Judicial History," 2–5. The numbers are 1823: 9/12 petit jurors, or 75 percent; 1824: 15/16 grand jurors, or 93.8 percent; 1826: 20/22 grand jurors or 90.9 percent and 28/36 jurors or 77.8 percent.

[42] "Book A," 1830–32; and sample court cases, Crawford County Courthouse, Prairie du Chien. Jury lists for this period are rare and fragmentary.

[43] *U.S. v. J. Barrell*, May 1824, Michigan [Territory] Circuit Court (Iowa County) Criminal Case files, 1824–36, Wisconsin Historical Society Library, Platteville, Iowa Series 20, folder 4 (The name is spelled as both Barrel and Barrell in the court documents); Brown, "Judge James Doty's Notes of Trials and Opinions: 1823–1832," 33. This trial probably took place on May 11 or May 12, 1824.

The men who sat on the jury in 1824 had ancestors from both nearby and far-flung locales. They were multilingual in French, English, and sundry Native languages. They included not only men of French and French Canadian ancestry such as Louis Rouse, Edward Pizanne, and Denis Courtois, but also Anglo-Canadian John Simpson, as well as Henry M. Fisher, of Scots ancestry but born in the United States. Through their wives and mothers, some were connected to Native cultures and communities: for example, juror George Fisher (Henry's son) was Odawa and Illinois as well as French on his mother's side; John Kinzie's mother, Nelly Lytle, had been adopted among the Senecas; and Hyacinth St. Cyr's wife, Keenoukau, was Ho-Chunk. Similarly Pierre Hurtibise's mother was from the nearby Dakota nation, and Augustin Grignon's ancestry was French and Odawa.[44]

Doty had lectured the grand and petit jurors before sending them to their deliberations, exhorting them "to the suppression of grog-shops, or irregular Taverns." He had also had insisted that the jurors adhere to both the *intent* and the *details* of the new territorial laws. And they had ignored his advice, and found John Barrell *not guilty* of selling spirituous liquor by small measure without a license.[45]

The circumstances of this particular case were that John Barrell – a Vermont man who had served in the army from 1814 until 1819 – was filling in for tavern keeper James Reed for a few months. As discussed previously, taverns in the Great Lakes region were community centers, places for local people to socialize with their neighbors, for travelers to find accommodations, and even sometimes for religious services and courts to meet.[46] Reed's stepson Antoine Grignon later characterized

[44] Les and Jeanne Rentmeester, *Wisconsin Creoles* (Melbourne, FL: Privately published, 1987), 246, 330–331; "Narrative of Morgan L. Martin," *Collections of the State Historical Society of Wisconsin*, Vol. XI (1888), 386; Juliette Kinzie, *Wau-Bun: The "Early Day" in the North-West* [1856] (Urbana: University of Illinois Press, 1992), 143–154; Peterson, "The People in Between," 161, 163; Elizabeth Baird, "Memoranda," typescript, Baird Papers, Box 4, Folder 1, Wisconsin Historical Society Library, Madison; James L. Hansen, "Two Early Lists of Mixed-Blood Sioux," *Minnesota Genealogical Journal* 6 (Nov. 1986): 5. The jurors were John Kinzie, Lewis Rouse, H. M. Fisher, Hyacinth St. Cyr, George Fisher, H. Boyer, Edward Pizanne, John Simpson, Pierre Hurtibise, Augustin Grignon, James Lyon, and Denis Courtois. Simpson and Hurtibise signed with an X. *U.S. v. J. Barrell*, May 1824, Iowa Series 20, Folder 4, WHSL, Platteville.

[45] *U.S. v. J. Barrell*, May 1824, Iowa Series 20, Folder 4, WHSL, Platteville.

[46] Harry Ellsworth Cole, *Stagecoach and Tavern Tales of the Old Northwest* (Cleveland: Arthur H. Clark, 1930), 17, 237–298. A more recent study by Elliott West made similar conclusions about the far west: *The Saloon on the Rocky Mountain Mining Frontier* (Lincoln: University of Nebraska Press, 1979).

Reed's establishment in just this way.[47] Reed, who was also the deputy sheriff, coroner, and county tax collector, had been granted a one-year tavern license on May 12, 1823, by the county court.[48] Although Reed had needed to leave town for two months, he was required by law to maintain the tavern, so he had recruited Barrell to look after the business.[49] Judge Doty felt that the license had not been properly worded, recorded, or granted by Crawford County's officials, and that "a license cannot be transferred." The petit jurors, however, disagreed, and found the defendant not guilty.[50] The frustrated judge wrote in his notebook, "I consider this verdict as contrary to law and evidence."[51] For the jurors, however, justice demanded that they ignore the advice about law and evidence. Through trials like this one, men like Doty learned that imposing control on the Creoles was not easy when they could use the system to assert their own sense of justice.

The case against John Barrell and, by implication, James Reed, expressed a number of tensions between the Yankee colonizers and the local community. Why did the jury rule in favor of Barrell and against Doty's advice? First, it was a matter of protecting one of their own. The case as presented by Doty criticized Reed for improperly conducting his tavern and by hiring Barrell.

Was someone picking on Reed? In the same week that the *Barrell* case came to trial (perhaps even on the same day), Reed appeared as a defendant in another case. Although Reed had a tavern license, he had been charged three months earlier in February 1824 on complaint of Nicholas Boilvin that he "kept an improper house and that he was selling spirituous liquors and debauching away his servants." Justice of the Peace James Lockwood had taken Boilvin's complaint and depositions from three Creoles admitting that they had purchased liquor "by small measure less than one quart" from Reed, who had to post a $200 bond guaranteeing

---

[47] Eben Pierce, "Indians Knew Reed as a Fearless Man," *Galesville Republican*, July 15, 1915.

[48] CC Supervisors, 3; Carter, *TPUS*, Vol. 11, 383. Thanks to Jim Hansen for bringing this source about Reed's appointment as coroner to my attention. *History of Crawford and Richland Counties* (Springfield, IL: Union Publishers, 1884), Vol. I, 364.

[49] Doty, "Notes on Trials and Decisions," 33–34; "An Act to Regulate Taverns," [1819], *Laws of the Territory of Michigan* (Lansing: W.S. George & Co., 1871 and 1874), Vol. 1, 407. [Vol. 1 was published in 1871 and Vols. 2 & 3 in 1874]; U.S. Adjutant General's Office, "Registers of Enlistments in the U.S. Army, 1798–1817," National Archives microfilm M233, roll 1 as cited in James L. Hansen to Lucy Murphy, July 1, 2008.

[50] *U.S. v. J. Barrell*, May 1824, Iowa Series 20, folder 4, WHSL, Platteville.

[51] Doty, "Notes on Trials and Decisions," WHSL, typescript, 33–34.

his appearance at the May court. On May 12, Reed entered a plea of "not guilty" and the case against him was eventually dropped.[52]

Prairie du Chien residents considered Reed a member of the community. Although he had arrived with the army, he had married Marguerite Oskache (who was Potawatomi and/or Ojibwe), and he had since been discharged. Reed spoke French as well as several Indian languages, and while a soldier had worked at carpentering side jobs, helping to build many of the local houses, during which time he seems to have made friends.[53] He was also, as mentioned previously, a deputy sheriff, coroner, and county tax collector.

Second, a tension revealed by the trial was between two different approaches to controlling the consumption of alcoholic beverages. As discussed in the previous chapter, Yankees like Doty and the American territorial lawmakers viewed drinking *establishments* as wicked, but the Prairie du Chien community considered drinking as routine except when excessive, leading them to target drunks rather than vendors for control. Doty had heard that many in the local community were reluctant to prosecute barkeepers. "I am told, Gentlemen," he warned the grand jury, "that it is the opinion of many members of this society, that they owe no duty to the public upon this subject, except such as may chance to consort with their interest." However, he insisted that "the laws must be enforced."[54] He also explained his views of taverns to the grand jurors, views quite different from Creole understandings of taverns as places of convivial community gatherings. "Taverns are for the convenience of travelers, and under proper regulations can never be sunk into grog-shops," he explained, "and if any one should assume this latter character, it becomes a crying evil, and demands your immediate interference." Moreover, he described grog-shops and "irregular taverns" as "those places of resort for the idle and intemperate, and haunts of dissipation and almost every species of crime."[55]

[52] *United States v. James Reed*, Iowa 20, folder 69, Wisconsin Historical Society, Platteville. This case was marked "Nolle Prosequi, May 8, 1826 JH Lockwood."

[53] James L. Hansen, "Crawford County, Wisconsin Marriages, 1816–1848," *Minnesota Genealogical Journal* 1 (May 1984): 54, and Hansen, "Prairie du Chien and Galena Church Records, 1827–29," *Minnesota Genealogical Journal* 5 (May 1986): 18. Eben D. Pierce, "James Allen Reed: First Permanent Settler in Trempealeau County and Founder of Trempealeau [Wisconsin]," Wisconsin Historical Society, *Proceedings* (1914), 108; Eben D. Pierce, "Reads Like Romance: Life of James Reed," *Galesville Republican*, July 8, 1915; Pierce, "Indians Knew Reed as a Fearless Man," *Galesville Republican*, July 15, 1915.

[54] Brown, "Judge James Doty's Notes," 33.

[55] *U.S. v. J. Barrell*, May 1824, Michigan [Territory] Circuit Court (Iowa County) Criminal Case files, 1824–36, WHSL, Platteville, Iowa Series 20, folder 4; Brown, "Judge James Doty's Notes of Trials and Opinions: 1823–1832, 33.

An 1816 territorial law prohibited the sale of alcoholic beverages to minors, apprentices, soldiers, militiamen while in service, and to Indians, and an 1819 act required vendors of individual drinks to be licensed.[56] To complicate the matter, the laws prohibiting the sale of liquor to Indians (many of whom would suffer greatly from alcoholism resulting from the trade) created tensions between the fur traders who dispensed whiskey, tavern keepers, Indians who wanted to drink, Indians who didn't think they should, and government officials who felt they should protect Indians from the liquor trade. Furthermore, it must have been difficult for some vendors to determine whether a person of mixed ancestry was entitled to buy a drink, given the ambiguity about the evolving concepts of whiteness and race in the very mixed Creole community.

A third source of tension was a clash between *local* courts and their officials on the one hand, and the *territorial* court and Anglo outsiders on the other. Reed had been trying to comply with the law: he had gone to the county court for a license, which had been signed by the county clerk, and had gotten permission from Creole judges Joseph Rolette and François Bouthillier to move his residence during the year. Because the territorial law regulating taverns required that the inn be consistently maintained, he had arranged for Barrell to barkeep for him during his absence. Doty's complaint was grounded in technicalities, that there seemed to be no record of the county court's proceedings and that the license had not contained the exact language ("they made no 'resolve,' as is required") demanded by territorial statute. It also challenged the legitimacy of local rule. It implied that if some minor details demanded by lawmakers in far-away Detroit had been neglected, the efforts – and power of – local officials were null and void. It was an insult to Rolette, Bouthillier, and other local officials. The jury acting as a local men's council mediated the conflict themselves. In the spirit of Native collective leadership and the French reliance on basic behavioral norms, the group refused to punish Barrell. After all, no one had been injured and it was not a willful violation, merely a misunderstanding of new laws.

Doty had told the jurors how he thought they should rule, yet they refused to concede the territorial government's right to punish a local man based upon a strict interpretation of some new and complex territorial laws – when the man and his friend had clearly tried to comply. They

---

[56] *Laws of the Territory of Michigan*, 1871, Vol. I, 201, 407. Another law passed in 1821 reiterated the ban on selling liquor to Indians but also stipulated that anyone who did so had to give back to the Indian whatever had been given in exchange. *Laws of the Territory of Michigan*, Vol. I, 923.

refused to endorse a verdict that would have criticized, by implication, the local county court judges and local government administrators for imperfect implementation of the territorial laws – statutes expressing a philosophy about the control of alcohol that were at odds with the local approach to this issue.

Ironically, both Reed and Barrell had been soldiers of the conquering army, but Reed had become a respected member of the local community, had intermarried, and held several local offices. Little is known about Barrell, who seems to have left town soon after this, but a decade later in 1834, Reed would be elected tax collector for Crawford County, indicating his continued popularity with his neighbors.[57]

Cases like this one demonstrate the difficulty for Doty and other Anglo officials of trying to control the Creoles with laws intended to be enforced in the court system, especially when the *habitants* could as jurors hinder, modify, or block the legislation's implementation. Eventually, Doty and other officials would have to find ways of adjusting the system to limit the participation of the *habitants*.

### "Damned Rascally Court": Another Challenge

Jurors were not the only ones to protest domination by the additional circuit court and its judge. That same week, in May of 1824, during the inauguration of the additional court at Prairie du Chien, an incident took place involving elite fur trader Joseph Rolette that reveals more of the tensions in a system where local men were given some authority but were trumped by representatives of the new régime. Rolette's protest and punishment provide an unusually well-documented case illustrating the resentments between the Creoles and the outsiders sent in to implement and enforce the new laws.

Joseph Rolette was an elite Creole Prairie du Chien fur trader who badly wanted to maintain a position of authority under the new régime and seemed to be acquiring official recognition through political office. Although he had publicly supported the British during the War of 1812, as had a large percentage of the population, he gained U.S. citizenship through the courts in 1823 at Mackinac.[58] He had been appointed an

---

[57] Entry for Sept. 15, 1834, "Election Record of the Territory, 1823–37," Fort Crawford Museum archives, Prairie du Chien, WI.

[58] Martinus Dyrud, "King Rolette," typescript, n.p. and p. 1, Collection of Villa Louis Historic Site, Prairie du Chien [1823 timeline]; thanks to Michael Douglass for sharing this resource.

associate justice of the county court in 1821, a role that was combined with that of county commissioner.[59] In 1822, he was also elected warden (chair of the town council) of the Borough of Prairie du Chien, a post he still held in 1824.[60] Yet, he protested the imposition of Doty's additional circuit court in 1824.

Rolette must have felt betrayed by Doty. He had graciously invited Doty and his wife to stay in his home over the previous winter (1823–24), an invitation they accepted. Yet in October of 1823 when Rolette got into an argument with Alexis Bailly that resulted in Bailly bringing slander charges against Rolette, rather than mediating the conflict, Doty demanded bail in the amount of $5,000. To make matters worse, over the winter Doty tutored Rolette's rival James Lockwood in the law, urging Lockwood to accept the position of Crawford County Prosecutor.[61] Furthermore, Doty's court had concurrent jurisdiction with the county court, of which Rolette was one of the justices; Doty convened his court at the exact time the county court attempted to meet. Doty also appropriated some of its cases and jurors, so the county court had to recess for a week "for want of juries."[62]

Rolette mounted a public challenge to Doty as Doty heard an appeal in the matter of *Charles Giasson v. J. H. Lockwood*. As marshal of the Borough of Prairie du Chien (of which Rolette was warden and Lockwood 2nd burgess), Giasson had attempted to use the justice of the peace court to enforce a regulation against Lockwood.[63] It seems that Lockwood's chimney had become dirty enough to catch fire, in violation of a local ordinance, and Lockwood had been found guilty and fined by a justice of the peace. Doty reversed the judgment of the lower court based upon technicalities in the language and form of the indictment, and added the

---

[59] Territorial Papers of the U.S., Vol. 11, 135; Territory of Michigan, 139, from James L. Hansen, "Crawford County Public Office Appointments."

[60] Peter Lawrence Scanlan, *Prairie du Chien: French, British, American* (Menasha, WI: Collegiate Press, 1937), 190–191; Borough of Prairie du Chien, "By-Laws;" Territorial Papers of the U.S., Vol. 1, 135; Mi, Vol. 1, 139 from James L. Hansen, "Crawford County Public Office Appointments"; Territorial Papers of the U.S., Vol. 11, 135; Mi, Vol. 1, 139 from Jim Hansen; Martinus Dyrud, "King Rolette," ms., n. p., Collection of Villa Louis Historic Site, Prairie du Chien [re: 1822].

[61] Smith, *James Duane Doty*, 56–57; James H. Lockwood, "Early Times and Events in Wisconsin," *Wisconsin Historical Collections*, Vol. 2 (Madison: Wisconsin Historical Society,[1856]; reprint 1903), 175.

[62] Brunson, "Judicial History," 9; Smith, *James Duane Doty*, 58; Iowa Series 20 court cases (re: dates concurrent with county court).

[63] Doty, "Notes on Trials and Decisions," typescript, 36–38; Lockwood, "Early Times and Events," 175; Borough of Prairie du Chien, "By-Laws" for 1823.

further insult of ruling that the Creole marshal, Giasson, should pay the costs of both courts.[64]

While Doty's court was in session, Rolette stood outside loudly denouncing the "damned rascally court" and all who participated, warning Giasson that he could get no justice from Doty so he should demand a jury trial. Evidently, he objected to the outsider Doty and his court being able to challenge the actions of the local borough council's marshal and to negate a decision by a local justice of the peace. Further, his desire to have a jury decide the case suggests that Rolette felt local jurors were more likely to deliver justice than a Yankee judge. As the system of adjudication by elite traders such as Rolette crashed, the mediation-by-council model seemed preferable to Doty's inflexible system.

When Doty charged him with contempt of court, Rolette contritely claimed that he had been drunk and could not remember what he might have said. His punishment was a public scolding and a $10 fine.[65] Even so, Rolette was continued as a judge of the county court through 1826, suggesting that Governor Cass still needed his support for the new régime, and continued to pursue acquiescence through participation.[66]

## "He Prayed Surety of the Peace": Instruments for Individual Actions

At the same time they felt the courts as instruments used against them, Creoles used new institutions for their own ends. Some individuals used the courts to resolve their personal conflicts. A lawsuit for slander might be used in lieu of a duel, in the absence of other mediation. For example, Alexis Bailly's suit against Joseph Rolette in 1823 arose because Rolette had said that Bailly "was a liar, & a thief; that he had struck his father;

---

[64] William W. Blume Papers, Bentley Historical Library, University of Michigan, Ann Arbor, card file, Box 12.

[65] Doty, "Notes on Trials and Decisions," typescript 38–41; Smith, *James Duane Doty, Frontier Promoter*, 59. When Rolette excused himself by blaming the alcohol, he used a logic often found in Native communities. Peter C. Mancall, *Deadly Medicine: Indians and Alcohol in Early America* (Ithaca: Cornell University Press, 1995), 79–82.

[66] Brunson, "Judicial History," 2. After several years in which the county court did not meet, Governor Lewis Cass in 1830 reappointed Joseph Rolette as a county court judge, but several Anglos complained and he was subsequently removed, although he continued as justice of the peace through at least 1834. Lockwood, "Early Times and Events in Wisconsin," 172, Brunson, "Judicial History," 6; Hansen, "Crawford County Public Office Appointments," Territory of Michigan, Vol. 2, 32, 96.

and that he was a swindler."[67] A husband might use the court to try to control a wife. To illustrate, Prudent Langlois in 1825 went to Justice of the Peace James Lockwood to complain that his spouse, Margaret Manikikinik (probably a Native woman), had been sleeping with Louis Cardinal.[68] Had they been living in a Native community, family mediation and/or divorce would have been their options.

Others brought their disputes to the courts for resolution: Michel St. Cyr, for example, was upset in 1839 because Benjamin Boudrie ejected him from his family's land, a measure submitted to the court, in this case probably the justice court.[69] Couples who had married according to the law also needed the court's permission to divorce. Julia Grignon, for instance, went to court in 1833 to ask for the dissolution of her marriage to Chrysostome Antaya, whom she said had become "intemperate and neglected his business wholly – and frequented houses of ill fame."[70]

Individuals could also use the courts to complain of mistreatment by Anglos: for example, Antoine Paquette complained in 1831 that a man by the name of King had violently assaulted and beaten him at Gratiot's Grove, so a justice of the peace issued a summons to have Mr. King brought before him ("or some other Justice") "to answer unto the said Complaint and to be further dealt with according To Law."[71] In 1833 Amable Moreaux sought the assistance of Creole Justice of the Peace Joseph Brisbois in a conflict with an Anglo, testifying that "he hath been threatened by Henry Sleephack ... and is afraid that ... Sleephack will beat or wound him, he being in fear of his life, whereupon he prayed Surety of the Peace against him." So Brisbois ordered the sheriff to apprehend Sleephack "and bring him forthwith ... to find surety for his personal appearance at the next county court, and in meantime to keep the peace, especially toward the said Amable Moreaux."[72] Here Moreaux's revenge for the insult not only caused Sleephack's arrest but it also forced him to post a surety (guarantee or bond). This might have involved finding a sympathetic member of the elite to vouch for him.

---

[67] Doty, "Notes on Trials and Decisions," typescript, 14, *Alexis Bailly vs. Joseph Rolette*, Oct. 17, 1823.

[68] *U.S. v. Louis Cardinal*, Iowa Series 20, Folder 16, WHSL, Platteville.

[69] *Michel St. Cire v. Benj. Boudrie*, Mar. 6, 1839, filed Sept. 5, 1843, Crawford County Courthouse.

[70] *Julia Antaya v. Chrysastone Antaya*,[,] Petition for divorce, Jan. 23, 1833. Crawford County Courthouse.

[71] Iowa Series 16, #159, Miscellaneous Court Case Files, WHSL, Platteville.

[72] Crawford Series 4, County Clerk Board Papers, October 7, 1833, WHSL, Madison.

Cases such as Moreaux's revealed another paradox created by the imposition of U.S. rule. Although the colonizers could use the courts to challenge the Creole elites' authority, court cases also created power for wealthy patrons in the community who could sign surety bonds for those charged with crimes and those who lost suits. Although some elites were challenged by way of the courts, their wealth was called upon to give surety for accused criminals, in cases for debt, and to assure the performance of many public officials, thus building their authority as patrons in the community. To illustrate, when Margaret Brousell and Joseph Desmarrais were charged with adultery in 1839, Hercules L. Dousman (an elite Creole fur trader) signed bail bonds of $250 for each of them.[73] In addition, officials with access to public funds had to find wealthy people to sign as security for their conduct.

Furthermore, elites sometimes stepped forward to protect less powerful people in the community against mistreatment by powerful Anglos. For example, during the mid-1820s, John Marsh, "a graduate of some Eastern college" in the words of James Lockwood, was appointed a justice of the peace for Crawford County. Marsh "was in the practice of taking notes for collection, and issuing process on them" (enforcing IOUs), Lockwood later remembered. When Marsh issued a controversial decision in a matter of contested identity – there being two Creoles with the name of Benjamin Roy – Hercules Dousman threatened to report Marsh to Governor Lewis Cass if Marsh proceeded with the case.[74] Here we see a member of the Creole elite standing up to a new Anglo justice of the peace on behalf of a poorer man, an action that not only challenged the newcomers but also once again reinforced Dousman's influence and status in the community.

Disputes did not always occur along ethnic divides. Creoles might step forward to stop abuses they perceived from other Creoles. For example, Joseph Brisbois claimed that he took the role of justice of the peace only to serve the community and compensate for Rolette's shortcomings. "I took the Office of Justice of the Peace against my will," Brisbois explained in a letter; "it [h]as been only when I saw that there was at the time only J. Rolette Esqr and he refused process to several persons, for reason that he was interested, or that he had no form &c –."[75] Thus, the courts provided

---

[73] *U.S. v. Margaret Brousell* and *U.S. v. Joseph Desmarrais*, October 20, 1839, B91, Crawford County Courthouse.

[74] Lockwood, "Early Times and Events in Wisconsin," 169–170.

[75] Joseph Brisbois to Morgan L. Martin, December 10, 1832, Green Bay and Prairie du Chien Papers, WHS, micro., 144 (frame 340).

forums for airing personal grievances, mechanisms for conflict resolution, and opportunities for the enhancement of elites' power.

### "A Body of Public Accusers": Indictments

Not only did Creoles use the courts *individually*, but they also found ways to use them communally, often through their jury service. Grand juries could accuse people of unlawful behavior, issuing indictments. Those who were indicted would be tried, and might have their trials decided by a petit jury.

Creole grand juries could assert their power, and express political views, by indicting people who would be subjected to court appearances and possible trial by judges and petit juries. As Doty told the county's first grand jury in 1824, they were "a body of public accusers" and ought to direct their attention "to every species of crime." At least twelve of the seventeen jurors had to agree in order to generate an indictment.[76] Prairie du Chien's grand jurors seem to have taken this advice to heart in challenging officers of the occupying army. In two cases, grand juries seem to have expressed their disapproval of the military stationed in their community by indicting officers – including the governor's brother – for violent behavior.

These cases should be understood in the context of the tense relationships between the army and the *habitants*. Residents had endured martial law for two years by 1818, when a new civil authority was established at Prairie du Chien, as Crawford County was created in the region newly transferred from Illinois Territory to Michigan Territory.[77] The U.S. Army had, in Lockwood's words, "treated the inhabitants as a conquered people, and the commandants assumed all the authority of governors of a conquered country."[78] As mentioned in Chapter 1, for example, Charles Menard had been whipped and marched through the streets in humiliation for allegedly peddling alcohol to soldiers.[79]

---

[76] Brown, "Judge James Doty's Notes," 31, 32, 34.

[77] Scanlan, *Prairie du Chien*, 123. *TPUS*, Vol. 10, 803–804; Michigan Territory "Records," Vol. 1, 61; Smith, *The History of Wisconsin*, Vol. I, 201.

[78] Lockwood, "Early Times and Events in Wisconsin," 128–129.

[79] Lockwood, "Early Times and Events in Wisconsin," 129; similarly Keyes recorded on December 5, 1817, "A French Citizen confined and punished at the fort for selling whiskey to hirelings and soldiers contrary to orders." Willard Keyes, "A Journal of Life in Wisconsin One Hundred Years Ago," *Wisconsin Magazine of History* 3, no. 3 (March 1920): 356.

Given Prairie du Chien residents' lingering resentment at the domination of civilians by the army, it should not be surprising that as jurors they used the new court to reverse the power dynamics of the martial law era and to assert their new ability to punish soldiers' transgressions, even to the point of insulting the territorial governor's brother. In addition to the case of *U.S. v. Cass*, mentioned in the introduction to this chapter, a grand jury in 1825 indicted Lieutenant Henry Clark, of the Fifth Regiment, "a person of wicked and malicious disposition," for attacking a Creole man in a local tavern.[80]

These grand juries demonstrated that they had the power to force the officers – even the brother of the governor – to answer to a panel of civilians – people whose community their army was occupying. They also used the formulaic language of indictments to insult these men.[81] Unfortunately, the surviving court records do not reveal whether Clark and Cass were convicted.

### "Power of the Court over the Consciences of Jurors": Petit Juries

Of course, petit juries sometimes issued decisions with which the judges and officers of the court disagreed, as in the case of *U.S. v. Barrell*. Doty criticized not only the Barrell jury but also another. In a civil suit between two fur traders, the jury arrived at a verdict awarding a settlement "by making an average of the several sums proposed by each juror." This creative solution to the problem of compensation illustrates how the jury – as a men's council – experimented with community mediation. Although Judge Doty disapproved (and it is unclear why), he refused the motion for a new trial. He wrote, "It is with great reluctance that I give way.... It is of doubtful utility to the public to permit the Secret of the jury room to be thus exposed. But the scandalous conduct of jurors appears to have rendered it sometimes necessary. This power of the court over the consciences of jurors (of whatever stuff they may be composed) is extremely doubtful."[82]

Doty was not the only Anglo to complain about Creole jurors, whose literacy and devotion to the legal system other Anglos also questioned. Joseph Street, U.S. Indian Agent, anticipated a trial fearfully, writing in

[80] *U.S. v. Henry Clarke*, May 11, 1825, Iowa Series 20, Folder 21, WHSL, Platteville.
[81] James Duane Doty, Green Bay, to J. W. Webb, New York, March 26?, 1831, Letterbook, 136, Doty Papers, microfilm, Bentley Library, Ann Arbor.
[82] Doty, "Notes on Trials and Decisions," typescript, 91–92. *Dousman v. Bailey*, Motion for a new trial, July 23, 1828.

1830 that the population of Prairie du Chien was "made up principally of ignorant Canadian French and mixed breed Indians, not one in 20 of whom can read or write. Many of these ... know little about the law, and care less, so long as they are not made to feel its penalties. Of this motley group the jury will be made up. From such materials I cannot even hope an impartial panel can be obtained."[83]

Of course, as Street was painfully aware, the laws and courts regulated property, and Creole jurors made decisions affecting their neighbors' material well-being. Juries had a substantial amount of power when they were asked to decide on civil suits in which there was a disagreement over debts, cases that could prove costly for either party. For a short time, a revised system was established in which juries could consist of six members instead of twelve.[84] When John Hammer sued Jean Brunet for debt in May of 1831, six jurors, including five Creoles decided that "John Hammer should be unsuited." Half of the jurors signed with an X.[85] Later that same year, three of six jurors were Creole who were summoned to consider the case of *John Hammer v. Louis Arriandreau* for debt, with Justice of the Peace Joseph Brisbois, another Creole, presiding.[86] Hammer lost again. His bad luck with juries continued: he was convicted and fined $50 that year for selling liquor by small measure without a license, and in 1832 the county court's grand jury issued four indictments against him for breaking the same laws. Convicted on one of the charges, he was fined $100 and costs.[87] The saga of John Hammer suggests widespread disapproval of him, expressed in ways that seriously affected his pocketbook: if men like Hammer felt ethnic tension underlay unsuccessful and costly court experiences, their resentment might be expressed as complaints against Creoles.

In addition to being criticized for lack of both education and loyalty to the legal system, the *habitant* jurors were criticized on the basis of both their language skills and objectivity. To illustrate, in September of

[83] Joseph Street, U.S. Indian Agent, to John H. Eaton, Secretary of War, February 22, 1830, Letters Received by the Office of Indian Affairs, Prairie du Chien Agency, microfilm reel 696; Smith, *James Duane Doty*, 74–76.

[84] *Acts of the Legislature of Wisconsin [Territory] passed during the Winter Session of 1837–8 and the Special Session of June, 1838, in the city of Burlington* (Burlington, Iowa: James G. Edwards, 1838), 167.

[85] Crawford County Court Records, *John Hammer v. Jean Brunet*, May 20, 1831, Crawford County Courthouse, Prairie du Chien.

[86] Crawford County Court Records: Jury Summons Oct. 27, 1831, Crawford County Courthouse, Prairie du Chien; Ira Brunson, "Judicial History," 6–7.

[87] Brunson, "Judicial History," 6–7.

1828, D. D. McNutt's lawyers asked for a continuance of his murder trial because "the jurors upon the present panel do not understand English – are not impartial."[88]

Still, juries continued to thwart some of the intentions of the laws. In 1833 and 1834, a case involving a defendant charged with "keeping a disorderly house" twice failed, once because a member of the jury suddenly disappeared, and when the case was bound over to the next term, a member of the jury "answered not," so the case was dismissed. Here was the rub about petit juries: complete consensus was required, unlike grand juries, which required less than unanimity to put forward an indictment. But even grand juries sometimes avoided charging their neighbors with wrongdoing. In 1835, the grand jury found no indictments at all.[89]

The U.S. Attorney for Michigan Territory, Daniel LeRoy (who was not Creole), in 1833 seemed surprised at the noncooperation of juries and their general lack of devotion to the régime and its legal system, blaming the influence of "Indian agents, traders, [and] owners of Saw Mills in the Indian Country." Even though these Creoles had been "placed in profitable business by the Government," they seemed to demonstrate no loyalty, being "the first to oppose its interest and violate its laws." Not only were they ingrates who didn't pay for their appointments and licenses with obedience to the régime but they also used their authority against it and set negative examples, encouraging the disobedience of their neighbors. "Almost the whole community on the frontiers is under their influence and very many of them Guilty of the same violations of the Laws," LeRoy lamented. "It would therefore be very rare that a Jury could be found to give a verdict of guilty even in a plain case."[90]

Although their participation as jurors was initially needed in order to implement the court system and (in Doty's words) "to inspire every one with a confidence in the laws and institutions of the country, and secure obedience to them," Creole jurors did not blindly obey the directives of judges or conform to expectations regarding process.[91] They were

---

[88] Doty, "Notes on Trials and Decisions," typescript, 102, *US v. McNutt*.

[89] Ira B. Brunson, "Judicial History," 9

[90] LeRoy to Lewis Cass, 1833 or 1834, quoted in Smith, *James Duane Doty*, 131; William Wirt Blume, ed., *Transactions of the Supreme Court of the Territory of Michigan, 1814–1824* (Ann Arbor: University of Michigan Press, 1938), Vol. I, 21.

[91] Brown, "Judge James Doty's Notes," 32.

often ambivalent about the laws and legal system and even resisted the laws by refusing to answer, indict, or convict those the authorities wanted punished. But they also rendered decisions that were costly to men who considered themselves better educated, more loyal and righteous, and wealthier than the *habitants*. Acts such as these generated efforts to reduce Creole participation in the system.

### "Such Number as can be Found Competent": Excluding the Creoles

During demographic transitions accompanied by power struggles, as in conquest and colonization, policymakers often pay a great deal of attention to the "people in between" (to use historian Jacqueline Peterson's term), and sometimes to those who were marginalized in other ways.[92] American colonizers (when a minority) needed coalitions with Creoles in order to assert dominance over the indigenous people. Once the numbers of non-Creole residents were great enough, the indigenous peoples removed or so reduced as not to pose a threat, and the political institutions strong enough to maintain control, the Anglos no longer needed the "people in between." If the Creoles had been troublesome and resistant, they were edged out. This was the case with jurors in Prairie du Chien's Crawford County.

During the 1820s and 1830s, demographic change came about after there were two major violent conflicts between Native and non-Native peoples. The 1827 Winnebago Revolt and the 1832 Black Hawk War demonstrated Native outrage and the government's incomplete control of the indigenous people. (See Chapter 5 for more on these conflicts.) Both were put down with massive mobilizations of militia and regular troops (including Creoles as militia members, interpreters, and mediators). By the mid-1830s, the removal of local tribes shifted the balance of power in favor of the colonizers, whose population surged in response to Indian removals, as, reassured of their safety, they took over formerly Native land.[93] By 1837, the Creole population of Prairie du Chien dipped

---

[92] Jacqueline Peterson, "The People in Between."

[93] Donald Jackson, ed., *Black Hawk, An Autobiography* (Springfield: University of Illinois Press, 1955); Roger L. Nichols, *Black Hawk and the Warrior's Path* (Arlington Heights, IL: Harland Davidson, 1992); Lucy Eldersveld Murphy, *A Gathering of Rivers: Indians, Métis, and Mining in the Western Great Lakes, 1737–1832* (Lincoln: University of Nebraska Press, 2000); Michael J. Sherfy, "Narrating Black Hawk: Indian Wars, Memory, and Midwestern Identity" (Ph.D. diss., University of Illinois, 2005).

below 50 percent due both to massive immigration of Anglo-Yankees and others and a smaller trend of Creole out-migration (see Table 2.2 and Map, Figure 3.1). As these shifts took place, the government would have less need for the support of the troublesome Creoles in its courtrooms. Creole voters had lost influence when they became a minority in Prairie du Chien; similarly, demographic changes eroded Creoles' power to influence the judicial system with their own notions of justice.

As the influx of newcomers changed the population balance, Anglo-Americans began to limit Creole jury participation. It is possible to track jury participation over time and compare it to population change. After 1839, the Creole participation rate was low, even relative to their proportion of the population (see Graph, Figure 3.2).

There were four ways that Creoles were excluded. First, county officials selecting men to summon for jury service excluded many Creoles from the lists of potential jurors. This was an effective way to minimize, if not eliminate, Creole participation. Officials were able to do this when Creoles became a minority of the citizens in the Prairie du Chien region. The social and economic implications of this demographic change were enormous; the political implications were predictable given the territorial implementation of a democratic electoral system emphasizing majority rule (but excluding Indians, African Americans, and all women from the electorate). The proportion of Creoles among both elective and appointive officials declined after 1836. By 1845, for example (as we have seen in Chapter 2), only 11.2 percent of county officials were Creole.[94]

Most relevant to the selection of jurors, fewer and fewer Creoles were elected as supervisors and assessors (the officials charged with nominating men to serve on juries) and this seems to have led to discrimination in juror nominations. Although petit juries between 1823 and 1833 had been between 59 percent and 92 percent Creole, after 1838 Creoles constituted less than 21 percent of the *potential* jurors, that is, those whose names were recommended by the commissioners, supervisors, and assessors to serve as jurors (see Graphs, Figure 3.2 and Figure 3.3). (However, bystanders were often impaneled to substitute for absentees, so men who had been left off the venire lists might still be drafted to serve.)

---

[94] In 1825, of the men mentioned in the Crawford County Commissioners minutes as serving in official roles, six out of eleven were Creole. In 1835, four out of six men named in that source were Creole, some of them serving in several different capacities. By 1845, however, fifty-five Anglos and seven Creoles were recorded as serving in seventeen official roles for the county government. CC Supervisors, 9–12, 35–37, 181–208.

FIGURE 3.1. Indian land cessions. Based upon Nancy Oestreich Lurie, *Wisconsin Indians* (Madison: State Historical Society of Wisconsin, 1980), 18; Charles C. Royce, *Indian Land Cessions in the United States* (Washington, DC: Government Printing Office, 1900; reprint, New York: Arno Press, 1971), 707–821, *passim*.

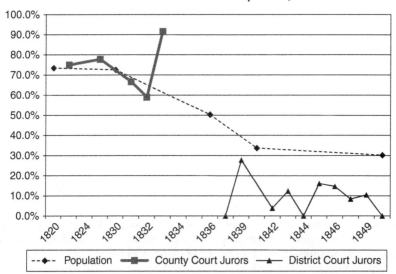

FIGURE 3.2. Prairie du Chien Petit Jurors and population. Percentage Creole, 1820–1850. When Wisconsin Territory was formed out of Michigan Territory in 1836, the county court system was replaced with a territorial district court system.

*Sources*: Jurors: 1823, 1824, 1826, and some of 1838 from Ira B. Brunson, "Judicial History"; 1831, 1833, and some 1838 data are from sample cases, Crawford County Courthouse (less complete than the other data); 1832 data are from Crawford County Courthouse, "Book A" 1830–32, 2 cases; Other data on petit juries are from "Crawford County Supervisors," [minutes], 54–342, *passim*. Population data, James L. Hansen, "Prairie du Chien's Earliest Church Records, 1817," *Minnesota Genealogical Journal* 4 (1985): 329–342; James H. Lockwood, "Early Times and Events in Wisconsin," State Historical Society of Wisconsin, *Collections*, Vol. 2 (1856), 125–126; M. M. Hoffmann, *Antique Dubuque, 1673–1833* (Dubuque, IA: 1930), 51–59; U.S. Congress, *American State Papers: Documents, Legislative and Executive, of the Congress of the United States ...*, 38 vols. (Washington, DC, 1832–1861), Class VIII, *Public Lands*, 8 vols., ed. Walter Lowrie et al., Vol. 5, 47–98, 270–272, 283–328; Donna Valley Russell, ed., *Michigan Censuses 1710–1830* (Detroit: Detroit Society for Genealogical Research, 1982), 146–147; Elizabeth Taft Harlan, Minnie Dubbs Millbrook, and Elizabeth Case Erwin, transcribers and eds., *1830 Federal Census: Territory of Michigan* (Detroit: Detroit Society for Genealogical Research, 1961); [C.W. Butterfield,] *History of Crawford and Richland Counties, Wisconsin* (Springfield, IL: Union Publishing, 1884), Vol. I, 294–295; *Sixth Census of the U.S., 1840* manuscript, Crawford County, WI, microfilm; *Seventh Census of the U.S., 1850*, manuscript, Crawford County, WI, microfilm; U.S. Census Office, *Population of the United States in 1860; Population* (Washington, DC: Government Printing Office, 1864), 534, and manuscript, Crawford County, WI, microfilm.

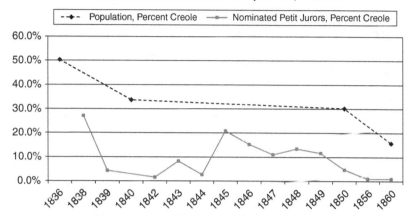

FIGURE 3.3. Nominated Petit Jurors and population, 1836–1860. For population data, see Figure 3.2; for jury nominees, "Crawford County Supervisors," except 1856, 1860, from "Journal A, 1849–65, Crawford County Supervisors Meetings minutes," 182–185, Fort Crawford Museum archives.

Second, as petit juries were impaneled in court for a specific case, men could be dismissed based upon the challenges of either party. Two could be dismissed with no reason; others could be challenged based upon language competency, prejudice, having an interest in the outcome, or being related to those involved in the case.[95]

Third, Creoles were excluded from additional circuit court juries by moving the court's meeting place to a town with a largely Anglo population. In order to shift authority from Creole to "American" jurors, the additional circuit court was moved away from Prairie du Chien to a different location. Doty wrote in a letter to Congressman William G. Angel of New York in March of 1830, "in the month of October last, the County of Crawford was divided by an act of the Legislative council. I do not think there is a sufficient number of Inhabitants, within the boundaries of that county at present, who are American citizens and who understand the English language, to form the juries required by law. The term of the court heretofore fixed at Prairie du Chien should be transferred to the new County of Iowa *which is settled by Americans*, and be held in the month of October next"[96] (emphasis added).

[95] *Laws of the Territory of Michigan* (1874), Vol. 2, 467–470.
[96] Doty to William G. Angel, March 7, 1830, *TPUS*, Vol. 12, 142.

Doty probably exaggerated the scarcity of qualified jurors. Language need not have been an issue, as interpreters had been used in the local courts for years. The 1827 law about juries *allowed* challenges based upon language competency but did not *require* that jurors be fluent in English; the revised 1828 law did not mention language as a cause for challenge at all.[97] Furthermore, there seem to have been enough men available to serve on juries. Territorial laws recommended that the fifteen grand jurors and twelve petit jurors needed for a court meeting be selected at random from a list of over 100 qualified nominees, or "such number as can be found competent."[98] Although it did not note how many were citizens, the 1830 Census for Crawford County had counted sixty-two household heads, and 188 nonmilitary "white" men, aged twenty and up. (As we have seen, men of mixed Native and European ancestry were considered "white" for the purposes of voting, as long as they were not tribal members.)[99] Certainly three or four dozen men could have qualified as jurors there.

There were additional ways to ensure that jurors would be available. In 1828, Governor Cass had felt that there was an urgent need to move forward with the trial of Ho-Chunk Indians arrested for attacking the Gagnier family the previous summer during the Winnebago Revolt, writing to Secretary of War James Barbour,

It is highly important to the peace and security of that frontier that this flagrant outrage should not pass unpunished, and the conviction of the prisoners is not less essential to the objects of justice than it is to our influence with the Indians of that region. They of course know nothing of the machinery of courts, nor can they comprehend, why those prisoners were not killed as soon as they were surrendered for that purpose. If they are acquitted the result will be attributed wholly to fear on our part and the consequences may be most afflicting to that whole country.[100]

Cass requested that the federal government support some of the costs of prosecuting the Ho-Chunks and explained some of the difficulties of conducting trials in Prairie du Chien. "The whole country contains but about 450 inhabitants, men, women & Children, and but a small part of these

---

[97] *Laws of the Territory of Michigan* (1874), Vol. 2, 467–470, 653–657.
[98] *Laws of the Territory of Michigan* (1874), Vol. 2, 467, 653.
[99] *Fifth Census or, Enumeration of the Inhabitants of the United States, 1830* (Washington: Duff Green, 1832), 152–153; Elizabeth Taft Harlan, Minnie Dubbs Millbrook, and Elizabeth Case Erwin, transcribers and eds., *1830 Federal Census: Territory of Michigan* (Detroit: Detroit Society for Genealogical Research, 1961), 98–99.
[100] Lewis Cass, Detroit, to James Barbour, Secretary of War, January 7, 1828, Cass papers, microfilm, Bentley Library, Reel 58.

is competent to serve upon Juries. There is no publick prosecutor for the compensation is so inadequate, that no one will accept the office."[101]

To address these problems, Cass arranged for the Legislative Council of Michigan Territory to pass a law authorizing a special session of Doty's additional circuit court to be held beginning August 25, 1828 at Prairie du Chien, and stipulating that qualifications for jurors might be more lenient than the laws otherwise prescribed. Grand and petit jurors were to be "free white males" who had resided in the territory for one year; no citizenship nor taxpayer status was required. Furthermore, "if any juror ... does not possess a full knowledge of the English language, he shall not be discharged for such cause alone."[102] Cass got the convictions he wanted – Chickhongsic and Waniga were sentenced to be hanged – but President John Quincy Adams pardoned them.[103] Nevertheless, this series of events demonstrates that government officials such as Cass accepted Creole juries to try crimes in Prairie du Chien in order to establish the government's authority over Indians, even if they were uncomfortable having Creole jurors assert authority over "Americans."

After the region's additional court was moved to the lead mining district's Iowa County, few Creoles served on that court's juries. For example, during two regular sessions of the court and one special session in 1834 and 1835, the only French names among fifty-four grand jurors were Pascal Bequette and Pierre Teller. There was not one Creole on any of the petit juries that decided twenty cases, although four of the trials involved Creoles and one concerned an Indian accused of murder. Forty-three non-Creole men served on those petit juries, and another twenty non-Creole men were called but were not needed for the special session.[104]

Meanwhile, back in Prairie du Chien, juries were still needed for some of the county and justices' courts, but the process of minimizing the jury participation of the *habitants* there took a new tack.

### "All ... Shall Be in the English Language"

A fourth way to marginalize the Creoles was through the issue of language. Officials could not use "race" to limit Creole participation because

---

[101] Cass to Barbour, January 7, 1828.
[102] *History of Crawford and Richland Counties,* 374–375.
[103] *History of Crawford and Richland Counties,* 374.
[104] Journal 1834–36, Circuit Court of the United States for the Counties of Crawford and Iowa, typescript copy, William W. Blume Papers, Bentley Historical Library, University of Michigan, Ann Arbor.

the 1825 election controversy mentioned in the previous chapter had concluded that men with some Native ancestry who were not tribal members were "white" enough to vote, and the jury lists were drawn from the lists of voters. And many Creole men had no Native ancestry and could not have been excluded on that basis. But officials found a way to use culture to discriminate against Creoles based upon the most evident marker of their French ethnicity.

In the early years of the court system, Francophones participated freely in the courts system. Certain bilingual Creoles were recruited to serve as interpreters of French, English, and Indian languages and they were paid for their services.[105] But, in the 1838 trial of Chequweyscum, an Ojibwe accused of murdering a fur trader who had alienated the affection of his wife, two Anglo attorneys were appointed for the defendant, and, according to a former judge, "The parties agreed to have none on the Jury except those who could understand the English language," even though three interpreters who spoke French and Ojibwe languages (and presumably English) were employed for the trial.[106] It is interesting that although the law had allowed jurors to be challenged on the basis of language competency before, it was apparently not until this case that the court chose to use this provision to exclude Creoles from the jury box.[107]

Why did this change in 1838? Creoles had become a minority, and there were enough Anglos to fill the jury venire lists. So there was no need for Anglo officials to tolerate the independence of Creole juries or to be hampered by translations any longer. Wisconsin had become a territory in its own right in 1836, and the new circuit court judge for Crawford County, Charles Dunn, may have had his own preferences.[108]

Unlike the situation in 1828 when Cass needed the Creoles to help control the Ho-Chunk Indians by demonstrating a willingness to convict and punish those who attacked non-Natives on the frontier, this Indian could be tried without Creole assistance. By this time, eleven years after the Winnebago Revolt and six years after the Black Hawk War, the government did not need Creoles as allies in controlling Indians. (However, after the case was carried over to the next term, the non-Creole jury deliberated for two days and declared Chequweyscum not guilty.)[109]

[105] CC Supervisors, 91, 148, 193, 227.
[106] Brunson, "Judicial History," 11; *History of Crawford and Richland Counties*, 381.
[107] Brunson, "Judicial History," 1.
[108] *History of Crawford and Richland Counties*, 380, 382.
[109] Ira Brunson, "Judicial History," 11

Ironically, in spite of the exclusion of jurors deemed to be problematic, this trial does not seem to have been the model of propriety. One of the Anglo jurors who served for this case, John H. Fonda, left a memoir in which he recalled that during recesses, the jurors "were locked up in a grocery, where, for the sum of seventy-five cents each, we could have all the liquor we wanted." Not only the jurors, but also the judge and lawyers, drank to excess according to Fonda, and "the prisoner was the only sober man in the court room."[110] The issue of alcohol consumption had certainly taken a new turn here.

Nonetheless, the change in policy regarding language competency and jury participation seemed to stick. When Pierre Barrette sued Pierre Lachapelle in April of 1838 over a land dispute, François Gauthier was brought in to be an interpreter, but the twelve jurors did not include one Creole.[111]

New legislation and policies at the territorial and county levels supported the exclusion from the courts of those not fluent in English. After the Territory of Wisconsin was created, an 1839 law required that "all writs, process, proceedings and records in any court shall be in the English language."[112] In 1849, the Crawford County Board of Commissioners began rejecting the invoices of interpreters.[113] The following year the board decided not to pay for interpreters in the future.[114] After this, the burden was on those who did not speak English to find their own assistance with translation.

Despite the changes in legal practice, a few Creoles continued to serve on juries, presumably men who were both fluent in English and convinced that this was their civic duty (or wanted to earn the $1 per day allowed for jury service). That year, 1839, although only one of twenty-three prospective petit jurors selected by the county supervisors was Creole, five Creoles were among the eighteen who actually served, four of them apparently standing in for absentees.[115] Between 1842 and 1850, Creole jurors in the District Court of Crawford County ranged from 0 percent to 16.1 percent.[116]

---

[110] *History of Crawford and Richland Counties*, 381.
[111] Crawford County records: *Pierre Barrette v. Pierre Lachapelle*, April 1, 1838, Crawford County Courthouse, Prairie du Chien.
[112] *Statutes of the Territory of Wisconsin* (1839), 200.
[113] CC Supervisors, 286, 302.
[114] CC Supervisors, 305.
[115] CC Supervisors, 63–64, 67.
[116] CC Supervisors, 104, 124–127, 133–135, 141, 146, 177, 195, 222–223, 270–271, 287–290, 296–298. For 1842, one out of twenty-six jurors was Creole (1842: 1/26);

At mid-century, a handful of Creoles could sometimes be found on the juries, men like Michel and Domitille's son, George P. Brisbois (brother of the politically active Joseph) and François Labathe, a French and Dakota man who had served on Prairie du Chien juries since 1824. They were multilingual members of the old fur-trade families. Out of ten who served in November of 1849 and appeared in the 1850 census, seven were farmers, one a fiddler, one a tavern keeper, and one still involved in the fur trade. We may assume that all understood the English language reasonably well; at least two had translated Indian languages for the court before the practice ceased being valued enough to record in the supervisors' minutes. At least six had Native ancestry and most of their wives were also Native-descended.[117] But clearly these men were the most successful at adapting and assimilating to the new court system, the most determined to be involved. They may have been tokens, but other Creoles may have seen them as evidence that their kind was not totally excluded from the body politic and that their sons might participate if they acculturated well.

The Creole jurors of the 1820s through 1850s were members of families and communities with strong ties to Native culture, values, and political traditions. Whether they themselves were Native or not, their households and neighborhoods included many who had been raised by Native parents. The jurors had spent time in Indian villages as part of their work in the fur trade and had witnessed and even participated in many councils and gatherings, in which members took care to hear all sides and then took action that they believed was in the best interest of the community.

---

1843: 14/105; 1844: 0/44; 1845: 5/31; 1846: 6/41; 1847 (no data); 1848: 3/36; 1849: 15/144; 1850: 0/14. Data for 1842 and 1843 include both grand jurors and petit jurors because the supervisors' records did not differentiate. In 1844 the number of jurors included petit and grand jurors for the district court and five for the justice of the peace court. Clearly some of the juror lists were incomplete, probably because some did not submit their documents to be paid in a timely fashion.

117 CC Supervisors, 17. *Seventh Census of the U.S., 1850*, manuscript, Crawford County, WI; James L. Hansen, "Crawford County, Wisconsin, Marriages, 1816–1848," *Minnesota Genealogical Journal* (May 1984): 40, 41, 42, 45, 47; Les and Jeanne Rentmeester, *Wisconsin Creoles*, 190, 240–241; 281–282, 288, 320, 333–334; Hansen, "A Roll of Sioux Mixed Bloods, 1855–56," *Minnesota Genealogical Journal* 7 (Nov. 1987): 11; James L. Hansen, "Prairie du Chien's Earliest Church Records, 1817," *Minnesota Genealogical Journal* 4 (November 1985): 3, 5; James L. Hansen, "Crawford County, Wisconsin, Marriages, 1816–1848," 43; "Baptismal Records from Little Chute 1839," typescript, Peter L. Scanlan Papers, WHS Platteville MssD, Box 7, Folder 1, pp. 2, 3, 4; "Prairie du Chien and Galena Church Records," *Minnesota Genealogical Journal* 5 (May 1986): 424, 435, 438, 3; Forsyth, "Half-Breed" lists.

Sometimes their actions as jurors protested the behavior of an army offi-cer, contradicted the details of a judge's instructions, or failed to punish someone for violating a law they disagreed with. The Yankee court and jury system had offered opportunities for them to address community problems as a men's council.

Some Creoles continued to participate. A few stepped forward to serve as jurors, even when they were not summoned, filling the spots of absen-tees. If some of the courts' actions, such as prosecutions for adultery and fornication, forced Creoles to submit to government control in the insti-tutional regulations of their domestic affairs, the courts also lured the old residents into participation and thus tacit acknowledgment of the legiti-macy of the new régime.

## Conclusion

Paradoxically, the new judicial system was both harsh and inviting. Appointed by the president, officials of Michigan Territory used the courts as an instrument of colonization to assert the authority of the United States, to impose the laws, and to secure from the inhabitants par-ticipation and acknowledgment of the Americans' power and the legiti-macy of the new institutions. But even as the courts provided a site where men like Doty denounced the *habitants*, their relationships, and their Indian kin, and where the Anglos sought to implement the laws designed to control them, there was room for some Creoles, including those who were Native-descended, in the new régime.

Formal roles in both legislative and judicial institutions were strictly gendered. While women could attend town meetings, watch court pro-ceedings, and appear as plaintiffs, witnesses, or defendants, they could not serve as judges, lawyers, jurors, town councilors, territorial legisla-tors, or voters. At the same time that new institutions excluded women from positions of authority, however, guidelines were initially quite inclu-sive for men, extending to the non-elite opportunities for influence that had not been available in the old French Canadian justice systems. These new opportunities for humble Creole men to serve as voters, jurors, and in other capacities were parallel to those opportunities available to Native people in tribal communities in the sense of giving them a voice in community decision making and a chance to participate in formal and informal mediation.

The judicial system differed from the legislative arm of the government in one key respect when it came to community participation. American democracy provided that elective decisions would be made by the majority of the electorate, but the jury system expected decisions to be made by *consensus*, giving more authority to minority viewpoints. Although Creoles were able to maintain their membership in the electorate while Anglo-Americans and new European immigrants gained the ascendancy, most would be excluded from jury service when they lost their numerical edge because even as minority members, their authority could thwart the goals of the new majority.

Early on, Creole men were actively and formally included in the new régime because their participation and their support were needed for the United States to establish and maintain power in the region. As we have seen, some of them protested actively or passively, but enough took part to help establish the new régime. Eventually, many of them learned to use the system to their advantage to settle disputes or gain justice. At some moments publicly venting their frustrations with the Yankee system, at other times using what authority they had to influence outcomes, men like Rolette tried to negotiate the new political realities and shifting alliances. The county, circuit, and justice of the peace courts *did* provide Creoles with some opportunities for agency. In some cases, men like Hercules Dousman and members of the Brisbois family influenced power relations in the system, posting bail or bonds for people in trouble with the court or threatening a justice of the peace who was out of line, while enhancing their own authority. Furthermore, as jurors Creoles could sit in judgment of their non-Creole neighbors in a forum where unanimity was required for a decision to be made.

But Anglo prejudice during this time period ran deep and it was difficult for many to accept the independent Creoles as their peers, especially if interpreters were needed to dispense justice. So, when the proportion of Creoles in the population dropped, their influence declined. By the mid-1830s, sufficient Anglo immigration made it possible to marginalize most of the old *habitants*. Thereafter territorial and local officials reduced Creoles' participation in the courts by manipulating the structure and location of the county and circuit courts and by excluding them from juries. In an interesting twist, although the Creoles avoided being racialized, they would be discriminated against based on culture rather than race. This is one of the reasons that some of them would eventually come to identify as French rather than as Métis.

# 4

## Public Mothers

### *Women, Networks, and Changing Gender Roles*

Angelique Brisbois was the daughter of Michel Brisbois and his Ho-Chunk first wife, Chambreywinkau. Growing up in a bicultural fur-trade family, she learned not only about the business but also about both parents' cultures, and so she became bilingual and entrepreneurial. Because her mother came from an elite Ho-Chunk family and her father was an important man in fur-trade circles, she was highly respected, but with her high status came high expectations for community service. Angelique used her family connections to become a fur trader among the Ho-Chunks on the Fox River in east-central Wisconsin along with her husband Jean Baptiste Pion. They made their home in Prairie du Chien and raised two children. Angelique served her community as a mediator and hostess: Indian agent Nicolas Boilvin frequently recruited Angelique to serve as an interpreter, and when Ho-Chunks visited Prairie du Chien, they knew they could always find at Angelique's home a place to sleep and a warm meal.[1] Angelique's actions were typical of many of Prairie du Chien's Creole women, who reached out to Native and non-Native people, creating and tending connections that would benefit their community.

Angelique and her neighbors lived in the shadow of war. The War of 1812–16 had followed upon sporadic violent conflicts around the Midwest that stretched back for many decades. In addition, from 1822 through 1832, violence flared in the lead region to the south between American miners and Native people, erupting into the Winnebago Revolt of 1827,

---

[1] Linda M. Waggoner, ed., *"Neither White Men nor Indians:" Affidavits from the Winnebago Mixed-Blood Claim Commissions, Prairie du Chien, Wisconsin, 1838–1839* (Roseville, MN: Park Genealogical Books, 2002), 82.

followed by the Sauk rebellion known as the Black Hawk War of 1832. These convulsions of colonialism created tensions, fear, suspicions, and suffering that affected the attitudes of *habitants*, Natives, officials, and other Americans toward each other. The "white persons skulking" law had revealed some of these antipathies. Other events would contribute to ill feelings with the potential to harden relationships and social categories. But mediators – many of whom were women – offered alternatives to violence, and many were very successful. During, between, and after these violent times, governmental, demographic, and economic changes troubled the community of Prairie du Chien, but in spite of significant challenges, some women found both familial and communal means to compensate, repair, and resist disruptions. The scholar Ann Laura Stoler has argued that attention to the "intimacies of empire" – the personal, sexual, affective, and familial relationships at the points of colonization – can illuminate aspects of politics previously obscured. In addition, she argues, scholars may benefit by examining the ways that colonial regimes seek to regulate people's intimate relations and the categories such as race that evolve. Prairie du Chien, I believe, was one such "social and cultural space where racial classifications were defined and defied, where relations between colonizer and colonized could powerfully confound or confirm the strictures of governance and the categories of rule."[2] While the territorial government regulated Creole intimacies, many of Prairie du Chien's women defied racial classifications in personal and public ways.

While their brothers, sons, and husbands were lured into participating in the new American political and judicial institutions, women like Angelique and the mixed Meskwaki Antaya daughters of Pokoussee faced gendered political and social challenges. Increasingly restrictive Euro-American laws and social ideals negatively affected Creole women's status and power during the nineteenth century, but these women developed and maintained strategies that would help them to negotiate the new political, economic, and demographic realities that came with the colonization of the Midwest. Changes in marriage patterns decreased Creole women's ability to use kinship to reach across cultural divides, but they found other ways to mediate. They created social, political, and economic networks both locally and across long distances, modified marriage patterns, and used charity, hospitality, health care, and midwifery to connect peoples

---

[2] Ann Laura Stoler, "Tense and Tender Ties: The Politics of Comparison in North American History and (Post) Colonial Studies," *Journal of American History* 88, no. 3 (December 2001): 829–865. Quote is on 830–831.

of different backgrounds and to smooth intercultural encounters. The overlapping gender ideals of different groups regarding benevolence, nurturing, and healing created spaces for women to exert their influence, particularly those whose bicultural backgrounds gave them social tools such as multiple language fluency and experiences with mediation.

Native women like Chambreywinkau and Pokoussee had long enjoyed substantial authority and autonomy in tribal communities, and these traditions had persisted to a significant extent when they married fur traders like Pierre Antaya and Michel Brisbois and moved to fur-trade towns. Native communities encouraged marriages like theirs because such unions linked the fur-trade outsiders to tribal kin groups, creating bonds of obligation and incorporating them into tribal and village units. Wives learned and taught about cultural values, expectations, and behaviors, becoming cultural mediators, to use historian Clara Sue Kidwell's term. Marriage and adoption served to acculturate and assimilate the Euro-Americans into the world of the traders' customers.[3]

## The New Regime

Increasing Anglo immigration and the introduction of U.S. social and political systems changed the dynamics of political power, ethnicity, and social hierarchy in the Great Lakes region. Women's status in Creole communities was negatively affected. The U.S. colonization of the Midwest accelerated a challenge to Native women's roles that had begun under the French regime. During their lifetimes, women like Angelique Brisbois and Pokoussee experienced a decline in legal status and property rights.

---

[3] Some works on this topic include Jacqueline Peterson, "The People in Between: Indian-White Marriage and the Genesis of a Métis Society and Culture in the Great Lakes Region, 1680–1830" (Ph.D. diss., University of Illinois at Chicago Circle, 1981); Clara Sue Kidwell, "Indian Women as Cultural Mediators," in *Native Women's History in Eastern North American before 1900: A Guide to Research and Writing*, edited by Rebecca Kugel and Lucy Eldersveld Murphy (Lincoln: University of Nebraska Press, 2007), 53–64; Sylvia Van Kirk, *"Many Tender Ties": Women in Fur-Trade Society* (Winnipeg, MB: Watson and Dwyer, and Norman: University of Oklahoma Press, 1980); Jennifer S. H. Brown, *Strangers in Blood: Fur Trade Company Families in Indian Country* (Vancouver: University of British Columbia Press, 1980); Tanis Chapman Thorne, *The Many Hands of My Relations: French and Indians on the Lower Missouri* (Columbia: University of Missouri Press, 1996); Susan Sleeper-Smith, *Native Women and French Men: Rethinking Cultural Encounter in the Western Great Lakes* (Amherst: University of Massachusetts Press, 2001); Carolyn Podruchny, *Making the Voyageur World: Travelers and Traders in the North American Fur Trade* (Lincoln: University of Nebraska Press, 2006); and Lucy Eldersveld Murphy, *A Gathering of Rivers: Indians, Métis, and Mining in the Western Great Lakes, 1737–1832* (Lincoln: University of Nebraska Press, 2000).

Native wives like Pokoussee and Chambreywinkaw came from communities in which mature women had a substantial amount of autonomy in their personal lives and economic activity, both because they controlled key resources and forms of production and because the norms of Midwestern Native societies emphasized gender balance and individual autonomy for women and men. Native peoples' political traditions acknowledged women's right to have a voice in community decision making, and some tribes included both women's and men's formal political organizations and roles. There had even been the occasional woman chief.[4] Couples divorced without needing official approval if either spouse felt the need to terminate the marriage (although in a very few cases of diplomatic marriages, parents tried to prevent it).

Native wives not only owned personal and household effects separately from their husbands and other male relatives but their business transactions and debts were considered to be independent also. Indian wives kept accounts with traders separate from those of their husbands in this region. Usually, it is difficult to tell the relationships of people whose names appear in fur-trade ledgers, but when the traders had trouble remembering all their customers' names and instead recorded their relationships to those they knew, the independent nature of women's transactions becomes apparent. For example, an early nineteenth-century trader (who couldn't remember everyone's names – and used both French and English) kept separate accounts for a man named "Mau Nau kee jee kau," "La Veulle [*sic*] femme de [the old wife of] Mau nau kee jee kau," "Her sister" and "Her Husband Hay Kouge hee wee kau," and other married individuals. He also extended individual credits to women designated as mothers, daughters, and sisters of certain people.[5] Similarly,

---

4 Tanis C. Thorne, "For the Good of Her People: Continuity and Change for Native Women of the Midwest, 1650–1850," in *Midwestern Women: Work, Community and Leadership at the Crossroads*, edited by Lucy Eldersveld Murphy and Wendy Hamand Venet (Bloomington: University of Indiana Press, 1997), 95–120; and Rebecca Kugel, "Leadership within the Women's Community: Susie Bonga Wright of the Leech Lake Ojibwe," in *Midwestern Women: Work, Community and Leadership at the Crossroads*, edited by Lucy Eldersveld Murphy and Wendy Hamand Venet (Bloomington: University of Indiana Press, 1997), 17–37; "Speeches of the Sioux … ," *WHC*, Vol. 17 (1906), 399–408; Norman Gelb, ed., *Jonathan Carver's Travels through America, 1766–1768* [1788] (New York: John Wiley, 1993), 72–73; David Lee Smith, *Folklore of the Winnebago Tribe* (Norman: University of Oklahoma Press, 1997), 155–157.

5 "Dousman" Account Book, no date, Ayer North American Manuscripts, Newberry Library, Chicago. This may have been either Hercules Dousman or a relative of his, or one of his clerks.

another trader's financial ledger indicates separate accounts for husbands and wives during the 1830s.[6]

But Europeans brought different ideas about marriage with them to the Americas. Roman Catholic priests taught that women should be subordinate to men, especially wives to their husbands. They opposed both divorce and pre- or extramarital sexual relations, and expected that priests would perform weddings as religious ceremonies. Most other Europeans accepted patriarchy as a pattern for gender and family relations, but the realities of the fur trade in America made it necessary for some to adapt their views to conform to Native ways, especially when they intermarried. Native people tended to resist the patriarchal European ideas, although some were influenced by these norms.

Women's status in Creole communities was also influenced by the French legal code, the *Coutume de Paris,* in force during the French and British regimes in the Great Lakes and Illinois regions, roughly until the 1790s. This code was less permissive than Native practices, but more protective of wives' property than the United States laws.[7] Examining women's legal status in the Francophone Illinois country along the Mississippi River, Susan C. Boyle found that men arriving from the United States viewed Creole women as having an unusual amount of both respect from their husbands and input into decisions regarding finances and other family matters. Examining almost 400 estate records and 150 marriage contracts, she argues this was due to an unbalanced sex ratio (more men than women) and because the laws allowed wives to be co-owners of a couple's property. In addition, she finds that "the prolonged absences of their menfolk gave wives additional power and ample opportunity to function as deputy husbands, protecting their own interests and those of their families."[8] French law guaranteed widows at least half of the estate, but many couples also wrote prenuptial contracts, which might reserve some of the brides' property to their own control, or predetermine a larger dower in case of the husbands' death, or both. Widows

---

[6] John Dixon Account Book, April 29, 1830–January 1832, "Ho-Chunk, Potawatomi, and settler accounts," George C. Dixon Collection, Illinois State Historical Library, Springfield (microfilm). For example, Dixon recorded separate accounts for "Mrs. O's Ont's [aunt's] husband" and "Mrs. O['s] aunt."

[7] Allan Greer, *The People of New France* (Toronto: University of Toronto Press, 1997), 69–71; Susan C. Boyle, "Did She Generally Decide? Women in Ste. Genevieve, 1750–1805," *William and Mary Quarterly*, 3rd. ser., 44, no. 4 (Oct. 1987): 775–789.

[8] Boyle, "Did She Generally Decide?" Quote is on 785. The term "deputy husband" is from Laurel Thatcher Ulrich, *Good Wives: Image and Reality in the Lives of Women in Northern New England, 1650–1750* (New York: Oxford University Press, 1980).

were also protected from creditors. The *Coutume de Paris* and French Canadian patterns of gender roles had a similar influence in Wisconsin and Michigan, connected as they were to the Illinois Country and Quebec. James Lockwood recalled in his memoir of Prairie du Chien that many couples had prenuptial agreements drawn up at the time they wed. "The Coutume de Paris so far prevailed in this country generally, that a part of the ceremony of marriage was the entering into a contract in writing, generally giving, if no issue, the property to the survivor; and if they desired to be divorced, they went together before the magistrate and made known their wishes, and he, in their presence, tore up the marriage contract and according to the custom of the country, they were then divorced."[9]

Another indication of different gender practices relates to women's names. Native women in tribal communities, of course, did not use their husband's names. Creole women often retained their birth surnames when signing documents such as baptismal records or legal papers, suggesting that their identities were not by custom wholly subsumed under their husbands' as were the wives in Anglo-America.[10]

The transition to U.S. control of the region in the early nineteenth century brought a legal and social system that reduced women's rights, in addition to stigmatizing and marginalizing Creoles. The newly dominant society not only brought different gender ideals but also tried to enforce those values with laws and courts that constricted the rights of wives and rigidified the concept of marriage.[11] There had been two main forms of marriage for Creoles under the old regime: first, *a la façon du pays*, that is according to the custom of the country (according to Indian custom, without Christian ceremony or official licenses, essentially what Americans came to call common-law marriage), or second, by contract and with religious ceremony where possible. The first was based upon Native practices and the second was the custom derived from French Canada.

Pokoussee and Pierre Antaya's daughter Euphrosine ran afoul of the new "American" system in 1824. She and her second husband, Strange

---

[9] James H. Lockwood, "Early Times and Events in Wisconsin," *WHC*, Vol. 2 (1856), 121; James D. Hardy Jr., "The Superior Council in Colonial Louisiana," in *Frenchmen and French Ways in the Mississippi Valley*, edited by John Francis McDermott (Urbana: University of Illinois Press, 1969), 91–92.

[10] Examples may be found in documents such as James L. Hansen, "Prairie du Chien's Earliest Church Records, 1817," *Minnesota Genealogical Journal* 4 (1985): 329–342.

[11] A parallel situation was occurring in western Canada at a later date. See Sarah Carter, *The Importance of Being Monogamous: Marriage and Nation Building in Western Canada to 1915* (Edmonton: University of Alberta Press and University of Athabasca Press, 2008).

Powers, were targeted by the new court system with an indictment for fornication, even though they had been together for five years and had two children.[12] Even though local norms had recognized marriages contracted "according to the custom of the country," under the new regime these marriages were considered illicit, so couples in such partnerships came under the critical scrutiny of the new territorial courts.[13]

Fornication and adultery charges demonstrated the new territorial government's right to regulate people's intimate relations and also humiliated Creoles who followed Native domestic patterns. When Judge Doty instructed the grand juries to indict more than thirty men for fornication in Prairie du Chien and Green Bay, including many of the Creole elites, he ignored the prevailing acceptance of common-law marriage in both Creole communities (and by this time in the northeastern United States) and asserted the right of the new government to dictate the terms of couples' intimate relationships. At the same time, he challenged the very bases of Creole families and insulted Creole mothers and fathers.[14] The court's action against Euphrosine Antaya and Strange Powers caused her to file for divorce from her previous husband. After official court approval of the split, she formally married Strange Powers the following year.[15]

---

[12] *United States v. Strange Poze*, Indictment for Fornication, Circuit Court of the United States for the County of Crawford of the term of May 1824, courtesy of Dale Klemme; James L. Hansen, "The Pelletier dit Antaya Families of Prairie du Chien" (forthcoming).

[13] Greer, *The People of New France*, 69–71; Lockwood, "Early Times and Events in Wisconsin," 121–122, 176; Peterson, "People In Between," 1; and Ebenezer Childs, "Recollections of Wisconsin since 1820," *WHC*, Vol. 4 (1859), 167.

[14] Patrick J. Jung, in "Judge James Duane Doty and Wisconsin's First Court: The Additional Court of Michigan Territory, 1823–1836," *Wisconsin Magazine of History* (Winter 2002–2003): 31; and Peterson, "The People In Between," 1, counted thirty-six at Green Bay; Bethel Saler, "The Treaty Polity: Gender, Race, and the Transformation of Wisconsin from Indian Country into an American State, 1776–1854" (Ph.D. diss., University of Wisconsin, 1999), 259; William E. Nelson, *Americanization of the Common Law: The Impact of Legal Change on Massachusetts Society, 1760–1830* (Cambridge, MA: Harvard University Press, 1975), 110; and Kermit L. Hall, *The Magic Mirror: Law in American History* (New York: Oxford University Press, 1989), 154. The case was *Fenton v. Reed* (1809).

[15] *United States v. Strange Poze* (1824); Les and Jeanne Rentmeester, *Wisconsin Creoles* (Melbourne, FL: Privately published, 1987), 322–323 When the new "American" legal system was established, while some couples in Native-style marriages were charged with criminal behavior, others were confused by the absence of provisions for prenuptial property agreements. Lockwood explained, "When the laws of Michigan [Territory] were first introduced at Prairie du Chien, it was with difficulty that the Justice of the Peace could persuade them that a written contract was not necessary," Lockwood, "Early Times," 121.

By requiring couples to conform to American marriage laws, the U.S. courts ensured that Native-descended women like Euphrosine Antaya would be considered part of the American community, as would their children, potentially disengaging them legally from Native tribes, which were not required to submit to these laws. Officially licensed marriage acknowledged the domination of the U.S. government over Creole societies as well as their intimacies, and the domination of husbands over wives' property and behavior. The policy's impact was mixed: it declared that these women were part of the community, but the consequences meant that they were subordinated to the regime and to men.

The courts enforced this subordination of wives with forms of public humiliation. For example, in 1825 Prudent Langlois went to Justice of the Peace James Lockwood to complain that his wife, Margaret Manikikinik, had been sleeping with Louis Cardinal. Twice that summer she was summoned to answer to the court about her relationship with Cardinal; in each case witnesses testified publicly about her personal life.[16] Divorces were not easy to obtain under American law. They could be granted by the territorial legislature or a circuit court only for impotence, adultery, or bigamy, circumstances essentially requiring public scrutiny of intimate personal information.[17]

Under this system of *coverture*, Creole women additionally became wives who could not own property or make contracts on their own.[18] Thus, when Julia Gardipie was sure that François St. Jean had stolen "seven yards of blue nankin" cloth from her and took the matter to the local magistrate, she had to give a deposition stating that he had stolen the cloth from *her husband*.[19] Similarly, as discussed in Chapter 1, the land claims process under Isaac Lee required that women's land had to be patented in the names of their husbands, because wives could not own land separately. When Euphrosine Antaya married Strange Powers, her land and other property became his as well and came under his control.

It also became harder to be a widow than in the past. By contrast with the French Canadian laws, which allowed widows at least half of

[16] *United States v. Louis Cardinal*, Iowa Series 20, folder 16, Wisconsin Historical Society Library, Platteville.

[17] *Laws of the Territory of the United States North-West of the Ohio* (Cincinnati, OH: W. Maxwell, 1796), 182–183.

[18] Allan Kulikoff, *From British Peasants to Colonial American Farmers* (Chapel Hill: University of North Carolina Press, 2000), 231–232.

[19] Crawford County Clerk Board Papers 1817–1848, Box 1, Folder 2, Wisconsin Historical Society, Madison.

the couple's estate, once the United States took over, Prairie du Chien's widows were entitled only to one third of the couple's real estate and personal property and were not protected from creditors.[20] For example, Marie Louise Rocque was the daughter of La Bleue, a Mdewakanton Dakota woman, and French Canadian Joseph Roc.[21] When her husband Jean Marie Querie *dit* Lamouche died in 1826, Marie Louise expected that she would inherit the entire estate – worth about $600 including a house lot and farm – since they had been married by contract and did not have any children. When James Lockwood, by then both a lawyer and justice of the peace, told Marie Louise she would have to pay the estate's debts, she refused, "alleging that the contract of marriage gave her all the property." The court ordered her to pay $263.28 in debts and $81.37 in court costs, totaling $344.65 or 57 percent of the estate. Some of her land passed into the hands of Joseph Rolette and she eventually had to sell the rest of it to Rolette's clerk and protégé, Hercules Dousman.[22] Had her husband not died, or if she rather than he had died, more time might have been allowed to cover the debts, preventing the family from losing the land. This world with individualized land ownership, legal subordination of wives, and female vulnerability to property loss due to *couverture* was a very different system from the world of Marie Louise's Dakota grandparents.

Thus, women in Prairie du Chien twice experienced a decline in legal rights, first from Native to French, and later from French to American. Tribal women who joined the Creole society left a Native system of balance and autonomy in which they had a political voice, controlled key resources and made decisions affecting their lives and property, and kept separate accounts. Under the French Canadian system, wives had fewer opportunities for formal political leadership and became co-owners with their husbands of their property. Under the "American" system, while the

---

[20] *Some of the Acts of the Territory of Michigan with the Titles and a Digest of all the Acts of the Said Territory; Now in Force.* March 20, 1816 (Detroit: Printed by Theophilus Mettez, 1816), 61. Wives could veto the sale of land, however (p. 45). *Statutes of the Territory of Wisconsin* (Albany, NY: Packard, Van Benthuysen, 1839), 308–309.

[21] James L. Hansen, "The Origin of the Roc/Rock Family of Prairie du Chien and Wabasha: Frontier Genealogy among the Voyageurs," in *The Genealogist* 11, no. 1 (Spring 1997): 3–36. This spelling of Marie Louise's surname appeared in the court records, but other spellings of the name appear in other records, such as Isaac Lee's map of Prairie du Chien.

[22] Lockwood, "Early Times," 121–122; Probate book A, Crawford County Courthouse, Prairie du Chien, 23, 117; Detroit Public Library Burton Historical Collection, card catalog: Land Records – Wisconsin – Crawford County Deeds, May 10, 1826, September 6 and 7, 1836.

*political* rights of their husbands, sons, and brothers were expanding, women's were not. In addition, they lost property rights and became subject to governmental intrusion into their personal relationships.

### Changes in Intermarriage

Intermarriage had been an effective strategy that Native peoples in the Midwest used for connecting with newcomers, monitoring them, and influencing their activities. During the eighteenth century, marriages across racial, ethnic, and cultural lines had helped newcomers to assimilate and acculturate *to* Native communities, and wives became crucial cultural mediators. However, during the nineteenth century in Creole communities, the new American territorial laws, instead of facilitating assimilation of Euro-Americans into Native communities did the opposite: they drew Native wives into the U.S. body politic, subjecting them, their children, and their property to the control of their husbands and to the new government and its courts.

After the United States assumed control and as Anglos streamed into the region, Creoles sought to extend their networks as much as they could through intermarriage with Anglo men. For example, in 1823 tavern keeper, deputy sheriff, and tax collector James Reed was wed by Marguerite Oskache, who was Potawatomi and/or Ojibwe, and after her death, by Menominee métisse Agathe Wood in 1831. When he again became a widower, Reed in 1844 married Archange Labathe, who was part Dakota.[23] To further illustrate, Emilie Rolette, the daughter of Joseph and his first wife Marguerite Dubois, was joined in matrimony to U.S. Army Lieutenant Alexander Simon Hooe.[24] Reed and Hooe as military men connected these Native-descended women and their kin to the muscle of the new regime. Marriages like these continued the old tactics of

---

[23] James L. Hansen, "Crawford County, Wisconsin Marriages, 1816–1848," *Minnesota Genealogical Journal* 1 (May 1984): 48, 54, 55 (Archange married first Joseph Barrette, then Amable Grignon, before marrying Reed; 40, 48); and Hansen, "Prairie du Chien and Galena Church Records, 1827–29," *Minnesota Genealogical Journal* 5 (May 1986): 18. Eben D. Pierce, "James Allen Reed: First Permanent Settler in Trempealeau County and Founder of Trempealeau [Wisconsin]," Wisconsin Historical Society, *Proceedings* 1914, 108; Eben D. Pierce, "Reads like Romance: Life of James Reed," *Galesville Republican* July 8, 1915; Pierce, "Indians Knew Reed as a Fearless Man," *Galesville Republican*, July 15, 1915; Eben D. Pierce, "The Recollections of Antoine Grignon," *Proceedings of the State Historical Society of Wisconsin*, 1904, 173–177.

[24] Joseph Rolette Family Group Chart, Wisconsin State Genealogical Society, Villa Louis Archives, Prairie du Chien.

TABLE 4.1. *Crawford County, Wisconsin, Marriages, 1820–1848*

| Couple | 1820s | | 1830s | | 1840s | |
|---|---|---|---|---|---|---|
| | # | % | # | % | # | % |
| Francophone/ Francophone | 30 | 44 | 45 | 44 | 33 | 21 |
| Anglophone/ Anglophone | 16 | 24 | 33 | 32 | 104 | 65 |
| **Total endogamous\* marriages** | **46** | **68** | **78** | **76** | **137** | **86** |
| Francophone/ Anglophone | 12 | 18 | 20 | 20 | 18 | 11 |
| Indian/Francophone | 8 | 12 | 3 | 3 | 0 | |
| Indian/Anglophone | 1 | 1 | 0 | | 0 | |
| Other | 1 | 1 | 1 | 1 | 5 | 3 |
| **Total exogamous\* marriages** | **22** | **32** | **24** | **24** | **23** | **14** |
| | – | – | – | – | – | – |
| **Total couples** | **68** | **100** | **102** | **100%** | **160** | **100** |

\* Endogamous marriages are within one's ethnic group; exogamous marriages are to someone of a different ethnicity.

*Source*: James L. Hansen, "Crawford County, Wisconsin, Marriages, 1816–1848," *Minnesota Genealogical Journal* 1 (May 1984): 39–58.

incorporating outsiders into the local community and culture in peaceful ways, but such marriages grew fewer and fewer over the decades.

Marriages according to the new laws were registered in the courthouse of Crawford County, in which Prairie du Chien was located. These records, although they do not record marriages *a la façon du pays*, demonstrate some of the shifting patterns of intermarriage (see Table 4.1).

Proportionally fewer of the people moving into the Great Lakes region after the War of 1812 married Native or Creole spouses for a number of reasons. From the 1820s onward, the new migrants to the area more frequently included women, so that Euro-American men had more opportunities to find brides within their own ethnic groups. In addition, new prejudices affected these patterns. Although some Anglo fur traders, like their French Canadian counterparts, married Native women and accepted the practice of intermarriage, many of the agricultural and commercial settlers who colonized the Great Lakes region after the War of 1812 disapproved of this exogamy and voiced their opinions.

Negative attitudes about intermarriage were evident in the voting rights conflict mentioned in Chapter 2. After the 1825 election for

Michigan Territory (under which jurisdiction Prairie du Chien was located), a controversy erupted about whether men with Indian wives and mothers ought to have been able to vote. Supporters of Austin Wing (the candidate who eventually became the delegate to Congress) characterized "half-breeds" as members of "wandering" Indian families, living in "camps," and following lifeways unlike those of "whites," arguing that they should therefore be excluded from the right to vote.[25] Specific individuals were targeted "whose mothers were squaws," or who had married "their squaws." The term, "squaw," that critics used had race-specific pejorative connotations, implying sexual looseness, alcoholism, and/or a status as a degraded and overworked "drudge."[26] Even though in subsequent years many men of mixed ancestry were permitted to vote, this conflict made clear that some powerful men opposed intermarriage, which probably discouraged many Anglos from considering marrying Native-descended spouses. Furthermore, Anglo-Americans who married Native-descended women (even of mixed ancestry) sometimes faced the disapproval of their own families. For example, when Henry Baird married Elizabeth Fisher, his parents and sister accepted his part-Odawa bride only reluctantly, and his brother disapproved.[27]

West of Prairie du Chien in Iowa, a man demonstrated some of the reasoning that discouraged Anglos from marrying Native people. When his cousin Jo Walsh wanted to marry a Sauk woman, he warned that if Jo married her and took her home to Baltimore to their family, people would mock and disparage her. He said, "in Baltimore, as you know, there is a miserable rabble, and an Indian is to them a great curiosity. When you go into the street they will raise the cry, 'There goes Jo Walsh's Indian.' They will not know of the good noble qualities of your wife, and will not care."[28]

Some of the old strategies of coping with immigrants began to change. During the period from 1820 to 1848, official marriage records reveal

---

[25] Clarence Edwin Carter, ed. and comp., *Territorial Papers of the United States*, Territory of Michigan (Washington: U.S. Government Printing Office, 1943), Vol. 11, 738–748.

[26] Clarence E. Carter, ed., *Territorial Papers of the United States*, 28 vols. (Washington, DC: U.S. Government Printing Office, 1934–68) (hereafter *TPUS*), 11: 739, 747; Rayna Green, "The Pocahontas Perplex: The Image of Indian Women in American Culture," *Massachusetts Review* 16 (Autumn 1975): 698–714; David D. Smits, "The 'Squaw Drudge': A Prime Index of Savagism," *Ethnohistory* 29, no. 4 (Autumn, 1982): 281–306.

[27] Henry Baird to Henry Baird Jr., May 10, 1824, Henry and Elizabeth Baird Papers, Wisconsin Historical Society, Madison, Box 1, Folder 1.

[28] Hawkins Taylor, "Indian Courtship and White Weddings," *Annals of Iowa*, 1st series, Vol. 12 (1874), 156. According to Taylor, the woman was Black Hawk's daughter.

that the local tradition of incorporating newcomers into community networks of kin and obligation persisted in a limited way as intermarriage continued, but Indian-white unions – like that of Pokoussee and Pierre Antaya – became a smaller percentage of all marriages. And the mixed sons and daughters of fur-trade families were marrying each other more often than they married people either wholly Native or entirely European.

The 1850 U.S. Population Census allows us to take a closer look at Prairie du Chien with a cross-section of Creole couples living in the town, rather than seeing them at the time they were married. Whereas Table 4.1 had examined cross-ethnic or interracial marriage based on *ethnicity* of surname and remarks about *race* by those who recorded the weddings, we can with the census data look at the *places of birth* of couples. Creoles were identified as residents with French surnames who were born in Wisconsin, Michigan, Minnesota, Missouri, Illinois, or Canada before 1820, and their children *and/or* those who were known from genealogical and treaty records to be members of fur-trade families. Out of a total population in 1850 of 1,406 people in Prairie du Chien, 425 were Creole.[29]

The census reveals that many local Creole women married French Canadians and others from outside the region, continuing a different kind of exogamy. In 1850, there were sixty-three couples in which one or both of the partners were Creole. In eighteen marriages, both husband and wife were born in Wisconsin; in twenty-one couples, both were from outside the state, and in twenty-four cases (38%) one spouse was from Wisconsin (usually Prairie du Chien) and the other from elsewhere. Of these twenty-four geographically exogamous marriages, in twenty-one of them the wife was from Wisconsin and the husband from outside: (16 of these husbands were Canadian); in three the husband was local and the wife an outsider. Traditionally during the fur-trade era, men were the immigrants and women created the ties if for no other reason than that men were still more likely to migrate alone than were women.

Thus the 1850 census data show that Creoles continued the Native tradition of enlarging one's family and community with new kin ties and of using marriage to incorporate newcomers. Now, however, the outsiders were generally not Anglo but tended to be recently arrived French

[29] U.S. Census office, *Seventh Census of the U.S., 1850* manuscript, Prairie du Chien, Crawford County, WI, microfilm.

Canadians. These marriages were one of the ways to create and enlarge networks.

## Networks

The Antaya, Brisbois, Fisher, and Rolette families and their neighbors belonged to networks of kin, friends, and others connected by love, blood, adoption, obligation, clan, tribal affiliation, and god-parenting. As they raised their children, others moved to their communities and became similarly linked to these Creole families and towns. Like many social networks the world over, these webs connected Creoles to others across long distances and perhaps facilitated migration. As in other countries, Creole marriages were often arranged by parents (or other kin) and affected the social and political status and authority of both brides and grooms. In times of difficulty, kin and friends might help people to overcome health problems, political conflicts, and financial difficulties.

The networks of Creole women were, in some ways, similar to those of white frontier women. In studies of frontier Michigan and Ohio, historians have shown that white women, through visiting and correspondence, maintained relationships that served as a resource for all family members, but particularly for women made vulnerable both by laws and economic realities that limited their autonomy.[30] The same was true for Creole women. However, a key difference was that many Creoles approved of women's activism in a wide range of arenas, including independent economic management, religious leadership, diplomacy, and, to some extent, political participation.[31] Thus, many of the networks in which Creole women like Angelique Brisbois Pion and their children participated connected them to business partners, religious associates, and political allies, in addition to friends and relatives.

Another difference was that Native and Creole cultures valued exogamy (out-marriage). While Europeans and Euro-Americans ideally married within their class, religion, race, and ethnicity, Native and Creole

---

[30] Marilyn Ferris Motz, *True Sisterhood: Michigan Women and Their Kin, 1820–1920* (Albany: State University of New York Press, 1983);Tamara G. Miller, "'Those with Whom I Feel Most Nearly Connected': Kinship and Gender in Early Ohio," in *Midwestern Women: Work, Community, and Leadership at the Crossroads*, edited by Lucy Eldersveld Murphy and Wendy Hamand Venet (Bloomington: University of Indiana Press, 1997), 121–140; and Sleeper-Smith, *Indian Women and French Men.*

[31] For an extended discussion of this issue, see Lucy Eldersveld Murphy, "Public Mothers: Native American and Métis Women as Creole Mediators in the Nineteenth-Century Midwest," *Journal of Women's History* 14, no. 4 (Winter 2003): 142–166.

people in the Midwest encouraged and appreciated women who espoused well-connected outsiders. Midwestern Indians traditionally assimilated immigrants into their communities by arranging marriages for them, or, less frequently, by adoption.

## The Baird Network

Some Prairie du Chien women were part of a network that can be reconstructed from the correspondence of Elizabeth Thérèse Fisher Baird, the half-sister of Jane Fisher Rolette. Herself born in Prairie du Chien, Elizabeth had been a neighbor of the Antayas and Brisbois during her infancy. Elizabeth Thérèse Fisher Baird came from three generations of fur-trade marriages and was of Odawa, Scottish, and French ancestry.[32]

Taken together, this correspondence reveals that Elizabeth Baird's family and friends were part of a large network that connected people whose grandparents had lived in places as far apart as Switzerland and Missouri. They included Odawa, Dakota, Osage, Menominee, and Illinois Indians as well as immigrants from France, Switzerland, Ireland, Scotland, and Canada. Between 1825 and 1837, they were located in places as far-flung as Green Bay, Prairie du Chien, Portage, Mackinac Island, L'Arbre Croche, and Pittsburgh. Elizabeth and her relatives maintained ties to old friends in both Creole and indigenous communities, while connecting with the newest immigrants, settlers, soldiers, and priests.

The United States' conquest and colonization of the Midwest had disrupted Elizabeth's family. She had moved as an infant with her mother from Prairie du Chien to Mackinac Island to be with her grandmother and great-aunt when her father left for Canada to avoid U.S. rule during the War of 1812. In 1824, at the age of fourteen, she married a young Scots-Irish lawyer named Henry Baird and moved with him to Green Bay in present-day Wisconsin.[33] With this marriage, her family allied

---

[32] She was the daughter of Henry Monroe Fisher, a Scots-American father, and Marianne LaSallière, a mother of French and Odawa Indian ancestry; her father and brothers were fur traders, and so were her maternal grandmother and great-aunt. Her great-grandfather Jean Baptiste Marcotte had been a fur trader who enhanced his chances for business success and political authority by marrying Marie Nekesh, the daughter of an Odawa chief, around 1775. Peterson, "The People in Between," 161, 163; "Memoranda," Henry S. Baird Paper, Wisconsin Historical Society Library, Madison, Box 4, Folder 1.

[33] Probably, Marie Nekesh's mother was Mejakwataw. Peterson, "The People in Between," 161, 163; Elizabeth T. Baird, "Memoranda," Henry S. and Elizabeth Baird Papers, WIS MSS V, Box 4, Folder 1, Wisconsin Historical Society Library, Madison; Elizabeth T. Baird, "O-De-Jit-Wa-Win-Wing; Contes du Temps Passe," H.S. Baird Papers, Box 4, Folder 9.

themselves with a man who knew not only the new court language, English, but also the laws of the new courts. Fortunately for Elizabeth, the marriage was not only beneficial to her family but also affectionate, as her correspondence reveals. Her papers, preserved in the Wisconsin Historical Society, also tell of an extensive network connecting women and men of Prairie du Chien with people in and from communities widely dispersed.

Elizabeth Fisher Baird and her family members were linked across hundreds of miles, by ties of kinship, friendship, religious association, and business interests with an extremely diverse assortment of people. For example, within a year after her marriage and move to Green Bay, Baird's step-grandfather, George Schindler, wrote to her from Mackinac Island: "Dear Betsey, ... I am glad to see that you will be here shortly." The young bride was pregnant and planned to return to Mackinac where her kin could help her through the childbirth and teach her to care for her new baby. Schindler, who was from Switzerland, reported that "your mother [h]as passed the winter with the unfortunate Mrs. Bailley."[34] Elizabeth's mother, Marianne LaSallière Fisher, was probably at L'Arbre Croche, an Odawa village on the mainland, with Alexis Bailly's mother, Angelique McGulpin Bailly, another French-Odawa fur-trade daughter who had evidently experienced some misfortune. Elizabeth Baird's and Marianne LaSallière Fisher's traveling to be with family and friends in times of childbirth, disease, or distress was also typical of Anglo women and suggests that Creole women followed similar patterns.[35]

Members of this network might visit each other for extended periods of time. Elizabeth's great-aunt, Madeleine Laframboise (also known as Shaw-we-no-qua) at Mackinac, received a short letter written in French from Domitille Gauthier Brisbois of Prairie du Chien, inviting her to spend the winter of 1829–30 with the Brisbois family.[36] Madame Brisbois descended from Odawa and Illini nations of Indians, as well as from French Canadian fur traders. Historian Susan Sleeper-Smith has shown

[34] George Schindler to Elizabeth Baird, May 7[?], 1825, H. S. Baird Papers, Box 1, Folder 1; Angelique Bailly was an Odawa woman married to fur trader Joseph Bailly. "The Mackinac Register," *WHC*, Vol. 19 (1910), 141; and Sleeper-Smith, *Indian Women and French Men*, 155–159, 218 n. 56, 219 n. 69.

[35] Carroll Smith-Rosenberg, "The Female World of Love and Ritual: Relations between Women in Nineteenth-Century America," *Signs: Journal of Women in Culture and Society* 1, no. 1 (1975): 1–29; and Miller, "Those with Whom I feel Most Nearly Connected."

[36] Kappler, *Indian Affairs*, Vol. 2, 200. Domitille Brisbois to Madame Laframboise, June 29, 1829, Baird Papers, Wisconsin Historical Society Library, Box 1, Folder 2.

how Brisbois's grandmother's networks expanded from Cahokia in the Illinois Country to St. Joseph, Mackinac, and Green Bay.[37]

These complex Creole families maintained their older networks through correspondence while extending them with new connections. Elizabeth Baird's step-niece, Emilie Rolette of Prairie du Chien, was the granddaughter of a Dakota woman. Rolette married U.S. Army Lieutenant Alexander Simon Hooe, who had been appointed a commissary and quartermaster and had been posted to Fort Winnebago, located at Portage in present-day Wisconsin.[38] In July 1831, Emilie wrote to Elizabeth of her trip to her new home ("We had a delightful journey ... we had good weather, no musketoes") and of how pleased she was to find that "there is 9 married ladies and the two Miss[es] Low" living at the Fort. "I am delighted with this place ... it is near[er] home and the country about is beautiful, [I take a] great many pleasant walks around the fort."[39] Emilie's father, Joseph Rolette, was a prominent fur trader at Prairie du Chien. Her marriage to an army officer connected her family to the military force of the new regime, and she cultivated friendships with the other officers' wives.

The fondness of friends and relatives comes through in many of the letters. "It is impossible for me to say how much I miss you. For the first few days of your absence I felt really desolate," wrote Eliza H. Platt, a recent migrant to the Green Bay area from Vermont, while Elizabeth Baird was away in 1837. "When will you come back and cheer us by your presence?"[40] Soon enough, Elizabeth was back home in Green Bay after visiting friends and relatives in Mackinac. Many other people were mentioned in the correspondence, which even included some letters written in Native languages.[41]

This unusually large collection of letters demonstrates that literate Creoles in the nineteenth century maintained networks across long distances. The diverse nature of network members suggests that racial lines had not been formed. Given the frequency with which both literate and nonliterate Creoles traveled and spoke with travelers, it is likely that

---

[37] *WHC*, Vol. 18 (1908), 490, 492; Jacqueline Peterson, "The People In Between," 161; and Susan Sleeper-Smith, "Women, Kin, and Catholicism: New Perspectives on the Fur Trade," *Ethnohistory* 47, no. 2 (Spring 2000): 423–452.

[38] James L. Hansen, ed., "A Roll of Sioux Mixed Bloods, 1855–56," *Minnesota Genealogical Journal* 7 (November 1987): 603; and James L. Hansen, letter to author, April 9, 2007.

[39] Emilie Hooe to Elizabeth Baird, July 19, 1831, H. S. Baird Papers, Box 1, Folder 2.

[40] Eliza H. Platt, Navarino, to Elizabeth Baird, Mackinac, September 10, 1837, H.S. Baird Papers, Box 1, Folder 2.

[41] Baird Manuscript Collection, Wisconsin Historical Society Library, http://www.wisconsinhistory.org/baird/, accessed June 30, 2012.

those unable to read and write were also able to send messages to distant friends and relatives and to visit them with some regularity, maintaining ties. Literacy, of course, did enhance the ability to communicate. And these friends and kin were important not only for reasons of the heart but also as resources to help them to weather not only the universal challenges of life – such as childbirth or death – but also the changes brought by the new American regime. Historian Tamara Miller commented in her study of Anglo women in early Marietta, Ohio, that, "Women ... played a crucial role in cementing kinship ties. In doing so, women both mitigated the inequalities of the gender system and improved the quality of their lives."[42] This can also be said about Creoles, and one might add to those inequalities the challenges of Indian removal, political change, and Yankee prejudices.

### "Doing Good to His Creatures": Public Mothers

Although Creole women lost legal rights during the nineteenth century, and there were fewer chances for them to connect with the ascendant Yankees through intermarriage, they could draw upon their networks and traditional roles as intercultural mediators to help one another and to enhance their usefulness to their communities. Many of them served in roles that I refer to as "public mothers."[43] In a climate where patterns of authority, marriage, and gender were changing to the detriment of Creole women, they used traditions of outreach to create and maintain ties not only with kin and old friends but also with the newcomers. Although Anglo prejudices put Creole men at a disadvantage, Anglo, Creole, and Native ideals of womanhood intersected when it came to certain behaviors, making it possible for some women to connect people in ways that merited approval from all, and even earned them mention in historical sources that often overlooked the experiences of Creoles, and of women more generally.

Throughout North America, Native-descended women often served as "cultural mediators," according to historian Clara Sue Kidwell. She argued, "there is an important Indian woman in virtually every major encounter between Europeans and Indians in the New World." As lovers, wives, and interpreters, "Indian women were the first important mediators of meaning between the cultures of two worlds."[44] Throughout the

---

[42] Miller, "Those with Whom I feel Most Nearly Connected," 130.
[43] Murphy, "Public Mothers."
[44] Kidwell, "Indian Women as Cultural Mediators," 54.

Great Lakes region during the fur-trade era, women had connected people across cultures and smoothed relations in these ways. Anecdotal evidence from many communities reveals some of the ways that Creole women linked Native, Creole, Anglo, and other people, and Prairie du Chien certainly had its fair share of public mothers.

Angelique Brisbois Pion, as mentioned in the introduction to this chapter, was an interpreter for the U.S. government and the Ho-Chunks. Catherine Boilvin Myott provides another example of an important cultural mediator from the Prairie du Chien community. Her father was Nicolas Boilvin, the U.S. Indian agent there, and her mother was Wizak Kega of the Ho-Chunk nation. Catherine herself had married François Myott. Because she was a skilled linguist and spoke both Ho-Chunk and French, working with Indian Sub-Agent Henry Gratiot she was able to help smooth relations among Ho-Chunks, Creoles, and Yankees by helping people to communicate and negotiate, reducing violence and creating trust in one section of the mining region south of Prairie du Chien during the conflicted lead rush years of the late 1820s and 1830s. During the Black Hawk War, she served as an official interpreter and was instrumental in saving the lives of two hostages and three other people who had been threatened with death by Black Hawk and Wabokieshiek, known as the Winnebago Prophet.[45] Like Angelique Brisbois, Catherine Boilvin Myott had linguistic and cultural skills that enabled her to mediate among people who very much needed to understand one another.

Serving as linguistic and cultural interpreters, however, was just one way that women could continue to reach out to others. Some Creole women also took on activities related to charity, hospitality, healing, and midwifery. They nurtured their neighbors, newcomers, travelers, kin, and fellow clan and tribal members. They came from Native and Creole traditions in which women's roles – particularly those of elite women – could be at once public and private, social and political. Although political and economic roles for Creoles under the new regime were being constricted and the Anglo gender system being imposed was more restrictive than the systems of Creoles and Native Americans, some Creole women maintained quasi-public roles in transitional communities, because newcomers perceived them as praiseworthy females doing motherly work. Although there are many instances of elite Creole men making connections and

[45] Murphy, *A Gathering of Rivers*, 106–109; Waggoner, *"Neither White Men nor Indians,"* 91; Ellen M. Whitney, comp. and ed., *The Black Hawk War, 1831–1832,* 2 vols. (Springfield: Illinois State Historical Library, 1973), Vol. II, 324, 509, 456.

laboring to smooth intercultural relations, the role of Creole mediator is most evident in the actions of women.

As Creoles and the Native villagers in the Great Lakes region lost power and numbers, the work of Creole women's mediation often revolved around helping the unfortunate and serving the needs of neighbors and newcomers. For many, this was part of their religious obligations, whether traditionally Native or Christian, or both. Native people believed (and many still believe) that "we are all related," including all people, all living things, and the earth. And they believed that it was their obligation to help all in need.[46] For example, in northern Illinois trader Stephen Mack learned this from his wife Hononegah, who was Ho-Chunk. When she died, he wrote that "In her the hungry and naked have lost a benefactor, the sick a nurse, and I have lost a friend who ... taught me to reverence God by doing good to his creatures." He continued:

Her funeral proved that I am not the only sufferer by her loss. My house is large but it was filled to overflowing by mourning friends who assembled to pay the last sad duties to her who had set them the example how to Live and how to Die.[47]

Similarly, many understood Christian teachings to value compassion and charitable outreach. Examples of other Native and Creole women's efforts are numerous in the historical record.[48]

### Healers and Midwives

Some Creole women around the Midwest reached out to their communities as healers – roles women could hold in Native communities – and as midwives, a practice women monopolized among Indians. Native-descended women brought their knowledge of medicine, midwifery, and nurturing to the service of their neighbors; it is likely that bicultural women drew upon multiple medical traditions, making their range of treatment options greater than those available to people with access to only a single medical tradition. Creole women healers were appreciated enough to have been mentioned in Anglo memoirs and newspaper accounts. Their efforts frequently brought them into the homes of neighbors who were

---

[46] Clara Sue Kidwell, Homer Noley, and George E. "Tink" Tinker, *A Native American Theology* (Maryknoll, NY: Orbis Books, 2001), 41–51, 110.

[47] David Bishop and Craig G. Campbell, *History of the Forest Preserves of Winnebago County, Illinois* (Rockford, IL: Winnebago County Forest Preserve Commission, 1979), 35.

[48] For more examples through the Great Lakes region, see Murphy, "Public Mothers."

culturally different, creating ties of respect and affection, and sometimes enhancing the healers' status and authority. Numerous examples of such women can be found in Prairie du Chien and the surrounding area.

One of the earliest known healers in Prairie du Chien was Marie, a Dakota woman who died in 1814. An army officer remarked that her death was a "great loss to this village, she being an excellent old doctress, particularly for children."[49] Another was Marianne LaBuche Menard, Prairie du Chien's midwife and healer, "a person of consequence," according to an 1856 pioneer writer who knew her in the early nineteenth century. Of French and African descent and a native of New Orleans, she had thirteen children by three husbands. "She was sent for by the sick," the writer recalled, "and attended them as regularly as a physician, and charged fees therefor, giving them ... 'device and yarb drink' [advice and herb drink].... [S]he took her pay in the produce of the country, but was not very modest in her charges." After the U.S. army brought in a male physician who would attend to civilians, many still preferred "Aunt Mary Ann," as she was called, and she sometimes cured people despaired of by the army doctor.[50]

Her daughter Adelaide Limery carried on as a medical practitioner.[51] A neighbor's son later recalled, "my father used to tell me of when Mrs. Limery ... used to get my father to go with her and gather ... different kinds of roots, barks and berries, and seeds for different ailments. She had learned this from the Indians." (And no doubt from her mother.) He related the experience of a logger who, like many others, had come down from the north woods to winter at Prairie du Chien, and "in a drinking brawl, this man was stabbed, the full length of a knife blade in his side, and it punctured his lungs." After the town's male doctors despaired of curing the logger and he was almost dead, Madame Limery contracted to take him home and cure him, earning $200 for her successful efforts.[52]

Another noted healer was Angelique Desmarais, of Ojibwe and French ancestry. She and her husband Louis and children lived for a while in Prairie du Chien before moving to Chippewa Falls. One of her Anglo

---

[49] Thomas Anderson, "Capt. T. G. Anderson's Journal, 1814," *WHC*, Vol. 9, 241.

[50] Lockwood, "Early Times," 125–126.

[51] Adelaide's maiden name was Gagnier. Correspondence from James L. Hansen, Wisconsin Historical Society genealogy librarian, July 15, 2010.

[52] Albert Coryer, interview, broadcast, and anecdotes, Wisconsin Historical Society Library, Madison. Madame Limery's husband Jean Limery also provided services to their neighbors with a faith cure he had brought with him from Canada. Coryer interview, typescript 17.

neighbors later recalled, "She was a woman of uncommon natural abilities, and with education and culture would have graced a high social position in any community. She was a born physician, and for many years the only one in the valley; and in making a diagnosis of disease, and her knowledge of the healing properties and proper application of many of the remedies used in the Materia Medica, exhibited extraordinary insight and skill in her practice. She was frequently called to attend upon myself and family, and her prescriptions were simple, natural, and always efficacious."[53]

Another example of this pattern may be found in a family genealogy compiled by Mary Martell during the 1940s, which recalled her ancestor, Mary La Pointe La Tranche, born in Prairie du Chien about 1838, who married and moved across the river to Iowa during the late 1850s. Madame La Tranche "would go around with an old Indian woman doctor and do the talking for her as this lady could not speak one word of English – only made the Indian sign signals. In doing this, Mary learned a great deal about taking care of the sick and in later years she went herself. She brought a good many of the now [1950] old-timers ... into the world. Many a cold, stormy night she braved the storm to go to someone in distress. She kept up this practice until she was quite old."[54] Clearly, both the "old Indian woman doctor" and Madame La Tranche were reaching across the cultural borders from Native to Creole to Anglo in their community. There are many similar examples of this type of health care–related mediation in accounts by both Anglos and Creoles around the Midwest.[55]

Those without unique medical talents sometimes stepped forward to assist sick neighbors as best they could. For example, Jane Fisher Rolette Dousman volunteered to nurse smallpox patients at Prairie du Chien when others were afraid to do so, according to a reminiscence of her granddaughter.[56] Madame Dousman, according to one obituary, "always

---

[53] Thomas E. Randall, *History of the Chippewa Valley* (Eau Claire, WI: Free Press Print, 1875), 17–18; *History of Northern Wisconsin* (Chicago: Western Historical Company, 1881), 193. There are numerous spellings of the family name, including Demarie.

[54] Mary Martell, *Our People the Indians: A Genealogy of the Indians and French Canadians, 1750–1950: in the areas of Prairie du Chien, Wisconsin, Harpers Ferry, Iowa, and Pembina-Red River of the North in N. Dakota and Minnesota* (n.p.: Privately published, ca. 1950), 7.

[55] Murphy, "Public Mothers," 148–149.

[56] Martinus J. Dyrud, "King Rolette, Astor Fur Trader on the Upper Mississippi," unpublished manuscript, Villa Louis archives, WHS, Prairie du Chien, 74; "Jane Fisher Rolette," Virginia Dousman Bigelow Papers, Villa Louis, WHS.

sought to alleviate suffering and assist the distressed."[57] Another stated that "She sought out the sick and suffering. Rich and poor alike felt her gentle influence in the hour [of] affliction."[58] Historian Joan M. Jensen has found similar instances of Native and Euro-American women healers in northern Wisconsin during this period and afterward.[59]

## Hospitality

Like Native communities, where generosity was among the greatest of virtues and elites provided hospitality for visitors, in Creole fur-trade communities such as Prairie du Chien, people expected prominent families to welcome travelers. They housed and fed friends, kin, and tribesmen, but also miscellaneous strangers.[60] In doing so, they became the newcomers' patrons but also served their communities by supervising the outsiders' behavior. Thus, women and their husbands opened their homes to visitors on short notice. Angelique Brisbois Pion, as we have seen, was one who provided hospitality to fellow Ho-Chunks. Her widower told officials that "while his wife lived, his house was always open to the Indians and they 'slept at his fire and ate at his board.'"[61]

Although as time went on there were proportionately fewer Native brides in frontier communities, many older Native women and their daughters and sons continued to live in areas of mixed population, where they provided hospitality and charity for Indians suffering the effects of land seizures, late or inadequate annuities, poorly administered Indian bureau policies, disease, and other social, economic, and political disruptions. The case of Mahnahteesee, a Ho-Chunk woman living in Prairie du Chien, provides an instance of this. She was "the full sister of ... the most influential Chiefs of the Tribe" and thus an elite member of the fur-trade community from the Ho-Chunk point of view, according to the leading men of Prairie du Chien and Green Bay who testified in 1838–39 pursuant to a treaty earmarking money for Ho-Chunk "half-breeds." When her husband, a Canadian trader, died, she had considerable wealth, but

---

[57] "Obituary in Memory of Mrs. Jane F. Dousman,"? January 1882, *Crawford County [?] Courier*, Villa Louis Archives, WHS, Prairie du Chien.

[58] "Another Old Resident Gone, Death of Mrs. Jane F. Dousman,"? January 1882, *Crawford County [?] Courier*, Villa Louis Archives, WHS, Prairie du Chien.

[59] Joan M. Jensen, *Calling This Place Home: Women on the Wisconsin Frontier, 1850–1925* (St. Paul: Minnesota Historical Society Press, 2006), 163–189.

[60] Samuel Mazzuchelli, *The Memoirs of Father Samuel Mazzuchelli, o.p.* (Chicago, IL: Priory Press, 1967), 103.

[61] Waggoner, *"Neither White Men nor Indians,"* 82.

expended most of it providing the hospitality and generosity expected of an elite Native woman during a time of crisis for the tribe, facing removal and disease.[62]

Hospitality was also available to Meskwakis and other Native people. For example, Pierre Antaya and Pokoussee's granddaughter Clara LaPointe Hertzog (b. ca.1835), who married an immigrant from Luxembourg (another exogamous marriage), offered a campsite and friendship to Native people. Clara's daughter Adaline Hertzog Barrette was interviewed about Clara in 1949 and recalled, "I can remember ... the Indians dancing in our back yard, my mother never minded them at all, she herself had Indian blood and she knew their languages and was able to carry on a conversation with them, they always treated mother very well, and looked to her for advice and instructions, she was often invited to their abode to eat."[63]

Creoles frequently offered hospitality not only to Native but also to non-Indian travelers and newcomers. For example, when Zebulon Pike and his party of soldier-explorers arrived in 1805 and 1806, Henry Fisher and his wife Madeleine Gauthier invited Pike (and probably his aides) to stay with them twice, for five days each time.[64] Their daughter Jane carried on the practice of hospitality as an adult when she and her husband Joseph Rolette invited the new judge of the circuit court, James Duane Doty, and his wife Sarah Collins Doty to spend the winter of 1823–24 with them.[65] As the wives of elite men, such hospitality was expected of them. Although they certainly had the help of servants, these women no doubt had to extend extra effort to provide plenty of food, bedding, other provisions, and entertainment for their guests, but it was their husbands who got the credit. Pike, for example, recorded that he "took quarters at Capt. Fisher's and was Received politely by him," and commented about the "gentlemen residing at the Prairie des Chiens," that they "possess the spirit of generosity and hospitality in an eminent degree, but this is the leading feature in the character of frontier inhabitants."[66]

---

[62] Waggoner, *"Neither White Men nor Indians,"* 31–32. Emphasis in original.

[63] Mary Martell, *Our People the Indians,* 53.

[64] Donald Jackson, ed., *The Journals of Zebulon Pike* (Norman: University of Oklahoma Press, 1966), 22–25, 124–127.

[65] Alice Elizabeth Smith, *James Duane Doty: Frontier Promoter* (Madison: State Historical Society of Wisconsin, 1954), 53.

[66] Donald Jackson, ed., *The Journals of Zebulon Montgomery Pike* (Norman: University of Oklahoma Press, 1966), 22; Elliott Coues, ed., *The Expeditions of Zebulon Montgomery Pike* (New York: Francis P. Harper, 1895), 304–305.

Some newcomers to the region acculturated enough to learn the customs of hospitality. The French Canadian Carriere family had recently moved to the Prairie du Chien area to be near a cousin, when one winter day a band of Indians stopped by their farm and asked their hired man, Joseph Drew (who spoke their language), if they could stay the night. Lucretia Carriere's husband was away overnight, but she welcomed the travelers, cooked them a meal, offered them some potatoes, and welcomed the Native mothers and children to sleep in her small house while the men camped outside. By the time the visitors left the next morning, they had given her a large stack of venison quarters. In addition, each Indian mother showed her appreciation by draping a necklace around Lucretia Carriere's little son Joseph. Her grandson later wrote, "each mother that had slept in the hut gave Joseph a string of beads which loaded his neck to a breaking point and also thanked Mrs. very much for welcoming them as she did."[67] The Carrieres gave away most of the venison to their neighbors. Although the Carrieres were recent arrivals, Madame adjusted to the local Creole norms, and although she could not speak her visitors' language, she found someone who could, in order to facilitate this peaceful encounter.[68]

## Charity

In addition to gifts of lodging and food for sojourners, Creoles provided other assistance to their neighbors as well, extending to neighbors the generosity they showed to visitors. For example, when Madame Marie Chalifoux Vertefeuille interceded to help the Glass family, as we have seen in Chapter 2, she was reaching across cultures in a traditional mediator role to try to help a suffering family. To further illustrate, Archange LaBathe's husband Amable Grignon had been the son of an elite Ho-Chunk woman named Echauwaukah, so Archange and Amable were expected to provide hospitality for Ho-Chunk visitors. After Amable's death, a neighbor in 1839 testified that Archange "is very kind and hospitable to the [Ho-Chunk] Indians, at all times making them comfortable as in her power, and that her home is always considered their home."[69] No doubt she also welcomed her own people, the Dakotas.

A few years later she became the third wife of James Reed, the deputy sheriff, tavern keeper, and tax collector. She and James moved to

---

[67] Albert Coryer, "Short Stories," manuscript, Wisconsin Historical Society Library, 5–6.
[68] Albert Coryer, interview, Wisconsin Historical Society Library.
[69] Waggoner, *"Neither White Men nor Indians,"* 16.

Trempealeau County, Wisconsin, where her behavior (no doubt a continuation of similar efforts at Prairie du Chien) impressed an Anglo neighbor. Years later, he described her as epitomizing the "twin traits [of] generosity and hospitality" of the best frontier residents. He wrote, "Squaw though she was, she was an angel of mercy to the residents of Reed's Landing and Montoville. How distinctly I recall her commanding figure – going from house to house – not with words, for few could understand her broken French and native tongue – but with well filled basket, and ready hand – tender as only a woman's is – to cheer the sick."[70] Although this Anglo writer racialized and demeaned her as a "squaw," he viewed Archange LaBathe Reed's actions as appropriate, gendered behavior.

### "Tender as Only a Woman": At the Intersections of Anglo, Creole, and Native Ideals

Given the ambivalence, prejudice, and racism of so many pioneer writers, it seems surprising that the efforts of these Creole public mothers were deemed noteworthy enough to mention in their letters and memoirs. Why were these Creole women memorialized in Anglo discourse? That many of the public mothers were elite women probably contributed to their acceptance. More important, they had found a social space at the intersection of different cultural groups' gender ideals. This was no mean feat as ideals of womanhood varied widely between Anglos and Creoles.

Creole women did not act like ideal Anglo women. Anglo Northeasterners might find them lacking in purity and submissiveness, and their religious participation did not always strictly conform to Protestant concepts of piety (partly because they were usually Catholic). They seemed, however, to possess many of the virtues of domesticity and their relations with their neighbors sometimes resonated with immigrating Anglos as being appropriate and laudable.

In the eastern United States, changes in social relations since the mid-eighteenth century had altered some Anglo behaviors and expectations while creating in many people a sense of nostalgia for colonial-era hospitality, communalism, and perceived idealism. In the colonial era, charity had been one of the fundamental virtues expected of women, particularly elite women, but as the economy and society changed in the Northeast during the early national period, new gender ideals were being created.

---

[70] John McGilvray to B. F. Heuston, June 18, 1886, Heuston Collection, Murphy Library, University of Wisconsin – La Crosse, Wisconsin State Historical Society, LaCrosse.

Many people were ambivalent about the individualism touted as appropriate for men, mourning the loss of the communalistic ideal. Ideals for women, therefore, came to encompass the old communalism: the selflessness, empathy, and concern for the well-being of one's neighbor.[71] Charity continued to be seen as a positive attribute for women.

In the meantime, women's roles in childbirth and healing were changing. Before the early nineteenth century, communities typically included a number of women with healing skills, but male doctors increasingly took over midwifery and healing work, administering new therapies, and gradually closing women out of a professionalizing medical field, a change that must have made many people uneasy.[72] Creole women healers probably reminded emigrants of doctoring women and midwives in the pre-professional traditions.

Anglophone emigrants to the Midwest were people dissatisfied enough with their lives in older communities to leave them behind. Many had been displaced by an evolving market economy and its attendant social disruptions. They frequently had mixed feelings about changes in their home societies: on the one hand, they looked back nostalgically to the old communalism and hospitality of days gone by; on the other hand, they tried to recreate many innovations of the changing societies they had left. For example, community studies of places such as Sugar Creek, Illinois, and Trempealeau County, Wisconsin, emphasize the ways in which Anglophone "pioneers" idealized "good neighborship."[73]

The Creoles seemed weird and exotic to these emigrants who would come to call themselves pioneers. Creoles spoke different languages, practiced a different religion, dressed oddly, had people of color among their elites, tolerated uppity women, and farmed differently. The pioneers might

[71] Rhys Isaac, *The Transformation of Virginia, 1740–1790* (Chapel Hill: University of North Carolina Press, 1982), 71, 302–305; Laurel Thatcher Ulrich, *Good Wives: Image and Reality in the Lives of Women in Northern New England, 1650–1750* (New York: Oxford University Press, 1980), 59–65; Barbara Welter, "The Cult of True Womanhood: 1820–1860," *American Quarterly* 18 (1966): 151–174; and Mary P. Ryan, *Cradle of the Middle Class: The Family in Oneida County, New York, 1790–1865* (New York: Cambridge University Press, 1981), 210–218.

[72] Laurel Thatcher Ulrich, *A Midwife's Tale: The Life of Martha Ballard, Based on Her Diary, 1785–1812* (New York: Vintage Books, Random House, 1990), 62, 254–261; Gerda Lerner, "The Lady and the Mill Girl," in Lerner, *The Majority Finds Its Past* (New York: Oxford University Press, 1979), 15–30.

[73] Merle Curti, *The Making of an American Community: A Case Study of Democracy in a Frontier County* (Stanford, CA: Stanford University Press, 1959), 114–116; John Mack Faragher, *Sugar Creek: Life on the Illinois Prairie* (New Haven, CT: Yale University Press, 1986), ch. 14.

have had trouble waxing enthusiastic about Angelique Brisbois Pion's success as a businesswoman, but they were comforted by women who looked after their neighbors. This was appropriate behavior for women, even for Creole women. The settlers seem to have lauded Marianne LaBuche Menard, Archange LaBathe Reed, and other Creole women for their nurturing, mother-like behavior, as they understood the concept, and the ways that this activity corresponded to their ideals. Thus, public mothers like these mitigated Anglo prejudices enough to help prevent ethnic bigotry from becoming racism. By gaining the respect and friendship of their neighbors, they softened the social boundaries between the old fur-trade family members and others.

The Creole women serving as public mothers succeeded in gaining the appreciation of the pioneers while retaining esteem among their own, because their actions corresponded to congruities in the two groups' value systems. But the ideals of these two groups did have significant differences, and women could behave in ways that seemed appropriate to the Creoles but peculiar or even scandalous to the pioneers.

Although Creole gender ideals varied from family to family, region to region, and evolved during the course of the nineteenth century, as a whole they differed in significant respects from those of Anglo-Americans. In particular, Creoles approved of women's activism in a wide range of arenas, including economic management and innovation, political participation, and social network building. Even within local Catholic communities, some women played dynamic roles as they found ways to make the institution of the Catholic Church and belief system enhance their authority. Like Native women, many Creole women – even wives – could own, control, and convey property and manage independent businesses. In other words, they had the undisputed right to make economic decisions and often had a substantial amount of both personal autonomy and authority within their Creole communities and among the tribes of their Native kin.[74]

Indian traditions strongly influenced Creole ideals because Creole women were usually either Native or part Native. From the mid-eighteenth

---

[74] Rebecca Kugel, "Re-Working Ethnicity: Gender, Work Roles and the Redefinition of the Great Lakes Métis," in *Enduring Nations: Native Americans in the Midwest,* edited by R. David Edmunds (Urbana: University of Illinois Press, 2008), 160–181; Murphy, *A Gathering of Rivers*; Sleeper-Smith, "Women, Kin, and Catholicism"; Richard White, *The Middle Ground* (New York: Cambridge University Press, 1991), 66–75. Instances of Native and Métis women serving as unofficial Catholic lay ministers may be found in Elizabeth T. Baird, "O-De-Jit-Wa-Win-Wing; Contes du Temps Passe," H.S. Baird Collection, Box 4, Folder 9, and Mazzuchelli, *Memoirs*.

century onward, multicultural and multiracial families had been negotiating gender-role differences. Whereas Europeans and Euro-Americans tended to believe that families should be patriarchal, that men should farm and take over leadership in government, religion, and commerce, Indian women played more active roles in politics, religious leadership, and the management of many forms of production. Creole couples' and families' compromises fell in between these traditions.[75]

Creoles valued public mothers because their actions reinforced many of the ideals and values of their own culture. The multi-ethnic nature of Creole families and communities meant that mediation and negotiation were fundamental to human behavior. Women were at the nexus of Creole families, as scholars of the fur-trade era make clear, linking immigrant men into large family, clan, and community networks. Women learned and taught their husbands and Native relatives about one another's languages, customs, beliefs, values, and expectations. They interceded with each side on behalf of the others, translated, and negotiated local and family economic matters contributing to the creation of syncretic cultures. They and their husbands raised multicultural, multilingual children who continued to have ties to both Indian and Creole communities, and they taught their daughters and sons to honor intermediaries.[76]

Creole people's ideals were distinctly communal: they built their homes close together, valued friendly cooperation, and scorned people who were argumentative. Creole communities may have been more socially cohesive than those of Anglo-Americans; *habitants* strongly valued congenial social interaction with their neighbors, as reflected in their closely spaced

---

[75] Juliette Kinzie, *Wau-Bun; The "Early Day" in the North-West* [1856] (Urbana: University of Illinois Press, 1992), 48; Donald Jackson, ed., *Black Hawk, An Autobiography* (1833; reprint, Urbana: University of Illinois Press, 1990), 104; Roger L. Nichols, *Black Hawk and the Warrior's Path* (Arlington Heights, IL: Harlan Davidson, 1992), 89; Smith, *Folklore of the Winnebago*, 155–157; Gelb, *Carver's Travels*, 69, 70; Helen Hornbeck Tanner, "Coocoochee: Mohawk Medicine Woman," *American Indian Culture and Research Journal* 3, no. 30 (1979): 23–41; Kugel, "Leadership within the Women's Community"; Nicolas Perrot, "Memoir on the Manners, Customs, and Religion of the Savages of North America," in *The Indian Tribes of the Upper Mississippi Valley and Region of the Great Lakes* [1911–1912], edited by Emma Helen Blair (Lincoln: University of Nebraska Press, 1996), Vol. I, 75; Thomas Forsyth, "Account of the Manners and Customs of the Sauk and Fox Nations of Indians Tradition," in *The Indian Tribes of the Upper Mississippi Valley and Region of the Great Lakes* [1911–1912], edited by Emma Helen Blair (Lincoln: University of Nebraska Press, 1996); and Murphy, *A Gathering of Rivers*.

[76] Peterson, "People in Between"; Van Kirk, *Many Tender Ties*; Brown, *Strangers in Blood*; Kidwell, "Indian Women as Cultural Mediators"; Sleeper-Smith, *Native Women and French Men*; and Murphy, *A Gathering of Rivers*.

village settlement patterns.[77] These attitudes evolved from communal agricultural practices, both French colonial and Native. Like their Native kin, neighbors, and customers, Creoles tended to value generosity and leisure rather than acquisitiveness, economic ambition, and excessive industriousness.[78] Because Creoles valued women and men who were community-minded, they appreciated that public mothers did more than create personal links between themselves and other individuals. These women's actions had specific meaning for the community as a whole: their efforts served social welfare and educational functions, facilitated social control, provided intergroup diplomacy, promoted peace, and served to acculturate and assimilate newcomers into the community.

## Institutionalizing Charity

Charity became institutionalized under the new regime, up to a point. The Glass family crisis, discussed in Chapter 2, demonstrated the ways that residents tried to use the new laws and governmental forms to help a family in economic distress. Individuals – Nicolas Boilvin and some army officers – gave donations, in traditional charitable behaviors. But the county commissioners first threatened to place the children with foster parents, then changed their minds and released Joseph Glass from jail so that he could work, while Michel Brisbois gave a surety bond guaranteeing that the parents would provide for the children. In the mid-1830s (as we have seen in Chapter 2) the local government was paying residents to take care of the poor, but when officials established a tax to fund this program in 1835, residents protested until the tax was reduced.

By the mid-1840s, Crawford County auctioned off its paupers. The county commission accepted bids to take care of Tunis Bell and Joseph Deschantier, and awarded contracts to the lowest bidders. At various times during 1844, one woman and five men were given contracts to care for paupers: Euphrosine Antaya Powers, three other Creoles, and two Anglos essentially took turns looking after the paupers. In 1845, four Creole men (including Bernard Brisbois and Jean Lemiry) submitted the

---

[77] Carl Ekberg, "Agriculture, *Mentalités*, and Violence on the Illinois Frontier," *Illinois Historical Journal* 88 (Summer 1995): 101–117. Ekberg suggests that this dedication to the community, based on communal agricultural practices, created an aversion to violence, in marked contrast to frontier Anglos.

[78] Ekberg, "Agriculture, *Mentalités*, and Violence"; Jacqueline Peterson, "Goodbye, Madore Beaubien: The Americanization of Early Chicago Society," *Chicago History* 9 (Summer 1980): 101.

winning bids. No doubt the wives and daughters of these contractors were involved in the paupers' care, making sure they were fed, clothed, and had clean laundry and warm bedding.[79]

This was an interesting shift in the gendering of charity, which had been a predominantly female function. The male members of the county commission decided who would get public funds to care for the indigent, while male voters weighed in on the question of a tax that would apply only to adult male residents. Although women were surely providing most of the services, wives under the system of *coverture* couldn't make contracts, so their husbands submitted the bids and signed the agreements. Euphrosine Antaya Powers, because she was a widow, was permitted to make her own contract with the commission. One can only speculate whether it was this shift in the gendering of poor relief, its institutionalization, or something else that had upset the voters in 1835.

Pokoussee and Pierre Antaya's daughter Euphrosine was also involved in another religious charitable contribution. St. Gabriel's Catholic Church was built between 1839 and 1858 on land that had belonged to Euphrosine Antaya before she married Strange Powers. Due to *coverture*, however, the deed of gift for the land was from Strange Powers to Frederick Rose, Bishop of Detroit.[80] Although historians have credited Strange Powers alone with donating the land, it seems probable that Euphrosine was at least an equal donor.[81] This was quietly recognized after Strange's death, when she was excused from paying the pew rentals expected of other parishioners.[82]

Official histories of American community development have often neglected to mention the many efforts of women. In 1987, historian Susan Armitage explained that in the West, women were extremely

---

[79] Wisconsin Territorial Papers, County Series, Crawford County, "Proceedings of the County Board of Supervisors, Nov. 29, 1821–November 19, 1850" (Madison: Wisconsin Historical Records Survey, 1941), 155, 181–208.

[80] Nov. 1, 1823, "Claims at Prairie du Chien," Woodbridge Papers, Burton Historical Collection, Detroit Public Library; Deed Book B, 159. A decade later Euphrosine signed a document relinquishing her dower right to the land. Deed Book E, 411, Crawford County, Register of Deeds Office, Prairie du Chien.

[81] Sources crediting Strange Powers: Marcella Cornford, "Saint Gabriel 1836–1986," alternate title: "1986 Directory and History of St. Gabriel the Archangel Church in Prairie du Chien, Wisconsin on the Occasion of Its Sesquicentennial" (Cleveland, TN: Majestic Marketing Associates, 1986); Marianne Luban, *Lucien Galtier, Pioneer Priest* (Ogden, UT: Pacific Moon Publications, 2010), 136.

[82] Pew rental and seating charts for 1861–62 and 1864–65, St. Gabriel's Church archives, Prairie du Chien. Thanks to Sandy Halverson for bringing these documents to my attention.

active in creating new institutions and often took leadership in drives to improve cultural and educational opportunities. She argued that women were not passive and that "They played an active role in building their communities. They selected community projects, lobbied for them, and raised money for them. But when the moment of formal organization came, the women stepped – or were pushed – back. Men were elected as officials and were often given credit for the entire enterprise. The official story and the informal story are not the same."[83] Standard histories credit the priests, Fathers Samuel Mazzuchelli and Lucien Galtier, and donors Strange Powers, Joseph Rolette, and Hercules Dousman with creating the church.[84] Church records, however, record that at least eighty-eight donors contributed.[85]

Like the new government, the Catholic Church also institutionalized charity during the late 1830s because the new building was an expensive undertaking. A number of organizations were established to help support the church, including a Ladies' Association and a Men's Association by 1839, a building committee ca. 1840, and a *"Societé de Bienfaisance"* (a Charity Society) by 1847.[86] While the first two groups were clearly segregated by gender, without detailed information about the latter two it is difficult to know whether they consisted of both women and men, but all seem to have had fundraising as one of their main activities.

Another St. Gabriel organization was initiated by the French priest Lucien Galtier, a confraternity of the Scapular, which between 1855 and 1865 admitted forty-nine members. Confraternities were organizations of lay church members that had charitable or devotional objectives, or both. Scapulars were pieces of cloth that members wore over their shoulders, either under or over their clothes.[87] Prairie du Chien's

---

[83] Susan Armitage, "Through Women's Eyes: A New View of the West," in *The Women's West*, edited by Susan Armitage and Elizabeth Jameson (Norman: University of Oklahoma Press, 1987), 13.

[84] Cornford, "Saint Gabriel;" Peter Lawrence Scanlan, *Prairie du Chien: French, British, American* (Menasha, WI: Collegiate Press, 1937), 200–201; Luban, *Lucien Galtier*.

[85] "Account of Money received to Erect a Catholic Church at Prairie du Chien" [ca. 1839], St. Gabriel's Church archives.

[86] "Account of Money received to Erect a Catholic church at Prairie du Chien" [ca. 1839]; "D'epence et Maniére que L'argent prelevé par la Societé de Bienfaisance à Etté depensé" [1847]; receipts for payment for material and labor on the church, 1839–41 in folder "Old Documents: Marriage Records and dispensations, etc." St. Gabriel's Church archives, Prairie du Chien.

[87] Charles George Herberman, *The Catholic Encyclopedia: An International Work of Reference on the Constitution, Doctrine, Discipline, and History of the Catholic Church* (Google eBook, Universal Knowledge Foundation, 1913), 13: 508–514.

Scapular confraternity may have originated as a society for English-speaking female members of St. Gabriel's who had recently arrived and who may have had difficulty participating in existing organizations dominated by French-speaking members. (A church history mentions that the priests "met with no little difficulty owing to the different languages and nationalities" of St. Gabriel's in the late nineteenth century.)[88] For the first seven years, this was an organization of mostly Irish and English women, but in 1863 the roster of names began also to include Anglophone men and Francophone Creole women and men. By 1865 when the record ends, fifteen of the forty-nine Scapular members were Creoles and the organization included eleven men (five of them Creole).[89]

These benevolent groups mentioned fleetingly in scarce church documents seem to have been gendered, at least initially. During the early years when St. Gabriel's church membership was overwhelmingly Creole, there were separate women's and men's associations, reflecting a practice one could find in Native communities around the Midwest, where economic and political life was structured according to gender. In the Northeastern states, Anglo and African American women were forming a variety of charitable groups around this time, too.[90]

Creole communities in other parts of the Midwest had women's religious and charitable organizations. At Sault Ste. Marie a Ladies' charitable organization was organized by 1828 to provide clothing for poor Indians. In 1830, a Creole Catholic women's prayer group in Green Bay sent their respects and prayers to a Mackinac women's religious organization which included Creoles.[91] These Native-descended women who organized Christian women's groups seem similar to the Ojibwe groups that historian Rebecca Kugel described for the later nineteenth century. She found that in Minnesota, Ojibwe women's politically active

---

[88] "History of Parish from beginning," manuscript, St. Gabriel's Archives. According to this document, by 1890, the church had 159 Bohemian, 138 English-Irish, 43 Germans, and 91 French families, for a total of 2281 "souls."

[89] "The Scapular," St. Gabriel's Church archives, Prairie du Chien.

[90] Nancy F. Cott, *The Bonds of Womanhood: "Woman's Sphere" in New England, 1780–1835* (New Haven, CT: Yale University Press, 1977), ch. 4.

[91] The latter group, called St. Mary's Ahmo Society, took its name from the Ojibwe word for bee and had as its main activity sewing to provide clothing for poor Indians. It may have been affiliated with St. Mary's Catholic Church there. E. S. Russell to Henry R. Schoolcraft, January 17, 1828, Schoolcraft Papers, Library of Congress, Reel 19, frame 10024; Henry Rowe Schoolcraft, *Personal Memoirs of a Residence of Thirty Years with the Indian Tribes on the American Frontiers*, Part 7 out of 15, January 17, 1828; Rosalie Dousman to Madame Laframboise, [?] October 1830, Baird Papers, Box 1, Folder 2.

traditional councils were transformed into women's church groups after the adoption of Episcopalian Christianity. These Ojibwe groups participated in community political discourse and continued seeking to influence local politics, to the dismay of male Anglo church leaders. The rare references to Catholic women's organizations at Prairie du Chien, Green Bay, Mackinac, and Sault Ste. Marie raise questions we cannot answer as yet about whether they, too, had political agendas.[92] In spite of the institutionalization of charity, of course, many Creole women continued independently to act as public mothers, to reach out to their neighbors and to strangers in need.

### Teaching and Acculturating

Clearly mediators such as these public mothers intended (whether consciously or not) to create bonds of affinity and mutual obligation between their own families and kin networks on the one hand, and the families and kin networks of those they assisted on the other hand. They were also doing what they had been taught was the right thing for people to do, "to reverence God by doing good to his creatures," as Stephen Mack interpreted the labors of his wife Hononegah. The alliances they sought were not just for themselves and their families, but for the good of their communities. As such, these were very public actions.[93]

Some Creole women reached out to newcomers and to those in need, creating ties of affection accompanied by bonds of obligation, integrating outsiders into their communities in ways that minimized socially disruptive alienation. These Creoles in greeting travelers gained information about them, then became their patrons and/or mentors, providing social welfare functions such as charity and health care. Their hosting of visitors served as a form of social control. At both the personal and intergroup levels, public mothers promoted peace.

Public mothering also served educational functions. Customs of hospitality passed from parent to child in this region, but the hospitable tradition could also be passed from host to immigrant as a form of socialization or acculturation by demonstrated behavior. As such, women like

---

[92] Kugel, "Leadership within the Women's Community," 17–37. Interestingly, Father Samuel Mazzuchelli, the priest who ministered to the region, did not mention these groups in his memoir, though he did acknowledge Métis women's important roles as cathechists. This suggests that the women's groups were self-initiated rather than organized by the priest or the church. Mazzuchelli, *Memoirs*.

[93] Thorne, "For the Good of Her People."

Archange LaBathe Reed were not only integrating strangers into the group but also modeling appropriate behavior.

Furthermore, public mothering was educational in that it facilitated cross-cultural learning, as both helpers and helped gained knowledge from their contacts with each other. Contacts between Creole healers, hostesses, and charity workers, and their beneficiaries, could dispel suspicion, ignorance, and intolerance. In addition, some Creole women educated their neighbors in religious traditions.

Some women of mixed Ho-Chunk and French Canadian ancestry served as lay ministers, according to Father Samuel Mazzuchelli. He explained that several of them, "having some knowledge of Christian doctrine and speaking the tribal language, would make their way into the lodges to speak of religion."[94] This evangelizing was similar to the actions of Elizabeth Baird's mother Marianne Lasallière Fisher and great-aunt Madeleine Laframboise in northern Michigan. Fisher translated Catholic texts into Odawa, and Laframboise was active in promoting Catholicism, serving as a lay minister to teach church doctrines to many women and girls in the area. Laframboise regretted that she had not received an education, so she hired tutors for other young women and encouraged them to attend school.[95]

## The Focus of Relationships

Challenges abounded for the old fur-trade families during the nineteenth century. As they became minorities in their hometowns, they lost status and economic and political control, and were disparaged by the ascendant newcomers as ignorant and "perfectly destitute of ambition or worthy pride." There was a real need to adapt mediation skills in order to smooth relations with the Anglos and European immigrants.

Marriage had been one way to create ties. Indian peoples in the Midwest had approved of – and even encouraged – intermarriage. Although Native women who married Euro-Americans during the fur-trade era facilitated peaceful and productive personal and economic relations between the two groups, after the War of 1812, Indian and mixed-ancestry wives often mediated among three cultures: Indian, Creole, and the Anglophone colonizers from the eastern United States. Many wives served as translators and cultural interpreters for neighbors, husbands, kin, and whole communities.

[94] Mazzuchelli, *Memoirs*, 83.
[95] Elizabeth T. Baird, "O-De-Jit-Wa-Win-Wing."

Some Creoles created links by promoting and arranging marriages between their children and Anglo immigrants. These marriages honored the Indian custom of incorporating outsiders into families and communities through marriage and mirror the historical experiences of some Spanish-speaking families in California and Texas during the transition to U.S. hegemony around the time of the Mexican War.[96]

But few Anglos married Native and Creole women; the decline in exogamy reduced opportunities for people to gain linguistic and cultural tools needed to create alliances. Even so, many Creoles responded to colonization by continuing to mediate not only between Indians and Creoles but also between these two groups and the immigrants. Indeed, the decrease in intermarriage in the face of surging Anglo immigration created a greater need for informal mediation within a community; public mothering thus seems to have created other bonds.

Jennifer S. H. Brown's research on Métis people in nineteenth-century Rupert's Land suggested that women were "centre and symbol in the emergence of Métis communities." She discussed evidence of "matriorganization," including matrilocality, matrilineality, and the transmission of crucial economic skills between female kin, patterns which are also apparent in the Midwest.[97] Brown also suggested that Canadian Métis families were "matrifocal," which means, according to Raymond T. Smith, who also found this pattern in some African families, that women were central to "economic and decision-making coalition[s]" with economically productive children, "whether the husband-father is present or not."[98] This pattern seems to have been the case with some Creole families at Prairie du Chien, such as those of Pokoussee, Angelique Brisbois Pion, and Mannetese. Smith also explained that in these types of kinship systems, "it is the women *in their role as mothers* who come to be the *focus* of relationships, rather than the head of household as such."[99] Many Creole women seem to have expanded their influence beyond their immediate families' economic concerns, using the Creoles'

---

[96] Darlis Miller, "Cross-Cultural Marriages in the Southwest: The New Mexico Experience, 1846–1900," *New Mexico Historical Review* 57 (1982): 335–359; Antonia Castañeda, "Presidarias y pobladoras: Spanish-Mexican Women in Frontier Monterey, Alta California, 1770–1821" (Ph.D. diss., Stanford University, 1990); Douglas Monroy, *Thrown among Strangers: The Making of Mexican Culture in Frontier California* (Berkeley: University of California Press, 1990).

[97] Jennifer S. H. Brown, "Woman as Centre and Symbol in the Emergence of Métis Communities," *Canadian Journal of Native Studies* 3, no. 1 (1983): 39–46.

[98] Raymond T. Smith, "The Matrifocal Family," in *The Character of Kinship*, edited by Jack Goody (London: Cambridge University Press, 1973), 121–144.

[99] Smith, "Matrifocal Family."

understanding of the mature mother's role to link neighbors as well as kin to each other.

Women's mediation during the fur-trade era conforms to Margaret Connell Szasz's concept of "the cultural broker." Although circumstances encouraged people to serve as intermediaries, Szasz argues that people were motivated by personality traits, including a particular "receptiveness" to cultural forms of "the other."[100] This cultural sensitivity bears a striking resemblance to the sensitivity evident in good healers and good mothers. Some scholars argue that women are both more empathetic and better able than men to interpret both the verbal and nonverbal expressions of others, suggesting that women develop these skills both because as mothers, they need to respond to infants, and as oppressed people, their survival may depend upon their accurate observations of dominant men. This sensitivity, it is argued, helps women to be good healers. These contemporary observations may apply to the nineteenth-century Midwest.[101]

If they were doubly oppressed – as women and as minorities – were they doubly sensitive? As people living in fur-trade communities founded expressly to link indigenous and alien cultures, they had been reared observing negotiation and mediation, hearing it praised, perhaps even trained in it. When the balance of power shifted as the United States colonized the region, the roles of women – especially Native-descended women – became increasingly at risk. Creoles' history suggested that these issues might be negotiable, as they had been during the fur-trade era.

## Conclusion

No doubt Creole people attempted a variety of forms of negotiation, public mothering being only one of them. Probably there were some efforts that failed and others that succeeded but were not publicly lauded. Racism could cause failure, particularly within religious institutions, according to several studies. For example, young Creole women in Midwestern Protestant mission schools aspired to leadership that could have allowed them to serve as intermediaries as teachers, missionaries, and interpreters, but white Anglo missionaries tried to channel women of color into

---

[100] Margaret Connell Szasz, ed., *Between Indian and White Worlds; The Cultural Broker* (Norman: University of Oklahoma Press, 1994), 295–296.
[101] Bobette Perrone, H. Henrietta Stockel, and Victoria Krueger, *Medicine Women, Curanderas, and Women Doctors* (Norman: University of Oklahoma Press, 1989), 4–5.

positions as domestic servants. However, there were opportunities for Creole women to serve Catholic communities in leadership positions, both informally and formally, and they used their roles as godmothers to create and reinforce fictive kin networks.[102] This may help to explain why many Creole people rejected Protestant missions, reaffirming their ties to the Catholic Church to such effect as to cause a nineteenth-century renaissance of Catholicism in the Midwest.[103]

The behaviors of Creole public mothers and the extent to which their efforts were appreciated and even valorized teach us that they actively reached out to their communities, and that in doing so, they had found a middle ground among the various ideals of womanhood held by the region's people. The fact that they found this intersection testifies to the continuation of Creole traditions of mediation. For the Creole people of the Midwest, the nineteenth century was a transitional era, and they experienced the imposition of increasing restrictions on women. The tribes and individuals who might be seen as non-white were at risk in the face of settler in-migration, new government policies, and economic changes. As mediators, many Creoles responded to such changes by continuing activities of negotiation, learning, and adaptation. A decrease in exogamy reduced one tool of mediation, but Creoles explored others. Some Creole women expanded the roles available to them by their matrifocal culture in which women's activities could be at once public and private, concerned with family and household while also for the benefit of the community. In the actions of hostesses, midwives, healers, and other caring neighbors, we see Creole communalism expressed by mature women creating and extending matrifocal networks. Their new Anglo neighbors – people who had themselves emigrated from transitional cultures – were particularly receptive to these women of color whose actions conformed to their evolving feminine and communalistic ideals.

These Creole women nurtured their neighbors, acting as public mothers to mediate among disparate groups in a multi-ethnic region. Their actions were in the best traditions of Native American, African American, and Euro-American women's activism. Although Creoles were frequently scorned for their perceived cultural, ethnic, racial, and economic differences, some Creole women succeeded in reaching across the cultural

---

[102] Kugel, "Re-Working Ethnicity"; Sleeper-Smith, "Women, Kin, and Catholicism"; Baird, "O-De-Jit-Wa-Win-Wing"; and Mazzuchelli, *Memoirs*.

[103] Keith R. Widder, *Battle for the Soul: Metis Children Encounter Evangelical Protestants at Mackinaw Mission, 1823–1837* (East Lansing: Michigan State University Press, 1999).

divides by navigating the intersections of gender ideals. In these ways they resisted the creation of hardened racial categories and helped to prevent the establishment of a monolithic non-white outsider category that could be used to permanently stigmatize and ostracize the *habitants*. Their actions were of central importance in determining the roles of Creoles in a changing community.

# 5

## "A Humble ... People"

### Economic Adaptations

When he was an old man, Antoine Grignon fondly remembered his child-hood in Prairie du Chien (Figure 5.1). Born there in 1828 to mother Archange LaBathe, who was Dakota and French, and Amable Grignon, who was Ho-Chunk and French, he grew up during the 1830s and early 1840s, a time of change for the community.[1] Nostalgia brought to mind Prairie du Chien in its fur-trade heyday. Grignon told an interviewer in 1904, "In looking over the departed years, I can see Prairie du Chien as it was when I played along its streets as a boy. The strange, wild life of the hunters, traders, and trappers thrilled me, and I was often on hand to see the fleets of canoes from the northland with their throng of painted Indians or, to see the voyageurs arrive with their bateaux of furs."[2]

Within a generation of his birth, scenes like this would become rare. Within a decade, Creoles became a minority in Prairie du Chien. During the first three decades of Grignon's life, Indian removal, fur-trade decline, Anglo-Yankee and European immigration, and commercial and occupa-tional changes added to the difficulties Creole voters, officials, and jurors faced (challenges discussed in Chapters 2 and 3). As Creoles' political

---

[1] Linda M. Waggoner, ed., *"Neither White Men nor Indians": Affidavits from the Winnebago Mixed-Blood Claim Commissions, Prairie du Chien, Wisconsin, 1838–1839* (Roseville, MN: Park Genealogical Books, 2002), 15–16; Eben D. Pierce, "The Recollections of Antoine Grignon," *Proceedings of the State Historical Society of Wisconsin* (1904): 173–177; Fred L. Holmes, "Early Wisconsin Industry Was Chiefly Fur Trading Up to Time of Territory," *Wisconsin State Journal*, Jan. 13, 1924; "Tells of Early Days on River," *Milwaukee Sentinel*, Dec. 7, 1902; E. D. Pierce, "When Trempealeau Was in the Wilds; The Days of Antoine Grignon, Fur Trader," *Galesville Republican*, April 25, 1929. The last three articles are available online at the website of the Wisconsin Historical Society.

[2] Holmes, "Early Wisconsin Industry."

FIGURE 5.1. Prairie du Chien in 1836. Wisconsin Historical Society, Image ID 41976.

authority declined, they sought ways to maintain as much economic autonomy as possible. They had to decide whether to stay and adapt or to move away, following the Native people and fur trade or looking for other opportunities to the north and west. This chapter focuses on the economic winds of change and the ways that some Creoles weathered these storms.

The old *habitants* coped in a number of ways. Former fur-trade workers and their families had to adapt their means of making their living if they chose not to move. Many explored wage labor, self-employment, and creative domestic economies. Most came to think of themselves as farmers, assimilating into the evolving agricultural sector of the economy. Some new French Canadian immigrants joined the community, usually as farmers.

### "From Far and Near to Trade": Before the Deluge

Antoine Grignon's nostalgia was for the community during the 1830s before the economic changes of subsequent years would significantly alter the community. His reminiscences can help us to visualize life on the island section of Prairie du Chien, one of four geographic areas that would by mid-century also include neighborhoods known as Frenchtown, Upper Town, and Lower Town. During his childhood, Grignon lived and spent much of his playtime on the island.[3] His father died when he was eight years old in 1836, and his mother would later marry James Reed, the tavern keeper.

Clearly describing life *on the island* section of the community during the 1830s, Grignon explained the town's role as a fur-trade depot. "Indians came from far and near to trade at Prairie du Chien, which was in reality a big post with stores and warehouses belonging principally to the American Fur company. From the north, the region along Minnesota and Chippewa rivers, and the upper Mississippi, came the Sioux, Winnebago, Chippewa and Menominee. Down the Wisconsin came bands of Indians belonging to different tribes. The Iowa, Sauk and Foxes came from the river below Prairie du Chien. The Indians traveled mostly by river in canoes, but a few came on ponies, afoot, and horseback from the interior."[4] Grignon's colorful memoir describes flotillas of between fifteen and forty canoes bringing a wide range of products to trade, including "furs, wild game, and pemmican made out of clean, fat venison pounded to pulp, or of buffalo meat.... Venison and buffalo meat that had been jerked, scorched and smoked. They likewise brought baskets, mats, wild honey, maple sugar, berries in season, and dried lotus-root, which when cooked tasted like a potato." Besides the mats and baskets, Native people brought other crafts including moccasins; buckskin; brooms made of birch, hickory, or ash; and sets of bows and arrows that appealed especially to the young white boys. Grignon commented, "With these commodities they bought or secured in barter flour, pork, coffee, tobacco, blankets, hatchets, knives, dress-goods, ribbons, ammunition and trinkets of many kinds."[5]

Having arrived at the old rendezvous grounds, Native customers did not leave right away. "These bands of Indians would remain a week or two to trade at Prairie du Chien and the surrounding neighborhood," Grignon explained. "While there they would feast and dance and enjoy life that had a tinge of civilization in it. You could hear the tom-tom beating all night when a dance was in progress."[6]

But these years were also a time of important events and demographic shifts that would bring change to the region. The Winnebago Revolt of

---

[3] Tax List 1843, Fort Crawford Museum archives, Prairie du Chien.
[4] Holmes, "Early Wisconsin Industry."
[5] Holmes, "Early Wisconsin Industry."
[6] Holmes, "Early Wisconsin Industry."

1827 and the Black Hawk War of 1832 traumatized all the people of the region in one way or other, through fear, anger, and – for some – direct experience with the violence that left over 500 Indians and over eighty non-Native people dead.[7]

### The Winnebago Revolt and the Black Hawk War

South of the Wisconsin River was a region rich in deposits of lead ore which Ho-Chunk, Meskwaki, and Sauk people had been mining for a long time and marketing to Euro-American traders since the late eighteenth century. When Anglo miners from the United States intruded into the mining region during the 1820s, Indian-white relations soured, leading to two violent conflicts that would affect Prairie du Chien.[8] The year 1827 was a tense one in Prairie because troops had been moved from Fort Crawford to Fort Snelling in Minnesota in 1826 just when conflicts between Ho-Chunks and Euro-American lead miners were heating up. In the early spring, a Creole family had been mysteriously murdered west of the Mississippi while making maple sugar, putting everyone on edge. In a separate incident, a group of Ho-Chunks responding to Anglo aggression in the lead district to the south and to rumors that Ho-Chunk prisoners at Fort Snelling had been killed, attacked the Gagnier family south of Prairie du Chien, killed Registe Gagnier and retired soldier Solomon Lipcap, and injured a baby. Then on June 30, when an Army keel boat passed north of the Prairie staffed by men who had reportedly abducted several Ho-Chunk women, a party of Ho-Chunks attacked. Two American soldiers were killed and ten or twelve Ho-Chunks died.[9]

In April of 1832, a group of about 1,100 Sauks and Meskwakis who had been forced to move west across the Mississippi River the previous year decided to come back to settle in a Ho-Chunk village at the latter's invitation. This "British Band" under Black Hawk included women and children in addition to about 500 warriors, who soon found that about 7,000 American soldiers and militiamen were sent to put down what

---

[7] Patrick J. Jung, *The Black Hawk War of 1832* (Norman: University of Oklahoma Press, 2007), 173; Peter Lawrence Scanlan, *Prairie du Chien: French, British, American* (Menasha, WI: Collegiate Press, 1937), 129–133.

[8] An extended study of this topic can be found in Lucy Eldersveld Murphy, *A Gathering of Rivers: Indians, Métis, and Mining in the Western Great Lakes, 1737–1832* (Lincoln: University of Nebraska Press, 2000), chs. 3–5.

[9] Scanlan, *Prairie du Chien: French, British, American*, 129–133, 161.

their leaders saw as an Indian insurrection. A number of battles and skir-
mishes ensued over the course of three months as the British Band first
tried to surrender and when attacked, fled through northwestern Illinois
and southwestern Wisconsin. At least half of these Indians lost their lives
before the events ended with the band's defeat and Black Hawk's surrender at Prairie du Chien.[10] Some of Prairie du Chien's residents served
as militia members, interpreters, a home guard, or in other capacities
in these conflicts, which terrified everyone in the region: Indian, Creole,
and Anglo.

The U.S. government responded to these events with increased pressure for Indian removal in the area, causing hardship for Native people
and their kin and traders. Furthermore, non-Native men from outside the
area who arrived with their militia units to put down the Indian resistance were enticed by the beauty and economic opportunities that the
lovely river region offered. After the pacification, some would come back
to settle, and others would invest in the idea of future settlement, specu-
lating in Prairie du Chien land during the late 1830s. Spikes in real estate
values offered opportunities for landed Creoles to cash in on their property and to move on if they chose.[11]

Yet change seemed slow to some people. During the late autumn
of 1836, J. H. Lamotte, an American stationed with the army at Fort
Crawford, wrote to a friend about Prairie du Chien, "Still the future city
of the prairie presents an unbroken aspect and still remains in that quiet
comatose state which has so long been its peculiar feature. Perhaps, on
this very spot, the hum of myriads and the confusion of a busy city may
one day greet the Traveller on the Upper Mississippi, but that you or I
will be bless'd with the vision is absolutely doubtful, I think."[12] During
the following quarter of a century, however, hum and confusion did come
to the Prairie.

## More or Less Indians at His House

Native and mixed-ancestry residents were still important members of the
community during the 1830s as made clear by testimony taken following
a treaty with the Ho-Chunk people. The treaty of 1837 had forced land
cessions but set aside money for the "half-breed" and "quarter-breed"

---

[10] Jung, *The Black Hawk War of 1832*.
[11] Scanlan, *Prairie du Chien*, 199–200.
[12] J. H. LaMotte, to – – Beaumont, November 16, 1836, Beaumont Collection, Missouri
Historical Society, St. Louis.

tribal members, and commissioners took testimony from the applicants themselves and from their neighbors about them. While one must take into consideration that most of those testifying hoped the applications for funds would be approved and thus accentuated applicants' worthiness or need, the comments do provide interesting details about some Ho-Chunk and Sauk residents of Prairie du Chien and the range of their circumstances.

When the Native visitors Antoine Grignon described came to town, they stayed with kin and friends, including his own family. His father Amable was the son of Echauwaukah, a sister of Ho-Chunk Decorrah chiefs, and as a nephew of chiefs, Amable was someone the tribe expected to provide hospitality. After Amable's death in 1836, Antoine's mother Archange Labathe (whose own mother had been Dakota) shared her home and resources with visitors from her late husband's Ho-Chunk tribe. A neighbor testified that she "is very kind and hospitable to the Indians, at all times making them comfortable as in her power, and that her home is always considered their home."[13] According to the local tax records, that home included a large lot and house worth $600 in the main village on the island.[14] Archange thus was in a good situation to serve as a public mother.

To further illustrate, Michel St. Cyr, the son of Hyacinth St. Cyr and Keenokou (daughter of an important Ho-Chunk chiefly family), also opened his home to tribal kin and friends. He had traded with the tribe at the Four Lakes, the region that became Madison, the Wisconsin territorial capital. St. Cyr had served the U.S. army during the Black Hawk War as an interpreter and "went on express on several occasions," that is, delivering messages. As the son of Keenokou, Michel also provided the hospitality of a cultural mediator. Living in Prairie du Chien in the late 1830s, he testified

that towards the Indians he has always extended the hand of hospitality and friendship – "That they have slept at his fire and eat at his board." That his home is their home when they visit this place, and that the necessaries of life are always divided with them – It frequently happened, that during the whole year he has more or less Indians at his house.[15]

Among them were not only his own sons Michel Jr. and Augustus, but also a Ho-Chunk woman named Seeaskah and her son Lewis Wood Jr.,

[13] Waggoner, *"Neither White Men nor Indians,"* 16.
[14] 1843 tax list.
[15] Waggoner, *"Neither White Men nor Indians,"* 39.

age three.[16] Indeed, the 1840 census showed him with a household of fourteen persons, including ten adults.[17]

### No Longer Able to Bear This State of Things

During the three decades from the 1830s through the 1850s, the U.S. government's project of removing the Indians caused suffering among the tribes that spilled over into the lives of Prairie du Chien's Creoles. At the same time, declines in the peltry business affected fur-trade workers and others whose livelihoods had been tied to this commerce and their families as well. The economic focus of the community shifted significantly. Nearby tribes were forced to relocate to the west, and in 1849, the troops stationed at Fort Crawford left for Fort Snelling in Minnesota and Fort Leavenworth in Kansas.[18] Many townspeople who had earned their living supplying the fort or the Indian trade had to decide whether to follow the troops or the tribes, or to stay and change the ways they earned their keep.

Tribal disruptions took a personal toll on some Prairie du Chien residents, as revealed by the treaty-related affidavits. The arrival of large numbers of Euro-Americans and Europeans had caused significant problems for tribal communities in the area, including intrusions into hunting, gathering, and planting areas. These were exacerbated by epidemic diseases, violence, and cultural challenges posed by missionaries and government agents. The violence of the Winnebago Revolt and the Black Hawk War traumatized Native and non-Native people. Indian removal affected all the tribes in the region.

Native people living near Prairie du Chien were moved farther and farther westward during the period from the 1820s through mid-century. After the Black Hawk War of 1832, the nearby Sauk and Meskwaki people were forced west of the Mississippi to central Iowa, until 1845 when they were removed to Kansas.[19] The government forced other tribes in the region of southern and central Wisconsin to sign treaties during the

---

[16] Waggoner, *"Neither White Men nor Indians,"* 58.

[17] Population Schedules of the Sixth Census of the United States, 1840, manuscript, microfilm, Reel 580, Crawford County, 6.

[18] Bruce E. Mahan, *Old Fort Crawford and the Frontier* [1926] (reprint, Prairie du Chien: Howe Printing, 2000), 240.

[19] William T. Hagan, *The Sac and Fox Indians* (Norman: University of Oklahoma Press, 1958), 80–81, 205–232, 261. During the 1850s, about 100 Meskwakis, unhappy with the situation in Kansas, returned to Iowa and bought land to establish a community at Tama. (Later on, in 1869, the Kansas members of the Sac and Fox Tribe were moved from Kansas to Indian Territory, but about 200 joined their relatives in Tama.)

late 1820s and 1830s, insisting that they move westward. This included the Ho-Chunk, Odawa, Potawatomi, Ojibwe, and Dakota people.[20] (See map, Figure 3.1 in Chapter 3.) Ho-Chunks occupied a reservation from 1832 to 1846 just west of the Mississippi River very near Prairie du Chien, then were moved to central Minnesota, before being moved again in 1855, and farther west in 1863. A Dakota reservation directly west of the Mississippi River and about 100 miles north of Prairie du Chien lasted only from 1830 to 1851, after which the Dakotas were forced to migrate farther west.[21] Smallpox epidemics in the region ravaged Native and non-Native residents alike during 1832–36, but the mortality among Native people was twice that of the settler population, the Indians losing as much as one third of their populations. In addition, the cholera epidemics of 1832–34 affected some of the Native communities, adding to the grief of removal.[22]

Many Creole people living in Prairie du Chien were traumatized by the violence, disruptions, removals, and epidemics. For example, Mahnahteesee lived in Prairie du Chien with several of her children, the youngest of whom was a son Alexis, age fifteen. She was a sister of the Ho-Chunk Decorah chiefs and probably the granddaughter of Glory of the Morning, an important female chief of the Ho-Chunk tribe.[23] Her first husband Jean L'Ecuyer had died in 1809. The two of them had resided (and probably traded) at the Portage and perhaps for a while at Green Bay.[24] The widow, left with four children, had a relationship with Augustin Grignon and became the mother of two more. Finally, she moved to Prairie du Chien and married Michel Payeur (aka Payet), with whom she had a son, but Michel went off to the west and did not return.

In 1839, six prominent men (including Hercules Dousman) testified that Mahnahteesee had acculturated to Euro-American culture after she married L'Ecuyer: "Madame Lequyér soon adopted much of the manners

[20] Nancy Oestreich Lurie, *Wisconsin Indians* (Madison: State Historical Society of Wisconsin, 1987), 18–19.

[21] Helen Hornbeck Tanner, ed., *Atlas of Great Lakes Indian History* (Norman: University of Oklahoma Press, 1987), 164–167; Lurie, *Wisconsin Indians*, 18–20.

[22] Helen Hornbeck Tanner, ed., *Atlas of Great Lakes Indian History* (Norman: University of Oklahoma Press, 1986), 173–174; J. H. Lamotte to William Beaumont, September 2, 1836, Beaumont Collection, Missouri Historical Society, St. Louis.

[23] [Henry S. Baird?], "A Famous French-Winnebago Resident," Henry S. Baird Papers, Box 4, Folder 4, State Historical Society of Wisconsin, 2. [The person referenced was also known as Madame Lequyer, Therese Payeur, and Monatice.]

[24] Waggoner, *"Neither White Men Nor Indians,"* 6–7, 30–32; Les and Jeanne Rentmeester, *The Wisconsin Creoles* (Melbourne, FL: Privately published, 1987), 244–245.

& customs of White people, and became a good & discreet housekeeper, & exemplary wife, thus exercising, by her example, a beneficial influence over the Indians."[25] She and Jean had apparently been successful as traders and farmers, as the men stated that "when she was left a widow ... about thirty some years since, they had a fine lot of goods, horses, wagons, fine stock of cattle, and was considered wealthy."[26]

Mahnahteesee had followed Native and Creole custom by serving as a public mother, welcoming tribal members to her home. As we have seen, Native people expected their elite families to be especially generous and hospitable, and the Ho-Chunks were no exception. So, "having plenty in the world, her house was called the home of the naked & hungry Indian," according to Dousman and the others, so much so that her wealth was depleted to assist tribal members who were suffering as a result of illness and economic disruptions caused by land loss, Anglo intrusions, and violence. Dousman and the others explained that Mahnahteesee's "farm stock, with all her valuable property left by her deceased husband, was sacrificed in support or harboring of Winnebago Indians, who applied to her in all cases for relief, as being the hospitable sister of their principal chiefs."[27]

Julia Grignon was Mahnahteesee's fifth child and youngest daughter, and unlucky in love. In 1828, when she was about fifteen years old and living at the Portage of the Fox and Wisconsin rivers, Fort Winnebago had been built there under the leadership of Major David Twiggs (the man whose report to President Jackson cost Judge Doty his job). Julia apparently had a relationship with him resulting in the birth of her son David Twiggs Jr.[28] It is unlikely that Major Twiggs took a paternal interest in his namesake. Unable to support her child, Julia gave him to her brother Jacques L'Ecuyer and his wife Margaret Brunette, when David was about one year old. They lived in the Green Bay area.[29] Julia told the commissioners that "the father of Said David Twiggs has not been herd [*sic*] from for several years, & that he is supposed to be dead."[30]

At Prairie du Chien in 1839, Julia was about twenty-six years old and separated from her husband, Christopher Antaya, "an habitual

[25] Waggoner, *"Neither White Men nor Indians,"* 31.

[26] Waggoner, *"Neither White Men nor Indians,"* 31.

[27] Waggoner, *"Neither White Men nor Indians,"* 31.

[28] [Henry S. Baird?], "A Famous French-Winnebago Resident," 1.

[29] Waggoner, *"Neither White Men nor Indians,"* 50–52.

[30] Waggoner, *"Neither White Men nor Indians,"* 32.

drunkard." The friends who testified for her stated that "Julia has generally lived with her mother as her friend & companion, & they have continued to extend kindness and hospitality to the Indians to the fullest extent or beyond their ability." Julia's house at Prairie du Chien had been "the resting place of the Winnebagoes when in the Village." Julia and her mother had tried to help their tribesmen, but the suffering had become overwhelming. "Julia Grignon has given her last loaf of bread to hungry Indians, & on some occasions *sold her own clothes to relieve their distress*. The mother and daughter, no longer able to bear this state of things, are now living with the brother," Dousman and the others testified. Apparently, this was Mahnahteesee's son Simeon L'Ecuyer, who was thirty-three years old and had recently moved with two small children to Prairie du Chien from Tete des Mort.[31]

Another local family affected by the tribulations of the 1830s included little Mary Ann Mitchell and her mother Ukseeharkar (who was Ho-Chunk and Sauk), who had barely escaped with their lives at the end of the Black Hawk War. They were among approximately 500 Indians trying desperately to retreat during the Battle of Bad Axe, swimming across the Mississippi River while hundreds of U.S. troops fired on them. Ukseeharkar pushed her pony into the river, hoisted her four-year-old daughter on her back, and swam desperately amid the whizzing bullets and artillery fire for the western shore as her horse drowned. Unlike over 260 of the other Indians who were killed during the massacre, Ukseeharkar and Mary Ann managed to survive.[32]

A year later, Ukseeharkar indentured her daughter Mary Ann as an "apprentice" to Lieutenant Thomas Hill of the U.S. army, stationed at Fort Crawford.[33] The mother, now a student at the Winnebago school, had asked the Indian agent to have her daughter Mary Ann Mitchell "bound to some respectable person who would have her brought up as a white person," and said "she had selected Lieut. Hill for that purpose."[34] The contract promised that Mary Ann would be taught the "arts of domestic industry and housewifery according to the improvements of civilized life so far as she shall be capable of receiving instruction," and

---

[31] Waggoner, "*Neither White Men nor Indians*," 31, 33. Simeon L'Ecuyer is on the 1843 tax list with personal property worth $100 and a building worth $300.

[32] Jung, *The Black Hawk War of 1832*, 170–174; Ida M. Ferris, "The Sauks and Foxes in Franklin and Osage Counties, Kansas," *Collections of the Kansas State Historical Society*, vol. XI, 1909–1910, 333–395, 355.

[33] Also spelled Uxcharkar, Uxehackar.

[34] Waggoner, "*Neither White Men nor Indians*," 57.

that Thomas M. Hill agreed to "treat her at all times with humanity and kindness, and teach her to read and write."[35]

Mary Ann lived with Hill's family until Mrs. Hill died and the army transferred the lieutenant. Mary Ann was then sent to the Winnebago school for a time until at age nine her indenture was taken over by Dr. Joseph Moore, an army physician residing at Fort Crawford, and his wife Eliza. No doubt Mary Ann's labor contributed to the housework for the families with which she lived. It is unclear whether she was considered more of a servant or a family member, but the indenture promised that she would remain with the Moores until she was age eighteen.[36] No mention of Mary Ann's father appeared in the testimony. After the ordeal at the Bad Axe, we may wonder what the psychological impact on Mary Ann was of being transferred from mother to first one and then another set of masters. And what circumstances caused Ukseeharkar to feel she needed to place her child with others rather than raise Mary Ann herself? Clearly the mother and daughter had been traumatized by the war. Ukseeharkar continued in 1839 to live at the school and model farm at Yellow River.[37] Placing her child with a "white" family and staying at the school were ways to avoid removal and violence, at least for a while.[38]

Yet another example of the tragedies of the Indian removal era may be found in the family of Thérèse Crelie Paquette, a Sauk and French granddaughter of Pokoussee and Pierre Antaya. She had moved to Prairie du Chien from the Portage of the Fox and Wisconsin Rivers where she had lived with her former husband, trader Pierre Paquette, whose Ho-Chunk mother, Ho A Me No Kau, was the sister of the Rock River Band's principal chief, White Crow. Thérèse had been living in Prairie du Chien with her two children on land that had been patented to Pierre who had lost the land. Thérèse testified after his death in 1836 that because of the smallpox epidemic and the hardships it caused for the Ho-Chunk people,

---

[35] Waggoner, *"Neither White Men nor Indians,"* 56. It was located "in the Neutral Ground on the north side of the Yellow River below the bluff, about three miles above the United States sawmill." Mary Elise Antoine, "Winnebago School on the Yellow River, 1832–1840, a Focus of Cultural Contact," in *Cross Currents: The Intersection of Native and European American Cultures in Southwest Wisconsin,* edited by Geoffrey M. Gyrisco, Proceedings of the Tippesaukee Symposium 2003 (Blue River, WI: Friends of Tippesaukee, 2005), 95–106.

[36] Waggoner, *"Neither White Men nor Indians,"* 55–57.

[37] Waggoner, *"Neither White Men nor Indians,"* 56.

[38] Joseph Moore received $1,000 from treaty monies for Mary Ann Mitchell and invested it in 1842 by loaning it to Levi R. Marsh at 7 percent interest "until she shall become of full age." Part of Farm Lot 32 secured the loan. Mortgage Book A, Crawford County Register of Deeds Office, Prairie du Chien.

Pierre went into debt to help the Indians and had to sell his property at Prairie du Chien to pay his creditors.[39] Thérèse testified and the leading men of the region affirmed that Pierre, who had served as a government interpreter, had "rendered misc. services and more assistance to the Indians than any other half breed of the Nation – Was always exceedingly kind and generous to them on all occasions. In addition,

In 1836 when the Small Pox was raging among the Tribe of Winnebagoes after he had given all he had to them, he exhausted his credit at this place in purchasing the necessaries of life for them, and then traveled into far distance places, purchasing supplies for them by which means, the lives of many were saved, who must, had it not been for his unceasing efforts, have perished from famine and disease – And by these his acts of unbounded philanthropy and liberality, which he saved the lives of hundreds – he utterly & completely ruined his own fortune and that of his children, as for the very debts he contracted for supplies given to the Indians. The property which he left behind him has been sold, and his wife & children left dependent for their support.[40]

After all of these efforts to save the Ho-Chunks, Pierre had been murdered, and Thérèse lost her home.

These glimpses into the experiences of Creole families reveal some of the difficulties they faced as a result of tribal disruptions, the presence of transient populations, and economic uncertainty. Euro-American husbands deserted their wives at a time when tribal disruptions left these women with little support available from friends or family. An army officer fathered a child and left a teenage mother unable to care for her baby; another mother traumatized by war felt compelled to give her young daughter up as an indentured "apprentice," absent the child's father. A fur trader went off to the west, deserting his Native wife and children. Alcoholism disrupted one family; many others did all they could to help their Native kin whose needs were extreme, even to the point of exhausting their own resources. Even some of the elite and more comfortable families were overwhelmed by the suffering and poverty of so many tribal members facing settler encroachment, epidemics, and forced removal. These difficulties help to explain why some of the Native-descended Creoles moved away.

Because some officials alleged that fraud in the distribution of treaty funds had fattened the bank accounts of several attorneys-in-fact and

---

[39] Waggoner, "*Neither White Men nor Indians*," 5; on Paquette genealogy, Rentmeesters, *Wisconsin Creoles*, 316–317; J. H. Lamotte to William Beaumont, September 2, 1836, Beaumont Collection, Missouri Historical Society, St. Louis.

[40] Waggoner, "*Neither White Men nor Indians*," 5.

guardians at the expense of naïve "half-breed" Ho-Chunks, an investigation delayed payment into 1839 and the early 1840s. Eventually Julia Grignon, Antoine Grignon, the Lecuyers, David Twiggs Jr., Alexis Payeur, the Paquette children, and Mary Ann Mitchell each received a few hundred dollars as settlements from the treaty of 1837.[41] Most of them seem to have moved away within a few years, apparently unable or unwilling to transform these funds into lands or other resources that could provide a foothold on the Prairie, or unsure that if they stayed, their fractured families would be able to support themselves. The payments did little to help them. Broken families, traumatized by the violence, poverty, and disease of the Indian removal projects, depleted their resources and felt they had to look elsewhere for sustenance.

### Decline of the Fur Trade

The American Fur Company's (AFC) post at Prairie du Chien would decline in importance as the tribes whose members hunted and trapped and processed furs were removed farther and farther away, and as the animal populations declined. As a result, fur-trade leaders Joseph Rolette and Hercules Dousman diversified their business pursuits between 1834 and 1854, shifting into flour mills, lumbering, banking, general merchandising, steamboat and railroad lines, and land speculation.[42] After John Jacob Astor retired and the American Fur Company reorganized in 1834, Joseph Rolette – who had formerly managed the AFC's Western Outfit (later called the Upper Mississippi Outfit) by himself – became partner with Hercules Dousman and Henry Sibley, trading in southern and western Wisconsin and along the Mississippi and its western tributaries from Iowa to southern Minnesota.[43] By 1840, however, the fur trade was suffering. Dousman complained in a letter that "times have never been so hard on this river since it was settled."[44]

Joseph Rolette's wealth in real estate was divided when he legally separated from his wife Jane Fisher Rolette, much of it going to her cousin

---

[41] Waggoner, "*Neither White Men nor Indians*," 101–114, 117–120. The investigation was inconclusive: no fraud was proven.

[42] Peter Scanlan, "Jean Joseph Rolette," Scanlan Papers, Platteville Area Research Center of the Wisconsin Historical Society, Box 10, Folder 9; Mary Elise Antoine, "Hercules L. Dousman," 1987, unpublished paper, Villa Louis Archives, Prairie du Chien.

[43] Rhoda R. Gilman, "Last Days of the Upper Mississippi Fur Trade," in *People and Pelts: Selected Papers of the Second North American Fur Trade Conference*, edited by Malvina Bolus (Winnipeg: Peguis Publishers, 1972), 105–107.

[44] Dousman to Henry H. Sibley July 12, 1838, quoted in Gilman, "Last Days of the Upper Mississippi Fur Trade," 112.

FIGURE 5.2. Hercules Dousman. Wisconsin Historical Society, Image ID 2620.

Bernard Brisbois in trust for her. When Rolette died in 1842, his partners Dousman and Sibley found ways to use most of the remaining estate to pay the Outfit's debt. Before long Dousman (Figure 5.2) married the widowed Jane Fisher Rolette, acquiring control of her properties, which her cousin had controlled before.[45]

During the 1840s Dousman and Sibley's Upper Mississippi Outfit expanded its goals to include trade not only with Indians but also with the growing settler population.[46] Traders like Dousman made great profits from government payments to Indians at the treaty grounds and when the Indians' annuities were paid since their Native customers had purchased significant amounts of goods on credit. Dousman was investing in a sawmill by 1838 and also in steamboats about the same time.[47]

[45] Antoine, "Hercules L. Dousman"; Scanlan, "Jean Joseph Rolette."
[46] Gilman, "Last Days of the Upper Mississippi Fur Trade," 113.
[47] Gilman, "Last Days of the Upper Mississippi Fur Trade," 128.

After Dousman withdrew from the fur trade in 1846, Bernard Brisbois and Henry Rice took over as managers of the Upper Mississippi Outfit, but Brisbois was relegated to a subordinate role two years later.[48] By the mid-1850s most of the elite fur traders of the upper Midwest had pulled out of the trade and turned their efforts to other pursuits.[49] Thereafter the fur trade continued only in a small way as merchants bought pelts from professional Native and non-Native trappers and from settlers supplementing their other work.[50] Bernard Brisbois invested in real estate and carried on a general merchandising business for many years.[51]

Historian Kathleen Neils Conzen argues that as the "fur trade" became the "Indian trade," men like Dousman and Sibley used political connections and relationships with the Ho-Chunks to manipulate the Indian removal process in order to amass enormous sums of money earmarked for annuities, moving expenses, and treaty-related provisions, funds they invested in the development of towns and cities up and down the Mississippi River. As the Ho-Chunks (also known as Winnebagos) were subjected to a series of treaties and removals, the government promised to compensate them for the loss of resources they had used to sustain themselves by paying them annuities, yearly payments in cash and/ or goods. Merchants who had formerly sold blankets, guns, kettles, and other products on credit to Indians in anticipation that they would hunt and bring in furs could now sell on credit anticipating that their Native customers would receive annuity payments and be able to repay their debts. In addition, these merchants made money selling annuity goods to government agents at inflated prices, purchased Indian land claims and resold them, earned attorney fees, invested Indians' trust funds, and sold them illegal liquor.[52] Conzen argues, "For the traders, the annuity system was a bonanza that promised all the profits of the fur trade with few of its market uncertainties."[53] Men like Dousman and Sibley invested these profits in real estate speculation, promoting the development of Prairie du Chien, St. Paul, La Crosse, St. Cloud, Winona, and other communities.

---

[48] Gilman, "Last Days of the Upper Mississippi Fur Trade," 116, 117, 119.

[49] Gilman, "Last Days of the Upper Mississippi Fur Trade," 105.

[50] Gilman, "Last Days of the Upper Mississippi Fur Trade," 130.

[51] B. W. Brisbois Estate, 1886, "Oath of Appraisers & Appraisal of Lands to be Sold. 3 July 1886," Crawford County Courthouse; obituary, Prairie du Chien *Union*, June 18, 1885.

[52] Kathleen Neils Conzen, "The Winnebago Urban System: Indian Policy and Townsite Promotion on the Upper Mississippi," in *Cities and Markets: Studies in the Organization of Human Space*, edited by Rondo Cameron and Leo F. Schnore (Lanham: University Press of America, 1997), 269–308.

[53] Conzen, "The Winnebago Urban System," 274.

She states, "It can clearly be argued that the federal funding that flowed through the Winnebagos to their traders, employees, and suppliers, and then on into real estate investments, urban promotion, and railroad development, played a critical role as seed capital in the development of the Upper Mississippi urban system."[54]

Besides Brisbois and Dousman, who stayed on at Prairie du Chien, other people who had made a living trading with the Natives, provisioning the fort, and selling liquor to the soldiers either moved away or shifted their focus increasingly to other types of work, chiefly farming.

### Emigration Overtakes It

In 1852, "J. Y. S.," a traveler, wrote about Prairie du Chien that it was "one of the loveliest localities" in the state, but explained,

For many years it was the principal trading post of the American Fur Company on the Mississippi. When this trade was in its glory, and a large garrison stationed here to protect it, it was a place of very considerable business; but losing both of these resources before emigration could supply their places, it has been struggling, for some years, under a reverse of fortune, a reverse very common to Indian trading posts upon the evacuation of the country by the red man, but seem to be repaid with interest so soon as emigration overtakes it.[55]

Migration into Prairie du Chien, as we have seen, increased after the War of 1812 and accelerated somewhat during the 1830s, but it would not be until the 1850s that a major boom and economic transformation took place. Some Creoles adapted to the shift, while a few were even able to thrive. Many, however, became marginalized, and others chose to leave the area, either following the fur trade west or northwest or seeking alternative homes in the Mississippi Valley. As many Anglo Yankees and western Europeans moved into Crawford County, so did some French Canadians from locations that included Red River as well as other locales (see Table 5.1).

The newspapers that were published in Prairie du Chien, Madison, Milwaukee, and Galena provide much useful information about the economic shifts in this community during the 1830s, 1840s, and 1850s. It is hard to find much evidence of the Creole presence in these papers, however. Francophone Creoles probably did not read them. The Yankee

---

[54] Conzen, "The Winnebago Urban System," 293.
[55] J. Y. S., "Prairie du Chien, July 14, 1852," *Crawford County Courier*, Aug. 4, 1852, p. 1, reprinted from the Madison *Argus and Democrat*.

TABLE 5.1. *Prairie du Chien Population, 1816–1860*

| Date | Population | Percentage Creole (%) | (Estimated) Creole Population |
|------|-----------|----------------------|------------------------------|
| 1816 | 600 | 83.3 | 550 |
| 1830 | 692 | 72.6 | 450 |
| 1840 | 1,267 | 33.7 | 427 |
| 1850 | 1,406 | 30.2 | 425 |
| 1860 | 2,398 | 15.8 | 380 |

*Note*: Percentages are for household heads only for 1820, 1830, 1840. Creoles include residents with French surnames who were born in Wisconsin, Michigan, Minnesota, Missouri, Illinois, or Canada before 1820, their children, and/or those who were known from genealogical and treaty records to be members of fur-trade families. Data for the years before 1850 were for those with French surnames. All residents appeared in the records without ethnic or racial designations or as "white."

*Sources*: For 1816: Population figures based on Coues, *Expeditions of Pike*, 304; Daniel S. Durrie, "Annals of Prairie du Chien," *Early Out-Posts of Wisconsin* (Madison: State Historical Society of Wisconsin, 1873), 5; for 1816 percentage, James L. Hansen, "Prairie du Chien's Earliest Church Records, 1817," *Minnesota Genealogical Journal* 4 (1985): 329–342; James H. Lockwood, "Early Times and Events in Wisconsin," *State Historical Society of Wisconsin* 2 (1856): 125–126; Hoffmann, *Antique Dubuque*, 51–59; Lowrie et al., ed., *Public Lands*, Vol. 5, 47–98, 270–272, 283–328; Donna Valley Russell, ed., *Michigan Censuses 1710–1830* (Detroit: Detroit Society for Genealogical Research, 1982), 146–147; Elizabeth Taft Harlan, Minnie Dubbs Millbrook, and Elizabeth Case Erwin, trans. and eds., *1830 Federal Census: Territory of Michigan* (Detroit: Detroit Society for Genealogical Research, 1961); [C.W. Butterfield,] *History of Crawford and Richland Counties, Wisconsin* (Springfield, IL: Union Publishing, 1884), Vol. I, 294–295; Population Schedules of the Seventh Census, 1850, manuscript, Crawford County, WI, microfilm M432, Reel 995; Population Schedules of the Eighth Census, 1860 manuscript, Crawford County, WI, microfilm M653, Reel 1402; U.S. Census Office, *Population of the United States in 1860* (Washington, DC: Government Printing Office, 1864), 534.

editors and contributors wrote for their Anglo neighbors but were also keenly aware that issues of the paper found their way to readers throughout the Midwest and to points east, and that articles about the community would be reprinted for potential migrants. Thus, when reading them one must take into consideration not only the disinterest in the Creoles but also the "booster" mentality and the Yankee confidence that all growth and development were positive signs of "progress."[56]

By 1840, significant in-migration by non-Creoles had shifted the population balance in Crawford County, and Creoles were about only one

[56] James L. Hansen, *Wisconsin Newspapers, 1833–1850: An Analytical Bibliography* (Madison: Wisconsin Historical Society, 1979), provides an overview of the early Wisconsin press.

third of the residents (see Table 5.1.). A description of Prairie du Chien appeared in a Galena (Illinois) newspaper, informative both for its expression of Anglo "progressive" attitudes as well as for its data on the physical and economic state of the town. The article explained, "Until within a few years, the population consisted almost exclusively of Canadians of French descent, and half-breed Indians, who derived their principal support by hunting, and the Indian trade – leading a life of occasional toil and hardship, strangely intermixed with periods of genuine Canadian jollity and indulgence." The author wrote approvingly of the recent "powerful current of emigration," which included "some of the sons of the 'universal Yankee nation,'" and introduced "a new state of things."[57]

Cultural differences had clearly influenced this Anglo, as is evident in the ethnocentric comment that "new and handsome stores and dwelling houses constructed of frame work, or handsomely hewn stone were erected – thus forming a curious contrast to the rare old odd-looking log huts of the old French settlers." In addition, the article asserted that the "new Anglo-American settlers," who were more "industrious, temperate, and ... refined," had improved "the moral state of the community." Who could argue that "new" and "handsome" and morally superior shouldn't supersede the "rare old odd-looking" French, in spite of their "Canadian jollity" – or perhaps because of it?

The article went on to survey the community's buildings, businesses, organizations, and some of the workers, providing more details than the 1840 census did:

About 100 houses: 30 in "Old Town" [also known as the Main Village, on the island]
 65 in "New Town" or St. Friole [this would become Upper Town]
 the rest in "Lockwood's addition" [this would become Lower Town]

- A large Court House
- A military Hospital
- A Post Office
- A Roman Catholic Cathedral
- 4 different religious societies
- 1 temperance society

---

[57] "Prairie du Chien," *Wisconsin Enquirer*, Madison, February 26, 1840, p. 1, reprint from the Galena *Gazette and Advertiser*. Additional sources on economic development include Mary Elise Antoine, *Prairie du Chien* (Charleston, SC: Arcadia Publishing, 2011), and Mary Elise Antoine, "Main Street, Prairie du Chien," Prairie du Chien *Courier Press*, April 8 and April 13, 2009.

- 2 schools
- 3 taverns
- 1 temperance hotel
- 4 groceries
- 8 dry goods and grocery stores
- 2 physicians
- 1 licensed auctioneer
- *no lawyers* [emphasis in original]
- several river pilots
- 2 master masons
- 1 painter
- 1 tailor
- 2 gun & blacksmiths
- 7 carpenters[58]

In 1840, the population of Prairie du Chien was 1,267, about one third Creole, with about 427 *habitants*.[59]

Yet, as "J.Y.S." had pointed out, Prairie du Chien was in a prime location to serve as a depot and transportation hub, the reasons that it had become a popular rendezvous point and fur-trade town in the eighteenth century. Its "commercial advantages" had chiefly to do with location, J.Y.S. argued, because it "commands the valley of the Wisconsin, extending 300 miles into the interior, with all its lumbering and agricultural resources, ... commanding ... a large share of the lead trade; and then four or five hundred miles of river navigation northward and westward on the Mississippi and St. Peters, draining the trade and travel of Northern Iowa, Northern Wisconsin, and the whole of Minnesota."[60]

With a typical progressive and ethnocentric perspective, the author was certain of divine approval for economic development plans: "And

---

[58] "Prairie du Chien," *Wisconsin Enquirer*, Madison, February 26, 1840, p.1, reprint from the Galena *Gazette and Advertiser*. The dry goods stores included "the Sutler's store in the Fort and the large three story establishment owned by the American Fur Company which always contains a large and extensive assortment of every kind of goods belonging to the Indian trade." The count of thirty houses in "Old Town" may be an overestimate: the 1843 Tax List noted only twelve lots with buildings on them, although some lots may have included more than one dwelling.

[59] Includes 197 in army. There were 1,502 in the county. Sixth Census of the United States, 1840, Crawford County, Wisconsin Territory, Population Schedules, Microfilm Roll 580; "1840 U.S. Census, Crawford County, Wisconsin Territory," James L. Hansen typescript (thanks to Jim Hansen for sharing this); Clark S. Matteson, *The History of Wisconsin from Prehistoric to Present Periods* (Milwaukee: Wisconsin Historical Publishing, 1893), 259.

[60] J. Y. S., "Prairie du Chien, July 14, 1852."

let no one imagine that these regions are designed by the Creator only as the abodes of wild beasts and savage men. 'He created them not in vain;' He formed them to be inhabited. They are capable of sustaining a dense population and giving scope to a vigorous enterprise; and for the trade of all this upper region, no point on the Mississippi can compete with Prairie du Chien."[61]

By the mid-1850s, the community consisted of three hamlets, and a fourth neighborhood – semi-rural in character – which had come to be known as "Frenchtown." The Milwaukee *Sentinel's* correspondent explained in 1855 (ignoring the old town on the island): "Prairie du Chien occupies the lov[e]liest site on the banks of the Upper Mississippi. The surface is dotted over with farm houses mostly occupied by descendants of the old French settlers, while in the two villages, the Upper and Lower Towns, as they are called, and a mile or two apart, are to be found most of the business men and recent settlers."[62] Indeed, the Upper and Lower Towns were the areas that would attract those sons (and daughters) of "the universal Yankee nation."

During the mid-1850s when it became clear that Prairie du Chien would be the terminus of a railroad being built from the east, hopeful investors and businesspeople streamed into town in large numbers and initiated a building boom. Builders scrambled to construct new homes and businesses at breakneck speed. In September of 1857, just a few months after the arrival of the first railroad train, the local newspaper announced a tally of new buildings that had either been completed during the year or were currently under construction:

- On the Island: 17 (also known as "Old Town," or "Main Village")
- French Town: 6
- North of Fort: 161 (Upper Town)
- South of Fort: 143 (Lower Town)[63]

These buildings – all constructed in less than one year – included not only private homes and small shops but also six hotels, several business blocks, two churches, a two-story schoolhouse, four warehouses, a steam sawmill, and a machine shop, but this tally does not include a number of railroad buildings. The article also estimated that during the previous year, "our city has doubled in wealth and the number of its inhabitants. It

---

[61] J. Y. S., "Prairie du Chien, July 14, 1852."
[62] "A Stranger's Impressions of Prairie du Chien (From the Editorial Correspondence of the Milwaukee Sentinel)," Prairie du Chien *Courier*, Aug. 25, 1855, p. 2.
[63] "The Growth of Prairie du Chien," Prairie du Chien *Leader*, Sept. 19, 1857, p. 2.

has quadrupled its business."[64] In fact, the population of Prairie du Chien grew from 1,406 in 1850 to 2,398 in 1860.[65]

## "This Class of Persons": Ethnocentrism

These data strikingly express the rapid infusion of migrants and capital and the diversification of the economy, but they also point to the economic marginalization of the Creole population. The *habitants* became concentrated in the Frenchtown neighborhood and on the Island, where new construction was limited. Likely the ethnic residential clustering was partly in response to Anglo prejudices against both Creoles and Indians.

Economic marginalization both fueled and was fed by ethnocentrism and cultural differences, evident in the local press. The Galena reporter's biases, mentioned earlier, were also evident in the Prairie du Chien newspapers. In addition, the local press, with their reporting, *erased* the Creoles who remained from public awareness.

The newspapers of Prairie du Chien, written and published by Anglos who had moved in during the 1830s and '40s, were already beginning to create their version of the community's history in the 1850s. Discussing the removal of Indians from the region and of troops from Fort Crawford in the late 1840s, the Crawford County *Courier* in June of 1852 stated:

Since that time a new class of inhabitants have taken the places of those who were accustomed to hang about military posts and Indian trading towns. As a general thing they [the old residents] were a race wholly destitute of enterprise, industry or frugality, as the appearance of the town will fully confirm.[66]

An article in the same paper in May of 1853 asserted:

It is true many worthy citizens were here at that time; but the majority were such as not only to neglect all real advantages, but deter an enterprising emigration. This class of persons – perfectly destitute of ambition or worthy pride – have been gradually dying out, before the onward march of civilization; and as their prey and associates retired, they have nearly all followed the Indians and troops to their new homes. Their places have been gradually filled by a healthy immigration; and where sloth, stupor and vice once ruled, now sturdy farmers, and busy mechanics are instilling a new life.[67]

---

64 "The Growth of Prairie du Chien," Prairie du Chien *Leader*, Sept. 19, 1857, p. 2.
65 Population Schedules of the Seventh Census, 1850, manuscript, Crawford County, WI, microfilm M432, Reel 995; U.S. Census Office, *Population of the United States in 1860* (Washington, DC: Government Printing Office, 1864), 534.
66 "The Past – The Present – The Future of Prairie du Chien," Crawford County *Courier*, Prairie du Chien, June 2, 1852, p. 2.
67 "Local Business," Crawford County *Courier*, Prairie du Chien, May 17, 1853, p. 2.

It would be hard to find language more contemptuous of the old fur-trade community anywhere: neglecting advantages, destitute of ambition, without pride or cause for it, stupefied slothful vice-ridden predators! The booster author could hardly find more reason to celebrate the arrival of the healthy study farmers and busy mechanics. The truth was that the Creole population was slightly less than 30 percent at this time, and about two thirds of them were farmers – some of them probably pretty sturdy themselves.[68]

The negative attitudes toward Creoles evident in the newspapers continued the Anglo prejudices that had been evident earlier (discussed in the previous chapter). There were exceptions: Creole elites such as Hercules Dousman and Bernard W. Brisbois, and farmer/ferryman Pierre Barrette, were treated respectfully in the newspapers, probably because they were financially successful.[69] Notwithstanding the few positive comments about these men, a general pattern of ethnocentrism and disrespect probably contributed to ethnic segregation.

Bigots in the Northeast, with their anti-Catholic prejudices and nativist sense of the superiority of ethnic English, "native-born" citizens, occasioned much discussion nationwide, and these sentiments reached Wisconsin by the 1850s. The "Know Nothing" or American Party's political efforts may have been part of the anti-Creole sentiment. Someone wrote to the Prairie du Chien *Weekly Courier* in 1856 complaining of tension in his or her neighborhood. The exact nature of the conflict is unclear, but "S" hoped for "good fellowship and kind feeling amongst all classes," and observed that "division, discord and bad feeling, the natural offspring of little and conceited minds, in the end produces nothing but ruin." He or she added, "I regret to say that a little of this blighted feeling exists in my immediate neighborhood, tinctured with know nothingism."[70] The reference, of course, is to the "American Party," a secret political organization known as "Know Nothings" because when asked, members were supposed to reply "I know nothing about it." The nativist movement, which was both anti-immigrant and anti-Catholic, had originated in Pennsylvania and New York in 1837. By 1855, the American Party

---

[68] Population Schedules of the Seventh Census, 1850, manuscript, Crawford County, WI, microfilm M432, Reel 995.

[69] On Brisbois, Prairie du Chien *Leader*, Sept. 12, 1857. A new hotel would be finished soon. "We were gratified to learn that it has been proposed to name it the Brisbois House, in honor of our esteemed townsman Col. B. W. Brisbois. No better name could be selected, and none which would commend it more favorably to our citizens."

[70] Prairie du Chien *Weekly Courier*, Sept. 4, 1856, p. 3.

had lodges in Wisconsin, supported a widely read Milwaukee newspaper called the *Daily American,* and may have mobilized as many as 20,000 votes in the gubernatorial race, in which "Know-Nothingism" was a significant source of controversy.[71] This anonymous letter to the editor suggests local tensions based upon ethnic and religious differences, possibly targeting the Catholic Creoles. Ironically, although the Creoles were Catholic, the Protestant Anglos were immigrants into Prairie du Chien. Ethnic residential clustering, of course, could also be a positive action as a means of fostering community, a topic to be explored further in a subsequent chapter. But the *habitants* also found hope and community in the institutions of their church and schools.

## "Souls Well Counted": Church and School

Unlike many fur-trade centers around the Great Lakes area, Prairie du Chien had not had a Christian mission before the War of 1812, and it was not until the early nineteenth century that priests spent any notable time there. By force of personality, it seems, the Italian missionary Father Samuel Mazzuchelli convinced his superiors to support his vision of a large and beautiful church to be built at Prairie du Chien. A popular story behind the founding of St. Gabriel's church told how Joseph Rolette, Hercules Dousman, and Strange Powers were caught in a canoe when a wild and frightening storm suddenly threatened to plunge them into the roiling waters of the Mississippi River. As they fervently prayed for the Almighty to deliver them safely home, they promised that if saved, they would provide the land and construction funds for a beautiful church, and the three honored their promise.

Strange Powers donated the land on which to build St. Gabriel's Catholic Church in 1836 and Euphrosine relinquished her dower right to it in 1845.[72] Eighty-eight people gave money to fund construction during the late 1830s, most of them francophone. A look at the list of donors gives us a glimpse of the wealth and religious hierarchy among Prairie du Chien's Catholics. The most generous donor was Joseph Rolette, who gave $739.28, followed by Hercules Dousman and François Chenevert

---

[71] Joseph Schafer, "Know-Nothingism in Wisconsin," *Wisconsin Magazine of History* 8 (1924): 3–21.

[72] Deed from Strange Powers to Frederick Rose, Bishop of Detroit, February 16, 1836. Deed Book B, 159; Deed of Relinquish of Dower from Euphrosine Powers to John Henri, Bishop of Wisconsin, December 4, 1845. Deed Book E, 411. Crawford County Register of Deeds Office, Crawford County Building, Prairie du Chien.

Sr., who each gave $100. Other generous donors were Rolette's daughters Elizabeth Rolette and Emilie Rolette Hooe, François Labathe, and François Deschouquette, who each gave $50. Others gave what they could: Antoine Grignon, for example, gave one dollar, and Domitille Brisbois gave ten. Joseph Brisbois was the church's secretary-treasurer during this time, his clear and graceful penmanship recording church income and expenses.[73]

The church would become a central cultural institution for the Creole community and a locus of activities. As early as the 1830s, Men's and Ladies' Associations were formed, and they were able to raise an additional $446.75 to support the costs of building the church. As we have seen in Chapter 4, other organizations were created during the middle of the nineteenth century, including a building committee, a "*Societé de Bienfaisance*" (a Charity Society), and a Confraternity of the Scapular.[74] Soon, it was possible for someone to record that the St. Gabriel Parish had "250 Families or about 1100 souls well counted. 300 communicants in the year [1839?]."[75]

By the end of the 1850s, the church's seating chart formalized a hierarchy within the Catholic community. People rented specific pews, the more expensive ones at the front of the church going to the community's most prominent members. Jane Fisher Dousman, wife of Hercules, reserved three pews at the front, paying $11 for each per year. Behind her and her family sat the Leclercs, the Hooes, the Barrettes, and so forth, each paying slightly less for their pews than those who sat in front of them. Euphrosine Powers sat six rows back but was not charged for her pew, in apparent recognition of the land donation she and Strange had made.[76]

## "Advantages for Education"

Throughout the Midwest after the United States asserted its hegemony, many families sought to help their children gain the skills they would

---

[73] "Account of Money received to Erect a Catholic church at Prairie du Chien," St. Gabriel Catholic Church archives. Thanks to Sandy Halverson for assistance in locating this and other related documents.

[74] "Account of Money received to Erect a Catholic church at Prairie du Chien" [ca. 1839]; "D'epence et Maniére que L'argent prelevé par la Societé de Bienfaisance à Etté depensé" [1847]; Receipts for payment for material and labor on the church, 1839–41 in folder "Old Documents: Marriage Records and dispensations, etc." St. Gabriel's Church archives, Prairie du Chien.

[75] "Account of Money received," written on the back.

[76] Pew List, "May 1859 & part of 60," St. Gabriel Church Archives.

need to succeed in a changing world. Native peoples in the region had long valued cultural and political mediators and had respected people who were skilled in learning and using different languages because they facilitated understanding among the increasingly diverse peoples of the region. As another way of creating links, many Creoles seem to have extended the region's tradition of valuing the acquisition of languages by urging their children to learn English, as a first step in personal diplomacy and acculturation. Schools might assist with this, but before 1812 the only schools were on the fringes of the area, in Mackinac or St. Louis. A few elite children were sent to Montreal. After this time, a few schools began to offer English instruction. For example, in 1812 the *Louisiana Gazette*, published in St. Louis, ran an advertisement in French for a new school for young ladies, listing all the subjects to be taught and adding that if parents wanted their daughters to learn English, the schoolmaster would have an assistant give additional instruction in this second language.[77] A memoir written by an Anglo man who remembered his school days in Detroit between 1816 and 1819 wrote that "in the school were many large French boys trying to learn English from the few books then in use."[78] Anglo Protestant missionaries who established schools in St. Joseph and Mackinac, Michigan, during the early decades of the century found they had many métis students; other schools in the south and east also accepted some elite children as boarding students.[79]

In the years before 1817, Prairie du Chien parents had to home-school their children or send them to boarding schools in distant towns, and through the middle of the century some parents continued to send older children to be educated outside the region. For example, the Rolettes sent Joseph and Virginia to school in New York during the 1830s.[80] In 1829, another young Prairie du Chien resident, the French-Dakota métisse Therese LaChapelle, at age fifteen went to live with her sister at Mackinac Island to attend a Presbyterian mission school.[81] Schooling

---

[77] Louisiana *Gazette*, May 9, 1812.
[78] B. O. Williams, "My Recollections of the Early Schools of Detroit that I Attended from the Year 1816 to 1819," *Michigan Pioneer Collections,* Vol. 5 (1882), 547–548.
[79] Keith R. Widder, *Battle for the Soul: Metis Children Encounter Evangelical Protestants at Mackinaw Mission, 1823–1837* (East Lansing: Michigan State University Press, 1999).
[80] Jane Fisher Rolette to her brother, Henry Fisher, 24 Juillet (July) 1836, reproduced in Martinus J. Dyrud, "King Rolette, Astor Fur Trader on the Upper Mississippi," unpublished manuscript, Villa Louis archives; Bruce M. White, "The Power of Whiteness, or the Life and Times of Joseph Rolette, Jr.," *Minnesota History* 56, no. 4 (Winter 1998–99): 179–197, 189.
[81] Widder, *Battle for the Soul,* 156–157.

after 1817 was private and intermittent until a public (district) school was built in 1846. Throughout, only two or three dozen scholars studied at a time, and sessions seem to have run no more than three to five months per year.[82]

Antoine Grignon's educational experiences illustrate the patchwork nature of schooling available to even the most fortunate youngsters. Antoine's father Amable Grignon worked for Colonel Zachary Taylor at Fort Winnebago as an interpreter, so he prevailed upon Taylor to enroll Antoine in a school at the fort during the 1830s. Antoine told his interviewer in the early twentieth century that

I next went for two terms to a private school conducted by a Mr. [Cadle], then John Haney became my teacher. There were no public schools in that day at Prairie du Chien and the parents of the pupils in the private schools paid the teacher a certain amount each month for their instruction. I remember, too, my French teacher, a Mr. Gibault, who also taught English, and a lady by the name of Mrs. Crosby, who held school in her home. When I was a little past twelve years of age [about 1840] I went to school to Rev. Joseph Cretin, a Catholic clergyman.... By the time I was fifteen years of age I had a fair education in the common branches of English and was ready to go out into the world better equipped than most French Canadian boys of my time.[83]

Grignon's education introduced him not only to the "three Rs" but also to Anglo- American culture. In addition, it helped him perfect his fluency in both English and French. (In addition, Antoine also spoke Dakota and Ho-Chunk.)[84]

A Presbyterian school for the Ho-Chunks educated both "full-blood" and mixed-ancestry children on the west side of the Mississippi near Prairie du Chien from 1834 through 1840, and some of Prairie's Creole children between the ages of seven and fourteen probably attended for a year or two. This was the school to which Ukseeharkar went for refuge after the Black Hawk War and where her daughter Mary Ann Mitchell was briefly enrolled.[85]

[82] Scanlan, *Prairie du Chien*, 182, 203–206.

[83] Eben D. Pierce, "When Trempealeau Was in the Wilds; The Days of Antoine Grignon, Fur Trader," Galesville *Republican*, April 25, 1929, Wisconsin Historical Society Library F902T7/PI. Pierce paraphrased Grignon's words.

[84] Eben D. Pierce, "The Recollections of Antoine Grignon," *Proceedings of the State Historical Society of Wisconsin*, 1904, 176.

[85] Mary Elise Antoine, "Winnebago School on the Yellow River, 1832–1840, A Focus of Cultural Contact," in *Cross Currents: The Intersection of Native and European American Cultures in Southwest Wisconsin*, edited by Geoffrey M. Gyrisco, Proceedings of the Tippesaukee Symposium 2003 (Blue River, WI: Friends of Tippesaukee, 2005), 95–106.

By 1850, Crawford County had five public schools and five teachers to serve a school-age population of about 750 children.[86] The Crawford County *Courier* lamented in August of 1852 that "the educational advantages are very limited. The young people who have grown up here are far behind the age in acquirements."[87] Two months later, the paper's editor, Buel Hutchinson, commented in a way that suggests ethnic tensions related to educational issues:

It has been a matter of deep regret that the advantages for education in our midst, are so very limited. Now that the apathy which has hitherto hung like a plague over our town, and restrained every improvement, has been succeeded by a healthier, impulsive and enterprising spirit – the same change which attends every other town of this description, when its population becomes Americanized – it is a disgrace upon the citizens, a shame to each and every man in [the] community, that we are so poorly provided with common school advantages.[88]

Although educational opportunities had been limited, some Prairie du Chien Creoles might have had attitudes resistant to formal education. Indians and mixed-ancestry people elsewhere in the western Great Lakes region had been skeptical about missionaries and government agents sent to teach them Euro-American culture and economic practices, rejecting the outsiders' ethnocentrism and insistence on religious and economic change. Predominantly Catholic Creoles often resented the Protestant missionary teachers' prejudices and efforts to convert students. Historian Mary Antoine has found that two of Prairie du Chien's traders, Joseph Rolette and James Lockwood, opposed the Presbyterian establishment of a mission school nearby because they distrusted Indian agent Joseph Street, who was promoting it.[89] Many fur-trade families, however, understood that literacy could help people to achieve higher positions and success in the mercantile hierarchy, although there are a few examples of illiterate traders who managed to achieve good results.[90]

---

By fall 1837, there were forty-one children attending the school. It was moved to Turkey River when the Ho-Chunks were moved again in 1840.

[86] *The Seventh Census of the United States: 1850* (Washington, DC: Robert Armstrong, Public Printer, 1853), Vol. I, 927; Vol. IV, 327.

[87] "Common Schools," *Crawford County Courier*, August 4, 1852, p. 2.

[88] "Common Schools," *Crawford County Courier*, October 13, 1852, p. 3.

[89] Antoine, "Winnebago School on the Yellow River," 95–106.

[90] Widder, *Battle for the Soul*; Willoughby M. Babcock, "Louis Provençalle, Fur Trader," *Minnesota History* 20 (Sept. 1939): 259–268; John E. McDowell, "Madame LaFramboise," *Michigan History* 56 (Winter 1972): 271–286; Lucy Eldersveld Murphy, "Public Mothers: Native American and Métis Women as Creole Mediators in the Nineteenth-Century Midwest," *Journal of Women's History* 14, no. 4 (Winter 2003): 142–166.

The schools were institutions serving some of the same purposes that marriage and adoption had traditionally served in the Midwest during previous centuries. Both introduced the culture of immigrants to the region's residents and created linguistic as well as cultural interpreters. Many Creoles, as traditional mediators, were quick to understand that as had previously been the case, those who spoke many languages and understood many cultures would fare better in society and economy. Indeed, literacy and education became even more valuable under the new régime. As we have seen in a previous chapter, English language fluency was used as a method of marginalizing Creoles as jurors.

### "Far Behind the Age in Acquirements"

The 1850 census suggests dramatic differences in the literacy rates of Prairie du Chien residents. The census taker was to indicate "persons over 20 y'rs of age who cannot read & write." For 1850, 1.8 percent of adult non-Creoles were listed as illiterate, while 28.9 percent of Creoles were so listed. This was not supposed to distinguish between people whose first languages were their only differences. Census guidelines stipulated that those who were literate in a language other than English be included among the lettered.[91]

It is possible, however, that language difficulties affected the accuracy of the census returns. John Thomas, a Vermont-born flour merchant (who, from his own enumeration of his children's birthplaces and ages, appears to have moved to Wisconsin between 1834 and 1845), performed both the 1850 and 1860 census interviews. From his large number of errors in spelling both French given and surnames, he was apparently not particularly familiar with the French language himself. For example, a branch of the Ducharme family was listed as "Jusheaume," and one Gauthier household became "Gochy," while Guillaume became "Geome." Hypolite became "Paulette" and Hyacinthe Rivard was "Yusuret Revoir." This suggests that Thomas had trouble communicating the census questions and understanding the answers, and that some of the old francophone fur-trade families had trouble with English, although many Creoles were multilingual not only in French but in Ojibwe and other Indian languages.

[91] Lee Soltow and Edward Stevens, *The Rise of Literacy and the Common School in the United States; a Socioeconomic Analysis to 1870* (Chicago: University of Chicago Press, 1981), 159.

Yet this alone probably doesn't explain the jarring difference in the reported illiteracy rates of Prairie du Chien Creoles in 1850 and 1860. While John Thomas reported in 1850 that 28.9 percent of Creoles over age twenty could not read or write, in 1860 he indicated that *68.5 percent* of adult Creoles were illiterate. Checking the returns of sixty-eight adults over age twenty in 1850 who appeared in both the 1850 and 1860 enumerations reveals that fifteen were literate in both years, thirteen remained illiterate during the decade, four somehow acquired the ability to read and write in the interim, but thirty-six *declined in their abilities*, according to the records. Did thirty-six people forget what they had known a decade earlier? Probably not. More likely Thomas's methods of making the determination about literacy changed, although instructions to enumerators did not change from 1850 to 1860. Did his general view of Creole ability levels become altered over the course of the 1850s, making him increasingly convinced that Creoles were ignorant? Did social, political, and economic changes during the decade increase the level of skill required to be considered adequately literate? He was one of thirteen men who organized a Prairie du Chien Academy in 1854, indicating that he had been thinking about issues related to education during the years between these two censuses.[92]

Overall, school attendance rates were low for both ethnic groups in 1850. Only 11.1 percent of Creole children under age nineteen attended school, similar to 12.6 percent of non-Creole youngsters. Looking at the prime attendance years of ages ten through twelve, 21.9 percent of Creoles and 24 percent of non-Creole youngsters were reported in 1850 to have "attended school within the year."

By 1860, however, *47 percent* of Creole children under age nineteen had been to school during the previous twelve months. The highest rate of attendance for Creole children in 1860 was from ages ten to twelve, when *86.8 percent* spent some time in a classroom. This pattern reflects dramatic shifts in both opportunities for schooling and attitudes toward education on the part of parents. By comparison, one study of northern U.S. families in 1860 found that only farm families with wealth exceeding $1,000 sent their ten- to fourteen-year-old children to school at rates exceeding 74 percent.[93] In 1860, ten-year-old students such as Serapha Cherrier were the children of parents such as Flavian and Louisa Lessard

---

[92] Scanlan, *Prairie du Chien*, 205–206.
[93] Soltow and Stevens, *The Rise of Literacy and the Common School in the United States*, 123.

Cherrier who had been born in Wisconsin and Canada during the 1820s and grown up to be illiterate adults during the transition to U.S. control of the region. These parents were probably keenly aware of inequalities in the evolving society and no doubt hoped that sending their nine children to school would give them better opportunities than the parents had experienced, even though the children's efforts would have been needed on the family farm.[94]


## Work

As the old fur-trade families around the Midwest watched thousands of newcomers move into their towns, they also noted that the economy was changing. In Prairie du Chien in the era when Creoles were being marginalized politically and when Anglo prejudices were freely aired in public forums such as the local press, when the fur trade declined and was replaced by Yankee-style commerce, many of the old *habitants* adapted their work lives to new realities. Farming became a fall-back option for many Creoles whose education and language skills were insufficient to qualify them for skilled work and whose finances provided little capital for enterprise. When Prairie du Chien in 1857 became the terminus of the railroad for people and products traveling west or along the Mississippi, many newcomers took advantage of opportunities for business and employment in hospitality, warehousing, forwarding, banking, and other enterprises related to transportation, but Hercules Dousman was the only member of the old fur-trade families to invest in these concerns.[95] Some Creoles such as Bernard Brisbois and Euphrosine Antaya Powers became involved in the real estate business, and a few others found work in the construction of the many new homes and commercial buildings.[96] Building the new St. Gabriel's Catholic Church from 1839 to 1858 also provided economic stimulation through construction jobs. In addition, the increase in the local and regional populations provided markets for farm produce.

A review of Prairie du Chien's workers reveals the ways that literacy, language, culture, and experience shaped the community's labor patterns

---

[94] Population Schedules of the Eighth Census, 1860 manuscript, Crawford County, WI, microfilm M653, Reel 1402, dwelling #476.

[95] Antoine, *Prairie du Chien*, 25.

[96] Bernard W. Brisbois Estate, 1886, "Oath of Appraisers and Appraisal of Lands to be Sold. 3 July 1886," Crawford County Courthouse, Prairie du Chien; on Euphrosine Antaya Powers, see Chapter 6.

and influenced the economic roles available to Creoles and how they changed. The federal censuses of 1850 and 1860, together with anecdotal evidence, provide glimpses of the old fur-trade families at work.

Women's paid and unpaid work, of course, is most difficult to find sources for, at least in part because their occupations seldom appeared in the population censuses. Still, we can piece together some of the options using other records. Certain types of work could be done by women of all ethnic backgrounds. Most looked after their families. Some also earned money taking in boarders at two dollars per week, and some women such as Euphrosine Antaya Powers were paid by the county to care for the community's paupers.[97] Women could also be domestic servants, earning a dollar per week with board, according to the census.[98] Fourteen-year-old Frances LaPointe, for example, was a servant living in the household of Joseph and Elizabeth Grimard in 1860, probably helping with the housework and care of their infant and toddler.[99] While Frances LaPointe appeared in the census as a wage-earner, most women working within the family economy or part-time for others did not attract the attention of the census taker.

Creole women often used their multifaceted cultural knowledge to earn money while serving in mediator roles as public mothers. As we have seen in a previous chapter, women could be healers and midwives: Adelaide Limery provides an example of a Creole who provided medical services to her neighbors for compensation. Women such as Catherine Myott and Julia Grignon were sometimes hired to serve as interpreters. Some women had been active fur traders, including Angelique Brisbois Pion, who had not only traded with the Ho-Chunks on the Fox River but also served as an interpreter for Indian agent Nicolas Boilvin.[100]

In one rare instance, a woman was given a government appointment. Emilie Rolette Hooe, forty-two-year-old daughter of Joseph Rolette and Marguerite Dubois, was appointed Postmistress in May of 1853.[101] Being

---

[97] 1860 Wisconsin Federal Census, Schedule 6, Wisconsin Territorial Papers, County Series, Crawford County, Proceedings of the County Board of Supervisors, Nov. 29, 1821–Nov. 19, 1850 (Madison: Wisconsin Historical Records Survey, 1942) (hereafter, CC Supervisors), 155. In 1844, Euphrosine Powers earned $2.50 per week for looking after Tunis Bell and Joseph Deschantier, who were probably elderly and in poor health. According to the county commissioners' minutes, services included providing board, lodging, washing, nursing, and beds.

[98] 1860 Census, Schedule 6.

[99] 1860 Wisconsin Federal Census, Household 388.

[100] Waggoner, *"Neither White Men nor Indians,"* 82.

[101] Crawford County *Courier*, May 3, 1853, p. 2. Dyrud, "King Rolette," 47.

both the widow of a U.S. army officer and a step-daughter of Hercules Dousman's wife Jane may have helped her to secure the appointment, but as an educated and literate woman who was fluent in both English and French, she also had the appropriate skills. Yet this was part-time work. In 1860, Hooe was evidently taking in boarders, too, according to the census. Included in her household were an Anglo banker and his wife and two children.[102] As we shall see later in the chapter, farm women were active members of their family economies as well.

The range of occupational opportunities was greater for males, but Creole men appear in the 1850 census with patterns somewhat different from those of non-Creole men. Occupations were given for 451 Creole and non-Creole men: the sixty-eight job titles ranged from assistant miller to wood chopper and included the usual array of farmers, petty merchants, artisans, unskilled workers, and government officials.

As the fur trade moved west and northward, there were fewer opportunities for Creole people who stayed behind to apply their biculturalism, tribal ties, tradition of mediation, and fur-trade experience to their work. The majority of them, like their Anglo and European neighbors, identified as farmers. In 1850, 66.2 percent of Creole men and 63.7 percent of non-Creole men were listed as such by the census taker (see Table 5.2). This was an occupation that did not require literacy, knowledge of the English language, or formal education – but it did require access to land.

Beyond farming, many of the differences between Creole and non-Creole men's occupational patterns are striking. The data demonstrate that Anglo immigrants were beginning to dominate the changing economy and filling the more elite roles in government and business.

Literacy, language, and educational achievements could limit one's occupational options. In the 1850 census, all ten professionals, all seven government workers, and all three clerks were non-Creoles. These were occupations in which English language fluency and literacy were important requirements. Professional careers (as teachers, physicians, clergymen, and editors) required a type of formal education that had not been available in Wisconsin earlier. By 1850 Creoles were seldom elected to office, and when they did take official roles, those roles tended to be occasional or part-time, not appearing in the census.

Although commerce had been a key feature of the fur-trade era, only three of fifteen merchants listed in 1850 were Creole. We might expect

---

[102] 1860 Wisconsin Federal Census, 61.

TABLE 5.2. *Prairie du Chien, 1850, Occupational Categories of Men*

| | Creole | | Not Creole | | Total | |
|---|---|---|---|---|---|---|
| | # | % | # | % | # | % |
| Farmer | 92 | 66.2 | 199 | 63.7 | 291 | 64.5 |
| Merchant | 3 | 2.2 | 12 | 3.8 | 15 | 3.3 |
| Professional | 0 | 0 | 10 | 3.2 | 10 | 2.2 |
| Government | 0 | 0 | 7 | 2.2 | 7 | 1.5 |
| Clerk | 0 | 0 | 3 | 1.0 | 3 | 0.7 |
| Accommodations | 1 | 0.7 | 4 | 1.2 | 5 | 1.1 |
| Artisan | 13 | 9.4 | 48 | 15.4 | 61 | 13.5 |
| Transportation | 2 | 1.4 | 2 | 0.6 | 4 | 0.9 |
| Musician | 2 | 1.4 | 0 | 0 | 2 | 0.4 |
| Laborer | 24 | 17.3 | 25 | 8.0 | 49 | 10.9 |
| Other | 2 | 1.4 | 2 | 0.6 | 4 | 0.9 |
| Total | 139 | 100 | 312 | 99.7 | 451 | 99.9 |

*Source:* Population Schedules of the Seventh Census, 1850, manuscript, Crawford County, WI, microfilm M432, Reel 995. Due to rounding, some totals do not add up to 100%.

Creole men to have continued in occupations related to the old fur trade such as transportation workers, interpreters, and so forth, but there were in 1850 only four men – a ferryman, a (boat) pilot, a hunter, and a tavern keeper – in occupations that related to travel or hunting, and only four in 1860.

One travel-related occupation not recorded in the census was that of mail carriers who took letters and packages from Prairie du Chien to other towns. Strange Powers was one of these men in the 1850s.[103] Louis Barrette, interviewed in 1919 when he was ninety-five years old, told about carrying the mail when he was a teenager, about 1838. Three years earlier, his father Pierre had contracted for the mail route from Prairie du Chien south to Platteville, traveling three times per week – a task he was able to delegate to his son. According to the article about Louis, the Barrettes' horse swam the Wisconsin River while Louis "would pole himself across on a raft" and then continue "over blazed trails through the timber and over the prairies."[104] Before long, Pierre established a ferry, which was noted in the local press.[105]

[103] Crawford County *Courier*, Feb. 2, 1853, p. 2.

[104] "Lewis Barrette to Celebrate His 95th Birthday," *Crawford County Press*, Prairie du Chien, Feb. 26, 1919, from Wisconsin Historical Society Library [F902 3BA 44].

[105] *Courier*, Aug 18, 1852, p. 3.

Another reflection of the educational disparity can be seen in that Creoles were overrepresented among unskilled laborers (17.2 percent of Creoles versus 8 percent of non-Creoles did this type of work) but were underrepresented among artisans (9.4 percent to 15.4 percent). During the fur-trade era, there had not been a strong craft tradition (in the formal European sense) in the region, and most young people did not have access to apprenticeship with skilled artisans. The result was a disparity in incomes. Wage rates for the community were reported by the census taker in 1860: a male farm hand earned $12 per month with board, a day laborer $.75 per day with board or $1 without, while a skilled carpenter earned $1.50 per day without board.[106] Construction work of this type thus could yield $30 per month or more during the warmer months if the work was steady.

Some Creole men had enough woodworking skills to pick up intermittent construction jobs when employers were willing to hire them. Evidence from the archives of St. Gabriel's Church for the period when the parish buildings were under construction provide a few details. Nicolas Chenevert, for example, earned $12.75 ($1.50 per day) for eight and a half days of work building St. Gabriel's church or rectory in 1840. Jean Baptiste Pion Jr. earned slightly less – about $1.37 per day, for four days' work as a joiner building the St. Gabriel's parish house in 1841. Church construction added to the incomes of other Prairie du Chien residents as well: Pierre Lachapelle earned $3.00 for hauling six loads of boards to the worksite in 1840, and Flavien Cherrier and Nicolas Chenevert were both paid for stone cutting.[107] Chenevert, Cherrier, and Lachapelle appeared in the 1850 census as farmers, however, demonstrating that they – or the census taker – considered farming rather than construction or hauling to be their primary occupations. Given the building boom of the 1850s, one would think there would be more work for Creoles in construction, but in 1860 only two listed their main occupation as carpenter. This raises the possibility that non-Creole employers actively discriminated in hiring.

Of course, there were probably some (mostly female) Native artisans among Prairie du Chien's residents making baskets, moccasins, snowshoes, and other items, but this type of work is not revealed in the census tally of occupations because women's work was ignored, because of

[106] 1860 Wisconsin Federal Census, Schedule 6.
[107] "Receipts for payments for material & labor on church," 1839–41, in Folder "Old Documents: Marriage Records and dispensations, etc.," St. Gabriel's Catholic Church archives. Some of the receipts are in French and still use the term "piastres" for dollars.

particular Euro-American ideas about what constituted an "occupation," and because of the difficulty of enumerating part-time work.

Some inequality in real estate ownership was also evident by 1850. It was an American custom to attribute a family's land to the head of household, usually male. Among Creole men age eighteen and older, 51 percent were landless, while only 42 percent of non-Creole adult men claimed no real estate. By 1850, Creoles were 30.2 percent of the population but only 28 percent of 238 landowners, according to the census. And they owned only 24 percent of the $138,219 worth of real estate valued in the 1850 population census. (Chapter 6 will consider shifts in land ownership.)

## "Turn Our Attention More to Farming"

The majority of Creoles, like most non-Creoles, identified as farmers. This was an occupation that was generally self-directed, allowing *habitants* to avoid discrimination in employment. Farming did not require much in the way of English language skills or literacy, although it did require access to land. Many longtime Prairie du Chien residents still had land remaining from the days of Isaac Lee's survey claims three decades earlier – land that had been patented in their own or their parents' or grandparents' names – so they turned to these resources. Some outsiders had married into the Creole landed families, of course, and some francophones from Canada and/or the Illinois country found their way to Prairie du Chien and bought land. Some who did not own real estate rented, or worked on a family member's place. Raphael Boisvert, for example, lived with Antoine Boisvert's family in 1850, apparently cultivating the fields while his brother or uncle Antoine and wife Domitille ran a tavern. To further illustrate, eighteen-year-old Gabriel Brisbois helped his father George and mother Catharine on their small farm; elsewhere Joseph and Monica Lessard were either squatting on or renting the parcel they cultivated.[108] But finding land was only part of the equation. In order to be able to make a living at agriculture, Creoles learned new skills, added commercial agricultural products, developed collaborative work routines, and found numerous ways to supplement their subsistence and farm income with nature's bounty and occasional side jobs.

Earlier in the century, as the fur trade declined, merchants and voyageurs around the western Great Lakes considered the appeal of agricultural

---

[108] Population Schedules of the Seventh Census of the United States, 1850, Microfilm M432, Roll 995, dwelling 32, 81, 114.

production. In 1824 Mackinac trader Michael Dousman wrote to Green Bay's John Lawe, "produce has taken a rise[;] furs are none two good ... and in fact[,] friend Law[,] we will have to turn our attention ... more to farming and rase our Bred and Pork."[109] These sentiments no doubt circulated among many of the Prairie's old fur-trade families, but they posed a bit of a dilemma since farming required a different set of skills from those needed in the fur trade. One observer commented that Prairie du Chien's Creole men "had generally been so long in the Indian trade that they had, to a great extent, lost the little knowledge they had acquired of farming in Canada so that they were poor cultivators of the soil."[110] And while Native wives might have learned indigenous agricultural practices, the crops and methods differed from Euro-American types of cultivation.

But there was increasing demand for agricultural products in and around Prairie du Chien by the 1840s as the settler population grew while Native farming villages were dislocated. Indian Removal had caused not only suffering for Native people and their Creole relatives, and the decline of the fur trade, but it had also affected the availability of certain foods in Prairie du Chien. Earlier in the century, fur traders had bought food from Native producers. The women farmers of Native villages in the region had long sold a great deal of agricultural produce to Prairie du Chien residents, as Antoine Grignon's narrative had pointed out.[111] In 1820, for example, a U.S. Army officer stationed near Rock Island reported that the Sauk and Meskwaki women living along the east bank of the Mississippi River cultivated 300 acres of land. "They usually raise from seven to eight thousand bushels of corn, besides beans, pumpkins, melons, &c. &c. About one thousand bushels of the corn they annually sell to traders & others," he wrote.[112] In fact, the residents of Prairie du Chien had been so dependent on Native communities for corn that they had grown very little of it, even when they grew other crops.[113] By the end of the 1830s, however, the disruptions of Native communities and Indian removal reduced Native agricultural output and thus the amount of food that Prairie du Chien residents could buy from Indians.

---

[109] Michael Dousman to John Lawe, May 28, 1824, Green Bay and Prairie du Chien Papers, Wisconsin Historical Society, Madison, microfilm, frame 10154.

[110] James H. Lockwood, "Early Times and Events in Wisconsin," *Wisconsin Historical Collections,* Vol. 2 (1856), 105.

[111] Elliott Coues, ed., *The Expeditions of Zebulon Montgomery Pike* (New York: Francis P. Harper, 1895), Vol. I, 294.

[112] "Morrell Marston," Thomas Forsyth Papers, Lyman Draper Manuscripts, microfilm, State Historical Society of Wisconsin, Madison, 1T:58.

[113] Lockwood, "Early Times and Events in Wisconsin," Vol. 2, 112.

At the same time, some Creoles migrated *to* Prairie du Chien and began to work the land. Many of the Prairie's farm families included francophones born north of the border who had arrived since the War of 1812. In 1850, 103 people told the census taker they had been born in Canada, while seven gave Hudson's Bay and ten gave Red River as their birthplaces[114] They would add different perspectives and skills as they joined the Creole community. For example, retired Canadian *voyageur* Julian Carriere and his wife Lucretia Lessard had come to Prairie du Chien after living in St. Louis, Dubuque, and Galena. A typical chain migration (where friends and relatives followed one after another across the landscape) had brought Lucretia's uncle Pierre Lessard to Prairie du Chien before 1820, in time to marry into the Antaya family and earn one of the land claims on Isaac Lee's map. Lucretia's brothers Jean Baptiste and François Lessard came to town selling horses around 1840, stopped to visit uncle Pierre, and were enchanted by the town and surrounding area. They decided to settle there and persuaded Lucretia and Julian to come up, buy land, and farm. Eventually, they were also able to convince their brother Joseph, sister Marianne, and their mother Marie Rose to join them.[115]

Lucretia Lessard and Julian Carriere (see Figure 5.3) shared a language and Creole background with most of the *habitants* whose families had been in Wisconsin and Michigan for two or more generations by mid-century, but they did not have direct connections to the land or the indigenous people of the area (except through uncle Pierre Lessard's wife, Julie Crelie, a granddaughter of Pierre Antaya and Pokoussee).[116] This was not a disadvantage, however. They and other Canadian immigrants joined the existing Creole community in the middle of the nineteenth century when kinship was changing, as connections to Midwestern tribes strained with Indian removal. During the fur trade, kin connections with tribal people had been distinct advantages, but in the post–fur-trade era, there was little to be gained. Indeed, suffering Native kin could deplete a family's resources, as the experiences of Mahnahteesee, Julia Grignon, the Paquettes, and others make clear.

By the 1830s and 1840s, family members from different cultural traditions learned, recovered, and adapted skills, often negotiating gender

---

[114] Population Schedules of the Seventh Census, 1850.
[115] Albert Coryer, interview, broadcast, and anecdotes, Wisconsin Historical Society Library, Madison, typescript, Side 1, 3.
[116] Julie's mother was Francoise Antaya, the daughter of Pierre and Pokoussee. James L. Hansen, "The Pelletier dit Antaya Families of Prairie du Chien" (forthcoming).

FIGURE 5.3. Julian Carriere. Prairie du Chien Historical Society.

roles. Some brought either Native or French farming patterns they had learned from their parents, while others had gained skills as workers on the farms of men such as Joseph Rolette. Creole variations gradually developed as spouses learned from each other and from their neighbors, as children grew up, as households grew in size, and as newcomers from other cultures contributed additional skills, traditions, and markets. The communally owned land of 1820 was not approved by Congress, but the *habitants* had for many years jointly kept a common fence around contiguous fields of crops such as corn, wheat, and potatoes.[117]

Prairie du Chien's Creole farm families worked the long prairie farm lots facing the old Indian Trail and parcels back up in the hills east of the bluffs. Peter Barrette's large farm was to the south, along the Wisconsin River; most others were either close to the Mississippi or to the east of

[117] Maj. Stephen H. Long, *Voyage in a Six-Oared Skiff to the Falls of Saint Anthony in 1817* (Philadelphia: Henry B. Ashmead, printer, 1860), 62.

Frenchtown. In 1843 according to a tax list, thirty-eight Creole and forty non-Creole taxpayers were cultivating land. A few had large fields of crops – three Creoles and ten non-Creoles had tilled fifty or more acres. Most plots, however, were smaller – ten to twenty acres in size.[118]

At mid-century non-Creoles tended to have more valuable land holdings than Creoles. The federal agricultural census shows that in 1850 an average value for Creole farms was $423. There were three Creoles with moderately large holdings – Flavien Cherrier and Louis and Peter Barrette, with properties worth between $1,000 and $1,200. Fourteen others had farms worth an average of $271 in 1850. By contrast, the average value overall for the sixty-four non-Creole farms was $865 – twice the average value of Creole farms.[119]

What was farm life like for the *habitants*? To get a good picture of Creole farming, we look for sources to the census, newspapers, visual images, and scattered anecdotal evidence. The most colorful stories of Creole life, including farm practices, come down to us from the Carrieres' grandson Albert Coryer, a farmer, laborer, and avid storyteller who as a septuagenarian from 1948 to 1951 shared the reminiscences he had heard from his parents, grandparents, and Creole neighbors about life in the latter half of the nineteenth century.[120] These myriad sources help us to understand the families that maximized their use of the area's abundant natural resources, often working communally for mutual benefit.

Creole farmers produced a variety of agricultural products in patterns that were in some ways similar to those of their non-Creole neighbors but did exhibit a few distinctive elements. Given the Native heritage of so many Creoles, we may wonder if they responded to the decreased availability of Native foods by using Native agricultural methods. Native farmers had grown corn, beans, and squash (the "three sisters") together in small mounds of earth, and sometimes other plants, cultivating the ground with hoes, neither plowing nor raising cereal grains such as wheat, oats, or barley. Traditionally they had not kept livestock although some Native people owned horses by mid-century.[121]

[118] 1843 Tax list.
[119] 1850 Wisconsin Federal Census, manuscript, microfilm P76–5836, Wisconsin Historical Society.
[120] Albert Coryer interview, 1951 and Albert Coryer, "Short Stories," manuscript, Wisconsin Historical Society Library; Copy of Albert Coryer map, Phil Gokey, "Four French Family Reviews," CD-Rom, privately published, 2003, Fort Crawford Museum, Prairie du Chien; Albert Coryer map, 1948, Villa Louis Historic Site library, Prairie du Chien.
[121] Donald Jackson, ed., *Black Hawk, An Autobiography* (1833; reprint, Urbana: University of Illinois Press, 1990), 90–92.

FIGURE 5.4. Prairie du Chien farms. Watercolor by Seth Eastman. Minnesota Historical Society.

Prairie du Chien's *habitants* did indeed retain some Indian practices. Holdovers included controlled burns, crop selections, and pooling of labor. Native people had set fires to keep the brush down, a practice the *habitants* continued in order to facilitate farming.[122] The results are evident in a watercolor painted by army officer Seth Eastman sometime between 1846 and 1848 showing the Prairie's farms, possibly based on a sketch made in 1829.[123] (See Figure 5.4.)

The watercolor shows an old gabled farmhouse, a log barn with a thatched roof, five cattle, a two-wheeled cart, and in the background to the north, the high bluffs intersecting with the Mississippi River behind clusters of other farm families' homes and outbuildings. The wide open prairie in the painting's background indicates that those controlled fires kept the brush and saplings from intruding on the fields. At the same time there was a French Canadian element, too: the distinctive two-wheeled "Red River cart" identifies this as a Creole farm – Anglos used four-wheeled wagons.

---

[122] Coryer, "Short Stories," 8–9.
[123] The painting is owned by the Minnesota Historical Society. It may be based on a sketch done in 1829 when Eastman was stationed at Fort Crawford, according to historian Mary Elise Antoine. Antoine personal correspondence, July 26, 2012; Marybeth Lorbiecki, *Painting the Dakota: Seth Eastman at Fort Snelling* (Afton, MN: Afton Historical Society Press, 2000), 93.

Rail fences also divide this landscape; the long fence on the center right going off in the distance may have marked the edge of the common fields. These barriers around the fields were to keep the livestock out. Coryer wrote, "all that was fenced was the land that was under cultivation." [124] The painting shows a man splitting rails to fix the fence.

Did Creoles grow the "three sisters": corn, beans, and squash? Although the agricultural census didn't record squash crops, we know that the Barrettes were having good success with theirs. The local newspaper recorded in early November of 1852: "'SOME PUMPKINS' – Or Squash – Mr. Pierre Borette, residing at the Ferry, six miles from this village, raised three monsters of the pumpkin family, which surpass anything we have ever seen. Call them *Squash* or *Pumpkin*, whichever you will, (and they look like a cross of the two,) the largest of the three weighs 106 1/2 lbs., and the smallest about 70. – Pass this round – the *story* we mean, not the squash."[125] In the Pion family, corn and pumpkins were grown together, according to a descendent.[126] This might have been a continuation of Native methods of growing corn, squash, and beans together in hills.

Information on other crops is available in the special census about agricultural practices, gathered by the census taker John Thomas in 1850 about eighty-one farms, and in 1860 about forty such properties; he did not collect information on every farm. It is a bit puzzling that the number of farms Thomas recorded in the special agricultural census declined, but perhaps with more people to enumerate on the population schedules, he ran out of time. Why were these agriculturalists selected for extra questioning, and not others? Probably these were the more successful farms, and perhaps the ones most easily accessible to the census taker. It may also have been an accident of fate – was someone at home who spoke English or who would patiently show John Thomas the livestock and crops in the field? So it is unclear how typical they were.

The census taker found Creole farmers at mid-century producing both Native and European foods. Like their Native predecessors, Creole and Anglo farmers included corn as one of their main crops in 1850 but they also grew wheat, oats, and potatoes, and most people produced more oats than corn or wheat.[127] An interesting change took place between

[124] Coryer, "Short Stories," 9.

[125] *Crawford County Courier,* Nov. 3, 1852, p. 2.

[126] Lucy Murphy interview of Myra Lang, August 2, 2002, Prairie du Chien.

[127] 1850 Wisconsin Federal Census, Schedule 4. The corn crops of both 1850 and 1860, however, were short, that is, less successful than in most years; 1850 Wisconsin Federal

1850 and 1860 when Creole farmers began growing "peas and beans." Only one Creole and five others had reported growing them in 1850, and then in very small quantities. But by 1860, all of the Creoles reported significant quantities of them, an average of 44.7 bushels each, while only a handful of other farmers grew any, and then in tiny amounts.

Peas, it seems, became an ethnic food that would become a distinctively "French" element of Creole cuisine and may have been emphasized by the more-recent French Canadian immigrants. Nationwide, most U.S. farmers raised beans for *people* to eat, but grew peas either to feed livestock or to plow under as a means to enrich the soil, according to an essay included in the compendium for the 1860 census.[128] At Prairie du Chien, according to historian Mary Antoine, Creoles ate the peas (a yellow variety used for soup, sometimes known as "pease") but used the vines as fodder for their livestock.[129] In addition, while both beans and peas could be dried for storage, cooking with dried peas required less preparation time because there was little need to soak them beforehand. And they had been a popular crop in cooler climates such as their Canadian ancestral lands.

Pea soup was a distinctively Creole dish. James Lockwood remarked that "the Canadian peasantry ... live mostly on pea soup, seasoned with a piece of pork."[130] Folklorist Mary Agnes Starr named her 1981 book about French culture in Wisconsin *Pea Soup and Johnny Cake*, commenting in her introduction,

There was a saying current in the French-Canadian community in which we lived: "Pea soup and Johnny-cake makes the Frenchman's belly ache!" ... After trotting home from school ... it was comforting to be greeted by the mouth-watering savor of bubbling hot pea soup which had been simmering all afternoon, blending with the appetizing aroma of corn bread baking in the oven of the old woodburning range![131]

Census, Schedule 6, and 1860 Wisconsin Federal Census, manuscript, microfilm P73–4450, Schedule 6. Wheat had been ground by handmills until about 1809 when a horse mill was set up. Within a few years, water power mills were introduced. William Arundell, "Indian History," Galena [IL] Miners' Journal, 30 October 1830, State Historical Society of Wisconsin, Madison, File 1809 (typescript); Lockwood, "Early Times," 120.

[128] Eighth census of the United States, 1860, vol. 2: Agriculture (Washington, DC: Government Printing Office, 1864), lxxv.

[129] Mary Elise Antoine to Lucy Murphy, email, Nov. 8, 2011.

[130] Lockwood, "Early Times," 110.

[131] Mary Agnes Starr, *Pea Soup and Johnny Cake* (Madison, WI: Red Mountain Publishing House, 1981), xi. Thanks to Bette Beneker for bringing this source to my attention. Some nutritionists stress that peas, like beans, are foods that when combined with corn, produce protein in the diet, something the Creoles seemed to realize. "Protein," Centers for

Several descendants of Prairie du Chien's Creole families remember that pea soup and cornbread or johnnycake were frequently on the menu at home when they were growing up.[132]

So the "three sisters" continued to be tended at the Prairie but adapted: indigenous pumpkins, corn, and beans with the European peas. We don't know whether most of the Creoles (besides the Pions) grew them together, or who tended them. But pea soup and johnnycake seem to be a culinary adaptation, an example of the syncretic practice scholars call creolization. Instead of three sisters, we might call this a traditional sister and a Canadian cousin.

Creole husbands and wives – or perhaps their parents and grandparents – probably negotiated gender roles. In Native society, farming was considered women's work and people did not keep livestock; in Euro-American society the inverse was true. Couples in which the wife was Native and the husband Euro-American in ancestry and cultural outlook sometimes had different expectations about who would do what type of work. Would Native women, who came from communities without a tradition of keeping dairy cattle and where the population was overwhelmingly lactose intolerant, milk cows and make butter?[133] Absent a tradition of working with yeast in the kitchen, would they bake bread that would suit the expectations of their spouses?

Early in the century Creole couples in Green Bay and Prairie du Chien sometimes resolved these differences by hiring workers to milk cows and do other farm work, and by buying bread and butter when they could, rather than producing these items themselves.[134] As we have seen, Michel

---

Disease Control and Prevention, posted October 4, 2012. http://www.cdc.gov/nutrition/everyone/basics/protein.html, accessed Dec. 21, 2012.

[132] Personal correspondence, Lois Coorough Harwood to Bette Beneker and Lucy Murphy, Nov. 6, 2011; Geri Phillips to Lucy Murphy, Nov. 8, 2011; Virginia Powell to Lucy Murphy, Nov. 8, 2011.

[133] N. S. Scrimshaw and E. B. Murray, "The Acceptability of Milk and Milk Products in Populations with a High Prevalence of Lactose Intolerance," *American Journal of Clinical Nutrition* 48, no. 4 (1988): 1079–1159; Jimmy L. Smart, "Lactose Intolerance: Exploring Reaction Kinetics Governing Lactose Conversion of Dairy Products within the Undergraduate Laboratory," *Chemical Engineering Education* 42, no. 2 (2008): 82–90; ERIC EBSCOhost, accessed October 14, 2011; John D. Johnson et al., "Lactose Malabsorption among Adult Indians of the Great Basin and American Southwest," *American Journal of Clinical Nutrition* 31 (March 1978): 381–387; Frederick J. Simoons, "Primary Adult Lactose Intolerance and the Milking Habit: A Problem in Biological and Cultural Interrelations," *American Journal of Digestive Diseases*, New Series, 14, no. 12 (Dec. 1969): 819–836.

[134] For further discussion of couples negotiating gender roles, see Murphy, *A Gathering of Rivers*, 59–67.

Brisbois set up a bakeshop around 1810 and hired Strange Powers to produce loaves for the residents and Native visitors, so that families did not have to make their own. Hercules Dousman established another bakery in 1855.[135] Eventually Creoles learned to bake their own bread, according to Louis Barrette, who remembered, "They made 'gallett' or bread by mixing the dough and rolling into a ball, put it in hot ashes and covered up until it had baked."[136]

But Creole women were taking up butter making during the middle of the nineteenth century as their families invested in cattle. Although there had been some cattle on the Prairie early in the century, animal husbandry became increasingly important. [137] Livestock raising was often more profitable than growing grain. A newspaper editorial in 1852 urged farmers in Crawford County to focus on dairying because wheat was vulnerable to "the frost of winter, the drouth [sic], and the many other accidents attending its culture." The editor suggested that farmers consider that "Thousands of broad ravines, yielding a most excellent herbage would furnish an everlasting range for cattle, and employment for five acres of white headed children to hunt them up. Here is a ready market for all the butter and cheese that you can make." He added that one could also make healthy profits from selling oxen and "milch" cows.[138] Apparently, Creole and non-Creole farm families alike – whether their children were brunet or "white headed" – thought this sounded like good advice.

During the boom decade of the 1850s, farm women took up dairying on a commercial basis. Before the boom, in 1850, only about one fourth of all farms – whether Creole or not – reported producing butter.[139] The market for butter increased with the non-Creole population but there were cultural issues to contend with in adopting this form of production.

In European and Euro-American communities of eastern North America, people generally considered dairying to be women's work, although men might otherwise care for the cows. Native Americans, however had no such traditions since they had not kept cattle. Historian Rebecca Kugel has found that to the northwest in present-day Minnesota,

---

[135] Mary Antoine, "Hercules Dousman," 6.
[136] "Lewis Barrette to Celebrate His 95th Birthday."
[137] Mary Antoine, personal correspondence, email, July 26, 2012.
[138] *Crawford County Courier*, Oct. 6, 1852, p. 2.
[139] All the Creoles kept milk cows, but only four of the seventeen Creole farmers reported producing butter, and only seventeen of the sixty-four non-Creoles did. 1850 Wisconsin Federal Census, Agricultural returns, microfilm, Wisconsin Historical Society reel P76–5836, 65–71?

Ojibwes were wary because they believed the cattle to have spiritual power, which could become malevolent.[140] Furthermore, there were biological reasons for Indians not to drink milk. Native adolescents and adults often have difficulty digesting dairy products, and because this is likely due to a genetic trait, it was probably true in the nineteenth century. Studies have found lactose intolerance in 90–92 percent of Native people with no European ancestry, but people of mixed Native and European ancestry are less likely to have trouble, perhaps half as likely.[141] Jane Rolette Dousman's half-sister Elizabeth Baird, who was of French, Scottish, and Odawa ancestry, still had a problem with lactose intolerance, writing that milk disgusted her. A resident of Green Bay, she remembered bitterly a time when her Scots-Irish husband and his parents expected her to process milk for others. "All who know of my great dislike of milk, especially cream, may imagine what I suffered in taking care of milk and making butter."[142]

Earlier in the century, in couples where the wives were Native and the husbands not only believed that dairying was inappropriate work for men but didn't have the skills themselves, butter making could only evolve when Creoles learned from neighbors, relatives, or teachers at missionary schools how to produce it. Certainly negotiations would be necessary. By mid-century, however, Creole wives had acquired the skills; furthermore, they were more likely to have some European ancestry, and so there were probably fewer with a genetic disposition to dislike consuming and processing milk.

Whether or not they ate butter themselves, farm women came to recognize it as a valuable commodity for a cash-poor family. By 1860, all but one of the Creoles and all but three of the non-Creole farm families reported butter production. Creole families produced an average of 157 pounds each that year (slightly less than the 218 average pounds

[140] Joan M. Jensen, *Loosening the Bonds: Mid-Atlantic Farm Women, 1750–1850* (New Haven, CT: Yale University Press, 1986), 93; Rebecca Kugel, "Of Missionaries and Their Cattle: Ojibwa Perceptions of a Missionary as Evil Shaman," *Ethnohistory* 41, no. 2 (Spring 1994): 227–244.

[141] Scrimshaw and Murray, "The Acceptability of Milk and Milk Products"; Smart, "Lactose Intolerance: Exploring Reaction Kinetics"; Johnson et al., "Lactose Malabsorption among Adult Indians"; Intolerance and the Milking Habit." H. S. Baird Papers, Box 4, Folder 9, ch. 26. S. A. Simoons, "Primary Adult Lactose Intolerance and the Milking Habit."

[142] Elizabeth T. Baird, "O-De-Jit-Wa-Win-Wing; Contes du Temps Passe," H. S. Baird Papers, State Historical Society of Wisconsin, Madison, Box 4, Folder 9, ch. 26.

per non-Creole farm). If they produced about three pounds of butter per week, they could trade it for provisions at a local store. According to Coryer, "grocers bought dairy butter but paid no cash, the farmer had to trade it out." (Similarly, he said eggs and potatoes could be sold for store credit; only wheat brought cash.)[143] Creole farm women thus by 1860 were adopting Anglo-American dairying in a way that the Native wives and mothers of the 1820s did not. When more wives were mixed or Euro-American than Native, the incidences of people with lactose intolerance probably dropped. At the same time, the market for butter increased with the non-Creole population, encouraging all farm women's selective acculturation to dairying.

While there was a significant increase in butter production linked to cattle raising, there was an apparent decrease in the production of an older commodity, maple sugar, probably because the individualization of landholding limited Creole access to maple groves. Sugar making had long been an important part of Great Lakes Indians' seasonal economy, and Native families had traditional sugar camps they visited in the early spring where they spent several weeks each year tapping sugar maple trees to drain the sap, boiling it into concentrated form and packing the maple sugar into boxes made out of birch bark. This was a festive time of year when women took charge of the process, which proceeded twenty-four hours a day. Men provided security, hunted for food for the workers, often chopped wood to feed the fires under the kettles, and probably helped to keep an eye on the children. Creole families had continued the practice in the early part of the century, combining Easter festivities with sugar production; Easter eggs and crêpes with maple syrup fed the denizens of the sugar bush, and fiddlers inspired the dancers. It was often a time of courting, and Creole girls gave their boyfriends maple sugar candy wrapped in a strip of birch bark that they called a *billet doux* (love letter, literally a "sweet note").[144] Native mothers had passed along to their daughters the sugar skills and usufruct rights to the groves. Sugar production, however, declined by around 1850, according to the agricultural census, with only one non-Creole farmer reporting having made any, and no Creoles.

---

[143] Coryer, "Short Stories," 12–13. Quote is from p. 12. Coryer's memoir is borne out by a *Crawford County Courier* advertisement by general store keeper S. A. Clark in 1852, "Cash Paid for Wheat, Hides, Furs, Peltries, Beeswax, Flaxseed, &c. &c." *Crawford County Courier*, Nov. 3, 1852, p. 2.

[144] Murphy, *A Gathering of Rivers*, 65–67.

Between 1850 and 1860, however, one family developed this product in a big way. The Barrettes reported producing 650 pounds of maple sugar, plus 30 gallons of syrup – much more than anyone else. Leander Lessard produced six pounds of sugar that year, and an Anglo reported twenty pounds, but the Agricultural Schedule credits no one else with producing any maple sugar. Pierre Barette and his wife Thérèse had a large family with three adult children and two teenagers at home and an extended family nearby including many Native-descended relatives.[145] Among them was daughter-in-law Caroline Powers, whose parents were Strange and Euphrosine, and whose grandmother was Pokoussee. In fact, Euphrosine seems to have lived near her daughter and the Barette family in 1850.[146] Euphrosine had taught her daughters how to make sugar.[147] Although it is purely speculation, it would not seem to be very much of a stretch to imagine that Euphrosine introduced the others to Pokoussee's ancestral sugar groves and supervised the process of tapping the trees and boiling the sap.[148] It should not surprise us that this extended family was able to mobilize the kinfolks to revive a traditional Native form of production. The surprising thing is that so few others did the same, raising questions about whether the other sugar groves had fallen into the hands of people without sugar making traditions and skills. (Another possibility is that other sugar production nearby escaped the notice of the census taker.)

While they were increasing spring sugar production, the Barrettes, who were spending a considerable amount of time running their ferry across the Wisconsin River, reduced the amount of horses, beef cattle, and swine they tended during the decade. Other Creoles, however, continued to devote their energies to animal husbandry.

Farm families had to consider the utility of livestock relative to the energy and costs required to maintain them, and cattle keeping necessitated a degree of wealth and effort that might be a challenge for some Creoles. Livestock raising, of course, had been introduced by Europeans; Native people had not kept domesticated animals besides dogs, but Prairie du Chien's *habitants* had been involved in animal husbandry since at least the beginning of the century. According to Coryer, keeping cattle required farmers to have barns to house them during the winter months,

---

[145] Population schedules of the Eighth Census, 1860, dwelling 423, p. 57.
[146] Population schedules of the Seventh Census, 1850, ms. Microfilm M432, Reel 995, 496–497.
[147] Personal correspondence, Virginia Powell to Lucy Murphy, Nov. 9, 2011.
[148] Hansen, "The Pelletier dit Antaya Families."

which limited the attractiveness of beef cattle for those without the time or resources to construct large barns.[149] In 1850, most of the seventeen Creole farmers reported six or fewer beef cattle; only Pierre Barrette had thirty. In 1860, Creoles reported few herds: only Francis Lessard and Flavien Cherrier kept about a dozen beef cattle each, more than most of their neighbors.[150]

But raising horses, by contrast, was not an expensive or time-consuming proposition. Early in the century, Creoles had developed the habit of letting their horses roam in the common areas during the summers as they were seldom needed during the warm months when canoes provided better transportation.[151] According to Coryer this practice continued later in the century. "All they had to do in the spring of the year when the grass got good enough so they could pick their living, was to turn them loose, let them go out on the prairie and in the hills. Then all they had to do was get feed for them during the winter."[152] One-horse carts with two wheels – Red River carts – were useful for local hauling. In the winter, the horses worked the most, pulling sleighs.[153]

Horse racing had long been a popular pastime in Prairie du Chien and as Coryer pointed out, faster horses brought better prices. The local newspaper reported in 1856 that hired hands in the southern part of town were surreptitiously racing their horses, afterward holding contests of speed between the cows and the horses.[154] In both 1850 and 1860, three Creole families each had about a dozen horses, many more than other Creole and non-Creole farmers who generally kept three or fewer.[155]

Everyone – Creole and non-Creole – kept hogs. Typical of their neighbors, the Creoles reported an average of eleven each in 1850, and in

[149] Coryer, Bittner interview, 20.

[150] 1860 Wisconsin Federal Census, 217–218.

[151] Long, *Voyage,* 62.

[152] Coryer, Bittner interview, 12–13.

[153] Albert G. Ellis, "Fifty-Four Years' Recollections of Men and Events in Wisconsin," State Historical Society of Wisconsin, *Wisconsin Historical Collections,* Vol. VII (1876), 219, refers to Green Bay, but his observations are borne out for Prairie du Chien by Coryer's anecdotes.

[154] Willard Keyes, "A Journal of Life in Wisconsin One Hundred Years Ago kept by Willard Keyes of Newfane, Vermont," *Wisconsin Magazine of History* 3, no. 3 (March 1920): 353; Lockwood, "Early Times," 120; Prairie du Chien *Weekly Courier,* Sept. 11, 1856, p. 2, "A New Race Ground."

[155] 1850 Wisconsin Federal Census, Agricultural returns; 1860 Wisconsin Federal Census, Agricultural returns.

1860 the number of swine ranged from five to twenty two.[156] According to Coryer, during the warm months the farmers let the hogs range freely near the river and on islands, where they ate acorns, nuts, wild artichokes, roots, grass, weeds, clams, and crawfish.[157] It was customary for each owner to notch the ears of his or her sow in a distinctive way, much like western ranchers would later brand their cattle. "One farmer's mark was a round hole in the left ear[;] another[']s mark was a hole in the right ear[;] another was a V cut out in left ear[;] the other was a V in right ear." In the fall there would be a communal hog roundup: "when they rounded them up whatever pigs followed a sow those pigs belonged to the owner of the sow."[158] Creoles took the swine home and fed them grain for a while, "otherwise the meat would taste fishy after those hogs living in islands on clams and claw-fish and roots out of the water."[159]

Then around December, the "silk hat" men came down from the lumber camps, Coryer explained:

The old-timers called them, "silk hats." They all wore those silk hats and a black silk handkerchief around their necks, and long black coats dressed, of course, as the wealthy men did in the cities at that time.[160]

Their mission was to buy pork (and what beef they could).[161] Communal butchering took place when the weather was cold enough to freeze the meat. Coryer remarked,

As soon as the river got frozen strong enough, ... they'd butcher their hogs and they'd haul them north, to the lumber woods. They'd go up the river, about forty teams at once, loaded with pork. They'd line up and had men ahead of the teams with axes to test the ice so that the teams wouldn't break through, and every ten minutes the head team would pull out and the next team would take the lead and the head team would drop in back so that would rest the teams, because of course there were no roads tracked – deep snow – and that's the way they got their meat up to the north woods for lumbering at the time.[162]

Thus, Creole families with land were able to make their living in a post–fur-trade world. If they grew some of the Native crops like their

---

[156] 1850 Wisconsin Federal Census, Agricultural returns; 1860 Wisconsin Federal Census, Agricultural returns.
[157] Coryer, "Short Stories," 45.
[158] Coryer, "Short Stories," 46.
[159] Coryer, "Short Stories," 48.
[160] Coryer, Bittner interview, side 1, 20.
[161] Coryer, Bittner interview, side 1, 44.
[162] Coryer, Bittner interview, side 1, 20.

predecessors and ancestors – such as squash, corn, and beans – they raised plenty of Euro-American crops such as wheat and oats, and they added dairying to their routines when their non-Creole neighbors did in the 1850s. They reintroduced distinctively ethnic foods with Canadian-style peas and even, in the case of the Barrettes, Native maple sugaring. Access to land was central to the efforts of these families.

## Supplemental Income

Whether engaged in agriculture or not, like many families of all ethnic backgrounds in most of America, Creoles added to family incomes by providing services for their neighbors. Julian Carriere and his son Joseph, for example, broke land for others, probably those who did not keep their own draft animals. According to Albert, "By the time Joseph was 12 years of age Julian had three good yoke of oxen and had all the land he wanted to till broken and he broke or ploughed land for others.... It was quite a job after this land was plowed[;] those sapling's and hazel brush had to be shaken out and piled up and burned before the land could be harrowed ready to plant or sow to crops.... Joseph drove three yoke of oxen at the age of 12 yrs whilst his father held the plow."[163] It is unclear how much the Carrieres earned from this work, but according to the 1860 census, in Crawford County the average wage to a day laborer without board was one dollar per day.[164] The earnings of Madame Limery, the doctoress, and people like Euphrosine Antaya Powers who took in paupers, we have already mentioned.[165] One could also bring in a few dollars by taking in boarders, or – for men – serving as a juror or minor local official from time to time. Jurors, for example, generally earned a dollar per day.[166] Some people traded labor for credit of one kind or another. This is illustrated in documents recorded in probate when Jean Baptiste Pion died in 1842 or 1843. He owed Joseph Brisbois for sugar, tea, gunpowder, and for a collection of joiners' tools Brisbois had purchased for him at auction. He had paid most of his debt with cash, but was also credited for "3 days work" worth $4.50.[167]

---

[163] Coryer, "Short Stories," 28.

[164] 1860 Wisconsin Federal Census, Schedule 6.

[165] Limery's husband was said to have brought a faith cure to Frenchtown which he taught to a few select others, but these healers were not supposed to collect any money for their efforts. Coryer, Bittner interview, side 2, 6–11.

[166] For example, CC Supervisors, 133–135.

[167] Probate Record, Jean Baptiste Pion, Crawford County Courthouse, Prairie du Chien.

### Harvesting Nature's Bounty

Earlier in the century, all the land not specifically being cultivated had been considered common areas where people could let their livestock wander and where they could gather wild grasses, fish, and other natural products, a practice reflected in some of the earliest local ordinances. On the eve of the Civil War, Creoles still had a keen sense of the resources provided by the prairie, forests, rivers, creeks, and marshes, and harvested them as part of their family economies.

The area's abundant natural resources could with effort be converted into cash. Coryer explained that the Creoles cut cordwood that they sold to the steamboats, sometimes taking it without permission from one of the many properties owned by Hercules Dousman, land that might have seemed temptingly reminiscent of the old common areas. Reconstructing a typical encounter in which Dousman challenged a man cutting trees from his land, Coryer voiced the woodcutter's usual arguments:

"Well, I'm sorry. I didn't realize I was cutting on your land, Mr. Dousman." "Well," Mr. Dousman would say, "I'll have that wood hauled home. I need fuel too. And you'll have to cut some more and cut it on your own land." "Well, now, Mr. Dousman, I have to have that money. I have to have it soon, too, because it's about time that I should haul it, before the roads break up and the sleighing plays out. I've got to have that money for taxes and other things that I need, for buying clothing for my children, and also other things about the house. I'm sorry, I can't very well spare that wood. Can't you let me have it?" "Well, yes, you take the wood this time. Don't you cut any more now. Don't cut any more wood on my land." "All right, Mr. Dousman, I'll do that. I'll be careful." And in a short time the thing was repeated again and again but Mr. Dousman was always willing to forget and never punish.[168]

In the spirit of the declining fur trade, some people continued to sell products of wild game as part of the family economy. In 1852, even though the Indian trade had shifted westward, B. W. Brisbois still advertised for furs: "All kinds of furs & skins wanted. I still keep open at my old stand on the Steamboat Landing, where I am prepared to pay, as usual, the highest cash prices for **Furs and Peltries!**" (emphasis in original).[169] Oliver Grimard, according to Coryer, earned a living by hunting, fishing, and trapping. "Trapping is really where he made his money mostly – and also shooting ducks and geese and then selling the meat ... to hotels and places in Prairie du Chien and people who didn't go out hunting.

[168] Coryer, Bittner interview, side 1, 7.
[169] Crawford County *Courier*, Aug. 4, 1852, p. 3.

And also the feathers – at that time the feathers were worth a whole lot and he made money by that."[170] The feathers found their way into comfortable bedding.

The natural world provided resources not only to sell but also for family consumption. Passenger pigeons, before they became extinct, flew overhead so densely that Lucretia Carriere could catch some for dinner very easily, according to her grandson. "She had a long slender pole and she would get where those flocks come over by standing in the hazel brush[;] the pidgeon would fly all about her[.] [S]he would soon have all the pidgeon she wanted by striking at the flock with her pole. Some [people] would catch them with nets[;] they would skin the pidgeon[s] and merely save the breast and legs and pickled them for winter use."[171] Other resources were wild fruit, nuts, and of course, maple trees for making sugar.[172]

The river was among the most important features of the landscape, and of both the local history and economy, providing many resources. The river offered waterfowl and fish. Coryer told his interviewer, "they speared fish by night[;] they would peel birch bark; this bark would burn the same as if it had been soaked in oil. They would get a green stick of wood about 5 ft. long and 3 in. in diameter fasten it on the end of the boat and put the birch bark at the other end of the stick and light it; this would give a light so the men could see the fish in the water quite a distance."[173]

Like the farmers who let their hogs run wild on the islands or shoreline of the river, Frenchtown residents used the uninhabited islands in the way their grandparents had used the old common fields of the eighteenth century, including harvesting wild hay. Coryer remarked that among the people who used this resource was a resident of Frenchtown: "a Mr. Thomas which raised horses to sell ... [he] made much hay in the islands[;] this hay was not very nutritious but kept the animals from hunger and answered the purpose by feeding grain with it."[174]

The Mississippi's tributaries also offered resources. Trout swam in Mill Coulee ("coulee" is a term for a creek or stream), available for boys to catch, evading Hercules Dousman who owned the coulee and would confiscate any fish from people he caught there. Afterward, according to

[170] Coryer, Bittner interview, side 2, 16.
[171] Coryer, "Short Stories," 32–33.
[172] Coryer, "Short Stories," 7, 36.
[173] Coryer, "Short Stories," 53–54.
[174] Coryer "Short Stories," 108 (misnumbered as p. 90).

Coryer, "the boys would leave and go on towards home for a short distance, then stop and watch Mr. Dousman disappear, go back and catch whatever trout they needed for themselves and go home and have their trout. And that happened many a time."[175] That the folklore emphasized both Dousman's claims to proprietorship of the creek and certain lands and the common person's ability to appropriate the resources anyway expresses both a sense of independence and the resonance of the communal right to the resources.[176]

As presented by Coryer sharing the old community lore, Frenchtown was remembered as a place where people worked together, making a living on their farms and utilizing resources available to all – on the hills where their ponies ran freely; on the islands and river bottoms where they cut hay and set their hogs to wander; on the river and creeks where they fished and hunted – even on Hercules Dousman's lands and streams, where they cut wood and stole trout.

## Conclusion

During the 1830s through 1850s, Prairie du Chien's economy changed dramatically, as Indian tribes suffered land loss, famine, disease, and removal, and as the fur trade shifted away from Prairie du Chien to the north and west. Anglo and European immigrants moved into the area to farm and establish new businesses, numerically overwhelming the Creoles, becoming dominant in politics and economy, bringing their anti-Creole attitudes with them. These changes accelerated during the 1850s with the arrival of the railroad, and the old rendezvous grounds became not only a locus for river traffic but also a depot for rail transportation east and west.

Some of the old fur-trade families moved away; the rest lived their lives on the island, in Frenchtown, or on farms up in the hills. Some former fur-trade workers became farmers; many became laborers, while a few adopted various transportation-related occupations such as operating a ferry, carrying mail, opening taverns or inns for travelers – in other words, jobs that gave them a fair amount of autonomy and/or allowed them to use skills developed during the fur-trade era. Only a few, like Hercules Dousman and Bernard W. Brisbois, worked in the more elite

---

[175] Coryer, Bittner interview, side 1, 6.
[176] No doubt Coryer was careful about what he said about Dousman, sensing that his interviewer wanted to hear good things about the man.

and profitable occupations that required education, English language proficiency, skilled training, or capital. Most who remained, however, identified as farmers, independent people with a paradoxical tradition of communalism. Albert Coryer said of them, "the old French settlers were a humble class of people. They didn't try to accomplish very much, but they always had in mind of being generous and friendly to one another, and enjoy themselves."[177] He may not have realized how hard his parents and grandparents and their neighbors worked, but his characterization of them as humble and generous has a profound ring of truth.

---

[177] Coryer, Bittner interview, 11.

# 6

## Blanket Claims and Family Clusters

### *Autonomy, Land, Migration, and Persistence*

Euphrosine Antaya Powers came into the courtroom on March 17, 1840, and told Judge James Lockwood that she needed still more time to pay off the debts. She had been trying to settle her late husband's estate for eight months and had sold Strange's personal effects but that had not earned enough to cover the financial obligations. So she asked the court for permission to sell some of the couple's real estate, the old Meskwaki land.[1] This was the beginning of Euphrosine's journey into the world of real estate dealing, of selling, buying, giving, subdividing, mortgaging, losing, defending, and haggling over Prairie du Chien lots, "half-breed" treaty claims, and bounty lands. Like many of her neighbors, she faced the many challenges of the mid-nineteenth century creatively, learning to mobilize the resources at her disposal, including land, family, and tribal ties. Two decades later, many of the Creoles had moved on, but she was still in Prairie du Chien with the Dousmans, Brisbois, and some of the other early fur-trade families.

During the middle of the nineteenth century, hundreds of Creoles like Euphrosine Antaya Powers and her family faced hard choices. Would they follow the fur trade north and westward and leave behind their old homes at the Wisconsin and Mississippi rivers? Would they follow the tribes – parents, siblings, cousins, and friends – as they were removed to the west? Would they move to "half-breed" lands or cash in on their real estate? Or would they stay and find ways to make a living in the changing economy, by wage labor, business management, farming the land, and/or

---

[1] Probate Book B, 14–15, Crawford County Courthouse, Prairie du Chien.

241

FIGURE 6.1. Euphrosine Antaya Powers. Courtesy of Phil Barrette.

drawing their sustenance from the river and nature's other gifts, as did the neighbors we examined in the previous chapter?

In the context of Prairie du Chien's economic development, as discussed earlier, this chapter explores Creole efforts to achieve and maintain autonomy, chiefly through land usage and residential patterns that enabled people to draw on the assistance and resources of family and friends. The complexities of land ownership are explored through a case study of one woman's efforts over three and a half decades to retain as much ancestral land in her family as possible while organizing it and using it as a resource in the face of life's challenges. The chapter concludes with an examination of Creole persistence patterns.

## Land

As the old fur traders such as Dousman, Rolette, and the Brisbois were diversifying their business practices, they were – like their neighbors, the entrepreneurial newcomers – ready to acquire the lands of Indians and *habitants* in myriad ways, both simple and complicated. Yankees like James Lockwood were in the ascendancy, increasingly controlling the government and the courts, which were set up in ways that could facilitate the transfer of land, usually to the detriment of the tribes and the Creoles.

There were four basic ways that land was transferred, and they were sometimes combined. First, tribes ceded land to the government, often under duress or otherwise less than freely. Subsequent to treaties, the federal government partitioned and sold or gave title to individuals, generally non-Native people. Second, the tribes gave land to specific individuals, usually their relatives. The original Prairie du Chien grant had come from the tribes to the traders – mostly husbands of tribal members – and had later been individualized and recorded by Isaac Lee. In other Midwestern locales, tribal leaders requested during treaty negotiations that some of the ceded land be given to friends and relatives, including "half-breeds" of the tribe. Third, owners with titles to particular lots could sell them to others; sometimes they divided the land into smaller parcels before giving or selling them. Finally, the courts could forcibly transfer land from one owner to another, usually to satisfy debts. Of course, when women married, the legal doctrine of *coverture* transferred control of their lands to their husbands, until the law was changed in 1850.[2] Euphrosine Antaya Powers, the daughter of Meskwaki mother Pokoussee and trader Pierre Antaya, was a party to all of these types of land transfer. Many of her Prairie du Chien neighbors would be affected by most of them.

## Marriage, Courts, and Land

Anglo-Americans brought with them in the early nineteenth century a legal and social system that reduced women's rights and stigmatized and marginalized Creoles. As mentioned in a previous chapter, the newly dominant society not only brought different, patriarchal gender ideals, but its representatives also tried to enforce those values with laws and courts that constricted the rights of wives and rigidified the concept of marriage.

[2] *Some of the Acts of the Territory of Michigan, with the Titles and a Digest of all the Acts of the Said Territory; Now in Force.* March 20, 1816 (Detroit: Printed by Theophilus Mettez, 1816), 61. Wives could veto the sale of land, however, 45. *Statutes of the Territory of Wisconsin* (Albany, NY: Packard, Van Benthuysen, 1839), 308–309; Theodora W. Youmans, "How Wisconsin Women Won the Vote," *Wisconsin Magazine of History* 5 (1921–1922): 3–32; see 4.

Euphrosine Antaya, Pokoussee's daughter, had been awakened to this system in 1824. Euphrosine had married James Fraser, a fur trader who moved away and didn't come back, so after a while Euphrosine married, according to the custom of the country, the man with the wonderful name of Strange Powers.[3] She and Strange Powers were among couples charged under the new court system with an indictment for fornication, even though they had been together for five years and had two children.[4]

Even though local Creole norms had viewed such relationships as legitimate marriages, under the new American regime these unions were considered illicit.[5] Such fornication and adultery charges were ways that the new American territorial government asserted its authority to regulate people's intimate relations, while humiliating Creoles who followed Native domestic patterns.

Because of the court's action, Euphrosine Antaya filed for divorce from Fraser and, after court approval of the split, formally married Strange Powers the following year.[6] The U.S. courts, by enforcing the marriage laws in this way, ensured that Native-descended women like Euphrosine Antaya would be considered part of the "American" community and subject to U.S. laws, as would their children, potentially disengaging them legally from Native tribes. Women such as Euphrosine Antaya also became subject to American legal doctrines such as *coverture*, the legal construct that wives could not own property or make contracts separately from their husbands.[7] By bringing women like Euphrosine Antaya under American law, the United States also extended its legal control over

---

[3] Both individually claimed parcels of land – his name is on the map, hers in a claim for a different parcel approved in 1823. Nov. 1, 1823, "Claims at Prairie du Chien," Woodbridge Papers, Burton Historical Collection, Detroit Public Library.

[4] *United States v. Strange Poze*, Indictment for Fornication, Circuit Court of the United States for the County of Crawford of the term of May 1824, courtesy of Dale Klemme; James L. Hansen, "The Pelletier dit Antaya Families of Prairie du Chien" (forthcoming); Les and Jeanne Rentmeester, *The Wisconsin Creoles* (Melbourne, FL: Privately published, 1987), 322–323.

[5] Allan Greer, *The People of New France* (Toronto: University of Toronto Press, 1997), 69–71; James H. Lockwood, "Early Times and Events in Wisconsin," *Collections of the State Historical Society of Wisconsin*, Vol. 2 (1856), 121–122, 176; Jacqueline Peterson, "The People in Between: Indian-White Marriage and the Genesis of a Métis Society and Culture in the Great Lakes Region, 1680–1830" (Ph.D. diss., University of Illinois at Chicago Circle, 1981), 1; and Ebenezer Childs, "Recollections of Wisconsin since 1820," *Collections of the State Historical Society of Wisconsin*, Vol. 4, 167. In eastern states, common law marriage had been officially recognized by the courts, but not on this frontier.

[6] Hansen, "The Pelletier dit Antaya Families."

[7] Allan Kulikoff, *From British Peasants to Colonial American Farmers* (Chapel Hill: University of North Carolina Press, 2000), 231–232.

women's property. Once Euphrosine and Strange Powers were legally recognized as married, her property officially came under the control of her
husband.

Strange Powers died on Christmas Day, 1838, and was mourned by his
family.[8] The former fur-trade worker, baker, mail carrier, and carpenter
left Euphrosine a forty-two-year-old widow with three married daughters
and six other children under the age of thirteen, including an infant who
was ten months old.[9] How was Euphrosine going to support herself and
her children? Even with a large garden, she would need income, probably
at least $300 to $400 per year to provide for the family.[10] She had two
main resources: her family and land. (As a widow, she could own and
sell land, although she might need permission from a judge as long as the
estate was not settled.)

When someone died, the law required that the court be notified and the
deceased person's debts be counted and settled, even though the widow
had children to provide for. Strange's estate was "greatly indebted,"
according to Euphrosine, who with family friend François Chenevert
was named co-executor in 1839. Neither she nor Chenevert could read
or write. A combination of Euphrosine's official marriage to Strange, the
U.S. legal system, and a $2,000 bond put forward by Louis Barrette guar-
anteed that Strange Powers's debts would not go unpaid.[11] In the process of settling the couple's financial obligations while providing for her
herself and children, Euphrosine would lose much of her land. But not
without strategic efforts to maintain as much as possible for as long as
she could.

From Strange's death in 1838 until her own demise about 1869, the
widow's life was closely tied to bits and pieces of her ancestral homeland.
Euphrosine would struggle with debt and would find creative ways to
leverage her claims to real estate – to parcels of the Meskwakis' terrain –
to support herself and to satisfy the demands of creditors. Land would

---

[8] Strange Powers Bounty Land Warrant Application No. 29702, National Archives,
Military Bounty-Land Warrant Application File (NATF 85C).

[9] Hansen, "The Pelletier dit Antaya Families."

[10] Steven Dubnoff estimated that a family of four in 1860 required a minimum annual
income of $441 to provide for its needs. Steven Dubnoff, "A Method for Estimating the
Economic Welfare of American Families of Any Composition: 1860–1909," *Historical
Methods* 13 (Summer 1980): 177.

[11] Probate sources: Second Record [Probate] Book A, 312–313, 320, 321; Book B, 14–15,
103, 154–155, 156, 165–166, 230, 306, 340, 360, 395; *Some of the Acts of the Territory
of Michigan* 1816, 61.

educate her children, support her church, and sustain a residential cluster of her kin. But she would also lose much of that land in spite of her best efforts to maintain it.

When Strange died, the couple owned two sizable parcels of land going back to the days when Isaac Lee registered the Prairie's land claims: farm lot 28, and village lot 14. The former had been *her* land going back to the days of Isaac Lee and she had managed to emerge from a land dispute against Joseph Rolette with a clear title. The latter had been part of the Antaya spouses' claims to the village of St. Friole.[12] Euphrosine also had rights to land in the Sac and Fox Half-Breed Tract in Iowa.

Under the laws of the territory, widows were entitled only to one third of the couple's real estate and personal property, with the rest going to other heirs. The estate was not protected from creditors.[13] Minutes of court hearings about the estate's administration show evidence of Judge Lockwood's concern for the creditors but also reveal he had no interest in protecting Euphrosine's dower rights.[14] And the court had a great deal of authority over the process of settling the estate. The judge mandated that the Powers property not be sold for less than its appraised value, and each time Euphrosine wanted to sell some land, she had to get the permission of the court.[15]

For fifteen years the process of settling the estate continued, as Euphrosine and Strange Powers's debts by far exceeded the value of his and Euphrosine's property, including the land, which was sold off piece by piece.[16] Year after year she and Chenevert returned to the court to ask for more time and to report on their efforts to liquidate enough assets to pay the creditors. It is possible that Widow Powers and her friend Chenevert were intentionally stalling, purposely dragging out the process. There might be debts owed, but Euphrosine still needed to support her family, and it is likely that the court-approved land sales provided income. We

---

[12] Nov. 1, 1823, "Claims at Prairie du Chien," Woodbridge Papers, Burton Historical Collection, Detroit Public Library; Isaac Lee map, "Plan of the Settlement at Prairie du Chien," 1820, Wisconsin Historical Society WHi-79654.

[13] *Some of the Acts of the Territory of Michigan*, 1816, 45, 61. *Statutes of the Territory of Wisconsin* (Albany, NY: Packard, Van Benthuysen, 1839), 308–309.

[14] Probate book A, 110, 312, 313, 320, 321, Crawford County Courthouse, Prairie du Chien.

[15] Probate book A, 320–321; Probate Book B, 14–15, 156, 165–166.

[16] Probate Book B, 14–15, 103, 154–155, 156, 165–166, 230, 306, 340, 360, 395. At one time they owned Farm Lots 28, 34, 35, and Upper Village Lot No. 14, but had sold some during Strange's life. M. E. Fraser, "Early Families of Prairie du Chien," [1919] Wisconsin Historical Society, Madison, SC 2743, 19.

know that Euphrosine in 1844 had some income for looking after a local pauper, but beside that, land sales may have been her best way to get money to pay for food, clothing, and the other necessities of life.

During the middle of the nineteenth century, this Native-descended woman became adept at real estate trading. In 1840 under pressure to settle the estate, Euphrosine Antaya Powers created a subdivision of one lot, which she had owned long before marrying Strange Powers, into what became known as the "Euphrosine Powers Town Plot." Evidently the family tried to hold onto the land once again as they had in 1820– 21: her sons-in-law and a niece's husband bought some of the land, but had trouble keeping up with tax payments.[17] During 1840 and 1841, Euphrosine sold nineteen lots for just under $400 in all. In 1843, court records noted that the estate still owed $376, so the widow and Chenevert requested permission to sell more land. After Lockwood approved, they sold more lots, giving credit of three and six months.[18]

In 1844 at one of the many hearings at which Euphrosine and Chenevert asked for extensions on the estate, Euphrosine said "she is going down to the payment of the annuities of the Sacs & Foxes Nation where she expects to receive money and she will be able to make final settlement of said estate."[19] Was she expecting to receive payment as a tribal member? During this time period, Sauks and Meskwakis were supposed to receive annuities averaging about $170 each, but because of controversies surrounding the distribution processes, it is unclear whether someone like Euphrosine who did not live in the tribal community received any or all of these funds, which were distributed at the discretion of certain chiefs.[20] On the other hand, she may have wanted to be present when people who owed her money got *their* cash. The leading businessmen such as Dousman came away from these payments with a great deal of money in

---

[17] Powers Plat, roll file No. 57, Crawford County Register of Deeds Office (This was part of Farm Lot 28); Assessment Roll of the territory 1843, Fort Crawford Museum archives, Prairie du Chien, #1998.006.017; Hansen, "The Pelletier dit Antaya Families"; "Crawford County Delinquent List." Crawford County *Courier* June 2, 1852, p. 3.

[18] Deed Book D, 379, 380–381, 398–399, 400, 401, 408–412, 429–431; Probate book B, 156,165–166, 230.

[19] Probate Book B, 340. See Treaty with the Sauk and Foxes, 1836.
Sept. 28, 1836. | 7 Stat., 517. | Proclamation, Feb. 27, 1837. From 1837 for the next ten years the government made annuity payments each June at the treaty ground opposite Rock Island. Charles J. Kappler, comp. and ed., *Indian Affairs: Laws and Treaties*, Vol 2, Treaties. Originally Government Printing Office, 1904, now available at http://digital. library.okstate.edu/kappler/, accessed Oct. 29, 2010.

[20] Michael D. Green, "The Sac-Fox Annuity Crisis," *Arizona and the West* 16 (Summer 1974): 141–150. (Data are on 151; population estimated at 2,348.)

their coffers. Why not someone like Euphrosine who was waiting to be paid for real estate she had auctioned?

Tribal annuity payments, it seems, affected the value of real estate in and around Prairie du Chien because these payments boosted the local economy as the money was used to pay off debts to traders and to make new purchases. To illustrate, a year after Domitille Brisbois died in 1847, her son Bernard told the court that as executor of the estate he would prefer to wait to sell her land for a little while. "By postponing the sale, till some time after the payment of the Winnebago annuities[,] the property would likely sell for a better price – money being now very scarce."[21]

Widow Powers had promised to settle the estate after the annuity payments, but it was not to be. At another hearing late that year, she and Chenevert stalled again, commenting that "at the last sale made ... they had to sue one man for the collection of what he owed and they have not yet collected."[22] In June of 1845 they needed another extension, explaining that "there was several lots sold to three individuals, which they always promise to pay ... from day to day."[23]

Euphrosine tried to hold onto some of her land as long as possible, mortgaging it when necessary. According to genealogical researcher, Reverend M. E. Fraser, "in 1850 at the final settlement of the estate, the assets were given as $340 and the liabilities were $680[,] most of which was claimed by H. L. Dousman."[24] In 1850 when the land on which her house stood was auctioned for $50 to settle Strange Powers's estate, Euphrosine bought back the property for $100 and mortgaged it.[25] (Once the estate was settled, a widow such as Euphrosine could own and sell land without court approval.)

But Euphrosine managed to hang onto some of her land until 1854, when she sold a town lot to her son-in-law Louis Barrette and another parcel to her daughter Marie Domitille Brisbois; she also sold part of her village lot to Hercules Dousman for $300.[26] As we have seen, the former fur-trade magnate was diversifying his business practices and owned

---

[21] Domitille Brisbois Probate file, entry for August 21, 1848, Crawford County Courthouse.

[22] Probate Book B, 360.

[23] Probate Book B, 395.

[24] Fraser, "Early Families of Prairie du Chien," 19.

[25] "National Register of Historic Places Inventory – Nomination form," for Strange Powers house, 2; Dale Klemme, "So, What Do We Know?" Thanks to Dale Klemme of Prairie du Chien for sharing this with me; Deed Book F, 447, 471.

[26] Deed Book G, 398, 464, 467, Register of Deeds Office, Prairie du Chien. This latter sale may have been part of the estate's settlement.

more and more of the real estate throughout the region. But Euphrosine was able to keep at least some of the Meskwakis' land in the family by selling it cheaply to family members.

She later borrowed against the town lots she still owned and used other land to secure promissory notes. During the 1857 economic depression, she was unable to pay her daughters' tuition and pledged three lots to cover that debt.[27] That same year, she mortgaged two of the other town lots she owned, losing one to foreclosure five years later.[28]

Although Euphrosine and Strange had donated the land for St. Gabriel's Church, she was not absolved from her obligations to another arm of the Catholic Church. In 1860, the Sisters of Charity of the Blessed Virgin Mary sued Euphrosine Antaya Powers because she could not pay the $750 worth of back tuition for her daughters Adrienne and Jane who attended their Dubuque school, St. Mary's Academy. I. P. Perret Gentil, a local attorney who had been asked to collect the debt, wrote, "I think they are very Poor and have nothing but an old house and three town lots.... Value probably $200[;] at present property has no worth at all."[29] In the 1860 census, Euphrosine Powers was listed as having $500 in real estate and $100 in personal property. Her daughter Adrienne Cowden, age twenty-five, and son John, age twenty-two, lived with her. None of them had an occupation listed.[30] As treasurer and assessor for Prairie du Chien, Gentil tried in 1868 to auction off Euphrosine's four remaining lots to pay these obligations, but no one bought them. Perhaps by refusing to bid, her neighbors were protecting her. Finally, in 1869, to satisfy Euphrosine's debt of $750, two of the lots were awarded to Sister Mary F. Clarke of the Sisters of Charity; a few months later Clarke sold them to Gentil for $250.[31]

But Euphrosine Antaya Powers had not yet exhausted her opportunities for gaining real estate, because in a striking irony, Euphrosine was granted another parcel of land in 1860. Land that the U.S. government had taken from the Sauk and Meskwaki Indians in 1804 and from the Ho-Chunks in 1837 was available not only to people who would pay for

[27] Mortgage Book D, 341.

[28] Mortgage Book B, 456, Mortgage Book C, 183, Deed Book 17, 114.

[29] I. P. Perret Gentil to T. J. Donoghoe, February 25, 1860, Folder 19, Item 14, Sisters of Charity Archives, BVM Center, Dubuque, Iowa, courtesy of Virginia Powell. This later became Clarke University.

[30] 1860 Wisconsin Federal Census, Schedule 6, 15, dwelling #120.

[31] Virginia Powell, personal collection; Consul Willshire Butterfield, *History of Crawford and Richland Counties* (Springfield, IL: Union Publishing, 1884), 636, 639.

it, but also as a gift to veterans of the army.[32] Land bounties had been available since the Revolutionary War, but by 1855 the federal government was willing to give up to 160 acres to any man who had served in a military unit for at least two weeks. Sergeant Strange Powers had served with the militia for twenty-eight days during the "frontier disturbances" in 1827, putting down the "Winnebago Revolt," a brief rebellion against American pressures to remove Native people. Euphrosine, as his widow, applied for and in 1860 received 146.89 acres of land in Seneca Township, north of Prairie du Chien. Thus, Indian land came full circle back into the possession of a Meskwaki woman's daughter. But instead of keeping it, she turned it over to Ira Brunson, either for money or to compensate Brunson for surveying her other lots.[33] Brunson turned around and sold the land for $195.[34]

### "Half-Breed" Treaty Lands

Although Euphrosine lost land because she had sent her children to boarding school, she gained land because she was Meskwaki on her mother's side. As we have seen, this was not the first time the tribe had developed strategies to keep land control with family members. When the local tribes had granted permission for traders to establish a community at Prairie du Chien, they gave that permission to men who had married into the tribes, including Pierre Antaya, Pokoussee's husband and Euphrosine's father. Antaya family efforts in the early 1820s had ensured, at least temporarily, that Meskwaki lands would stay with Meskwaki kin, at least for a while. Thus when the southern part of the Prairie was divided up under Isaac Lee's scrutiny in a system where wives could not own land independently, Antaya husbands and cousins got most of the land patents.

---

[32] Nancy Oestreich Lurie, *Wisconsin Indians* (Madison: State Historical Society of Wisconsin, 1987), 18; John G. Rice, "The Effect of Land Alienation on Settlement," *Annals of the Association of American Geographers* 68, no. 1 (Mar. 1978), 63.

[33] Strange Powers, Warrant No. 29702, June 15, 1860, Bureau of Land Management, General Land Office Records Online. www.glorecords.blm.gov, accessed Aug. 23, 2010. At least two other Creoles received land for this service: Private John B. St. Martin and Private Charles Menard. G. R. Frakes, "Partial Michigan-Wisconsin Black Hawk War Rosters," Michigan Territory (Wisconsin) Militia, American Armed Forces of the Black Hawk War, Black Hawk War Message Board, http://blackhawkwar.proboards.com/index.cgi?action=display&board=michigan&thread=659&page=1, accessed August 23, 2010.

[34] Map of Crawford County, Wisconsin / S. Briggs, R. C. Falconer, 1878, Wisconsin Historical Society Library Archives, Madison; Deed Book L, 560, Deed Book N., 639. Thanks to Josh Wachuta for locating this information.

Midwestern tribes' other strategies to retain control of the Native landscape came to light in the bargaining that took place before designated tribal leaders touched the quill to paper. As tribes were forced to cede lands to the U.S. government, negotiations surrounding the treaties they signed provided opportunities to reserve some of the land for their friends and intermarried relatives. These reserved tracts and parcels could become bases for those required to move west, places where kin remained to tend the landscape and host homecoming visits from time to time.

Numerous treaties with Midwestern tribes stipulated that portions of the ceded land would be given to friends and relatives. For example, the 1817 treaty with the Wyandots, Senecas, Delawares, Shawnees, Potawatomis, Odawas, and Ojibwes gave land grants to blood and adopted kin. To further illustrate, in 1821 and 1833 the Odawa negotiated land grants for specific people.[35] In some cases, people who had been helpful to the tribes, or to whom the tribes owed money, received grants. Thus, for example, in the treaties of 1829 and 1832, the French and Potawatomi interpreter Antoine LeClaire and his Meskwaki-French wife Marguerite LePage LeClaire received three land grants in the vicinity of Saukenuk which allowed them to found the towns of Davenport, Moline, and LeClaire and become wealthy and prominent community leaders in Davenport Iowa.[36] Afterward, Marguerite hosted annual visits of Meskwaki at her home. A local historian wrote, "For years, large delegations of the tribesmen came here every fall, whole villages at a time, and camped near [the] house and enjoyed the hospitality of the family."[37] These kinsmen "were always made welcome, entertained as long as they wished to remain, and when leaving, always carried away as a free gift what necessaries they required – corn, flour, etc."[38]

Several treaties affected Prairie du Chien residents: An 1824 treaty with the "Sac and Fox" (Sauk and Meskwaki people) allocated a portion of the ceded land in Iowa for unidentified members of mixed heritage; and Winnebago/Ho-Chunk treaties of 1829, 1832, and 1855 specified that land in ceded areas would be reserved to particular children of mixed parentage.[39] Sometimes mixed people received land scrip – allowing them to select parcels anywhere federal land was available. In 1856,

---

[35] Kappler, *Indian Affairs: Laws and Treaties,* Vol. 2, 145–147, 199–200, 392–393.

[36] Kappler, *Indian Affairs: Laws and Treaties,* Vol. 2, 298, 350.

[37] Harry E. Downer, *History of Davenport and Scott County, Iowa* (Chicago: S.J. Clarke, 1910), 403.

[38] Downer, *History of Davenport and Scott County,* 400.

[39] Kappler, *Indian Affairs: Laws and Treaties,* Vol. 2, 207, 301–302, 347, 692.

680 "Sioux half bloods" were listed as entitled to land scrip in lieu of land that had been promised in an 1830 treaty; seventeen of them were listed as living in Prairie du Chien.[40] All seventeen "Sioux half bloods" who received land scrip in the 1855 treaty were still in Prairie du Chien in 1860, but most were still very young. Other treaties, of course, did not offer land to mixed relatives.

The Sac and Fox Half-Breed Tract in southeastern Iowa may have been the brainchild of Maurice Blondeau (whose mother Keepaikeoa was Meskwaki and father Nicholas was French Canadian), or of a Meskwaki leader of mixed ancestry named Morgan.[41] Both tribes and the government approved of land grants to "half breeds." Tribal leaders indicated their support for it not only as signatories to the treaty but also through their correspondence with Superintendent of Indian Affairs William Clark.[42] But according to historian Thomas Ingersoll, the government also had reason to support giving land reserves for the mixed-ancestry kin of Indians being forced to move away. He argues that because "mixed bloods" were effective as leaders in resisting removal and other forms of government pressures, federal officials sought to separate them from the other tribal members. Furthermore, separating the more acculturated métis from the "full bloods" made the latter appear culturally more conservative and supported the contention of pro-removal advocates that the "civilization" program was not working, according to Ingersoll.[43]

But mixed-ancestry Sauk and Meskwaki people who had put down roots in other places or who envisioned a future for themselves in other locales hesitated to make their homes in Iowa and were sometimes tempted

---

[40] James L. Hansen, "Two Early Lists of Mixed-Blood Sioux," *Minnesota Genealogical Journal* 6 (Nov. 1986): 1–6; Hansen, "A Roll of Sioux Mixed Bloods, 1855–56," *Minnesota Genealogical Journal* 7 (Nov. 1987): 1–20.

[41] B. L. Wick, "The Struggle for the Half-Breed Tract," *Annals of Iowa*, 3rd series, 7, no. 1 (April 1905): 18; Thomas Forsyth, "A List of the Sac and Fox half breeds, who claim land according to the Treaty made at Washington City with the Chiefs Sac and Fox Tribes on 4th August 1824," Thomas Forsyth Papers, Lyman Draper Manuscripts, microfilm, 2T, 21–23, State Historical Society of Wisconsin, Madison. On Morgan as leader, see William T. Hagan, *The Sac and Fox Indians* (Norman: University of Oklahoma Press, 1989), 100,108, 117, 146.

[42] Forsyth papers, Draper Papers, Wisconsin Historical Society Library, microfilm, 2T, 21; "Dr. Galland's Account of the Half-Breed Tract," *Annals of Iowa* 10 (July 1912): 454–455. The argument that the "civilization" programs were not working was used to justify Indian removal.

[43] Thomas N. Ingersoll, *To Intermix with Our White Brothers: Indian Mixed Bloods in the United States from Earliest Times to the Indian Removals* (Albuquerque: University of New Mexico Press, 2005), 224–228.

to sell their rights to the Tract. Lieutenant Joseph LaMotte wrote a newsy letter from Prairie du Chien to his friend on September 2, 1836, reporting the latest gossip and recent land sales. Lamotte's letter commented on two "half-breed" claims that had come on the market. He remarked that "Dousman and Brunet have bought the claim of *Jeandron*, – at what price is unknown – they probably gave him a horse – a fiddle a hatband and a Song (with the privilege of singing himself!)" [emphasis in original]. He also remarked that "Powers, I understand, offers his halfbreed claim for $3000 – this is the best chance for Speculation that I have heard of here."[44]

The claims offered for sale were shares in the Half-Breed Tract that had been set aside as part of the 1824 treaty with the Sauks and Meskwakis.[45] It included 119, 000 acres of land in the southern part of Lee County, Iowa, and initially the land was not divided: it was communally owned.[46] Many people of mixed Sauk-Fox and European ancestry who were entitled to shares in the Half-Breed Tract lived at Prairie du Chien at one time or other, including the Antayas, Heberts, Giards, St. Jeans, Blondeaus, Johnsons, and Pierre Jeandron.[47] If Strange Powers was offering a half-breed claim for sale, it was his wife Euphrosine's and had come under his control because of the legal *coverture* of wives under the American laws.

A few of the mixed Sauk and Meskwaki people who lived in places other than Prairie du Chien did move to the land. For example, Mawwaiquoi, her husband Dr. Samuel Muir, and their children had a house at Puckeshetuck, which would later be known as the town of Keokuk.[48] By 1829, there were about twenty families living at Keokuk, where Maurice Blondeau, one of the "half-breed" recipients, had established a farm and tavern. The American Fur Company set up a trading post with several buildings and at least eight employees there.[49] The community, it seems, was developing into a typical frontier fur-trade town. Historian Jacob

[44] J. H. LaMotte to William Beaumont, September 2, 1836, Beaumont Papers, Missouri Historical Society.

[45] Kappler, *Indian Affairs: Laws and Treaties*, Vol. 2, 207.

[46] Wick, "The Struggle for the Half-Breed Tract," 17.

[47] Forsyth, "A List of the Sac and Fox half breeds," 1824.

[48] Isaac R. Campbell, "Recollections of the Early Settlement of Lee County," *Annals of Iowa*, 1st series, 5 (1867): 889–890; Jacob van der Zee, "The Sac-Fox Half Breed Tract," *Iowa Journal of History and Politics* 13 (April 1915): 151–165, 153; Forsyth, "A List of the Sac and Fox half breeds," 1824.

[49] Tanis Chapman Thorne, "People of the River: Mixed-Blood Families on the Lower Missouri" (Ph.D. diss., University of California, Los Angeles, 1987), 203; van der Zee, "The Sac-Fox Half Breed Tract," 155.

van der Zee wrote that "village life on the Half-Breed Tract was nothing if not sociable: card-playing, dances, horse-racing, and boxing matches afforded the mixed population their chief amusements."[50]

Originally, the "half-breeds" owned the land in common, and not individually. The 1824 treaty stated that they were to hold it "by the same title, and in the same manner, that other Indian titles are held."[51] Unlike in tribal communities, however, there was no organized government for the reserve, nor were there designated leaders, official council, or legal system.[52] This made residents feel that they were without leadership and had no protection against intruders or criminals.

### "Remove All the White People"

From an early date, problems of control prompted tribal leaders, "half-breeds," and their Euro-American kin to petition the federal government for help. In 1834, nineteen of the grantees complained that "The people of the Illinois and Missouri touching their very borders on the east[,] south and west, and the settlements of Debuk's Mines are not far on the north and settlers some of them unauthorized *intruders*, are constantly coming in, against whom your petitioners have no legal or delegated means of protection or redress."[53] In 1830, six Sauk and Meskwaki chiefs dictated to their agent a letter to Governor William Clark (Superintendent of Indian Affairs at St. Louis) about the Half-Breed Tract. Perchapaho, Pishkeenanie, Wabalalow, Taimah, Keokuk, and Mukkopaum visited their agent Thomas Forsyth and requested that he express their concern about squatters and liquor vendors on the Tract.

Father; we wish you to remove all the white people now on that tract of land which we intended for the use of the half-breeds of our nations and not to allow any white people of any description to settle and live on that land except a father, a husband or wife of any of the half-breeds or an agent or agents appointed by the President. Father; we wish you to prevent any white persons or half-breeds from keeping any spirituous liquors for sale on any part of the above mentioned

---

[50] Van der Zee, "The Sac-Fox Half Breed Tract," 159–160.

[51] Kappler, *Indian Affairs: Laws and Treaties,* Vol. 2, 207.

[52] Petition to the House of Representatives, August 25, 1829, "Sac-Fox Half-Breed Claims: Sept. 30, 1828, to June 9, 1837," Records of the Superintendent of Indian Affairs, St. Louis, Vol. 32, Kansas State Historical Society Microfilm, 3–9.

[53] "The petition of the undersigned half breeds descendants of the Sack and Fox tribes of Indians," ca. 1834, to Congress of the United States, Photostat copy in US Mss. BP, Wisconsin Historical Society, Madison. Thanks to James L. Hansen for sharing this document.

tract of land on any account whatever, but if any white people or half-breeds who wish to sell goods to Indians or others, we can have no objection to their being allowed to remain anywhere on the tract of land, provided you choose to give them a license.[54]

Not only were squatters and whiskey sellers invading the Tract but the woods were being looted also. An early resident in 1847 complained that "For the last ten years the timber on this tract has been esteemed as common booty, and within that time more than fifty thousand dollars damage has been sustained."[55]

### "Already Become Civilized"

If the intent was to set aside communally owned lands for the mixed ancestry members of the tribes to live on while their fully Native relatives were being forced to go west, this goal was not shared by all the grantees. Some of the adults, and the guardians of children entitled to shares in the reservation, did hope to make their homes there, but others wanted to be able to sell their claims.[56] The unwillingness of this latter cohort to be segregated as a separate group identified as "half-breeds" would doom the Half-Breed reservation but help ensure that they would avoid being racialized as non-white in the region.

Four of the Antayas – Maria, Chrysostome, Isaac, and Isidore – signed a petition in 1829 regarding the Half-Breed Tract. So did twenty-three others, including Euphrosine Antaya's husband Strange Powers (who presumed to sign on her behalf as part of the system of legal *coverture* for wives). The petitioners asked that the land be allotted rather than held in common, arguing that because they had become acculturated they would be hesitant to settle on the land unless it was individually owned. They explained that "most of them [had] already become civilized" and stated that while some were living in the traditional Meskwaki communities, others were "raised and educated in the habits, manners and customs of the whites," and "many have received good and some a very liberal education, & are in all respects, identified with the white population." Dividing the Tract into separate parcels, the petition argued, would "stimulate the industry and consequently promote the improvement and advance the happiness of the settlers," while providing a good example

---

[54] Forsyth papers, Draper Papers, Wisconsin Historical Society Library, microfilm, 2T, 21; "Dr. Galland's Account of the Half-Breed Tract," 454–455.

[55] "Dr. Galland's Account of the Half-Breed Tract," 457.

[56] Thorne, "People of the River," 205–207.

to "the Indians in the vicinity."[57] Similarly, the 1830 letter from the Sauk and Meskwaki chiefs requested that the lands be "surveyed and equally divided."[58]

The petition of 1829 also pointed out the lack of government on the Tract and the difficulties this situation posed in keeping order and in protecting themselves from squatters and other intruders: "The persons designated not being an organized community[,] tribe or nation, cannot be supposed to have rules[,] laws[,] or institutions of binding force, by which rights are to be determined, their possessions protected even against each other or to settle disputes among themselves, nor will they have any means to punish or prevent the intruders of the whites or others."[59]

The 1829 petition suggested that the "half-breeds" planned to keep the land rather than sell it. "Your memorialists ... are persuaded that the said reservation was made not to be used merely as bounty ground for a time, and then surrendered but to be enjoyed by them permanently and for beneficial purposes, for their improvement in agriculture & civilization."[60] Were some of them being disingenuous? It is hard to know.

If white squatters were unafraid to park their families on the Tract, some of the "half-breeds" were not so sanguine. John Connolly said that the grantees hesitated to "make improvements" or begin farming until a survey and division could happen.[61] Given the expectation that the lands would be divided, one can understand if grantees wishing to settle on the Tract hesitated to choose a building site without knowing if they would be confirmed on that location or forced to move. Furthermore, some of the grantees objected to the notion that the Half-Breed Tract should be allotted. Historian Tanis Thorne found that "the serious mixed-blood settlers became alarmed and petitioned the War Department to reverse the decision on the right to alienate property," but although the War Department tried to reverse Congress's permission to sell, the reversal was unenforceable.[62]

Who were the Sauk and Meskwaki "half-breeds" entitled to a share in the Tract? Unlike most treaties that gave land parcels to individuals, the

---

[57] Records of the Superintendent of Indian Affairs, St. Louis, Vol. 32, Kansas State Historical Society.
[58] Perchapaho and others to William Clark, June 9, 1830, Records of the Superintendent of Indian Affairs, St. Louis, Kansas State Historical Society.
[59] Perchapaho and others to William Clark, June 9, 1830.
[60] Perchapaho and others to William Clark, June 9, 1830.
[61] Van der Zee, "The Sac-Fox Half Breed Tract," 161.
[62] Thorne, "People of the River," 207.

treaty of 1824 did not list the grantees, creating a great deal of controversy and plenty of opportunities for fraud. Up and down the Mississippi River, over a hundred people in Iowa, Illinois, Wisconsin, and Missouri had their claims recorded, urged their friends and relatives to testify for them (Indian, métis, Canadian, or American), secured the services of justices of the peace and county clerks and anyone else who could write, and sent it all to Clark.

Between 1828 and 1837, William Clark collected ninety-two pages of correspondence, depositions, and notes about the Half-Breed Tract, mostly regarding the identities of the offspring of mixed marriages.[63] In dozens of letters, depositions, and documents, all kinds of frontier people became involved in the process of determining who would be the beneficiaries of the Half-Breed land grant of 1824.[64] Thus, for example, Denis Courtois, "sworn on the Holy Evangelist of Almighty God," on March 8, 1834, testified that "he has resided at Prairie du Chien since the year 1792 & that he was well acquainted with Pierre Antaya Senr., a Canadian by birth who resided at said place and who married a Fox woman Keezish (or the Sun) – the Pierre Antaya Jr. is the son of said Pierre Antaya Senr., by the said Fox woman ... and has two brothers viz Isaac and Chrysostome & three sisters, Mrs. Larriviere, Mr[s] Powers & Mr[s] Proveau ... and that said Pierre Antaya Jr is entitled to all the rights & priviledges of a half breed of the Fox nation." This deposition was recorded by Joseph Rolette, Justice of the Peace, and followed by a certificate from Crawford County Clerk Joseph Brisbois affirming that Rolette was indeed a justice of the peace.[65] And on February 4, 1834, Keokuk himself and eleven other Native men told a Hancock County, Illinois, justice of the peace that "Christostome alias Christopher Entaya is a half breed of the Sac & Fox Tribes of Indians, and ... is entitled to an equal share or proportion of the tract of land reserved by the said Tribes of Indians in their Treaty ... and that the mother of said ... Chrisostome ... was ... Po-Ko-See."[66]

[63] Records of the Superintendent of Indian Affairs, St. Louis, Vol. 32, Kansas State Historical Society.

[64] Clark recommended that claimants obtain depositions from those who knew them, to be recorded by a justice of the peace and accompanied by a letter from "a clerk of some court of record" certifying that the person recording the deposition was in fact a justice of the peace. William Clark, Superintendent of Indian Affairs, to Doct. L. Garland, January 7, 1834, Records of the Superintendent of Indian Affairs, St. Louis, Vol. 32, Kansas State Historical Society.

[65] Records of the Superintendent of Indian Affairs, 67–68. Keezish was apparently another of Pokoussee's names.

[66] Records of the Superintendent of Indian Affairs, 60–61.

To further illustrate, on April 30, 1834, Courtois, Louise Queré, and Michael Dubois testified about all the eighteen people they knew to be "half-breeds."[67] On December 12, 1833, Mah-me-ash-e-ko, "an old Sac man," swore that he "was personally known to Tus-se-sac-kuk, a Sac woman who was the wife of a Canadian Frenchman by the name of Baptiste Jaco, and during her residence with the said husband, she was the mother of a son by the name of Baptiste Jaco, but commonly called Baptiste Twome ... now residing at Ke-o-kuck town."[68] On December 12, 1833, Sher-a-no-quah, "an ancient woman of the Fox Tribe," recorded her acquaintance with Mas-sauk-que and her husband Joseph St. Jean, and their children Archange and Louisa. The interpreter added to the document an assurance that "the within facts were fully stated by the within deponent in the Sac tongue and appeared to be well understood by her."[69]

At the urging of John W. Johnson, the father of three of the "half-breeds," William Clark in 1832 appointed a man to survey the reservation, but although this work was completed by 1833, titles were not forthcoming.[70] Congress in 1834 and 1836 responded to pressure and gave the "half-breeds" permission to sell their claims.[71] By the latter date, occupants of the Tract included people with a wide range of backgrounds – some with sketchy claims. According to historian B. L. Wick, "there might be on the same land, half-breeds, Indians, speculators and squatters, all claiming title to the land through some pretext or other."[72]

In the meantime, land speculators were buying up "half-breed claims" to the Tract. Euro-Americans hoping to make a killing in the real estate market used both fair means and foul to get "half-breeds" to sign away their rights to part of the Tract. Echoing LaMotte's suggestion that Jeandron had received a horse, a fiddle, a hatband, and a song, Wick asserted, "It is stated on good authority that one Indian trader ... purchased claims worth several thousand dollars, for a horse, a pony, a saddle, or a barrel of whiskey.... So many transactions of this kind went on,

---

[67] Records of the Superintendent of Indian Affairs, 70–72.
[68] Records of the Superintendent of Indian Affairs, 55. Testimony was taken in Hancock County, Illinois.
[69] Records of the Superintendent of Indian Affairs, 56–57.
[70] Van der Zee, "The Sac-Fox Half Breed Tract," 163.
[71] "History of Early Title," typescript, Lee County Recorder, Abstracts in South Lee County, Fort Madison, Iowa; Thorne, "People of the River," 207.
[72] Wick, "The Struggle for the Half-Breed Tract," 21.

that all these land contracts became known in law, as 'blanket claims.'"[73] Some Creoles and Indians of "full blood" conspired, according to Wick, to present people of unmixed Native ancestry as entitled to shares in the Tract, to entice investors into purchasing sham claims.[74] In fact, the Index to the Lee County Deed Book for this period is full of Indian names, supporting this accusation.[75]

One couple that had been duped by a speculator in 1833 wrote to Indian Superintendent William Clark to complain. Amos Vanorsdal, whose wife Louisa Muir was a grantee, wrote, "Some time since[,] I was married to a Daughter of the late Doctor Muir and immediately after said marriage, a man by the name of Aldridge obtained a deed from us, for my wife's proportion ... – now sir when we signed said deed, we did not understand the matter at tall[*sic*]." Aldridge had apparently invited the couple to his home for dinner, given Louisa, "a few articles of clothing," and sent them on their way. Vanorsdal explained, "the whole was not worth more than fifty dollars."[76]

Soon the business of speculation became more sophisticated, as corporations organized to separate the grantees from their rights to the land. In 1836, the New York Land Company sent William Elliot Lee to the region to set up shop. Lee hired Isaac Galland to buy claims from the Sauk and Meskwaki métis, claims that were later resold for large profits.[77] The St. Louis Land Company was another player in the frenzy of speculation but was eventually taken over by the New York Land Company.[78] Yet another firm, the Des Moines Land Company, advertised in 1837 that it was offering land for sale in the Tract, including town lots in Keokuk and Montrose, on convenient terms: one fourth down payment in cash, and the balance divided into equal payments in two and three years at 6 percent interest. Potential buyers could be accommodated free of charge "with rooms, or dwelling houses, and stabling for horses and cattle ... for a reasonable time, to erect buildings on such lands as they may

---

[73] Wick, "The Struggle for the Half-Breed Tract," 20.

[74] Wick, "The Struggle for the Half-Breed Tract," 20–21.

[75] "Index to Lots and Lands 1," 1837–1850, Recorder of Deed Office, Lee County Courthouse, Keokuk.

[76] Louiza Muire and Amos Vanorsdall [sp?] to William Clark, May 18, 1833, "Sac-Fox Half-Breed Claims: Sept. 30, 1828 to June 9, 1837," Records of the U.S. Superintendent of Indian Affairs, St. Louis, Vol. 32, Kansas State Historical Society, microfilm.

[77] "Bank services began before there were actual banks," Fort Madison, Iowa, *Daily Democrat*, n.d. [2005]; source provided by Lee County Recorder, Keokuk, Iowa.

[78] Wick, "The Struggle for the Half-Breed Tract," 21.

purchase."[79] People from as far away as St. Louis, Mississippi, Delaware, Pennsylvania, New York, and Canada purchased land claims.[80]

The trouble was just starting, though, because the Half-Breed Tract had not been divided yet. So in April of 1840, Josiah Spalding and twenty-five others filed a "petition" in the District Court of Lee County, Iowa, at Fort Madison against Euphrosine Antaya and seven other grantees, requesting they agree to have the Half-Breed Tract partitioned. After much testimony was taken, the court in May of 1841 decided in the case of *Josiah Spaulding et al. vs. Euphrosine Antaya et al.* that there were 101 valid undivided shares in the claim. About *twelve* of them were held by the original "half-breed" grantees and the rest went to people who had purchased, cajoled, or cheated the métis Sauk and Fox people out of their rights in the land.[81] Josiah Spaulding, for example, said he had acquired a one half share from Margaret Antaya, a one half share from her sister Theotiste Antaya Prevost, one eighth share from Mary Giard, and a quarter share from Francis Blondeau.[82]

The Antaya family apparently was not all of one mind on whether to sell their shares of the Half-Breed Tract. Euphrosine Antaya Powers was the only defendant in the *Spaulding* case who never appeared in court.[83] Either she opposed the partition of the land or just decided to hold on as long as possible to the ancestral real estate, passively resisting by non-participation in the court proceedings. Certainly, she would have been aware of the situation as her neighbors and kin did appear in court to participate in the case. In 1841, a judge ultimately approved 101 people to get a share of the partitioned Half-Breed Tract – actual land deeds. But Euphrosine was the only member of the Antaya family to get "Half-Breed" land; the other siblings had apparently all sold out. Chrysostome Antaya, for example, sold his entire claim to Isaac Galland in 1840 for $122, a fraction of its worth.[84]

[79] Montrose *Western Adventurer*, August 19, 1837, reprinted in the *Annals of Iowa* 7, no. 8 (Jan. 1907): 637.
[80] "Dr. Galland's Account," 461.
[81] "Decree in Partition of the Half Breed Tract in Lee County, Iowa, 1840," rendered by Charles Mason, Chief Justice of the Territorial Supreme Court of Iowa, *Annals of Iowa*, 3rd series, 14, no. 6 (October 1924): 424–460.
[82] "Decree in Partition," 425.
[83] "Decree in Partition," 452; "History of Early Title," Part of Abstracts in South Lee County, Lee County Recorder, Fort Madison, Iowa.
[84] "Index to Lots and Lands 1," 1837–1850; Deed Book 8, 16, 329; Deed Book 9, 583–584, 611; Deed Book 10, 135, 260–262, 272–275, 615–616. Lee County Register of Deeds Office, Keokuk. Thanks to Betty Posz for help with these materials. The town of Nashville was later called Galland. Van der Zee, "The Sac-Fox Half Breed Tract," 157.

In 1841, three commissioners divided the Tract into separate parcels and allotted them to specific claimants.[85] Euphrosine Antaya Powers received eighteen separate properties: eleven town lots in the city of Keokuk, two in Nashville, and five parcels of land in rural areas, including about 1,270 acres. Between 1847 and 1850, she sold the land for $3,490 in eleven separate transactions.[86] None of this land was mentioned or considered in the records regarding the Strange Powers estate. Somehow she succeeded in shielding this property from the obligations to repay the estate's debts. That many of the Half-Breed Tract documents referred to her as Euphrosine Antaya rather than Powers may have helped her to keep these properties separate from those in Prairie du Chien subject to the probate court's control.

Of course, the judgment of partition in the 1841 court case *Josiah Spaulding et al. v. Euphrosine Antaya et al.* was contested, and the conflict wended its way through the courts until it was finally concluded in the U.S. Supreme Court in 1854, three decades after the Half-Breed Tract was established in the treaty.[87]

Who benefited from the creation of the Half-Breed Tract? Probably no more than ten of the mixed Sauk and Meskwaki people who were supposed to benefit actually lived on the land for very long. Perhaps four dozen of them sold their rightful shares for a consideration that might have ranged from $2,000 to a fiddle, a hatband, and a song.[88] Certainly a substantial number of non-Native speculators and lawyers lined their pockets as litigation dragged through the courts and as landsharks sought to make a killing on the process. Although few of the so-called half-breeds actually lived on the land, it served for more of them as a resource they could convert into cash when they needed it, even if they were often paid significantly less than its eventual value due to both greed and the uncertainties of titles to land tied up in a series of court cases. And because they did not move from mainstream communities like Prairie du Chien onto a segregated "Half-Breed" reservation, they avoided being permanently branded as racialized outsiders.

[85] "History of Early Title," Part of Abstracts in South Lee County, Lee County Recorder, Fort Madison, Iowa.

[86] "Index to Lots and Lands 1," 1837–1850; Deed Book 8, 16, 329; Deed Book 9, 583–584, 611; Deed Book 10, 135, 260–262, 272–275, 615–616.

[87] "History of Early Title," Part of Abstracts in South Lee County, Lee County Recorder, Fort Madison, Iowa; Wick, "The Struggle for the Half-Breed Tract," 25–26. *Coy v. Mason*, 1854, United States Supreme Court, http://supreme.justia.com/us/58/580/case.html, accessed Dec. 20, 2011.

[88] "Dr. Galland's Account of the Half-Breed Tract," 461.

## "None of Them Have Derived Much Benefit"

Prairie du Chien's Sauk and Meskwaki métis were not the only people of mixed ancestry living there who were supposed to get treaty land. An 1829 treaty with the Ho-Chunk identified thirty-eight "Winnebago half-breeds" – many of them living in Prairie du Chien – who would receive one or more sections of land in Wisconsin and Illinois, while their "full-blood" relatives were removed from the valuable lead mining region that had been invaded by Anglo lead rushers after 1822. It took eight years of bureaucratic foot-dragging and official bungling before parcels of land were assigned to the so-called half-breeds. By 1837 most of them had received title to parcels of 640 acres selected for them by strangers. The township grid system was used to assign the people almost randomly among five counties in two states.[89] But most of this land turned out to be located without reference to their priorities, kin, or attachments to particular places, and the lands did not have access to major rivers. So, most of the recipients sold it. Some even sold their land claims before the land parcels were identified.

In an examination of the real estate in Winnebago County, Illinois, given to the namesake tribe's peoples of mixed ancestry, county court-house records were located confirming that of sixteen parcels deeded to the treaty recipients, fourteen were sold by 1849, most for between $800 and $1,000. Eleven of the parcels were soon owned by two land speculators. In fact, the recipients sold nine of them *within two years* of receiving a patent. [90] In 1857, the Ho-Chunks' Indian Agent, J. E. Fletcher, concluded that "of the several sections of land reserved to" the so-called half-breeds, "none of them have derived much benefit from their reservations," except for three people whose "money is not yet squandered."[91]

Some of the people who received parcels of land may have been cheated out of it. For example, L'Avoine Grignon's heirs complained that, while

---

[89] Kappler, Indian Affairs: Laws and Treaties, "Treaty with the Winnebago, 1829," Vol. 2, 300–302; U.S. Bureau of Land Management, Springfield, Virginia, Misc. Vols., 471–473, "Donation," Vols. 9–12, and "Minnesota Winnebago," passim.

[90] The two land speculators were Daniel Whitney and Nicolas Boilvin. Source: records of Winnebago County, IL, county courthouse, Register of Deeds office. (I am grateful to Linda Waggoner for sharing her research files and to Jim McClurken for teaching me the research methods here.)

[91] J. E. Fletcher at Winnebago Agency to H. L. Dousman, Prairie du Chien, July 8, 1857. National Archives, RG75, Records of the Bureau of Indian Affairs, Records Relating to Claims, Records Concerning Indian Land Reserves, Reserve File Box A 401. The three were Bridgett St. Cyr Dougherty, and Frank and Joseph Thibault.

drunk, he had been duped into signing away his land to a Lieutenant McClure (then stationed at Fort Winnebago) for two bottles of whiskey and a pig.[92] In a striking example of the maxim "what goes around comes around," Lieutenant McClure was killed in 1834 during an attack against the Pawnees.[93]

One of the Ho-Chunk's daughters, however, found a way to transform the randomly allocated real estate into a resource for herself and family: Mary Gleason and her husband Jean Baptiste LaBorde in 1846 traded her 597 acres in Winnebago County, Illinois, for 100 acres on the Fox River in Wisconsin and $600 in cash. This would have been closer to where she had been living and would provide access to the river for transportation, drinking water, irrigation, and access to fish and other resources such as wild rice and water fowl.[94] Mary Gleason LaBorde, however, was unusual. Most of the grantees did not move to their "half-breed" allotments.

Treaties presented opportunities for some Native-descended people to hold onto small portions of ancestral lands when the majority of tribes were being removed. But mixed-ancestry Creoles were limited by the courts and government officials: the democratic political and judicial system that the Yankees had introduced during the 1820s exerted significant control over the distribution of treaty lands, at the local, territorial, and federal levels. If officials had intended that the "half-breed" land reserves would physically separate them from both the tribes and Anglo settler society, they failed. The "half-breeds" generally did not move to the reserves. For some of them, this may have been a way to resist being racialized by way of segregation. But some of them did derive funding by selling their land grants, funding that helped them to pay their living expenses to stay in Prairie du Chien or other communities. In order to mobilize the land as a resource, people like Euphrosine learned to work within – and in spite of – these systems.

## Families and Neighbors

The land that was supposed to provide homes for the mixed-ancestry peoples instead provided funds for some, and for others, the experience

---

[92] Affidavit of Louis Manaigre, Oct. 1857, National Archives, Res A, #389, Box 12.

[93] George M. McClure to John Wentworth, April 17, 1848, National Archives, Res A #389, Box 12. Thanks to Linda Waggoner.

[94] Winnebago County Courthouse, Book M, 215. She traded it to speculator Daniel Whitney.

of being swindled. It took many years – up to three decades – from the times of the treaties until titles were confirmed, and many got tired of waiting, lost faith that they would ever get the land, or had to cash in their claims to meet their economic obligations, and so sold out.

But even those who kept their claims until titles were issued and resisted the temptations to sell to speculators seldom moved onto the land. Why didn't the mixed Meskwaki, Sauk, and Ho-Chunk people want to live on their treaty lands? Most wanted to stay with their families, neighbors, and community. Families had become complicated – they had married people from many backgrounds and had complex ties to others in the community and surrounding regions.

There had been plenty of prejudice against the *habitants* in the nineteenth century. As we have seen, Anglos often brought a wide range of biases with them, whether they called the older residents "Canadians," "French," "half-breeds," or "Creoles." These negative attitudes, however, had been tempered by the actions of public mothers and the elite status of a few men such as Dousman and the Brisbois family, so the bigotry did not effectively marginalize the entire Creole population as racially "other." Yet during the period between 1830 and 1860 the Creole residents of Prairie du Chien were experiencing both this prejudice from the newcomers and the challenges of a changing economy. The resources they had available included not only whatever land they had been able to retain but also their sympathetic kin and neighbors.

Families like the extended Antaya Powers kin often responded by circling the wagons (to invert a pioneer trope) and organizing their homes close to one another. We can see this in the 1850 records of a census taker going door to door. We can get a sense of who lived in the same neighborhood, and if we add information about the women's maiden names to an analysis of the census records, we can see families living clustered together, often around the senior women.

Throughout the (doubtless oftentimes trying) years after Strange Powers's death, Euphrosine Antaya Powers and her relatives continued to reside near one another. The Antayas had arranged for the family to claim land together when Isaac Lee came around in 1820, and when Euphrosine had subdivided her land as she settled Strange Powers's estate, she had sold some of the lots to her relatives. In 1850, the family was still close. Euphrosine Antaya Powers was fifty-eight years old. Living next door on one side was her cousin Mary Antaya (widow of Francis La Pointe), with Mary's son Michel La Pointe, and five children. Living on the other side of Euphrosine Antaya Powers were three houses of the Barrette family, including Barrette wives Caroline Powers (Euphrosine's daughter) and Theresa La Pointe (whose mother was Susan Antaya).[95]

The residential pattern of Euphrosine Antaya Powers's family is typical of many other Creole families in Prairie du Chien. For example, dwellings 139, 140, 141, and 142 were those, respectively, of the Lessards, the Gauthiers, the Lessards, and the Cherriers. François Gauthier's wife, however, was Marianne Lessard and Flavian Cherrier's wife was Louisa Lessard. In between Marianne's house and Louisa's residence lived Joseph Lessard, a widower who was probably their father. Two doors down, in dwelling 144, was Lucretia Carriere *née* Lessard and her husband Julien, a child, and Oliver Carriere, probably Julien's brother.

Similarly, nearby was a cluster of three families in which the Canadian-born wives all had the maiden name of Ducharme. To further illustrate, Maria Laroque Menard and her husband and two children lived near Josephine Laroque Gagnier and her spouse and five children. Another extended kin group, Angelica Chenevert Benoit, her Canadian husband David and baby lived next door to two houses of older Cheneverts, probably her parents and grandparents. And in yet another, the LaPointe and Brisbois women were cousins: dwellings 29, 32, and 36 included Sophia LaPointe Cherrier, Domitille Henriette Brisbois Boisvert, Elizabeth LaPointe Richard, and their husbands and children.[96]

This pattern of female kin and their families clustering together may reflect the matrilocal residence patterns of many Midwestern tribes, and perhaps even Native women's habits of doing agricultural and other work in female kin groups. In addition, it suggests possible parallels with practices north of the border. Jennifer Brown has argued that Métis women in Rupert's Land were "centre and symbol in the emergence of Métis communities," and that their families were matrifocal in organization.[97]

---

[95] James L. Hansen, "Two Early Lists of Mixed-Blood Sioux," *Minnesota Genealogical Journal* 6 (November 1986): 4, 5.

[96] "Reverend Theodore Van den Broeck Founder of Little Chute in 1836 ... Baptismal Record, Little Chute, 1839," Peter L. Scanlan Papers, Wisconsin Historical Society, Platteville, Box 7, Folder 1, 2; Population Schedules of the Seventh Census, 1850, manuscript, Crawford County, WI, microfilm M432, Reel 995, 496–497; "Reminiscence of Theresa Barrette," in Mary Martell, *Our People the Indians: A Genealogy of the Indians and French Canadians, 1750–1950: In the areas of Prairie du Chien, Wisconsin, Harpers Ferry, Iowa, and Pembina-Red River of the North in N. Dakota and Minnesota* (n.p.: Privately published, ca. 1950), 52–53; James L. Hansen, "Crawford County, Wisconsin Marriages, 1816–1848," *Minnesota Genealogical Journal* 1(May 1984): 50.

[97] Jennifer S. H. Brown, "Woman as Centre and Symbol in the Emergence of Métis Communities," *Canadian Journal of Native Studies* 3, no. 1 (1983): 39–46.

These residence patterns at Prairie du Chien suggest that the pattern
Brown noted in Rupert's Land was sometimes practiced in Wisconsin.

### Ethnic Clusters

While the Creoles often clustered their homes with their relatives, they
also developed ethnic neighborhoods. Most of them followed one of
three patterns: (1) they moved to the countryside and took up farming in
earnest (as we have seen in a previous chapter), (2) they clustered on the
island that became known as Prairie du Chien's Fourth Ward, or (3) they
lived along the northern section of the town's main road in the neighborhood that would come to be called "Frenchtown."

### "A Little French Village": Fourth Ward

By the late 1830s, Prairie du Chien consisted of four distinct sections,
with significant ethnic clusters. In 1838, Bishop Jackson Kemper had visited Prairie du Chien and described two of the community's neighborhoods. On the island, he noted "a little French village on a sand bar."[98]
This was the section that had long been the commercial center for the fur
trade. To the east, "on the main land," Kemper commented, was "what
may be called the American village where there is the court House, post
office &c."[99] This "American village" was Upper Town, and south of it, a
neighborhood that would be known as Lower Town was being developed
and would seem to be "American" as well. To the north of Upper Town
was Frenchtown.

By 1861, the "French" island was sparsely populated, although the
Dousmans and Brisboises made their homes there. A visitor who stopped
at the Dousmans' home wrote, "you would never know it was a town,
unless previously informed of the fact – as the houses are scattered at
random over the prairie; with plenty of elbow, garden, & other kinds of
room."[100] Railroad buildings had been constructed on the lower end of
the island by the time the "Bird's-Eye View" map was created in 1870.[101]
(See Figure 6.2.)

---

[98] Bishop Jackson Kemper, "A Trip through Wisconsin in 1838," *Wisconsin Magazine of History* 8, no. 4 (June 1925): 423–445. Quote is on 426.

[99] Kemper, "A Trip," 426.

[100] David Courtenay, "Villa Louis in 1861, From D. Courtenay's Letter," *Wisconsin Magazine of History* 38, no. 4 (Summer, 1955): 254.

[101] Ruger and Stoner, "Prairie du Chien," Bird's-Eye View map, 1870, Madison, Wisconsin.

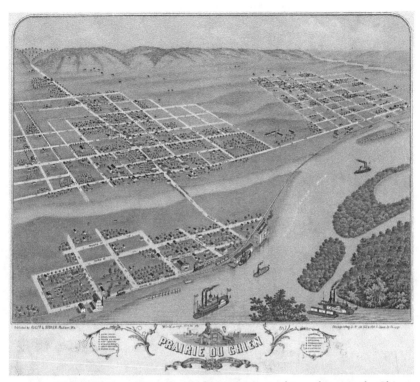

FIGURE 6.2. Bird's-Eye view map. In this 1870 map, three of Prairie du Chien's four neighborhoods are clearly evident: the Island, Upper Town, and Lower Town. North is to the left, and Frenchtown would extend in that direction. Ruger & Stoner, "Prairie du Chien," Bird's-Eye View map, 1870, Madison, Wisconsin. Wisconsin Historical Society Image ID 4111.

Eventually the island became the home of three extended families: the Valleys, LaBonnes, and Fernettes who developed a tight-knit community and family economies combining wage work with gardening, hunting and fishing on the river, and a few small businesses.[102]

### "Generous and Friendly to One Another": Frenchtown

To the north of Upper Town, however, was Frenchtown, a semi-rural neighborhood that would be warmly remembered by some of its residents, most notably Albert Coryer. We can visualize the relationship of

---

[102] Lucy Murphy interview of Dale Klemme, September 11, 2007; Lucy Murphy interview of Mary Valley and Bette Beneker, Sept. 3, 2003.

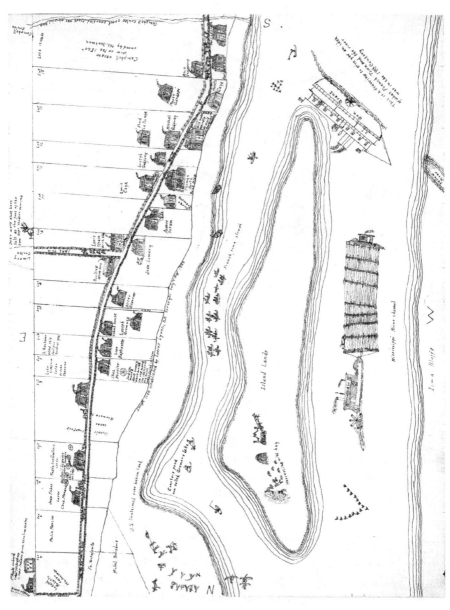

FIGURE 6.3. Albert Coryer map. Courtesy of Villa Louis Historic Site, Prairie du Chien.

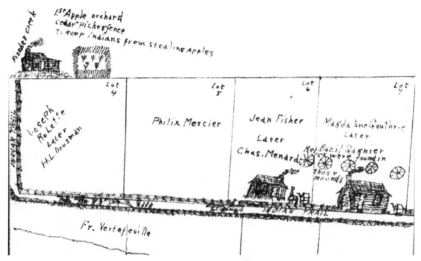

FIGURE 6.4. Coryer map, detail 1.

the *habitants* with the Frenchtown landscape, thanks to a remarkable document the elderly Coryer created in 1948. It is a map of what the Frenchtown neighborhood had been like around 1860, as it existed in his and his old neighbors' reminiscences.[103]

Coryer took pen to paper and drew his mental walk down memory lane – or to be more precise – along the north-south road that was called Indian Trail, and later Frenchtown Road in Prairie du Chien. This neighborhood was west of the farms his grandparents and great-uncles and great-aunts had established in the hills. This large, illustrated map, 19 by 24 inches in size, together with his interviews and stories, provide a unique, multifaceted view of this neighborhood as it existed in the memories of Coryer and his neighbors. (See Figures 6.3–6.5, Coryer map.)

By using it with care and corroborating the map and his memoirs against other sources such as the U.S. census, we can learn a great deal about the social and economic lives of the old fur-trade families and their descendants. It is this part of town that seemed to interest folklorists and historians in the mid-twentieth century looking for remnants of the town's fur-trade legacy. The name "Frenchtown" itself made it easy to identify this neighborhood with a particular ethnic group, those who had spoken French when the Anglophones had arrived. That the name itself was in English – Frenchtown rather than Ville Français – suggests a label facing

---

[103] Albert Coryer map, Villa Louis Historic Site library, Prairie du Chien.

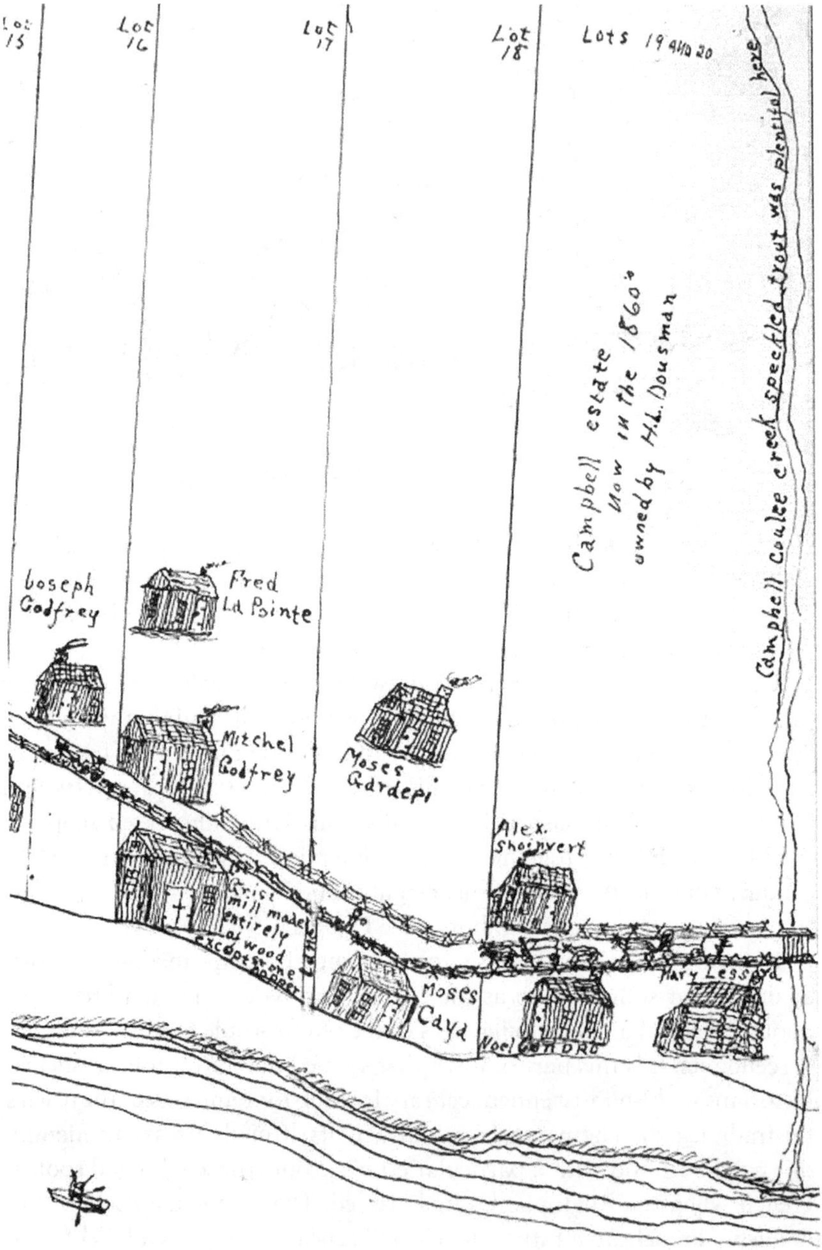

Lot 15
Lot 16
Lot 17
Lot 18
Lots 19 and 20

Campbell estate Now in the 1860's owned by H.L. Dousman

Campbell coulee creek speckled trout was plentiful here

Joseph Godfrey

Fred La Pointe

Mitchel Godfrey

Moses Gardepi

Alex. Shoinvert

Grist mill made entirely of wood except some copper

Moses Caya

Woolen Dno

Mary Lessard

FIGURE 6.5. Coryer map, detail 2.

FIGURE 6.6. "The Oyster Club." Most of the men pictured were members of the extended Barrette Family. Courtesy of Phil Barrette.

outward. We don't know, however, what the residents themselves called their neighborhood. Since Coryer's mother came from an Anglophone family, his English was good, and he had multiple perspectives of the past; but he seems to have identified primarily with the "French" population in depicting this neighborhood. It is interesting that the ethnic neighborhood was *not* identified as Métis, Indian, or "half-breed." This is a clear indication that, in spite of the prejudices of Yankees and other Anglos, the old fur-trade families had continued to avoid being racialized.

Coryer's stories, no doubt, had been told many times. His descriptions of the people and his drawings of their activities give a sense that he had considered them often and that they had been discussed in groups of old-timers sitting around their favorite beverages. (See Figure 6.6, photo of "the Oyster Club.") It is likely that Coryer presents a kind of collective community memory of the "old French people," as he called them. Certainly nostalgia colored the memories, and there is in addition a sense of auto-ethnography as Coryer tried to depict the culture and values – as well as the characters and incidents – in the lives of his parents and grandparents and their neighbors. Coryer thus shared both evidence about the events and economy of the community, and about the way the community was remembered. These sources provide an important counterbalance to the unflattering newspaper reports and letters written by their new Yankee neighbors. He clearly drew this map after consulting the Lyon's map of 1828, which was similar to the Isaac Lee Map, and it also seems to be a response to the Bird's-Eye View Map, which included Prairie du Chien's other three neighborhoods but omitted Frenchtown.

At the most basic level, Coryer's map and his stories recorded who and what was in Frenchtown in the late nineteenth century. Detailed drawings suggest the architectural styles of buildings, the location of wells and fences, and the roads along which travelers (represented by tiny people and their tiny wagons and horses) made their way in and out of town. An orchard and a salt lick, a trout-filled stream, fences, and ancient Indian mounds bring the neighborhood to life. In addition, Coryer drew and described the grocery store and the old mill. We learn from the map where the region's first bowling alley was located; we see where the school was, and that it was "an old-fashioned house with those boards, up and down wide boards with cleats nailed to it, and it was large enough to accommodate about thirty children. And of course an old box stove. I went to that school myself just a few years," he told his interviewer. [104] (See Figures 6.4 and 6.5, Coryer map details.)

He sketched the house in which his great-grandmother Marianne Lessard lived. Taking a cue from local customs, he labeled the other houses and lots by the names of the husbands, a reflection of the patriarchal land control patterns typical of his era even extending to the logic of street naming. At the same time we learn a bit about the residents. For example, "Limery Lane was named after Mr. John [Jean] Limery which lived opposite, west across the Indian Trail, and he also owned most of the Coulee [stream and surrounding land], the Limery Coulee.... Now this John Limery is the one that first introduced, or brought about, this faith cure here amongst the Canadians, and his wife had learned how to doctor with roots, herbs, and seeds."[105] Madame Limery we have met as one of the community's public mothers, the daughter of Marianne Labuche Menard. Her husband was one of a small group of "charmers," who sometimes used specific prayers to cure their neighbors. [106]

---

[104] Florence Bittner interview with Albert Coryer, 1951, Wisconsin Historical Society Library, Madison, 17.

[105] Bittner, Coryer interview, 17.

[106] Bittner, Coryer interview, 17.

In addition to creating a community portrait, Coryer tried to convey a sense of the values of the Creoles. He told his interviewer, "Well, the old French settlers were a humble class of people. They didn't try to accomplish very much, but they always had in mind of being generous and friendly to one another, and enjoy themselves. They would help one another whenever it was needed, in case one would get sort of handicapped some way through sickness or hard luck of some kind, get backwards with their work, why, the others would all pitch in and help them. They called this making a bee, working together." The *habitants* not only worked but also played together. "As far as enjoying themselves, they were a class of people who tried to be together as much as they could. They enjoyed one another's company, and they would get together especially during the holidays."[107]

The theme of looking out for neighbors and helping the unfortunate comes out in a number of Coryer's stories, as it does when I have spoken with descendants of the Creole residents during research trips to Prairie du Chien.[108] But Albert Coryer's map, anecdotes, and yarns were also meant to entertain. This story about one of the Frenchtown residents illustrates his point about communalism and adds evidence about gender expectations for domestic work, with a little twist. He said,

Right north of Joe Gremore's: One old party ... lived in Frenchtown, ... they were the oldest couple at that time, and I guess any time, in Frenchtown. The old lady was supposed to be 140 years old. [She had been] ... married four times ... he was past eighty. He still made the living for the two of them. He would work around for the neighbors on the farms and did some trapping and some hunting, and they made a living. But one spring it was getting on towards housecleaning time, and they realized the old lady couldn't clean her house herself, so the ladies of the neighborhood, those that knew her, got together – my mother was one of them – and they cleaned the house for her. The house was in terrible condition, of course. Finally they said they'd give the old lady a bath, and on giving her a bath, they found that she really had moss growing on her back.[109]

Similarly, Coryer shared another tale of community concern, and gave it another touch of humor:

Jean Baptisette, ... an old man and his son that lived there.... The son had gone to town one day and apparently the old man had – it was late in the fall, it was getting quite cold, and the old man had built quite a fire in the stove, and none of them had any brick chimneys, they just had a stovepipe going through the roof

---

[107] Bittner, Coryer interview, 10–11.
[108] This is a theme that one also finds in the Anglo Pioneers' narratives as well.
[109] Bittner, Coryer interview, 20.

and it had a piece of tin around it. And the roof had got afire and someone that just happened to be going by and noticed that roof flaming and so they run in and told Mr. B ... that his house or his roof was afire. 'Oh, is it?' he says, "Well, Charles is at town. When he comes back, I'll tell him. He'll put it out." Of course, the people that seen that realized that when Charles would come there wouldn't be any house there, it would be all burnt, so they got water from the well, and put the fire out.[110]

These communal expressions of concern and mutual assistance were good reasons for the Creoles to stay in Prairie du Chien, even as the economy was changing and prejudices persisted.

### Native Peoples

Coryer's memories and map not only sketch out the details of the social landscape of Frenchtown but also express changing relationships with Native people. Before the 1820s, nearly every woman living in Prairie du Chien was either Native or part Native. Many of the residents of Frenchtown, such as the Cheneverts, Jeandrons, and Gardipies, descended from the earlier intermarried fur-trade families and had ancestors among the Sauk, Meskwaki, and Menominee tribes.[111]

But intermarriage had declined significantly by mid-century [see Table 4.1 in Chapter 4] and so Mitchell Godfrey's full-blooded wife Ouia was unusual enough to be mentioned in Coryer's interview (and on another map he made later). Mitchell Godfrey and his Meskwaki wife, Coryer explained, had three children.

[She] soon got so that she lived the same as the other old settlers there, the French women, dressed and cooked and got along the same as the other women, and spoke the French language, of course. And still, when springtime came, she'd get lonesome for her old way of living with the Indians and also visiting her folks, so she'd tell Mitchell, "Now, you've got to take care of the children while I go visiting." And she'd put on her Indian attire and a blanket over her head and away she'd go, and she'd be gone three or four weeks. Then she'd come back to her husband.[112]

By 1860, it seems, Native people, were not usually community members, but they were not absent from the surrounding areas. In one part of Coryer's map, Native people would seem to be troublesome outsiders: the

---

[110] Bittner, Coryer interview, 17–18.

[111] Coryer spelled their names Shoinvert, Jondro, and Gardipi. Coryer map.

[112] Bittner, Coryer interview, 13.

"first apple orchard" was depicted with a "cedar picket fence to keep the Indians from stealing apples." On the river and the "unclaimed river bottom land," however, we see Indians in canoes or near their tents: one is even hunting a deer with a bow and arrow; another leads a horse with a travois attached. We also see the evidence of much older Native presence in the mounds inscribed on several lots, where Coryer also included references to excavations (see map detail).

The main street through town was labeled "Indian Trail," although on another map Coryer drew two years later, he labeled it "French Town Road" with the words (Indian Trail) in parentheses, suggesting a shift in the function, usage, and/or identity of the road, from one that brought Indians *into* town, to one that took outsiders *to* Frenchtown.[113] The shift may be interpreted as a change in Prairie du Chien's collective memory or its concept of outsiders: if fewer Indians came to town, or if their having laid out the road was forgotten, newer residents recognized the francophones as having an ethnic enclave apart from the center of the village of Prairie du Chien.

Other sources corroborate that Native people often traveled through, visited, and camped in the area, as we have seen in Chapter 4. Both Pokoussee's granddaughter Clara LaPointe Hertzog and Albert Coryer's grandmother Lucretia Carriere, for example, hosted traveling Indians.[114] Even as the Ho-Chunks and others were removed to the West, some of them remained surreptitiously or returned.

Coryer described the Courtois family for whom an Indian presence represented a paranoid delusion. Peter Gremore [Grimord], Coryer explained, "owned quite a patch of ground.... This land that he owned was really gotten through a man by the name of ... Charles [Courtois], and of course this [Grimord] married this [Courtois's] sister, and this Charles [Courtois] had gone daffy, or insane, it seems, so that all he done was walk up and down the Sandy Ridge around Gremore Lake, with a club in his hand, chasing Indians away. He said he was protecting the place from Indians. Of course, the Indians could have made away with him if they wanted to, but it seems they realized they shouldn't ... and the Indians never bothered him, and he just imagined that he was the one that was keeping the Indians away."[115] The lingering presence of Native

[113] Phil Gokey, Copy of Albert Coryer map, "Four French Family Reviews," CD-Rom, privately published, 2003, Fort Crawford Museum, Prairie du Chien.
[114] Mary Martell, *Our People the Indians*, 53.
[115] Bittner, Coryer interview, 18.

people in the area might have frightened Charles Courtois, but in the local memory, a man so fearful was not in his right mind.[116]

Yet paranoia aside, most of the Creoles in Frenchtown probably did not think of themselves as Indian most of the time. A few older adults, such as Euphrosine Antaya Powers, had been named in treaties and government documents as tribal kin (although they were "half-breeds"), and some such as her son George would eventually go to live with their tribes. Euphrosine and Strange's daughter Caroline Powers had married Louis Barrette, who had in 1919 told the newspaper reporter interviewing him that he and Caroline had both European and "Indian lineage" and that the family was "proud of it."[117] This indigeneity provided a sense of connectedness to this place. But most of the Creoles with mixed ancestry probably felt they were different from wholly Native tribal members, and thought of themselves as ethnically "French" – perhaps French Canadian – with a meaning that incorporated an understanding of the local and regional fur-trade history.

## Persistence

Places like "Frenchtown" and the island known as the Fourth Ward continued to be ethnic enclaves for the older generations of Creole people, their children, and even some culturally similar newcomers, but the Creole population declined both absolutely and in relative terms. While the *habitants* were half of the Prairie's people in 1836, they were just less than 16 percent by 1860 (see Table 2.2). The shifting ethnic balance in Prairie du Chien was clearly caused both by Anglo in-migration and by Creole out-migration. Between 1850 and 1860, 151 Creoles (35.5%) stayed in Prairie du Chien, at least 24 died (according to church records), and 249 Creoles (58.6%) disappeared, presumably having moved away.[118]

The Creoles, it would seem, were not quite so restless as many others around the region. This seems like a very low persistence rate, but throughout the Midwest, many people were on the move. By comparison, in John

---

[116] In this context, Coryer explained another change in the landscape, as Courtois Pond later became known as Gremore [Grimord] Lake.

[117] "Lewis Barrette to Celebrate His 95th Birthday."

[118] "Registre de Catholicite de la Prairie du Chien," 1840–1866, Saint Gabriel's Parish Record, translated, transcribed by Peter Scanlan, Peter Scanlan Papers, Wisconsin Historical Society, Platteville. Of course, there were probably other deaths that were not recorded in the church records.

Mack Faragher's study of Sugar Creek, Sangamon County, Illinois, only 22.2 percent of household heads persisted from 1850 to 1860; a comparable figure for Prairie du Chien would be that 42.9 percent of Creole men who were household heads persisted during that decade. Summarizing six other studies of Midwestern communities, Faragher states that rates lower than 30 percent were the norm.[119]

Not all the migration was outward. During the 1850s, 110 Creoles moved in: 49 born in Canada, 41 in Wisconsin, and 20 from various other places. This in-migration of Francophone Creoles is somewhat surprising, a pattern not noted by most authors who have commented on Creoles in the nineteenth century.[120] The existence of congenial ethnic francophone neighborhoods may have served as a pull factor for these migrants. And some may have been relatives of Creole residents, as we have seen with the example of the Carrieres and Gokeys whose initial link with the Prairie was through their kin, the Lessards.

What reasons contributed to Creole persistence in the face of the transition? Looking at the 1850 and 1860 censuses, the answer seems to be a combination of factors including family role, gender, birthplace, wealth, tribal affiliation, ties to early families, and marriage patterns. When household members were sorted by family role, it became clear that women who were wives and/or mothers were the most likely to stay in Prairie du Chien: 50 percent of them persisted, while 42.9 percent of men who were husbands and/or fathers, and 36.8 percent of children stayed during the decade. Others including boarders, employees, other relatives, persons living alone, and those in jail were much more likely to relocate when they could.[121]

Traditionally during the fur-trade era, men had been the immigrants and women created the ties. Creole *couples* at mid-century exhibited a few interesting patterns: local women seem to have married Creoles and others from outside the region, continuing the traditional exogamy. In 1850, there were sixty-three couples in which one or both of the partners were Creole. In eighteen marriages, both husband and wife were born in Wisconsin; in twenty-one couples, both were from outside the state,

---

[119] John Mack Faragher, *Sugar Creek; Life on the Illinois Prairie* (New Haven, CT: Yale University Press, 1986), 50, 249 n. 14.

[120] I have conflated "Canada," "Canada East," "L. Canada," and "W. Canada." Six of the newcomers gave "Red River" as their birthplace. Households 5, 6, 358, 359, 373, and 381 in the 1860 census.

[121] Persistence rates for these seventy-six other Creoles ranged from 0 (in jail) to 33.3 percent (boarders).

and in twenty-four cases (38%) one spouse was from Wisconsin (usually Prairie du Chien) and the other from elsewhere.

Of these twenty-four exogamous marriages, in twenty-one of them the wife was from Wisconsin and the husband from outside (16 of these husbands were Canadian); in three the husband was local and the wife an outsider. This continued the Native tradition of enlarging one's family and community with new kin ties and of using marriage to incorporate newcomers. (Of course, men were more likely to migrate alone than were women.) This pattern is illustrated in Coryer's tale about the Courtois family, where the Canadian-born Peter Grimord gained not only a wife (and a paranoid brother-in-law) but also land by marrying Elizabeth Courtois, whose family had land rights going back to Isaac Lee's 1820 property confirmation project.

And the persistence rates show that these connections could be strong: exactly half of all 126 who were married with a spouse present in 1850 were still there in 1860. Where both were from Wisconsin, 55.6 percent persisted; where only the wife was local, 61.9 percent stayed; where only the husband was local, 66.7 percent stayed; but only 31 percent of those from marriages in which both were outsiders stayed for ten years. It is interesting that those with one spouse from elsewhere were slightly more persistent than couples in which both were local, but perhaps the out-siders brought additional resources – or caution – from their previous homes.

Ties to the early Creole families and to the land seem to have influenced residents' decisions about whether to stay in Prairie du Chien. "Lyon's Map" of 1828 shows the Prairie du Chien lots and lot owners for that year; 241 of the 425 Creoles (56.7%) in 1850 had a surname, maiden name, or (for children) mother's maiden name appearing on Lyon's Map. Nearly three quarters (72.8%) of those who stayed had such land/surname ties, while only 45.2 percent of those who moved did.

Tribal affiliation was also a factor. Three fifths of Prairie du Chien's Creoles (255/424) could be identified with at least one tribe. Of 151 Creoles who *persisted* from 1850 to 1860, 75.5 percent had a tribal affiliation, while only 26.6 percent of the 249 who *moved* had Native kinship ties.[122] One's relationship to an Indian community could promote either persistence or out-migration, depending on a number of factors. Removal

[122] Forsyth, "A List of the Names of the Half-Breeds," 1824; Kappler, *Indian Affairs: Laws and Treaties*, Vol. 2, 300–302; Hansen, "Two Early Lists of Mixed-Blood Sioux," 523–530; Hansen, "A Roll of Sioux Mixed Bloods," 601–620; "Minute Book" 1849, Menominee Indian Papers, Wisconsin Historical Society Library, Madison.

was an event presenting challenges: if one's immediate family of origin was being relocated to a distant region, she or he might be tempted to accompany the family. On the other hand, one might try to stay and make a home for kin in order to help them resist removal and to maintain a presence on the ancestral land.

Ho-Chunks had the highest rate of persistence in Prairie du Chien; twenty-seven out of thirty people (90%) affiliated with them stayed out the decade, probably because the tribe had not been removed yet to the trans-Mississippi West. Mixed ancestry Ho-Chunk people seem to have shared the resistance of their kin: many members of this tribe responded to removal through the nineteenth century by hiding out and sneaking back to Wisconsin.[123] Even when they stayed at their designated reservations, they were not far from kin who lived at the Wisconsin River: during the mid-nineteenth century, although they were removed, they stayed relatively close to Prairie du Chien until the Dakota revolt of 1862. Relegated to a reservation just on the west side of the Mississippi River from Prairie du Chien from 1832 to 1846, the Ho-Chunks were relocated to a site in central Minnesota from 1848 to 1854, then were shifted south again to a reserve in southern Minnesota, where they lived 140 miles west of Prairie du Chien from 1855 to 1863. Persistence rates for other Native-related Creoles ranged from 34.7 percent (Sauk) to 43.1 percent (Dakota). The Dakota resided on a reservation about 100 miles north of Prairie du Chien from 1830 to 1851, but the Sauks and Meskwakis had by this time been removed farther west.[124]

As we might expect, wealthier people had higher persistence rates: all four people with more than $1,000 worth of real estate in 1850 lasted out the decade, as did three fifths of landowners with property values between $501 and $1,000. Persistence rates were not related to literacy: 35.7 percent of those who *could* read and write stayed, while 35.2 percent of those who could not remained in Prairie du Chien in 1860.

So the Creoles least likely to move away during the 1850s were wives and mothers, the married couples that had some local roots, the wealthy, and the Ho-Chunks' kin. Most of Prairie du Chien's Creole families lost at least some members to migration around this time. Examples abound and may help to express these data in human terms.

---

[123] Nancy Oestreich Lurie, *Wisconsin Indians* (Madison: State Historical Society of Wisconsin, 1987), 20.

[124] Helen Hornbeck Tanner, ed., *Atlas of Great Lakes Indian History* (Norman: University of Oklahoma Press, 1986), map 31, 163.

## Generations, Migration, and Persistence

Anecdotal evidence can flesh out the data for us about the ways that Creole families resolved the dilemmas of where to go and what to do in a changing world. Most of them stayed in the Midwest, moving north and west from Prairie du Chien. Some people moved to unsettled or sparsely settled areas away from the established (though evolving) economy and hierarchy of Prairie du Chien. Julia Grignon, who had sold her clothes to support the suffering Ho-Chunks, married another Creole, John (Jean) Mayrand Jr., moved to Stevens Point, Wisconsin, and worked as an interpreter for the Ho-Chunk's attorney, H. W. Lee.[125] Mary Ann Mitchell whose mother had saved her during the Black Hawk War by swimming across the Mississippi River while under fire, later attended a Quaker school in Philadelphia, and even later moved to Kansas when the Sauks were there. Her mother Ukseeharkar became known as Julia, married a white man named John Goodell who was the Sauk tribe's interpreter in Kansas, and became a classic public mother there during the 1840s through 1870s. According to the memoir of an acquaintance, "their home was an asylum for the orphans, the sick and the afflicted."[126] Julia Grignon, Mary Ann Mitchell, and Ukseeharkar seem to have found niches for themselves in affiliation with the tribes.

Archange Labathe, who was French and Dakota, and her husband James Reed the tavern keeper left Prairie du Chien and moved north, establishing a town that was first known as Reed's Landing and later as Trempealeau. Her son Antoine Grignon worked in the fur trade at St. Paul in Minnesota Territory, then kept store in Wabasha for Alexis Bailly. Later he served as an interpreter for the government, worked as an assistant surveyor, and enlisted in the militia's home guard during the Mexican War. He and his wife Mary Christine de la Ronde had fourteen children and settled in Trempealeau near his mother and stepfather. Grignon proudly told an interviewer late in life about his daughters: "when they were young ladies [they] were noted in this part of the country for their singing; one of them became a school teacher and was very successful in her work."[127]

[125] [Henry Baird?], "A Famous French-Winnebago Resident" Henry S. Baird Papers, Box 4, Folder 4, State Historical Society of Wisconsin, 1.

[126] Ida M. Ferris, "The Sauks and Foxes in Franklin and Osage Counties, Kansas," *Collections of the Kansas State Historical Society*, Vol. XI, 1909–1910, 333–395; see 355.

[127] Eben D. Pierce, "When Trempealeau Was in the Wilds," Proceedings of the State Historical Society of Wisconsin for 1914, 107–1 17.

When Antoine Grignon moved to Minnesota, he was traveling a popular migration route, following the fur trade. The business declined in Prairie du Chien, but maintained its vitality for a while to the northwest. The Minnesota fur trade lured many of Prairie du Chien's younger generations away, including some of Euphrosine and Strange Powers's offspring. By 1850 Harriet, Euphrosine Junior, Jean Baptiste, and George were all in Minnesota, although George would eventually settle with the Meskwaki tribe in Indian Territory (Oklahoma).[128] Euphrosine Junior was married to a *voyageur* named Thomas Provencal dit LaBlanc, and living in Wabashaw County, Minnesota Territory, with their two children. The census taker had asked people where they were born, and "Frezine" not only told him "Wisconsin," but also specified Prairie du Chien, which was duly recorded.

Quite a few former neighbors were living nearby. Twenty-two other residents in that county also said they came from Euphrosine's hometown, including Lucie Faribault Bailly who was with her husband Alexis and their children. Alexis Bailly, of course, had played a key role as a jury foreman in the early years of the court system (see Chapter 3). He was probably the employer of LaBlanc, and of Pierre and Michel Lariviere, who like LaBlanc gave their occupations as "*voyageur*." Like Lucie, many of the transplanted Prairie du Chien residents had Dakota kin connections and had probably moved north to be closer to the tribal villages.[129]

But some of the Powers children stayed close to home, as evidenced by the family cluster noted earlier. In addition to daughter Caroline Powers who married Louis Barrette and lived in Prairie du Chien until the 1880s, Euphrosine Senior was also connected to the Brisbois family: Domitille Fraser, her daughter by her first husband, married Joseph Brisbois and also stayed in her hometown.

Other members of the Brisbois family had varied residential patterns. When Bernard W. Brisbois died in 1886, according to his estate inventory, his and his wife Theresa LaChapelle's children and grandchildren had scattered. Although one daughter still lived nearby, son William was living in Montana Territory; another son had been confined to the state mental hospital in Mendota, Wisconsin; and a second daughter lived in

---

[128] Census of the Sac and Fox Indians of Sac and Fox Agency, Indian Territory, 1889, 19, Ancestry.com – U.S. Indian Census schedules, 1885–1940 – online. National Archives, Records of the Bureau of Indian Affairs, Record Group 75.

[129] Minnesota Territorial Census, 1850, edited by Patricia C. Harpole and Mary D. Nagle (St. Paul: Minnesota Historical Society, 1972), 71–74; Hansen, "Two Early Lists of Mixed-Blood Sioux," 523–530; Hansen, ed., "A Roll of Sioux Mixed Bloods," 601–620.

Chatsworth, Illinois. Yet another son had moved to Kansas City, Missouri, and died, leaving three children there.[130]

The Rolette family also included emigrants who found new homes, but a few did stay. Joseph had a sister Julie living in Prairie du Chien who married Jean Brunet, a fur trader, tavern keeper, and local official who would become involved in the lumber business. In 1837, Jean Brunet moved north to the Chippewa Valley to build a sawmill and stayed; soon his adopted son François Gauthier joined him. Julie stayed for a few years in Prairie du Chien before she moved up to join her husband. Their granddaughter Josephine (the daughter of Gauthier and the French-Ojibwe Sophie Jandron) later remembered Jean and Julie fondly, and explained that the migration was a gradual one. "Mr. Brunet did not bring his wife up from Prairie du Chien until after he had spent some years in the Chippewa Valley, but he used to visit her several times a year."[131]

Joseph Rolette's first wife Margaret Dubois was French and Dakota. Two of their three daughters married military officers, alliances likely to enhance the family's elite status and to connect a leadership family of the old regime with the new government. Henriette followed her husband to Baton Rouge, Louisiana, where she died shortly after her twenty-first birthday. Emilie Rolette Hooe was widowed and remained in Prairie du Chien with her children, taking in boarders and serving for a time as postmistress. Like Euphrosine she was sued for nonpayment of tuition, not having inherited very much from her parents, who had died by 1842. Emilie's sister Elizabeth never married but stayed in Prairie du Chien, as did their half-brother Michel, a farmer.[132]

Joseph Rolette Jr. was the son of Joseph and his second wife Jane Fisher and made quite a name for himself in Pembina, Minnesota, in the fur trade. He was elected to the Minnesota Territorial Legislature, where he served for several terms and was well known as a colorful character whose legislative accomplishments included preventing the capital from being moved from St. Paul to another city. Unlike those who stayed in Prairie du Chien, he sometimes presented himself as ethnically Métis,

[130] B. W. Brisbois Probate Record, 1886, Crawford County Courthouse, Crawford County, WI; Fraser, "Early Families of Prairie du Chien," 11.

[131] William W. Bartlett, "Jean Brunet, Chippewa Valley Pioneer," *Wisconsin Magazine of History* 5, no. 1 (September 1921): 33–42. Quote is on 39–40; James L. Hansen, "The Rolette Family of Prairie du Chien," unpublished genealogy, courtesy of the author.

[132] Hansen, "The Rolette Family of Prairie du Chien"; I. P. Perret Gentil to T. J. Donoghoe, February 25, 1860, Folder 19, Item 14, Sisters of Charity Archives.

posing for a portrait in *voyageur* attire. He served as postmaster and customs collector at Pembina while managing a fur-trade concern.[133]

Joseph Rolette Jr. was not the only Creole to achieve some political influence. Like him, Alexis Bailly was elected to the Minnesota Territorial Legislature.[134] A few of those who stayed in Prairie du Chien also exercised political leadership. A particularly sad case was Theophilus LaChapelle, who was Dakota and French, descended from a chiefly family. Probably Wisconsin's first Native-descended lawyer, he was admitted to the bar in 1841 and represented Crawford County in the Wisconsin Territorial Legislative Council from 1842 through 1844. Sometime before 1850, he became insane, murdered a man, and was institutionalized for the rest of his life.[135] It is hard to know whether personal, political, professional, or physiological causes pushed LaChapelle over the edge, but the fact that his nephew was also confined to the Wisconsin mental hospital suggests that there were hereditary tendencies in that direction in the family. His cousin, however, remarked, "He was a brilliant man and made insane by hard study."[136] Perhaps, however, given the tensions of the justice system, the marginalization of the Creoles, and the removal of the Indians, it should not surprise us that he snapped.

LaChapelle's brother-in-law was more successful. Bernard W. Brisbois (married to Theophilus's sister) was appointed a U.S. consul to Belgium in 1873 but stayed only a year or two due to homesickness and health problems.[137] His brother Joseph Brisbois (Euphrosine's son-in-law) served not only as a justice of the peace, associate justice of the county

---

[133] Dyrud, "King Rolette" [no page, filed under 1841]; Bruce M. White, "The Power of Whiteness, or the Life and Times of Joseph Rolette, Jr.," *Minnesota History* 56, no. 4 (Winter 1998–99): 179–197.

[134] Donald Chaput, "Bailly, Joseph," *Dictionary of Canadian Biography Online* (University of Toronto/Université Laval, 2000), Vol. VI, accessed July 14, 2009; "1821: Wisconsin Traders' Letters," *Wisconsin Historical Collections* (hereafter, WHC), Vol. 20 (1911), 197, n. 55.

[135] Lyman C. Draper, ed., "Traditions and Recollections of Prairie du Chien, Related by Hon. B. W. Brisbois," *WHC* (1882), Vol. 9, 285 "Reminiscence of Theresa Barrette"; Crawford County Supervisors (CC Supervisors), 296; Ira B. Brunson, " Judicial History of Prairie du Chien, Wis., 1823–1841," manuscript, Wisconsin Historical Society Library, Madison, p. 12; Butterfield, *History of Crawford and Richland Counties*, 356; Elizabeth T. Baird, "Reminiscences of Early Days on Mackinac Island," *Wisconsin Historical Collections* 15 (1900): 255.

[136] "Reminiscence of Theresa Barrette"; Butterfield, *History of Crawford and Richland Counties*, 564.

[137] Obituaries: Prairie du Chien *Union*, June 18, 1885; "An Old Settler Gone,"? *Gazette*, June? 1885; Wisconsin State Historical Library, Obituaries, "Col. B. W. Brisbois."

court, and clerk of the county court, but also as a representative in the Wisconsin Legislative Assembly.[138]

These men provided just enough examples to show that Creoles *could* participate in politics at the territorial and state levels of government, and even in the U.S. diplomatic corps, so that Creoles felt included in the body politic. But they were minorities in the government, and their influence was limited. Locally, of course, as the Creoles became a minority of voters, they held very few offices. By 1845, only 11 percent of county officials were Creole.[139] Significantly, by the time these men were officials, the *habitants* did not have a collective political identity and as minorities did not possess much clout. Creole politicians did not represent a cohesive ethnic constituency.

Interestingly, the most successful former fur trader did not seek elective office. Hercules Dousman, after the early years of the U.S. regime, avoided becoming a candidate for government posts. According to a eulogy by his friend Henry Sibley, "he made it a rule of his life to accept no public position." Still, Dousman had plenty of clout. As Sibley explained, "So widely and so favorably was he known, that his advice with reference to the management of Indian affairs in the northwest was eagerly sought by high dignitaries of the general government."[140] Devoting his attention to his businesses rather than the distractions of legislative affairs may have helped him to amass the wealth for which he became known. As we saw in the previous chapter, he gained wealth not only from the fur trade but also from other businesses such as railroad building and real estate transactions.

## Key Resources

The most successful of the *habitants* who *stayed* in Prairie du Chien were those who owned the land, and Hercules Dousman came to own more of it than anyone else. His partner and predecessor Joseph Rolette, as one of Prairie du Chien's preeminent traders had amassed a great deal of real estate in and around the Prairie. But Rolette lost some of it to his wife Jane Fisher at the time of their separation and much of the rest

---

[138] Crawford Series 4, County Clerk Board Papers, October 7, 1833, Wisconsin State Historical Library, Madison; *History of Crawford and Richland Counties,* Vol. I, 355; Hansen, comp., "Crawford County Public Office Appointments."

[139] CC Supervisors, 181–208.

[140] Henry H. Sibley, Memoir of Hercules L. Dousman, *Minnesota Historical Collections,* Vol. 3 (1880), 196.

to his debt to the American Fur Company. Hercules Dousman obtained Rolette's land in two ways: through the settlement and reorganization of the fur-trade outfit, and by marrying Rolette's widow Jane Fisher.[141] But Dousman acquired land in many other ways, as the example of the Strange Powers estate demonstrates.

Another of Albert Coryer's memoirs includes an anecdote about Dousman's near-appropriation of his grandparents' land that further illustrates Dousman's flexible methods of gaining wealth and authority. Julien Carriere and his wife Lucretia Lessard, and her sister Marianne and husband François Gauthier (aka Gokey) had squatted on land, created farms, and planned to purchase the land but had not been able to raise the cash needed to register their claims. One winter day, Dousman arrived at the Carriere home in his sleigh and told them that he himself was going to purchase the tracts and they would have to leave. According to the family legend, Julien protested with a not-so-subtle threat. "Now Dousman[,] I considered you a friend," Albert quoted," and if you did me and Gokey such a deal it makes me feel like not letting you go looking as fresh as you are now."[142] Dousman backed off, Albert recorded, saying, "Julian[,] it does me good to realize you still have the old fighting spirit you had when we worked for the fur company." Instead, Dousman loaned the two families the cash to register their land and a sleigh to take them to the land office ahead of two men Dousman knew were planning to purchase the farms that the Carrieres and Gokeys were building.[143] Thus the two families narrowly avoided losing their land twice – once to Dousman and next to the outsiders. In Albert's telling, his grandfather had forced Dousman to back down and reconsider, but Dousman had helped the Carrieres and Gokeys. While Dousman did not come to own this land, he must have earned interest on the loans, and he did acquire much of the surrounding land.[144] Furthermore, by lending the money and the sleigh and preventing the loss of the farms, Dousman earned the (perhaps grudging) gratitude and loyalty of the Carrieres and Gokeys. And these relative newcomers became firmly planted as members of the Creole community.

[141] Dictionary of Wisconsin History, Wisconsin Historical Society, online: http://www. wisconsinhistory.org/dictionary/index.asp?action=view&term_id=2472&search_ term=dousman, accessed Feb. 5, 2011.

[142] Coryer, "Short Stories," 24.

[143] Coryer, "Short Stories," 23–26. Quote is on 24.

[144] Map of Crawford County, Wisconsin / S. Briggs, R. C. Falconer, 1878. Wisconsin Historical Society Library Archives, Madison.

## Conclusion

It was land that sustained farm families like these and that helped to enrich and enhance the authority of elites such as Hercules Dousman. After the economic changes of the early nineteenth century, many of the old fur-trade families turned to farming as their means of support. Those who still held title to the farm lots from the era of Isaac Lee had resources for agriculture, or for real estate sales. And some, like the Carrieres and Gokeys bought land as did Yankees and Europeans. In addition, some Creoles gained title to lands in the Indian treaties' provisions for "half-breeds," when the Sauks, Meskwakis, Ho-Chunks, and other tribes in the region lost their territories to the American government's removal project, and tried to keep some of it in friendly hands. Yet the treaty grants which some Creoles received as "half-breeds" provided at best a measure of long-delayed income rather than places to call home. Like the tribes, many Creoles faced challenges trying to keep their land, as the example of Euphrosine Antaya Powers makes clear.

The case of Madame Powers's real estate dealings demonstrates the surprising ways that land could be organized, divided, and commodified in order to support a family. In some ways, her actions seem very similar to the behaviors of Yankee speculators on the frontier. But Euphrosine may have felt conflicted about selling her ancestral land. She did try to keep much of it in the possession of her family and friends when she sold it. And she did resist the allotment and sale of the Sac and Fox Half-Breed Tract. Sometimes when she needed money, she mortgaged rather than sold the land, hoping she would be able to get it back later. Yet whatever her feelings about this Euro-American way of manipulating possession of the earth, her experiences show that as the daughter of a successful fur-trade couple, Euphrosine had learned or inherited sufficient business acumen to manage this resource long enough to raise her many children. Just as Pokoussee and the other Meskwaki daughters had done in the time of Isaac Lee, Euphrosine adapted to the new land system in pursuit of her family goals.

The other important resources available to Creoles coping with social, political, and economic change were family and the fellowship of neighbors. In response to the pressures of political and economic marginalization and of Anglo prejudice, Creoles developed two ethnic neighborhoods. The island became known as the Fourth Ward and included homes of the dominant Dousmans and comfortable Brisbois but also of many families that were less successful. In Frenchtown, the families had more land and many farmed with some success. In both neighborhoods, Fourth Ward and Frenchtown, a strong sense of community neighborliness developed. In addition, family clusters – often matrifocal in their organization – helped Creoles to pool their resources. Community and kin ties gave joy to life and lightened the load, an experience common in many frontier settlements and ethnic enclaves of various kinds. But Creoles without these types of resources to help them adjust to Prairie du Chien's changes left this place behind.

# Conclusion

As the Great Lakes area was colonized in the early nineteenth century, the United States established its dominion over the old fur-trade communities. They also backed this up with the presence of the army and pressed most of the Creoles' Indian relatives to give up their lands and move away. By the middle of the century, the massive immigration of Anglos and other outsiders brought enormous changes to the region's economy, political and legal systems, and dominant social practices. Creoles faced a new government and court system, English as the court language, Protestant churches, and different forms of business and other economic practices. The fur trade went into decline. What this meant for the Creoles was that they eventually became minorities in their own communities, their livelihoods changed dramatically, and their access to authority and land shifted in complex ways.

The Creole men of Prairie du Chien, most of whom had supported the British side during the War of 1812, were not excluded from the government after the United States took over. During the demographic transitional stage in which the Anglo-Americans did not have a majority of the population, these newcomers needed the support and participation of the Creoles to control the Indians, to make the democratic institutions work, and to legitimize the government. So elite traders were appointed as local officials and judges, and ordinary Creole men served as voters and jurors. In the early years, because the Anglo-American judges, local Yankee officials, territorial governors, and members of the territorial legislative council needed Creole support and participation, they tolerated Creoles' protests, unfamiliarity with the system, inability to speak English, and assertiveness and noncompliance as jurors (although at the same time, many non-Creole officials complained bitterly).

As long as the new institutions required Creoles' participation in order to function, they exerted some agency in these roles. They were sometimes able to protect neighbors from powerful people or against aspects of the new institutions that seemed harsh or unjust. Creoles as jurors and as other participants in the court system might use it for protection or to effect their own concepts of justice, agendas separate from the objectives of officials like Doty and Cass who used the courts not only to resolve disputes and punish the wicked but also to establish the power of the United States and its territorial and state governments in Wisconsin.

As in-migration to Prairie du Chien increased, pushing the declining Creole population near the 50 percent mark, Creoles could continue to participate in electoral politics because they avoided being racialized in the 1825 election controversy. People of mixed Native and European ancestry were declared white enough to vote as long as they were not tribal members. Because electoral politics was based on the concept of majority rule, the Anglo-American hegemony would be assured once Creoles became a minority of the population after 1836. Creoles could still feel that they were part of the system, though, even if they were seldom elected to important political offices. However, after the *habitants* became a minority and Native tribes were removed or pacified, Creoles were increasingly excluded from the courts. Their support, as "people in-between," was no longer needed to maintain Anglo control. They might be white enough to vote but they were too French to serve on juries. The fact that language and residence – rather than race – were the criteria formally used to exclude them was one of the reasons Creoles evolved into a white ethnic group rather than a racialized out-group.

While their brothers, husbands, and sons faced the challenges of political and economic marginalization, Creole women experienced the constricting rights of the Anglo-American legal system. Native-descended women were forced to license their marriages to non-Native men, ensuring that they would be considered part of the American community and subject to U.S. laws, as would their children, potentially separating them from tribal membership. Married women also became subject to the American legal doctrine of *coverture*, under which they could not own property or make contracts separately from their husbands. Many of them became the cores of their families, as the matrifocal centers of strategic family clusters. And Creole women found ways to express their leadership outside the political system as public mothers. They were able to reach across cultural barriers and gain acceptance and even genuine respect through charity, hospitality, healing, and midwifery. Their actions helped to counteract many of the prejudiced attitudes of Anglo settlers and to prevent the Creoles from being racially marginalized.

At the beginning of settler colonialism, right after the War of 1812 when U.S. officials such as John W. Johnson arrived in Prairie du Chien, the newcomers were unsure of, but thinking about, the racial status of the Creoles. His comment that "the americans ... had to immagin them to be a white people" expressed both the officials' ambivalence and their flexibility.[1] Because the Creoles were needed, the Americans included them within the fold, but with some hesitancy. And the *habitants,* too, had been uncertain about racial concepts at first. Prairie du Chien's "skulking" law demonstrated that some Creoles in the 1820s had thought of "white persons" as dangerous "others" and outsiders, more threatening even than intoxicated Indians. For them, whiteness was identified with the unruly and oppressive soldiers at Fort Crawford and perhaps with U.S. officials like Johnson. Yet they came to avoid talking about race and in fact avoided all generalizations about themselves, never gaining a strong collective identity as indigenous or as an out-group.

Soon, after a challenge surrounding the 1825 election controversy, Creole men who had mixed ancestry or Native wives became legally "white" enough to vote. Thus, they avoided being racialized – and were not politically excluded based upon ancestry or appearance. The color line lost relevance, but the democratic system of majority rule created a system where their clout would be diluted once they became less than 50 percent of the population and electorate.

Yet the nature of jury service – based as it was on consensus decision making – presented a challenge to Anglos who disapproved of Creole's independent jury behaviors. To exclude the Creoles, they developed several techniques, including one that focused on language. The inability to speak English distinguished the French speakers. It would be French culture that would be the ethnic markers for the Creoles who would become known as "the French."

Language, literacy, and education became issues by mid-century. As the economy changed, non-farm jobs required different skill sets. No matter how many Native languages Creoles knew in addition to French, without English proficiency and literacy, they could not rise very far in

---

[1] John W. Johnson to George C. Sibley, April 28, 1817, Prairie du Chien, Sibley Papers, Missouri Historical Society collections, St. Louis.

the commercial or political worlds. The Brisbois men, whose English was imperfect but serviceable, and who were smart, diplomatic, and had clear, fine penmanship, were among the few who succeeded in the changing economic and political sectors.

Other Creole families compensated by sending their children to school so that they could not be excluded based on language, an emphasis on education that is reminiscent of many immigrant groups in U.S. history. The next generations, then, would have better English fluency and literacy skills, but like Albert Coryer would understand the importance of French Canadian heritage to their families.

### Creoles, Métis, and Mexicans

The old fur-trade families of the Great Lakes region emerged from the political, economic, and demographic transitions of the early nineteenth century with a status and an identity that was very different from those of the Canadian Métis and the Mexican-heritage populations of the Southwestern borderlands region. A brief look at those two groups and their history can explain why the Creoles generally became an assimilated white ethnic group within the United States, while the Métis and Hispanics generally did not.

There were certainly similarities among the three groups. In all, there had been previous colonization by France or Spain before the Anglo-American or Anglo-Canadian government took over. In all three, the previous colonial periods had been based on societies that included Native people as part of their economies, being what geographer Marvin Mikesell called "frontiers of inclusion."[2] All had been taken over by a new Anglophone government focused on settler colonialism, that is, systems emphasizing the displacement of Native peoples so that newcomers could settle on that land.

Identity, of course, develops both internally and from the outside. What people think about themselves matters and affects the ways they interact among themselves, with governments, and with those they perceive as outsiders. Historical circumstances and the attitudes of others certainly contribute to the creation of any specific group status and identity. Comparing these three groups may help us to understand how Creole identities were and were not affected by key events, situations, and policies.

[2] Marvin Mikesell, "Comparative Studies in Frontier History," *Annals of the Association of American Geographers* 50, no. 1 (1960): 62–74. Quote is on 65.

The situation in the Canadian West shows key similarities to the Great Lakes region in the origins of mixed-ancestry families with the international peltry business. Francophone fur-trade workers from the St. Lawrence River area traveled to the Great Lakes region in the late eighteenth and early nineteenth centuries, but some of them and their younger cousins *also* migrated to the Red River area of northern Minnesota and Rupert's Land, the latter a politically separate part of the British Empire until 1869.[3] Francophone fur-trade workers married Native women; so did some Scots. Many of these families later developed distinctive lifeways as self-employed hunters and/or farmers and created an identity for themselves as Métis.

By 1868, the British American colonies north of the United States had been confederated to create the modern nation of Canada, and the Hudson's Bay Company had sold the Rupert's Land region to the new nation. But people of mixed Native and European ancestry who identified themselves as Métis resisted the Canadian government in 1869–70 and 1885 under the leadership of Louis Riel. Among the fundamental issues leading to the rebellions and to the identification of Canadian Métis as a racialized out-group were political rights and land rights. During the first Riel resistance, they sought to establish their legislative rights and created their own provisional government for Manitoba, which the federal government did not recognize.[4] They also reacted against Canadian surveyors who indicated that the government had no plans to confirm the ribbon-style river lots of the Métis.[5] It is possible that their experiences were all the more frustrating because they knew that during the 1820s in the transition to settler colonialism, Creoles in Michigan Territory *had* negotiated a political and literal space for themselves.[6] Creole men

---

[3] Jennifer S. H. Brown, "The Métis: Genesis and Rebirth," in *Native People, Native Lands*, edited by Bruce Alden Cox (Ottawa, Canada: Carleton University Press, 1988), 136–147; Jennifer Brown and Theresa Schenck, "Métis, Mestizo, and Mixed-Blood," in *A Companion to American Indian History*, edited by Philip J. Deloria and Neal Salisbury (Malden, MA: Blackwell, 2002), 321–338; Rupert's Land Act, 1868, William F. Maton, Solon Law Archive, http://www.solon.org/Constitutions/Canada/English/rpl_1868.html, accessed Nov. 5, 2012.

[4] J. M. Bumsted, *A History of the Canadian Peoples*, 4th ed. (Don Mills, Ontario: Oxford University Press, 2011), 212; Alexander Begg, *The Creation of Manitoba* (Toronto: A. H. Hovey 1871), 110–111, 255–256, reproduced in Victoria Community Network, http://victoria.tc.ca/history/etext/metis-bill-of-rights.html, accessed Nov. 20, 2012, and Canada History, http://www.canadahistory.com/sections/documents/thewest/metisbillrights.htm, accessed Nov. 20, 2012.

[5] Maggie Siggins, *Riel: A Life of Revolution* (Toronto: HarperCollins, 1994), 95–97.

[6] Brown, "The Métis: Genesis and Rebirth"; Brown and Schenck, "Métis, Mestizo, and Mixed-Blood"; Chris Andersen, "*Moya 'Tipimsook* ('The People Who Aren't Their

working in the fur trade in the 1860s and 1870s surely knew what had happened in Michigan Territory, and that knowledge influenced their expectations. Men who traveled widely and shared with each other the stories of their travels must have known that many Creoles in Michigan Territory had gained title to ribbon lots and that men had political rights. After the first Riel resistance, some Métis did gain land titles but others did not. Many moved to the North-West Territory, where by the end of the 1870s, new waves of settlers and the issues of land and political rights again caused a revolt.[7]

The Canadian Métis coalesced with a sense of peoplehood as early as 1818 at Red River based on distinctive economic pursuits, including large-scale buffalo hunts and provisioning dried meat to the fur trade.[8] Grievances and conflicts with the fur-trade companies and later with the Canadian government pushed them to think of themselves as an opposition group. They also developed a sense of themselves as an indigenous people. An observer commented that they "look upon themselves as members of an independent tribe of natives, entitled to a property in the soil, to a flag of their own, and to protection from the British government."[9] After the Riel rebellions, although some Métis did receive land scrip or certificates, most became landless and many became chronically poor.[10]

If the Métis defined themselves in a certain way, their identity as a specific, non-white people also came from others. In the late nineteenth and twentieth centuries, other Canadians also generally perceived the Métis as a distinctive out-group, in part because they had rebelled against the government but also because of their poverty, and because of racism. Hatred toward people who were not "Anglo-Saxon," and particularly toward "half-breeds," was promoted by a group of Canadians whose movement was called "Canada First," founded in 1868. After the first Riel resistance

Own Bosses'): Racialization and the Misrecognition of 'Métis' in Upper Great Lakes Ethnohistory," *Ethnohistory* 58, no. 1 (Winter 2011): 37–63; Bumsted, *A History of the Canadian Peoples*, 212; Alexander Begg, *The Creation of Manitoba*, 110–111, 255–256; Siggins, *Riel: A Life of Revolution*, 95–97.

[7] Julia D. Harrison, *Metis: People between Two Worlds* (Vancouver: Glenbow-Alberta Institute, 1985), 39–43.

[8] Brown, "The Métis: Genesis and Rebirth," 139–140.

[9] William McGillivray to?, March 14, 1818, quoted in Brown, "The Métis: Genesis and Rebirth," 140.

[10] As they became more economically comfortable, especially those who were farming, some mixed-heritage people in Manitoba distanced themselves from their poorer neighbors and denied being Métis. See Nicole St-Onge, *Saint-Laurent, Manitoba: Evolving Métis Identities, 1850–1914* (Regina, Saskatchewan: Canadian Plains Research Center, University of Regina, 2004).

of 1869–70, this group stirred up the Canadian public, promoting racist prejudice against the Métis.[11]

It is also possible to make comparisons with the Southwestern borderlands region. In Mexico, Spanish colonists had long intermarried and formed liaisons with indigenous peoples (as well as Africans) and established multicultural communities often in proximity to Native villages. When they migrated to colonize northern New Spain, they developed missions, military posts, villages, and rural pastoral settlements incorporating Native people into these communities in a variety of roles, and sometimes they intermarried. These Hispanic peoples – including individuals whose ancestry might be purely European, indigenous, or African, or any combination of these backgrounds – developed identities as Californios, Hispanos, and Tejanos. After the Mexican-American War (1846–48), Latinos in California, New Mexico, Texas, and Arizona became subject to the U.S. government, lost their land, and became wage workers in economically changing economies. Although citizens among them had voting rights, they became minorities in their own communities and were unable to exert much political clout. Most became part of a poor underclass.

The Spanish-speaking peoples whose families had resided in the region for many years had a sense of community and distinctiveness that was heightened after 1848 as their neighborhoods, also known as *barrios*, became surrounded by Anglos and other newcomers whose housing styles, language, and other aspects of culture differed. In these ways, they were similar to the Great Lakes Creoles. But they formed formal ethnic groups such as Santa Barbara's *La Junta Patriotic Mexicana*, took steps to maintain distinctive cultural elements, and introduced new ones such as celebration of Mexico's Independence Day, September 16.[12] The Hispanics' proximity to Mexico helped to sustain a sense of separate identity and affiliation. And more people arrived from south of the new border seeking jobs, moving into the barrios, swelling the Hispanic population, and reinforcing Mexican cultural elements and identification. Even though they had a sense of peoplehood, they tried to reject racialization, and many overtly insisted that they were "white."[13] Still,

---

[11] Bumsted, *A History of the Canadian Peoples*, 217.

[12] Albert Camarillo, *Chicanos in a Changing Society: From Mexican Pueblos to American Barrios in Santa Barbara and Southern California, 1848–1930* (Cambridge, MA: Harvard University Press, 1979, 1996), 58–65.

[13] Linda Gordon, "Internal Colonialism and Gender," in *Haunted by Empire: Geographies of Intimacy in North American History*, edited by Ann Laura Stoler (Durham, NC: Duke University Press, 2006), 428–451; see 434–437.

they understood themselves as the victims of prejudice, discrimination, and racism, an understanding that created a perceived distance between themselves and others.

In addition, Mexican Americans were defined by others in ways that both contributed to and flowed from their marginalization. Historian Reginald Horsman's study of race relations in the nineteenth century found that a political ideology stressing the superiority of white "Anglo-Saxon" people over all others gained strength and crystallized with the Texas Revolution and the Mexican War. This ideology justified American expansion and aggression toward Mexico. Horsman wrote, "By the time of the Mexican War, America had placed the Mexicans firmly within the rapidly emerging hierarchy of superior and inferior races. While the Anglo-Saxons were depicted as the purest of the pure – the finest Caucasians – the Mexicans who stood in the way of southwestern expansion were depicted as a mongrel race, adulterated by extensive intermarriage with an inferior Indian race."[14] This bigotry supported Manifest Destiny, the idea that it was God's will for the United States to bring its freedom and democracy along with its settler colonialism across the continent, even if it meant taking over the northern half of a neighboring country. And the Anglos who brought these prejudices with them discriminated against the Mexican Americans in numerous ways, including politically.

During the early years after the Mexican War, Hispanic men were allowed to vote in many places. But when Hispanics became minorities in their own towns, as had the Great Lakes Creoles, their political authority plummeted. For example, according to historian Albert Camarillo, in Santa Barbara, California, the Californios voted and held local political offices until the mid-1870s. At that time, Anglo politicians reorganized the city government using a ward system, ensuring that Chicanos would be able to elect no more than one city councilman, given the segregated neighborhoods. And Chicanos seldom served on juries.[15] To further illustrate, in San Antonio, Texas, although Hispanic men were almost two thirds of the aldermen from 1837 to 1847, they were only 17 percent of the aldermen from 1848 to 1857, and there were absolutely no Hispanic men among the sixty aldermen who served between 1895 and 1904.[16]

---

[14] Reginald Horsman, *Race and Manifest Destiny: The Origins of American Racial Anglo-Saxonism* (Cambridge, MA: Harvard University Press, 1981) chs. 11, 12, Quote is on 210.
[15] Camarillo, *Chicanos in a Changing Society*, 71–77.
[16] Jerome R. Adams, *Greasers and Gringos: The Historical Roots of Anglo-Hispanic Prejudice* (Jefferson, NC: McFarland, 2006), 154.

Anglos sometimes expressed their prejudices in violent attacks. For example, during the California gold rush, a foreign miners' law drove Latinos out of the mines and helped to provoke Anglo miners to riot against them.[17]

Throughout the Southwest, however, one of the most consistent challenges for the Mexican Americans was the loss of land. They experienced this loss in several ways. For many, the bureaucratic and judicial processes set up for securing land titles proved too costly and difficult. In New Mexico, some landowners lost their holdings because they could not pay the taxes on them. Anglo officials often manipulated the system and helped Anglo elites – or themselves – to gain title to Mexican Americans' individual and communal lands. And, as scholar Mario Barrera has pointed out, "Perhaps the key point … is that the subordinate status of Chicanos in the Southwest put them in a particularly vulnerable economic position. Anglo capitalists and land speculators were best able to take advantage of this vulnerability to dispossess Chicanos of the land they had previously controlled." In spite of the variations in process and pace, he argued, eventually this dispossession "affected nearly all Chicanos."[18] When they became landless, they became economically and politically vulnerable. Soon Mexican Americans became a dependent class of wage workers, typically in low-paying, low-skilled jobs, and constituted "a racially stratified labor force," in Barrera's words. This economic status contributed to prejudice and discrimination in a vicious cycle. By the end of the nineteenth century, Mexican Americans were economically and socially segregated throughout the Southwest.[19]

There were some significant similarities between the Hispanics and the Great Lakes Creoles. In both areas, some families were more recently intermarried with indigenous people than other families whose Native ancestors were more generations back. Furthermore, in both areas, there was a small number of elites in each community (some of whom were Creole or Hispanic) for whom other less wealthy neighbors worked. In both of these regions, Hispanics and Creoles were Roman Catholic.

---

[17] Matt S. Meier and Feliciano Ribera, *Mexican Americans/American Mexicans: From Conquistadors to Chicanos* (New York: Hill and Wang, 1993), 71, 129.

[18] Mario Barrera, *Race and Class in the Southwest: A Theory of Racial Inequality* (Notre Dame, IN: University of Notre Dame Press, 1979), 32; Camarillo, *Chicanos in a Changing Society;*Miroslava Chavez-Garcia, *Negotiating Conquest: Gender and Power in California, 1770s to 1880s* (Tucson: University of Arizona Press, 2004), 143–150; Horsman, *Race and Manifest Destiny,* 279; Adams, *Greasers and Gringos,* chs. 19–24.

[19] Matt S. Meier and Feliciano Ribera, *Mexican Americans/American Mexicans: From Conquistadors to Chicanos* (New York: Hill and Wang, 1972, 1993), 71, 129.

(The Canadian Métis also included a large number of Catholics among their number.) This would prove to be significant both because churches could provide spiritual and social resources, but also because Anglo-Americans and Anglo-Canadians tended to be Protestants and often brought anti-Catholic prejudices with them.

The Great Lakes Creoles differed from the Mexican Americans in three key respects, all of which influenced the way they would be viewed by others. The first has to do with land. While most Mexican American landowners lost their land after the United States took over their region, many of the Creoles were able to hang onto their land, at least for a while. Second, while the majority of Mexican Americans became unskilled, underpaid workers employed by Anglos, most Creoles who remained in the community were able to be economically independent, generally working their land, economic behavior that did not really differ significantly from that of their non-Creole neighbors. Finally, in part because of their subordinate economic status, the Mexican Americans came to be seen by others as a non-white underclass, but in spite of prejudices and challenges, Creoles would be considered another white ethnic group and would be able to assimilate. Their political status as "white" and their generally independent economic status contributed to this situation. Furthermore, unlike the Canadian Métis or the Mexican Americans, the *habitants* did not coalesce as an oppositional group. They did not identify with Canada in the way the Chicanos identified with Mexico, and they did not rise up as a people against the government, like the Métis. But there were other factors at work as well.

The Creoles' own actions made a difference. They avoided using general terms of any kind about themselves. Their sense of the collective focused on family and (sometimes) church, and (later) neighborhood, but nothing larger. Political participation, at least in the beginning, had made them feel like insiders, and even though they would be marginalized politically and as jurors, they still could vote and a few still served on juries. They were not passive participants, however. Their political and judicial behaviors resisted the new regime, its values and ideals, and they asserted local concepts of justice as long as they could.

Emerging from Native and fur-trade cultures that valued inclusiveness and exogamy, that identified people not by race but by family, friendship, and economic networks, they continued to reach out. The Glass family crisis provides an example where the Creole community mobilized to help people who were outsiders. Public mothers reached out not only to their Native and Creole kin and neighbors but also to Anglos and other outsiders. These behaviors counteracted prejudices and social polarization.

Creoles probably benefited from the historic moment in which settler colonialism came to their doorsteps. In the early nineteenth century, the United States was new and shiny and the ideals of republicanism inspired policymakers who crafted the Northwest Ordinance and who hoped to extend the democratic process to the new territories. French Creoles from St. Louis and New Orleans and Illinois had since the late eighteenth century petitioned the government for political and land rights, laying the groundwork that would eventually bring Isaac Lee to Prairie du Chien.[20] In the early nineteenth century, the Midwestern tribes were viewed by the government as a significant threat, a factor that caused officials to need Creoles as allies. And while there was plenty of prejudice during the 1820s and '30s among American settlers and officials against Catholics, Indians, Africans, and suspiciously mixed people, it would be at mid-century that the super virulence of racism and Anglo-Saxon ideology affecting Hispanics and the Canadian Métis arose. By that time, the status of Creoles in the Great Lakes region was already settled.

## Creolization and Assimilation

Prairie du Chien's *habitants* show us the Native, creative, and resistant faces of the process of creolization. They maintained a sense of themselves as people whose families had been there before the U.S. takeover – and for many, before even the French had arrived. Louis Barrette, as we have seen in the introduction to this volume, stressed that his and his wife's ancestors included Indian women who had been born in this place as well as European men. The sensibilities of men who became involved in the new American political and judicial institutions brought values and practices from their contact with Native and French traditions and used them to counteract aspects of the Anglo system and its laws with which they disagreed. They even used the institutions to challenge men such as Charles Cass whose behavior had offended their sense of justice and propriety, demonstrating a creative adaptation of new institutions in combination with several cultural traditions. Women creatively counteracted their legal disempowerment and the decrease in opportunities for mediation caused by less-frequent intermarriage by finding the

---

[20] Jay Gitlin, *The Bourgeois Frontier: French Towns, French Traders and American Expansion* (New Haven, CT: Yale University Press, 2010), ch. 3.

intersections of gender ideals to reach across the cultural divides as public mothers.

Adapting to the new regime, Prairie du Chien's Creoles exhibited what scholars call "structural assimilation," by participating in the political system, by sending their children to school, and by joining church organizations.[21] But their tendency to live in ethnic neighborhoods and to continue speaking French and Native languages demonstrate what is known as "segmented assimilation," becoming incorporated into the larger society while deliberately maintaining their group's values and cohesiveness.[22] They were part of the American society although part of a "white" subgroup. Their unwillingness to move to "half-breed" reserves underscored this.

For most of those with Native ancestry, this would eventually lead to detribalization. When the tribes were removed, the choice was a difficult one. If the generations of the 1830s through 1850s managed to maintain ties with the tribes, it became increasingly difficult to do so after that. So those who stayed did their best to maintain ties to the land.

Land was central to their status. The land helped those who could keep it to maintain an accepted status within the Americanized community. For those whose land was challenged, like Euphrosine Antaya Powers, it provided a resource which even in its sale sustained families for a while. The ability to work one's own holdings helped Creoles to avoid becoming a racialized, dependent labor group, as many were part of the agricultural middle class. Settler colonialism had arrived in Prairie du Chien with the War of 1812, with newcomers hungry for land, and it dispossessed most of the tribes and many of the *habitants*; but a core group was able to persist in spite of all, thanks to historical circumstances but also to their Creole adaptability.

---

[21] Milton Gordon, *Assimilation in American Life: The Role of Race, Religion, and National Origins* (New York: Oxford University Press, 1964).

[22] Alejandro Portes and Min Zhou, "The New Second Generation: Segmented Assimilation and Its Variants," *Annals of the American Academy of Political and Social Science* 530 (Nov. 1993): 74–96; Clemens Krokeberg, "Ethnic Communities and School Performance among the New Second Generation in the United States: Testing the Theory of Segmented Assimilation," *Annals of the American Academy of Political and Social Science* 620 (Nov. 2008): 138–160.

# Epilogue

While Creoles in the nineteenth century drew their livings from the rivers and the land (and sometimes from both), by the turn of the twentieth century, other options had arisen. Caroline Powers (the daughter of Euphrosine Antaya and Strange Powers) with her husband Louis Barrette had farmed in the Prairie du Chien region until the 1880s and then followed the fur-trade migrations along the river north to Minnesota, as did many other Creoles. Some of their children went with them. But after Caroline died in 1817, Louis made his way back to Prairie du Chien to live on the farm owned by their son Samuel Barrette and daughter-in-law, Adeline Hertzog. It was here that Louis gave the newspaper interview mentioned in the introduction to this volume.[1]

Although the Barrettes moved away for three decades, many other Prairie du Chien Creoles remained to farm in the late nineteenth century and beyond. An 1878 map of land ownership in Crawford County shows Cherrier, Brisbois, Ducharme, Corriere, LaBonne, and other French names sprinkled across the landscape among names such as Kaiser, Rice, Brunson, O'Donnell, and Eggerton.[2] Members of the Barrette family continued on their farm until the 1970s.[3] Descendants of the Pion and Brisbois families farmed into the twentieth century as well.[4]

---

[1] Gina Mae Powell to Lucy Murphy, email, June 13, 2012; "Lewis Barrette to Celebrate His 95th Birthday," Crawford County [WI] *Press*, Prairie du Chien, February 26, 1919, Wisconsin Historical Society Library, F 902/3BA, 44.
[2] Briggs and Falconer Map of Crawford County, Wisconsin, 1878, Wisconsin Historical Society Library, Madison.
[3] Gina Mae Powell to Lucy Murphy, personal correspondence, email, June 19, 2013.
[4] Myra Lang interview with Lucy Murphy, August 14, 2002.

In Frenchtown, although some of the land came to be owned by people with non-French names like Jones, Cornford, Humphery, Wachter, and Beck, enough of the old Creole community spirit remained to nurture Albert Coryer during his youth in the late nineteenth century.[5] There he heard the old stories about the *habitants* who had lived in the neighborhood before the Civil War, some of whose children still lived along the northern stretch of the Prairie's main highway. Coryer, of course, recorded those tales during the first half of the twentieth century, gave handwritten copies to his relatives, and regaled anyone who would listen.[6]

Life in the neighborhood on the Island continued to be oriented toward the rivers. Once called the "old French village," the Island became the Fourth Ward after 1872, when the City of Prairie du Chien was incorporated; it superseded the Township of St. Anthony, which had replaced the Borough of Prairie du Chien.[7] Nowadays, former residents of the Fourth Ward remember it fondly as a close-knit community of families, most of them members of three extended kin groups.[8]

Many of the Fourth Ward residents were wage workers. Some were employed by the Dousman family until they left the mansion and moved away in 1913.[9] A woolen mill offered jobs for 135 local workers from 1891 through 1935, when the plant was converted into a sponge factory. A cannery also offered employment in the plant while providing a market for local farmers to sell their vegetables.[10] Later, during the 1940s, a meat packing plant provided similar opportunities.[11]

The rivers generously provided the means to make a living for many Creoles and their neighbors. Riverboats, bridges, and ferries needed

---

[5] Briggs and Falconer Map.

[6] See Chapter 5 of the present volume.

[7] Mary Elise Antoine, "Main Street Prairie du Chien," Prairie du Chien *Courier Press*, April 8 and April 13, 2009; for the comment about the "old French Village," Bishop Jackson Kemper, "A Trip through Wisconsin in 1838," *Wisconsin Magazine of History* 8, no. 4 (June 1925): 426.

[8] Dale Klemme interview with Lucy Murphy, September 11, 2007; Mary Valley interview with Lucy Murphy, September 3, 2003; Jeff Lessard, host, "Remember fourthward" Facebook page, accessed June 26, 2013.

[9] "Villa Louis celebrates 50th anniversary as a state historical site," Prairie du Chien *Courier Press*, May ? 2002, Collection of Bette Beneker.

[10] Mary Elise Antoine, *Images of America: Prairie du Chien* (Charleston, SC: Arcadia, 2011), 72–73.

[11] Jesse Aspenson et al., *Rivertown Memories: A Pictorial of Our Historic River Towns* (Prairie du Chien: Wisconsin-Iowa Shopping News, 2006), 71.

regular staff and frequent attention from repair crews. A steady stream of logs floating down the Mississippi from the northern woods needed guiding, watching, steering. Men who worked in the Fourth Ward's sawmill processed some of the thousands of logs that came this way. In addition, those who fished for clams provided thousands of shining shells to the button factory where seventy-eight lathe operators cut out blanks to be sent elsewhere for finishing. The sand and gravel beds along the river provided the raw materials for the Cement Products Company to use in making concrete bricks and tile. In the coldest part of winter, the frozen river itself became a commodity when workers cut it into blocks and packed it into sawdust to be sold to the railroads and to local residents and businesses. That ice kept thousands of gallons of ice cream cold at the local creamery.[12]

Mike Valley (some of whose ancestors were in Prairie du Chien well before 1817) grew up in the Fourth Ward and remembers how important the rivers were to his family and neighbors, providing opportunities for fishing, clamming, hunting, and trapping. During the third quarter of the twentieth century, he estimates, there were about thirty-two commercial fishermen living on the island at any given time who supplied his father Dallas's fish shop. He and his father and grandfather also hunted and sold the furs and meat, often to wholesalers. They collected antiques and arrowheads to sell for additional cash. Dallas carved beautiful duck decoys and taught his son; today Mike's decoys fetch hundreds of dollars each. Mike carries on the family's economic traditions – hunting, fishing, and with his wife Lisa running a successful fish shop in Prairie du Chien.[13]

On the mainland near the river, St. Gabriel's Catholic Church continued to be an institution central to the Creole communities. Children from the island crossed a footbridge to join mainland kids in its school; parishioners participated in numerous church activities. When large numbers of Bohemians made their homes in Prairie du Chien, they built their own house of worship, St. John Nepomuc Catholic Church.[14]

Creole identity slowly evolved over time. Although people like Albert Coryer kept the history and stories of Frenchtown alive, it was remembered as more French than Indian. Even Indian Trail – the main north-south

---

[12] Antoine, *Images of America*, 89–104.
[13] Mike Valley interview with Lucy Murphy, September 13, 2007.
[14] Myra Lang interview with Lucy Murphy, August 14, 2002.

route through the Prairie – had its name changed to Frenchtown Road.[15] By the middle of the twentieth century, young descendants of the fur-trade families spoke English as their first language, although their grandparents sometimes conversed in French.[16] Fourth Ward came to be identified more by lifestyle and social class than by ethnicity; perhaps half of the residents in the 1970s were ethnically "French," according to one observer.[17] In the same way that many American towns and cities kept their poor and working classes segregated on the "wrong side of the tracks," in Prairie du Chien the middle and upper classes looked down on the Fourth Ward residents living on the island and stigmatized them as "river rats." Children hearing this insult carried the hurt into adulthood, and its memory still stings today.[18]

Although the Mississippi River provided sustenance to hundreds of Prairie du Chien families, it was not always kind to the residents of the Island. While there had been occasional floods before the twentieth century, they increased in frequency and intensity from the 1930s on, possibly caused by locks and dams built elsewhere on the Mississippi. During these floods, streets on the island turned to rivers, yards into ponds until the rising water covered all but the roofs of houses (see Figure F.1). In 1965, a record flood reached 25.4 feet, covering most of the island and forcing the residents to flee. A child died. When the Army Corp of Engineers came in to assess the situation, they determined for the first time ever that there was really nothing they could do but move the residents off the island onto the mainland. So, in spite of much reluctance and many regrets, 128 families sold their property to the government during the later 1970s and relocated to the mainland, eventually settling in several different neighborhoods.[19] Most of the island was converted into park space including ball fields, but a number of historic buildings remain, including the old homes of Jane Fisher Rolette Dousman and Bernard Brisbois, and of Jane and Hercules Dousman's son Louis and daughter-in-law Nina Sturgis, which were preserved and restored as historic sites.

[15] Albert Coryer, Prairie du Chien map, Villa Louis archive; Copy of Albert Coryer map, Phil Gauthier, "Four French Family Reviews" (CD-ROM, published by the author, 2003).
[16] Interview with Myra Lang; interview with Rosemary Stephens, Geri Curley, Phil Barrette, and Doris Barrette, Prairie du Chien, Wisconsin, August 1, 2002.
[17] Dale Klemme interview.
[18] Interview with Lori Valley, February 21, 2004; interview with Bette Valley Beneker, September 3, 2003.
[19] Dale Klemme interview; Antoine, *Images of America, pp. 105–108*; film "Come Hell or High Water," University of Wisconsin-Extension Telecommunications Center, WHA-TV, Madison, WI, 1980, courtesy of Bette Beneker.

FIGURE E.1. Carl Valley, April 1951. This photo was taken in the Fourth Ward, on the Island, during a flood. Courtesy of Bette Valley Beneker.

The great-great-grandchildren of the fur trade who remained in Wisconsin identified by neighborhood and church, sometimes by occupation, and sometimes – like Albert Coryer – as French. Many acknowledged having some Native ancestry, but very few were tribal members although their families remember a few Native friends. When government forms asked them their race, they checked the boxes for "white." Today the Creoles' descendants are a small minority of Prairie du Chien's population. Out of almost 6,000 people in 2010, only 76 (1.3%) claimed French Canadian ancestry and 353 (5.9%) claimed French heritage, according to the U.S. Census Bureau, while only 0.4 percent were American Indian or Alaska Native.[20]

Their history, however, is very much on their minds and even provides another resource for residents. Historic sites such as the restored Dousman mansion Villa Louis, the Fort Crawford Museum, the Brisbois

[20] "Prairie du Chien (city), Wisconsin," State and County QuickFacts, quickfacts.census. gov/qfd/states/55/5565050.html; U.S. Census Bureau, American Fact Finder, "Selected Social Characteristics in the United States, 2007–2011," http://factfinder2.census.gov/ faces/tableservices/jsf/pages/productview.xhtml?src=bkmk

store, and the James Reed house draw tourists to this lovely community and provide jobs. Descendants of the Brisbois, Courtois, Limery,
and Menard families – and of many other Creoles – have worked or
volunteered at these historic sites. Local author and historian Mary
Elise Antoine, whose Belgian-French ancestors arrived during the nineteenth century, is president of the Prairie du Chien Historical Society
and designs exhibits for the Fort Crawford Museum. She lives in one
of the Prairie's earliest homes, where Catholic services were held before
St. Gabriel's Church was completed. Bette Valley Beneker, who descends
from Cheenawpaukie, one of the early Meskwaki wives, researches
Fourth Ward history, and Jeff Lessard hosts a Facebook site dedicated to
that community's memory.[21] The new director of the Villa Louis historic
site is Susan Caya-Slusser, whose ancestors include Marianne Labuche
Menard and Adelaide Limery.[22] Barrette family members Geri Curley and
Gina Powell research their genealogy, and Phil Barrette takes his metal
detector out to find forgotten pieces of the past in the wild places around
the Prairie. He has boxes of buttons, old coins, musket parts, and other
remnants of days gone by. Former Prairie du Chien mayor Cheryl Mader
and her husband Dale Klemme live in Euphrosine Antaya and Strange
Powers's old home. In his spare time, Dale acts as an amateur archaeol-
ogist, digging in the home's crawl space. He has unearthed hundreds of
beads, potsherds, broken toys, musket flints and balls, and other relics of
the site's colorful history.[23] Every year during Father's Day weekend, a
Prairie du Chien Rendezvous reenacts the days of the fur trade alongside
a large flea market.

Conscious of the past, descendants of Prairie du Chien Creoles remain
connected to their history. Still, they are part of the American mainstream,
neither tribal members nor part of a racialized, marginalized group. For
many of their ancestors, the border crossed them. Given the fluidity and
pervasiveness of America's historic borderlands, we may wonder how

[21] "Remember fourthward," Facebook page; Mary Valley interview, 3 September
2003; Scanlan, ed., St. Gabriel's Church records transcript, WHS, pp. 14, 113; Phil
Gauthier," Four French Family Reviews," (CD-ROM, published by the author, 2003);
Les and Jeanne Rentmeetster, *Wisconsin Creoles*, p. 272; James L. Hansen, "Prairie
du Chien's Earliest Church Records, 1817," *Minnesota Genealogical Journal*: 4
(November 1985) p. 10; Thomas Forsyth Papers, Lyman Draper Manuscripts, microfilm, 2T 22, State Historical Society of Wisconsin; Thomas Forsyth, Records of the
Superintendent of Indian Affairs, St. Louis, Kansas State Historical Society, vol. 32,
"Sac-Fox 1/2Breeds."
[22] Conversation with Susan Caya-Slusser, July 14, 2012.
[23] Dale Klemme and Cheryl Mader, personal conversations with the author.

different they and their ancestors were from other peoples of the heart-land, especially those in the small towns and rural areas where local histories have yet to be connected to a larger, complex narrative. In the early twenty-first century, American demographics are changing again: there may be lessons for us to learn from America's historic creolized people, places, and cultures about power, mediation, and social change, to guide us into the future.

# Index